THE STAIR SOCIETY

PERPETUITIES IN SCOTS LAW

by

ROBERT BURGESS LL.B.(Lond.), Ph.D.(Edin.)

EDINBURGH
THE STAIR SOCIETY
1979

© ROBERT BURGESS, 1979

ISBN 0 90229206 4

PRINTED IN GREAT BRITAIN BY WILLIAM HODGE AND CO., LTD., GLASGOW

CONTENTS

Preface	i
Table of Cases	viii
Office-bearers of the Stair Society	233
Constitution of the Stair Society	235
Publications of the Stair Society	237

Chapter I Perpetuities	1	Reconstitution and Restriction	105
The term 'Perpetuity'	1	Perpetual Settlements	110
Approaches to Perpetuities	8	Legality	113
The Factors Present for the Creation of a Perpetuity	8	Illegality	117
		Perpetuities and Perpetuity Rules	119
The Effects of Perpetuities on Beneficiaries	13		
The Attitude of the Courts to Perpetuities	17	**Chapter IV** Perpetuity Rules in Scotland	120
		The Common Law Rules	122
Chapter II Perpetuities in English Law	24	Origins of the Rules	124
		Effect and Extent	131
Alienation	24	Avoidance	135
Entails	28	Conclusions as to the Common Law Rules	146
Perpetual Settlements	32		
Conditions	33	The Statutory Rules	146
Contingent Remainders	35	Qualifying Beneficiaries	152
Executory Interests and Trusts	39	Effect	153
Rules Against Perpetuities	41	Powers of Appointment	158
Reasons for the Adoption of a Policy against Perpetuities	41		
The Relationship between the Rules	44	**Chapter V** Accumulations	162
		The Origins of Accumulation Settlements in England	162
The Effect of the English Law of Perpetuities in Scotland	45	Accumulation Settlements in Scotland	166
Chapter III Perpetuities in Scots Law	49	Objections to Accumulation Settlements	171
English Law and Scots Law	49	Rules against Accumulations	173
Alienation	51	The Legislation	174
The Control of the Feudal Superior	53	Scope of the Legislation	181
		The Legislative Restrictions	197
Legal Restraints on Alienation	58	Contravention of the Restrictions	205
The Reaction	61	Termination of Accumulations	222
Entails	62		
Origins—External Influences?	62		
Origins—Scots Feudal Law	69	**Chapter VI** Rules and Perpetuities	226
Developments to 1685	73		
The Act of 1685	80	The Role of the Rules against Perpetuities	226
The Judicial Approach to Entails	90		
The Legislative Approach to Entails	96	The Relevance of Perpetuity Rules at the Present Day	228

PREFACE AND ACKNOWLEDGEMENTS

'Perpetuities in Scots Law' has its origin in a Ph.D. thesis submitted to the University of Edinburgh in 1975 and comprises, with a few modifications, the first part (and main text) of that thesis. It represents a study of the origins and development of the perpetuity principle in Scotland, of the rules of common law embodying that principle and of the legislation enacted in reaction to it. It is a study intended primarily for a legal audience although it is hoped that professional historians will find something of interest in it.

Inevitably, in the production of a volume like this a great many favours and kindnesses have been extended to me. First, I should mention my colleagues in the Department of Scots Law at Edinburgh, many of whom submitted in some degree to my interrogations and in particular to Professor W. A. Wilson who bore the brunt of these sessions. Next, thanks are due to the staff of the Historical Search Room at Register House for their unfailing help and courtesy during my daily visits to plough through the two hundred and forty-seven dusty volumes that make up the Register of Entails. And last, but by no means least, my thanks are due to the two Literary Directors of the Stair Society involved with this volume, Professors I. D. Willock of Dundee and W. A. J. Watson of Edinburgh for their help in its production.

ROBERT BURGESS,
Department of Scots Law,
University of Edinburgh.
June, 1977.

TABLE OF CASES

Scottish Cases

Case	Page
A v B's Trustees 1941 S.L.T. 193	212
Earl of Aberdeen v ―――― 1683 M 13394	60
Agnew v Earl of Stair (1822) 1 Shaw's App Cas 355	89, 94
J. S. Aikman Petitioner 1968 S.L.T. 137	180, 203
Allardice v Allardice 1795 Bell's Cas 156	132, 141, 142, 146
Allen v Flint (1886) 13 R 975	143
Lord Ankerville v Sanders 1787 M 7010	95
Creditors of Earl of Annandale v Viscount Stormont 1662 M 6139	94-11, 18, 66, 69, 74, 75, 76, 78, 79, 82, 97
Duke of Atholl v Robertson 20th Nov 1800 FC	124, 152
Baillie v Carmichael 1734 M 15500	95
Baillie v Grant 1859 21 D 838	111
Baird v Baird (1844) 6 D 643	105
Barbour v Rudge [1947] SN 100	200
Baxter v Baxter 1909 SC 1027	148, 158
Beveridge v Beveridge's Trustees (1878) 5 R 1116	124, 137
Black v Auld (1873) 1 R 133	146
Brash v Phillipson 1916 SC 271	138
Brown v Countess of Dalhousie 1803 M App No. 19	93
Bruce v Bruce (1830) 4 W & S 240	85, 94, 114, 115
Burns' Trustees v McKenna 1940 SC 489	159
Bryson v Chapman 1760 N 15511	95, 113
Earl of Callendar v Lord John Hamilton 1687 M 15476	83
Campbell v Earl of Breadalbane 12th June 1812 F.C	55
Campbell v Campbell's Trustees (1882) 10 R (H.L.) 65	183
Campbell v Duncan [1913] 1 S.L.T. 260	142
Campbell v O'Neill 1766 M 4287	
Campbell v Wardlaw (1883) 10 R (H.L.) 65	150
Heirs of Campbell v Wightman 1748 M 15505	93, 95
Campbell's Trustees v Campbell (1891) 18 R 2	191, 200, 211, 214, 218
Cant v Borthwick 1726 M 15554	81
Carey's Trustees v Rose 1957 SC 252	191, 200, 201, 204, 218
Cathcart v Cathcart (1831) 5 W & S 315	86
Cathcart's Trustees v Heneage's Trustees (1883) 10 R 1205	186, 218
Chambers' Trustees v Smith (1878) 5 R (H.L.) 151	223
Chaplin's Trustees v Haile (1890) 18 R 27	150
Chisholm's Trustees v Menzies 1931 S.N. 41	179
Coats' Trustees v Coats (1903) 5 F 401	125
Colquhoun v Colquhoun's Trustees (1892) 19 R 946	210, 211, 215
Colville's Trustees v Marinden 1908 S.C. 911	143
Compton's Judicial Factor v Barnardo's Homes 1917 S.C. 713	225
Crichton Stuart's Tutrix 1921 S.C. 840	152, 154, 155, 156
Cripps' Trustees v Cripps 1926 S.C. 188	142, 143
Cumstie v Cumstie's Trustees (1880) 3 R 921	122, 124, 126, 128, 138, 140, 143
Cuthbertson v Thomson & Graham 1781 M 4279	124
Earl Dalhousie v Ramsay-Maule 1782 M 10963	111
Dalrymple's Trustees v Watson's Trustees 1932 S.L.T. 480 (O.H.)	124, 137
Dalyell v Dalyell 17th January 1810 FC	111
Davie v Davie's Trustees (1900) 8 S.L.T. 28 (O.H.)	149
Devlin v Lowrie 1922 S.C. 255	143
Dennistown v Dalgleish (1838) 1 D 69	137
Dewar v Campbell (1825) 1 W & S 161	214
Dickson v Cunningham 1786 M 15534	87, 88, 89
Dillon v Campbell 1780 M 15432	7
Donaldson's Trustees v H.M. Advocate 1938 S.L.T. 106 (O.H.)	215
Douglas v Ainslie 1761 M 4269	124
Douglas v Douglas & Drummond 1724 M 12910	123
Dowden's Trustees v Governors of Merchiston Castle School 1965 S.C. 56	216, 225
Drybrough's Trustees v Drybrough's Trustees 1912 S.C. 939	148
Dykes & Dykes v Boyd 3rd June 1813 FC	146
City of Edinburgh v Binny 1694 M 9107	116
Merchant Company & Trades of Edinburgh v Governors of Heriot's Hospital 1765 M 5750	116
Edmonstone of Duntreath v Edmonstone 1769 M 4409 1786 M 15534	87, 94, 95
Elder's Trustees v Treasurer of Free Church of Scotland (1892) 20 R 2	191, 208, 214, 218
Elmslie v Fraser (1850) 12 D 724	143
Ewan v Watt (1828) 6 S 1125	144
Falconer v Wright (1824) 2 S 633	129
Ferguson v Ferguson (1875) 2 R 627	141
Ferguson's Trustees v Hamilton (1860) 22 D 1442 affd. (1862) 24 D (H.L.) 8	124, 137
Fraser v Brown 1707 M 4529	135
Fraser's Trustees v Turner (1901) 8 S.L.T. 466 (O.H.)	124, 137
Creditors of Robert Frog v His Children 1735 M 4269	123, 124, 125, 127, 128, 129, 131, 132, 133, 134, 135, 136, 137, 138, 140, 141, 142, 144, 145, 146, 147, 148
G. v G's Trustees 1936 S.C. 837	212, 214
Viscount Garnock v Heirs of Entail 1725 M 15596	81
Gerran v Alexander 1781 M 4402	125
Gibson v Arbuthnot 1726 M 11481	123
Lady Gibson's Trustees—Petitioners 1963 S.C. 350	198, 207, 218, 221
Gifford's Trustees v Gifford (1903) 5 F 723	132, 137, 138

TABLE OF CASES

	Page
Gordon v Dewar 1771 M 15579	112
Gordon Cumming v Gordon 1761 M 15513	84
Gordon v Mackintosh (1841) 4 D 192, affd. (1845) 4 Bell's App. Cas. 105	124, 132
Graham v Graham's Trustees 1927 S.C. 56	225
Hall of Dunglas v Gow 1725 M 13395	60
Hamilton v McDowall 3rd March 1815 FC	82
Harvey's Trustees v Harvey 1942 S.C. 582	148, 149, 154
Hay v Erskine Balfour 1758 M 4406 M 15461	87
Henderson's Trustees v Anderson 1930 S.L.T. 346 (O.H.)	179
Creditors of Hepburn 1738 M 15567	81
Howdens v Rocheid 1869 7 M (H.L.) 110	111
Hunter's Trustees v Edinburgh Chamber of Commerce 1911 S.L.T. 287 (O.H.)	218
Hutchison v Grant's Trustees 1913 S.C. 1211 (O.H.)	191, 192, 206, 218
Hutton's Trustees v Hutton (1847) 9 D 639	124, 137
Innes' Trustees v Bowen 1920 S.C. 133	191, 192, 194, 195
Keating v Collins 1870 S.L.R. 548	144, 148
Keith's Trustees v Keith (1857) 18 D 1040	170, 175, 176, 177
Kempt v Watt 1779 M 15528	94
Kennedy v Allan (1825) 2 S 554	124
Ker v Law 1687 M 13395	60
King's Advocate v Creditors of Cromarty 1683 M 13393	60
Lord Kinnaird v Hunter 1761 M 15611	82
Lee's Trustees v Fringies (1897) 34 S.L.R. 613	191
Lillie v Riddell 1741 M 4267	138
Lindsay v Dott 9th Dec. 1807 FC	124
Lindsay's Executors v Forsyth 1940 S.C. 568	21
Lindsay's Trustees—Petitioners 1911 S.C. 584	183, 194
Lindsay's Trustees v Lindsay 1931 S.C. 586	179
Lockhart v Lockhart 1841 3 S 901	86
Lockharts v Stewart Denham June 8th 1811 FC	84, 85
Lockhart's Trustees v Lockhart 1921 S.C. 761	135, 138
Logan's Trustees v Ellis (1890) 17 R 425	143
Logan's Trustees v Logan 1896 23 R 849	191, 218
Lord v Colvin (1860) 23 D 111	189, 191, 194, 195, 218, 219, 221
Lucas' Trustees v The Lucas Trust (1881) 8 R 502	224
Mackellar v Marquis (1840) 3 D 172	124, 130, 131, 133, 134, 135
Mackenzie's Trustees v Mackenzie 1922 S.C. 404	148, 158
McClymont's Executors v Osborne (1895) 22 R 411	124, 138
McCullogh v McCullogh (the Barholm Case) 1752 Elch. Tailzie No. 48; 5 W & S 180-185 (Note)	8, 20, 112, 167, 169, 170, 175
Maccullogh v Maccullogh's Trustees (1903) 6 F (H.L.) 3	158, 225
McGowan v Robb (1862) 1 M 146; 2 M 943	145
McIntosh v McIntosh Jan 28th 1812 FC	123, 125, 145
McIver's Trustees v IRC [1973] S.T.C. 398	199, 200, 201, 203, 204, 214
Mackay's Trustees v Mackay 19090 S.C. 139	209, 210, 218
Mackenzie's Trustees v Mackenzie (1877) 4 R 962	191, 210, 216
McNair v McNair 1791 Bell's Cas. 546	8, 17, 19, 20, 62, 111, 113, 114, 115, 116, 117, 119, 141, 167, 169, 170
Mair's Curator Bonis v Inland Revenue 1932 S.C. 151	218, 219, 220, 221
Malcolm's Trustees v Malcolm 1950 S.C. (H.L.) 17	160
Marshall's Trustees v Findlay 1928 S.L.T. 560	160
Martin v Milliken (1864) 3 M 326	145
Mason v Skinner (1844) 16 Jur. 422	21, 22, 23, 118, 119, 170, 171, 178
Mason's Trustees v Mason (1899) 2 F 201	212
Maxwell v Gracie (1822) 1 S 509	124
Maxwell's Trustees v Maxwell (1877) 5 R 249	183, 191, 200, 206, 209, 210, 211, 215, 216
Mearns v Charles 1926 S.L.T. 118 (O.H.)	124, 157
Mein v Taylor (1827) 5 S 779	124, 136, 140, 143, 144
Menzies v Menzies 1785 M 15436	7
Miller's Trustees v Miller (1890) 18 R 301	222, 223, 224, 225
Middleton 1929 S.C. 394	151
Mitchell's Trustees v Fraser 1915 S.C. 350	183, 194, 195, 196
Moon's Trustees v Moon (1899) 2 F 201	191, 206, 218
Earl of Moray 1950 S.L.T. 188	153
Morice's Trustees v Yeats (1872) 10 S.L.R. 141	137
Moss's Trustees v Bramwell 1936 S.C. (H.L.) 1	190, 191, 192, 193, 195, 196
Mowbray's Trustees v Mowbray's Executors 1931 S.C. 595	224
Muir v Muir 1786 M 4288	124
Muir's Trustees v Williams 1942 S.C. 5; 1943 S.C. (H.L.) 47	17, 18, 45, 46, 47, 120, 155, 159
Muirhead v Muirhead (1890) 17 R (H.L.) 45	223, 224, 225
Mure v Mure 1786 M 4268	138, 140
Naismith v Boyes (1899) 1 F (H.L.) 79	150
Newlands v Creditors of Newlands 1794 M 4289	125, 131, 132, 136, 138, 139, 140, 141, 142, 146
Ogilvie's Trustees v Kirk Session of Dundee (1846) 8 D 1229	169, 175, 176, 200, 205, 209, 211, 215, 216, 222
Creditors of Paterson & Anderson v Douglasses 1705 M 4259	127

TABLE OF CASES

	Page		Page
Pearson v *Martin* 1665 M 4249	127	*Strathmore* v *Strathmore's Trustees*	
Perth Hospital v *Campbell* 1724 M 5729	116	(1831) 5 W & S 170	17, 19, 21, 22, 117, 168, 170, 171, 173, 175
Porterfield v *Graham* 1779 M 4277	124	*Lord Strathnaver* v *Duke of Douglas*	
Preston v *Wellwood* 1791 Bell's Cas 191	125, 126, 130, 138, 140, 144	(1728) M 15372	7, 84
Pursell v *Elder* (1865) 4 Macq. 992	191, 218	*Studd* v *Studd's Trustees* (1880) 8 R 249	121
Pyper's Trustees v *Leighton* 1946 S.L.T. 255 (O.H.)	218	*Suttie* v *Suttie's Trustees* (1846) 18 Jur. 442	8, 18, 19, 20, 21, 22, 113, 115, 117, 171
Duke of Queensberry v *Earl of Wemyss* 1807 M. Tailzie App. Part I 44	18	*Tristran* v *McHaffies* (1894) 22 R 121	143
Case of Queensberry Leases 1819 1 Bligh 339	91	*Thomsons* v *Lawson* 1681 M 4258	128, 140
Marquis of Queensberry v *Exors. of Duke of Queensberry* 1830 4 W & S 254	86, 94, 114, 115	*Thomson* v *Thomson* 1794 Bell's Cas. (Fol) 72	141
		Union Bank of Scotland v *Campbell* 1929 S.C. 143	198, 199, 200, 201, 203, 204, 217
Rait v *Arbuthnot* (1892) 19 R 687	137, 145	*Ure* v *Earl of Crawford* 1756 M 4315	84
Ranken and others (1870) 8 M 878	124, 137	*Veitch* v *Robertson* 1630 M 4256	126
Ranken's Trustees v *Ranken* 1908 S.C. 3	183	*Wallace* 1695 4 Bro. Supp. 65	84
Ramsay v *Beveridge* (1854) 16 D 764	132, 133	*Watson* v *Watson* (1854) 16 D 803	137
Reid's Trustees v *Dashwood* 1929 S.C. 748	152, 154, 156, 157	*Watson's Trustees* v *Brown* 1923 S.C. 228	188, 189, 191, 195, 217, 218
Robertson's Trustees v *Robertson's Trustees* 1933 S.C. 639	177, 182, 208, 218	*Watson's Trustees* v *Watson* 1913 S.C. 1133	225
		Wemyss v *Macintosh* 1672 M 7257	124
Earl of Roseberry v *Baird* 1765 M 15616	82	*Whitelaw* v *Stewart's Trustees* 1932 unreported	159
Case of Rosehaugh (See *McIntosh* v *McIntosh* 28th Jan. 1812 FC)	125, 130	*Williamson* v *Cochran* (1828) 6 S 1035	124
Ross v *Drummond* 9th February 1836	82	*Williamson* v *Williamson's Trustees* (1881) 19 S.L.R. 276 (O.H.)	124, 137
Ross v *King* (1847) 9 D 1327	136, 137	*Willison* v *Willison* 1726 M 15458	87
Rothes v *Melville* (1677) 3 Bro. Supp. 170	18, 62, 92	*Wilson's Trustees* v *Glasgow Royal Infirmary* 1917 S.C. 527	209, 210, 213, 215, 216, 218
Roxburghe v *Bellenden Ker* 1808 M App. (Tailzie) 18: 2 Dow 151	19, 90, 95, 96	*Young* v *Bothwells* 1705 M 15482	84
Roxburghe v *Don* (alias *Wauchope*) (1734) 1 Cr. and Sr. 126	199	*Young* v *Young* (1761) 5 Bro. Supp. 884	84
Royal Bank of Scotland v *I.R.* 1977 S.L.T. 45	183, 187	*Yuill's Trustees* v *Thomson* (1902) 4 F 815	223, 225
Russell's Trustees v *Russell* 1959 S.C. 148	198, 199, 201, 214, 217	*Earl of Zetland* v *Lord Advocate* (1878) 3 App. Cas. 505	69
Scott v *Price* (1837) 15 S 916	137		
Seton v *Creditors of Seton* 1793 M 4219	136, 144	**ENGLISH CASES**	
Sharpe v *Sharpe* 1835 1 S & M App. Cas. 594	93, 95	*Re AEG Unit Trust (Managers) Ltd.'s Trust Deed* [1957] Ch. 415	48, 181, 187
Sheill's Trustees v *Sheill's Trustees* (1906) 8 F 848	149, 158	*Bassil* v *Lister* (1851) 9 Hare 177	185, 186, 187
Smith v *Glasgow Royal Infirmary* 1909 S.C. 1231	214, 215, 216, 218, 219	*Berry* v *Geen* [1938] AC 575	219
Smith's Trustees v *Gaydon* 1931 S.C. 533	179	*Blease* v *Buigh* (1840) 2 Beav. 221	208
Smyth's Trustees v *Kinloch* (1880) 7 R 1176	184, 187, 191, 213	*Re Bourne's Settlement Trusts* (1946) 115 L.J. Ch. 152	203
Speid v *Speid* Feb. 21st 1837 FC	95	*Brent's Case* (1575) Dyer 339(b)	40
Lord Stair v *Stair's Trustees* (1826) 4 S 488	216	*Corporation of Bridgenorth* v *Collins* (1847) 15 Sim. 538	189
Stewart v *Fullarton* 1830 4 W & S 196	85, 94, 114, 115	*Bryan* v *Collins* (1852) 16 Beav. 14	202
Stewart v *Home* 1789 M 15535	93	*Bullock* v *Stones* (1754) 2 Ves. Sen. 521	164
Stewart v *Vans Agnew* (of *Sheuchan*) 1784 M 15435; 2nd June 1818	82, 88	*Butler* v *Butler* (1744) 3 Atk. 58	164
Stewart's Trustees v *Stewart* 1927 S.C. 350	198, 199	*Re Cababe* (1914) 59 Sol. Jo. 129	182, 220
Stewart's Trustees v *Whitelaw* 1926 S.C. 701	47, 152, 158, 159, 189, 191, 200, 207	*Cadell* v *Palmer* (1832) 1 Cl. & Fin. 372	41
		Re Cattell [1914] 1 Ch. 177	198, 202, 203
		Chapman v *Blisset* (1735) Cases temp. Talbot 145	164
		Cholmley v *Humble* (1595) unrep.	34
		Chudleigh's Case (1589-95) 1 Co. Rep. f. 120a	1, 2, 3, 4, 5, 38, 40, 41
Storie's Trustees v *Gray* (1872) 1 R 953	217	*Colthirst* v *Bejushin* (1551) Plowd. 21	5, 33, 37, 38

TABLE OF CASES

	Page		Page
Combe v Hughes (1865) 34 L.J. Ch. 334	210	Saunders v Vautier (1841) 4 Beav. 115	33, 223, 225
Corbet's Case (1600) 1 Co. Rep. f.83*b*	2, 34, 35	Scholastica's Case (1572) Plowd. 708	35, 69
Crawley v Crawley (1835) 7 Sim 427	182, 208, 220	Shaw v Rhodes (1835) 1 My. & Cr. 135	190
Re Deloitte [1926] 1 Ch. 56	212, 214	Shelley's Case (1581) 1 Co. Rep. f. 886	122
Case of Lady Denison's Will (1787) unreported	163, 165, 166	Stephen v Stephens (1736) Cases temp. Talbot 228	164
Elborne v Goode (1844) 14 Sim. 165	189	Studholme v Hodgson (1734) 3 P. Wms. 300	163
Ellis v Maxwell (1841) 3 Beav. 587	202	Taltarum's Case (1472) YB 12 Edw. IV 19	1, 3, 14, 25, 32, 90
Re Errington (1897) 76 L.T. 616	203, 204	Re Taylor [1901] 2 Ch. 134	202
Eyre v Marsden (1838) 2 Keen 564	208, 210	Tench v Clease (1855) 6 D.M. & G. 453	189
Fane v Fane [1913] 1 Ch. 404	159, 201	Thelluson v Woodford (1799) 4 Ves. 227: (1805) 11 Ves. 112 (H.L.)	162, 163, 165
Re Gardiner [1901] 1 Ch. 697	184, 185		
Re Garside [1919] 1 Ch. 132	183, 220		
Gartside v IRC [1968] AC 553	151	Travanion v Vivian (1752) 2 Ves. Sem. 430	164
Germin v Aiscot (1595) unrep.	34	Re Vaughan [1883] W.N. 89	186
Gibson v Lord Mountford (1750) 1 Ves. Sen. 485	164	Vine v Raleigh [1891] 2 Ch. 13	184, 187
Gibson v Rogers (1750) 1 Ves. Sen. 521	164	Re Watt's Will Trusts [1936] 1 All ER 1555	202
Gorst v Lowndes (1841) 11 Sim 434	200	Weatherall v Thornburgh (1878) 8 Ch. D 261	214, 215, 223
Green v Ekins (1742) 2 Atk. 473	164		
Green v Gascoigne (1865) 34 L.J. Ch. 268	209	Webb v Earl of Shaftesbury (1789) unreported	163
Griffiths v Vere (1803) 9 Ves. 127	207	Webb v Webb (1840) 2 Beav. 493	208
Haley v Bannister (1819) 4 Hood. 275	202, 208	Wharton v Masterman [1895] AC 186	226
Harrison v Harrison (1787) unreported	163, 165	Williams v Nixon (1840) 2 Beav. 472	208
Hawkins v Combe (1783) 1 Bro. C.C. 335	164, 166	Willion v Berkley (1562) Plowd. 225	70
Re Hopkins [1916] 2 Ch. 570	182, 220		
Hopkins v Hopkins (1749) 1 Ves. Sen. 268	164	Innominate Cases (in date order)	
Re Hurlbatt [1910] 2 Ch. 553	184	(1225) Bracton's Note Book No. 1034	24, 25
Jagger v Jagger (1883) 25 Ch. D. 729	198, 201, 202, 203	(1304) YB 32 & 33 Edw. I (Rolls Series) 329	36
Jeffries v Alexander (1860) HLC 594	118	(1306) 33-35 Edw. I (Rolls Series) 387	32
Re Knapp [1929] 1 Ch. 341	178		
Lampet's Case (1612) 10 Cro. Rep. 466	5	(1308) YB 2 & 3 Edw. II (Selden. Soc. vol. 19) 4	36
Langdon v Simon (1806) 12 Ves. 295	208		
Lambe v Stoughton (1841) 12 Sim 304	196	(1311) YB 5 Edw. II (Selden Soc. vol. 31) 17	31
Manning v Andrews (1575) 1 Leo. 256	3	(1331) YB 4 Edw. III Tri. pl. 4	12, 13
Manning's Case (1609) 8 Co. Rep. f. 946	5	(1336) YB Edw. III Michs. No. 8	37
Re Mason [1891] 3 Ch. 467	184, 185	(1341) YB 14 Edw. III (Rolls Series) 314	12
Mildmay's Case (1606) 6 Co. Rep. f. 40*a*	2, 12, 34, 78	(1344) YB 18 & 19 Edw. III 201	31
Miles v Dyer (1837) 8 Sim 330	208	(1346) YB 20 Edw. III (Rolls Series) ii 202	12
Mole v Mole (1758) 1 Dick. 310	164, 166	(1346) Lib. Ass. f. 73 ann. 20 pl. 17	14
The Duke of Norfolk's Case (1682) 3 Ch. Cas. 1	2, 6, 7, 17, 22, 41	(1350) YB 24 Edw. III 70 No. 79	121
O'Neill v Lucas 1838 2 Keen 313	208	(1352) Lib. Ass. f. 124 ann. 26 pl. 37	24
Pells v Brown (1620) Cro. Jac. 590	5, 40		
Perrot's Case (1595) Moo. 368	3, 38	(1355) Lib. Ass. f. 160 ann. 24 pl. 19	24
Perry v Phelips (1798) 4 Ves. 108	164	(1366) YB 40 Edw. III f. 9 No. 18	121
Re Phillips (1880) 49 L.J. Ch. 198	182, 220	(1388) YB 11 Ric II (Ames Foundation Volume) 283	37
Re Pope [1901] 1 Ch. 64	182, 220		
Mary Portington's Case (1614) 10 Co. Rep. f. 356	35, 37, 69, 76	(1409) YB 11 Hen. IV 74 No. 14	37
Pride v Fooks (1839) 2 Beav. 430	208	(1410) YB 12 Hen. IV 9	31
Purefoy v Rogers (1671) 2 Wms. Saunders 380	5, 39, 40	(1412) YB 14 Hen. IV f. 4 (Nich. pl. 6)	24
Re Ransome [1957] Ch. 348	204, 205	(1431) YB 9 Hen. IV 23 No. 19	37
Re Robb [1953] Ch. 459	188		
Re Lady Rosslyn's Trust (1848) 16 Sim 391	198, 203	COMMONWEALTH CASES	
Rudhall v Milward (1586) Moo. 212	35	Blair v Curran (1939) 62 C.L.R. 464	189
Sainsbury v IRC [1969] 3 All ER 919	151	Re Wood (1961) 28 D.L.R. (2d) 583	219

CHAPTER I

PERPETUITIES

The term 'Perpetuity'

It would seem that the term 'perpetuity' first became used in England towards the end of the first Elizabethan era. It was used to denote a particular type of settlement whereby land was tied up in such a way as to render it inalienable. The chronology and the meaning are vouched for by cases in the law reports of the time and in contemporary treatises. Thus in 'The Use of the Law', generally (although some say fallaciously) attributed to Bacon,[1] the following statement appears:[2]

"There is started up a device called perpetuity, which is an entail with an addition of a proviso conditional, tied to his estate not to put away the land from the next heir, and if he do so, to forfeit his own estate. Which perpetuities, if they should stand, would bring back in all the former inconveniences of entails."

The first reported case in which perpetuities are discussed at length is *Chudleigh's Case*[3] designated by Coke as the 'Case of Perpetuities'. It is clear from this case that although the term 'perpetuity' might only recently have come into use the end sought after by the creation of perpetuities, and the devices used in furtherance of that aim were of some antiquity, but were, nonetheless, contrary to the common law of England as an extract from that report shows.[4]

"The statute made 13 Ed. I de Donis Conditionalibus in a manner created perpetuities and it continued about 200 years, but in 12 Ed. IV 9 (5) by the resolution of the judges it was resolved that by a common recovery the estate tail should be barred for the mischiefs which were introduced in the commonwealth thereby. In the time of Rich. II, Justice Richel,[6] attempted to make a perpetuity, as it appears by Lit[tleton] in his Chapter on Warranty fol. 263 and 21 Hen. VI 33*b*. which has such in effect. Justice Richel, having divers sons, and intending that none of those sons should alien those lands, or to make a warranty to bar or hurt the others, made a deed intended to such effect, scil. that the lands and tenements were to be given to his eldest son in tail, etc. or if any of his sons should alien, etc. then that their estate should cease and be void and that then the lands should remain to his second son in tail, etc. and sic ultra the remainder to his other sons and livery and seisin was made accordingly. But all such remainders were void because the limitation of them were against the rule of law as appears by Lit[tleton]. And it appears in 21 Hen. VI that Thirning, Chief Justice of the Common Pleas made the like perpetuity for the continuance of his land in his blood, but the judges held it was against the law."

In other cases of the same period dicta to the same effect appear and so it appears quite clear that by the end of the reign of Elizabeth I, the English com-

[1] See esp. Morris and Leach—'The Rule against Perpetuities' at p.8; and Holdsworth 'History of English Law' vol. vii, p.197.
[2] Bacon's works (Spedding ed.) vol. vii at p.491.
[3] (1589-95) 1 Co. Rep. f.120*a*.
[4] 1 Co. Rep. at f.131*b*.
[5] *Taltarum's Case* 1472.
[6] Usually spelt Rickhill, and occasionally Richil (1), a judge of the Court of Kings Bench during the reign of Richard II.

A

mon lawyers were acquainted with both the term 'perpetuity' and its meaning.[7]

Put broadly that meaning amounted to this, that a perpetuity was really a refinement on the centuries old grant in fee tail. This refinement was felt to be necessary during the latter half of the sixteenth century since by 1536 at the latest[8] the English entail had become freely alienable by means of the joint use of the fine and the common recovery[9] and this in turn gave rise to a form of rationalisation by which the judges came to look upon the entail as possessing the inherent quality of being so barred.

The refinement, as appears from the extract from the report of *Chudleigh's Case* quoted above, was the introduction into the deed of entail of a clause or 'proviso' known as a 'clause of perpetuity' purporting to render the interests granted determinable at the occurrence of an action which could be construed as an attempted alienation.[10] It was the description given to this clause that came to be used to describe the settlement as a whole and the purpose behind that settlement.

The original meaning of perpetuity, then, relates to attempts to create an unbarrable entail in order to render the settled land inalienable. The reason why this should be so is that in early English Law an entail was practically the only way by which land was settled. Hence it would be the starting point from which conveyancers would work in any attempt to tie up land within a family.

Also during the sixteenth century, a second strand to the definition of perpetuity appears, a strand that is closely linked with the idea of the unbarrable entail. The point behind the settlements in this line of cases was comparatively simple: an unbarrable entail rendered the grantee in possession

---

[7] Thus in *Corbet's Case* (1600) 1 *Co. Rep.* f.83b, Glanville J in the course of his judgement referred to the attempts by Rickhill and Thirning to the effect that they "intended to have made perpetuities and upon forfeiture of the estate tail of one of their sons, to have given the remainder and entry to another, but such remainders were utterly void and against the law".

Again in *Anthony Mildmay's Case* (1606) 6 *Co. Rep.* f.40a, the judges resolved that "all these perpetuities were against the reason and policy of the common law; for at the common law all inheritances were fee simple . . . But the true policy and rule of the common law in this point was in effect overthrown by the statute de Donis Conditionalibus made anno 13 Ed. I which established a general perpetuity by Act of Parliament.

Although throughout the seventeenth century, as more devices were tried with varying success, and as the general concept of a perpetuity widened from simply an attempt to create an unbarrable entail to the more general idea of an attempt to render land inalienable, the definitions given by the courts frequently stressed the connection with entails. Thus, nearly a century after *Chudleigh's Case,* in *The Duke of Norfolk's Case* (1682) 3 *Ch. Cas.* 1 *at p*.31 Lord Nottingham L.C. gave what is considered to be the classic definition of a perpetuity. He said, 'A perpetuity is the settlement of an estate or an interest in tail, with such remainders expectant upon it as are in no sort in the power of the tenant in tail in possession to dock by any recovery or assignment, but such remainders must continue as perpetual clogs upon the estate; such do fight against God, for they pretend to such stability in human affairs as the nature of them admits not of and they are against the reason and policy of the law and therefore not to be endured."

See too, as late as 1721, the edition of 'Termes de la Ley' of that year which defines perpetuity as being "where an estate is so designed to be settled in tail, that it cannot be undone or made void". It is interesting that the original edition of this work, published in 1618 did not make mention of perpetuities at all.

[8] As a result of the Statute of Fines 1536 (the Second Statute of Fines).

[9] See Chapter II below.

[10] Compare the prohibition against alienation in the modern English protective trust, as contained in section 33 of the Trustee Act 1925.

and those following him with powers of enjoyment equivalent to those of a life tenant. Why not, therefore, settle the land directly on one's grantees for successive life interests? The first case in which this device appears is *Manning* v *Andrews*[11] where the settlor conveyed lands to feoffees to uses to the effect that his heirs were to take only life interests thereunder, creating behind a trust what came to be known as a perpetual freehold.

Holdsworth tends to regard this case as something of an oddity in that it occurred nearly twenty years before the great perpetuities cases, but, more importantly, in that the settlement in question was made as early as 1517, nearly forty years before the settlement in *Chudleigh's Case*.[12]

The answer is probably that suggested by Charles Sweet[13] that prior to the Statute of Uses 1535, settlements in perpetuity could be made (and were made) behind a conveyance to feoffees to uses and that this was simply an example of this practice. The point was that while, even as early as this, the common law was feeling its way towards a rule against perpetual settlements[14], the common law restrictions did not apply in equity with the result that such equitable perpetuities were valid. Certainly in *Manning* v *Andrews* the perpetuity point was not argued, discussion centering around the effect of the Statutes on the estate of the feoffees to uses, but it seems to have been assumed that, as the Statutes executed the uses, the limitations became subject to the common law which would have rendered them void as perpetuities. (However this particular rule had not yet been settled by the courts[15]). Weight is given to this interpretation by the fact that one of the objects of the Statute was "utterly to extirpate and extinguish" contingent uses of this kind, being "uses invented and limited in a new manner not agreeable to the ancient common laws of the land."[16] That this object was effected is clear from *Chudleigh's Case* where Popham C.J. explained:[17]

"If a feoffment be made to the use of A for life, and after to the use of every person who should be his heir, one after another, for the term of the life of every such heir only; in this case if this limitation should be good, the inheritance should be in nobody, but this limitation is merely void, for the limitation to have a use for a perpetual freehold is not agreeable with the rule of law in estates in possession."

The first case in which perpetual freeholds were directly linked with unbarrable entails was *Perrot's Case*[18] a decision which really turned on technical points of pleading. However the case is important in this context for the argument of Coke, who equated the settlement before the court with those of Rickhill and Thirning and, relying on *Chudleigh's Case*, argued against its

---

[11] (1575) 1 Leo. 256.
[12] The settlement in *Chudleigh's case* was made in 1556.
[13] (1899) 15 LQR at p.73 and authorities cited there.
[14] Examples of this are the cases of Rickhill and Thirning cited above, and of course, *Taltarum's Case* (1472) *YB* 12 *Ed. IV* 19.
[15] Nor was it until *Chudleigh's case* (1589-95) 1 *Co. Rep. f.*120a.
[16] ibid. at f.138a.
[17] ibid.
[18] (1595) Moo. 368.

validity.[19] Coke's line of reasoning was accepted as correct[20] and so in addition to definition by reference to unbarrable entails, perpetuities also came to be defined by reference to attempts to create perpetual freeholds. Thus Gilbert C.B. stated:[21]

"It is against the rules of common law that a perpetual freehold for life only should should descend, because it creates a perpetuity".

And later that:[22]

"A perpetuity is the settlement of an interest descendable from heir to heir so that it shall not be in the power of him in whom it is vested to dispose of it or turn it out of the channel."

In spite of the obviously hostile approach of the courts, as time went on the number of settlements attempting to create perpetuities increased and the devices employed became more varied.[23] To combat these the courts sought to apply by analogy the rules developed in connection with unbarrable entails and perpetual freeholds, and with these cases there evolved the wider, more general concept of a perpetuity as an attempt to render property inalienable. Holdsworth captures the essence of this process in the following passage:[24]

"It was only gradually that the courts came to appreciate the nature of this new problem with which they were faced, and to provide an effective solution. They laid down rules from time to time to meet the various devices employed by the landowners. Here, as in all other branches of English law, they advanced from precedent to precedent, till the repeated consideration of many cases gradually led them to a true understanding of the nature of the problem, and of the rules which were needed to deal adequately with it. Hence we get at different periods many different rules laid down, which represent different plans adopted to meet different devices to creat a perpetuity, and often these rules have little in common except the general object of frustrating the creation of unbarrable entails, and settlements of property upon a succession of limited owners in perpetuity. In fact the development of this branch of the law, having been left almost entirely to the courts has all the characteristic defects of case law. The ground has been encumbered, and to some extent still is encumbered, with many rules invented for the purpose of coping with devices employed to create perpetuities at different periods in the history of the law-rules propounded before the true nature of the problem was correctly appreciated. It is for this reason that it has been truly said that this

---

[19] *ibid*. at p.372:
"Il conclude ceo point que l'estate de franktenement en remainder al Sir Tho. Perrot est bon a luy et chescun fitz que fuit en esse durant son vie, mes nient ouster; et sic de tout les autre persons nosme en le remainder et leur fitz . . . Et il did que ceux *p* petuities ont estre touts temps *p p*vidence de Dieu defeat et pvent per l'act del ley, come en les cases de Thirning et Rickill esteant deux les Judges de ceo Realm. Et en le darrain temps les future uses and perpetual franktenements entend de faire *p* petuities ont este enfeable per les opinion des Justices en le *case* de Dillon and Freine communement appel Chudley's Case argue darreinmt per tout les Judges d' Angleterre et sur ceo adjudge ecnounter les *p* petuities en Bank le Roy.'
In this case the pleadings raised the question, "si touts les estates *p*-petualment limit en franktenemt pur vie al toutsles fitz soi bone ou void".

[20] See Sheppard's Touchstone (1600-1620) which is generally regarded as authoritative, and follows Coke by stating the law as follows:
". . . . . therefore if a feoffment be made to the use of A for life, and after to the use of every person that shall be his heir one after another for the terms of his life . . . these uses shall not be executed because these limitations are wholly void." It is interesting to note than in the 1820 edition of this work, prepared by Preston, a leading conveyancer of his period, the words 'being a perpetuity' were added to the passage quoted.

[21] Gilbert on Uses at p.77.
[22] *ibid*. at p.118.
[23] For a full account of these devices see Holdsworth H.E.L. vol. vii at pp.197-228.
[24] *ibid*. at p.194/195.

branch of the law 'is particularly distinguished by what the Romans termed *inelegantia juris*'[25]."

The most effective devices were created by way of trust and sought to guard against the possibility of alienation by postponing the vesting of the estate by fencing it round with conditions until some remote date in the future. The idea of postponed vesting was not new and was indeed exemplified by the successive grants for life. The original device was the contingent remainder.[26] Now the English common law had no problem in dealing with contingent remainders. It simply applied the doctrine that the law abhors an abeyance of seisin, which effectively meant, in this context, that if a contingent remainder was to be valid it had to vest before the prior estate, on which it was made to depend, ceased. Further, the rule was that the remainder could only be valid if the grantee of the precedent life estate was in esse at the date of the grant. Thus, in effect, the remainder, if it was to be valid had to vest within the lifetime of someone living at the date of the grant, with the result that at common law land could only be effectively tied up for a lifetime.

However if the fee simple was given to trustees no question of an abeyance of seisin could arise and, provided the Statute of Uses could be evaded[27] possibilities for the creation of perpetuities could be made to exist. The first development was that certain executory devises of terms of years were recognised as indestructable,[28] and in *Pells* v *Brown*[29] it was held that executory[30] interests in freeholds, other than those taking effect as contingent remainders were valid and indestructible.[31] Thus armed, settlors began to create settlements behind trusts whereby land was effectively limited so that the vesting of the ultimate remainder might be postponed until far into the future. In the mess of case law in the seventeenth century the judges reacted by applying by analogy various rules of common law, sometimes appropriately, sometimes not. Eventually in

---

[25] Williams on Real Property (22nd Ed.) at p.424.
[26] Contingent remainders were only finally declared valid as such in English law in 1551 in the case of *Colthirst* v *Bejushin Plowd*, 21.
[27] If it could not be so evaded the limitations would be subject to the common law rules re contingent remainders.
[28] *Manning's Case* (1609) 8 *Co. Rep.* f.94b; *Lampet's Case* (1612) 10 *Cro. Rep.* 46b.
[29] (1620) Cro. Jac. 590.
[30] 'Executory' refers to interests behind trusts (or uses) not yet 'executed' by the Statute; that is, not yet converted into legal estates.
[31] Under the dicta in *Chudleigh's Case* these would have been subject to the common law rules and therefore destructible as 'quasi' contingent remainders. However the decision in *Pells* v *Brown* effectively negatived the application of *Chudleigh's Case* to such interests. *Pells* v *Brown* however was not unanimously decided, Dodderidge J. feeling that the limitation in question created "but a possibility to have a fee and quasi a contingent estate which is destroyed by this recovery before it came in esse, for otherwise it would be a mischievous kind of perpetuity which could not by any means be destroyed".

Unfortunately Dodderidge was in a minority of one. Had his views prevailed it is doubtful whether the development of the modern rule against perpetuities would ever have taken place. (See Holdsworth H.E.L. vol. vii at p.218).

The last vestige of *Chudleigh's Case* as an operative rule of law was the rule in *Purefoy* v *Rogers* (1671) 2 *Wms. Saunders* 380, that if a limitation by way of use did not in fact break the common law rules as to the limitation of contingent remainders then it would be subjected to such rules. The result therefore was that a limitation which frequently broke the common law rules would escape. It was to deal with this situation that the modern rule was developed.

1681 the *Duke of Norfolk's Case*[32] was argued before Lord Nottingham in which the Lord Chancellor delivered the judgement that forms the foundation of the 'modern' rule against perpetuities, recognising the problem as the date of vesting. Having defined perpetuity[33] he went on:[34]

"But on the other side future interests, springing trusts or trusts executory, remainders that are to emerge and arise upon contingencies are quite out of the rules and reasons of perpetuities, nay, out of the reason upon which the policy of the law is founded in those cases, *especially if they be not of remote or long consideration*, but such as by a natural and easy interpretation will speedily wear out, and so things come to their right channel again."

It is to be observed that both the original and the modern rules against perpetuities had the same broad aim, but that the emphasis of the two rules is rather different. In the former, the reference is to the power of alienation: in the latter it is to the period (or remoteness) of vesting. In later years the importance of the modern rule outstripped that of the old rule and as a matter of practice "the restrictions imposed by the original rule on the creation of future estates ceased to be attributed to the doctrine of perpetuities and were stated as a rule of law forbidding the limitation of contingent remainders to the children of unborn persons. In other words 'perpetuity' lost its primary meaning of an unbarrable entail, or a limitation of successive estates for life to unborn descendents and acquired the sense of a limitation which is unduly remote in point of time,"[35] with a consequent shift of emphasis from the property settled to the interests subsisting or to subsist under the settlement.

We have, then, the three meanings which have been attributed to the term 'perpetuity' by the English courts in their development of a set of rules against the tying up of property indefinitely. Looked at historically perpetuities present few difficulties of understanding and such as there are usually stem from confusion as to what a perpetuity actually is. Perhaps one source of difficulty is that both the old and the new rules, with their different definitions and emphases were in use concurrently. Thus while the modern rule was founded by Lord Nottingham in 1682, for at least another century the courts continued to use the term 'perpetuity' in its original sense of an unbarrable entail or a perpetual freehold.

While in England the term 'perpetuity' is generally met in a negative context, in that it is something against which the policy of the law has always stood and can be seen to have stood for centuries, the situation in Scotland, at least until the perpetuities legislation of the nineteenth century, has not been nearly so clear, although the modern tendency is to present it as a contrast to the English position.[36]

However modern Scots lawyers may rationalise past trends, it is almost undeniable that when they speak of a 'perpetuity' they do so with reference to the English definitions; indeed it would appear that no definition of the term was attempted by a Scottish jurist until 1825.

---

[32] (1682) 3 Ch. Cas. 1.
[33] See above at note 7.
[34] 3 Ch. Cas. at p.31.
[35] per Charles Sweet (1899) 15 LQR at p. 76.
[36] per T. B. Smith in his chapter on Trusts in Studies Critical and Comparative at p.214.

The first occasion on which the term seems to have been used in Scots legal literature was the year the *Duke of Norfolk's Case* was being argued before Lord Nottingham, 1681, for in that year were published Stair's Institutions. The reference to perpetuities comes in the context of the author's discussion of entails. He writes:[37]

"The perpetuities of estates where they have been long accustomed have sufficiently manifested their inconveniency; and therefore devices have been found to render them ineffectual . . . . But these perpetuities in England are now easily evacuated; first by warrants to sell, purchased in Parliament, which pass without much difficulty; and if they become frequent with us, it is like we will find the same remedy; they are also evacuated by a simulate action of fine and recovery, whereby the purchaser pretends that he is unwarrantably dispossessed of such lands by the present fiar, who colludes and is silent, having received a price or other consideration, so that these sentences, though collusive, must be irrevocable."[38]

In spite of the authority of Stair's work the reports of decisions during the remainder of the seventeenth and almost the whole of the eighteenth century make little mention of perpetuities. Such mention as there is adds very little to Stair's view and is worthy of note only in that it confirms that the term and idea of perpetuity were considered within the context of the strict entail,[39] and indeed this state of affairs continues into the nineteenth century. The point was that the term was essentially English and was only really relevant in comparisons with English law. Thus as late as 1825 Bell's Dictionary and Digest contains the following definition:[40]

"In the law of England a perpetuity seems to have been originally equivalent to a Scotch entail."

Perhaps the first trace of a broadening of the idea of perpetuity is to be found in Bankton. He wrote:[41]

"Some of these strict entails tend to infer a perpetuity of the estate subject thereto which no doubt is an inconveniency; but at the same time, such settlements were allowed by the civil law, tho' the emperor Justinian at last made a kind of temperament in this case viz. that unless the will of the testator was very express, the fideicommissary settlement should not endure beyond the fourth generation . . . . [I]t is submitted to the wisdom of Parliament how far some such limitation might not be put to future settlements, that our strict entails may be reduced *as not to run into perpetuities*."

Although Bankton is clearly dealing with strict entails it is suggested that the use of the term in the last part of the passage quoted might contain the germ of a wider concept of a settlement rendering property inalienable, as opposed to simply a settlement by way of strict entail (which of course would have that effect).

---

[37] Book II Tit. III. 58.

[38] The first edition of Stair's work was published in 1681. In his revised edition of 1693, while amendments to the general text are made to take account of the Entail Act 1685, Stair's original views on perpetuities remained unaltered.

[39] Thus in *Lord Strathnaver* v *Duke of Douglas* (1728) M 15372 *at* 15377. "But in tailzies of lands the principal intention is to preserve the estate to the heirs in perpetuity and not to give the value to any one substitute."

In two other cases, *Dillon* v *Campbell* (1780) M 15432 and *Menzies* v *Menzies* (1785) M 15436 the reports mention the purpose of the entails in question as 'perpetuating' the entailer's name.

See also Erskine's Institutes (1773) Book III Tit. VIII; 25 where entails are equated to a 'perpetuity of liferents'.

[40] at p.725.

[41] Institute: Vol. I at p.585, para. 147.

Whether Bankton was referring to recent developments or perhaps pointing the way is uncertain. What is known is that about the time of Bankton's treatise, or shortly after, the trust came to be used with increasing frequency as a means of settling property, and of settling it in perpetuity. While the strict entail may have created interests equivalent to 'a perpetuity of liferents,' the actuality could be created behind a trust, the trust form overcoming the problem of the general rule that the fee might not be in pendente, by vesting it in the trustees. As Bell put it:[42]

"The trust will be effectual to sustain future or contingent interests or those of persons not yet existing; and the fee in the trustees will be effectual to all intents, as if those persons were actually in existence, or as if their right were already purified."[43]

It is on this account that trust deeds are made of so much use in family settlements and in marriage contracts where, if a single conveyance alone were used, the purposes of the arrangement would find an obstacle almost insurmountable, in the maxim that a fee cannot be in pendente.

As in England the analogy with entails was drawn and not only in perpetual liferent trusts. In three cases towards the end of the eighteenth century, limitations involving issues of remoteness of vesting were found,[44] particularly in accumulation trusts, and in these it became clear that the second stage in the English development of the perpetuity concept, that of a settlement, of whatever type, which effectively rendered the property settled inalienable, had been reached. However in spite of trusts involving problems of remoteness the third stage in the English development, the transition from considering perpetuities on the broad ground of alienation to the narrower aspect of remoteness never seems to have occurred. Accordingly, then, as far as the domestic law of Scotland is concerned the concept of perpetuity is essentially that of a settlement rendering the property subject to it inalienable.

Approaches to Perpetuities

It will have been noticed from the foregoing that the creation of a perpetuity was a very deliberate act; it was not simple to create, and a degree of precision and accuracy was required in the legal creation which is probably equalled in modern times only by that required for the drafting of instruments relating to tax avoidance schemes.

Given this, it would seem to be essential that there be some analysis of the attitudes of the various parties involved. Why, for example, should people want to create perpetual settlements, and how did their existence affect those subject to them? And above all what was the attitude of the law towards them and why was that attitude adopted?

The Factors Present for the Creation of a Perpetuity

There would appear to have been three principal factors involved in the creation of perpetuities.

---

[42] Commentaries vol. i p.38.

[43] The best example of a trust of perpetual liferents to come before the court was *Suttie* v *Suttie's Trustees* (1846) 18 Jur. 442.

[44] The first was the *Barholm Case, McCullogh* v *McCullogh* (1752) Elch. Tailzie No. 48; 5 W. & S. 180-185 (in a note); the second was that of *Lord Hyndford's settlement*, apparently unreported but discussed in the third case, *MacNair* v *MacNair* (1791) *Bell's Case* 546.

(*a*) Dynastic Ambition

The first is, in a sense, a positive one, consisting of gratifying the desire to 'found a family' and to endow it with land. In many cases this sentiment has been explained as manifesting an affection for one's descendants, but in truth it amounts to little more than an attempt to achieve immortality by establishing a permanent connection with that most permanent of assets, land. In a scholarly, if emotional, attack on the entail system in Scotland, Patrick Irvine disposed of this argument:[45]

"The strong affections of the human mind do not extend to many generations. If traced upwards the feeling of affection towards ancestors is soon lost in that of veneration or respect; and beyond the second generation, feelings towards descendants may more properly be denominated benevolence than strong affection. The motives which prompt men to endure privations, and which lead to vigorous exertions, are those which flow from self-love and from affection to immediate descendants, and to relations endeared by personal intercourse. Industry is not promoted by estimating the respectability of posterity a century hence;—however powerfully it may be stimulated by endeavours to raise an existing family in the scale of Society. Complete security for the enjoyment of property during the life of the possessor, with power to give a preference to a particular line of descendants after death and a right to secure the succession against imprudent management, during the limited period over which human affections extend, are sufficiently powerful motives to influence conduct. Many have persuaded themselves in making entails, that they act upon principles proceeding from affection for their posterity. But the principle on which they really act, in so far as regards remote heirs, proceeds from their anxiety to perpetuate their own names and to establish a connecting tie between themselves and their property. By assuming a right of management for their successors they seem to continue their possession after death . . . . The same predominating principle of perpetuating a name, by preserving a control over property, neither sanctioned by natural law, nor calculated to promote the benefit of future generations, pervades the whole system of entailing."

These dynastic ambitions generally manifest themselves after a successful career and the creation of perpetual settlements has generally followed the amassing of great wealth either by trade or in a chosen career.[46] The settlements of Rickhill and Thirning are generally considered to exemplify this, Rickhill especially, having come to England from Ireland to practice at the bar and having no especially noble antecedents.

But these two settlements were exceptional. The rash of perpetuities came to be effected in England during the Elizabethan era and before, a period described by one commentator as "that almost Victorianly commercial age"[47] when land became available fairly freely[48] and great fortunes could be made in trade, or from privateering, an age during which the New World was yielding forth its riches in abundance.

In Scotland too the creation of perpetual settlements by way of ential seems to have coincided with the increase in commercial activity and wealth generated by the industrial revolution of the late eighteenth and early nineteenth centuries,

---

[45] "Considerations on the Inexpediency of the Law of Entail in Scotland by Patrick Irvine, W.S. 2nd Ed. 1827 (Edinburgh and London) at p.16/17.
[46] Kames in his History of Property, Law Tracts at p.130 suggests that the wealth was derived from acquisitions in war.
[47] Farran at p.152.
[48] Especially after the Reformation with the freeing of Church lands.

a fact that can be verified by consulting the entries in the Register of Entails for the appropriate dates. Thus:[49]

between 1685 and 1735	there were	335	deeds recorded involving the settlement of land
,, 1735 ,, 1785	,, ,,	590	,, ,, ,, ,, ,, ,, ,,
,, 1785 ,, 1835	,, ,,	1114	,, ,, ,, ,, ,, ,, ,,
,, 1835 ,, 1885	,, ,,	1134	,, ,, ,, ,, ,, ,, ,,
,, 1885 ,, 1935	,, ,,	221	,, ,, ,, ,, ,, ,, ,,
since 1935	there have been	2	,, ,, ,, ,, ,, ,, ,,

We see, then, from this table that the great mass of new registrations occurred during the period of the industrial revolution, a period which saw an unprecedented upsurge in the generation of new wealth, a substantial portion of which was invested in land. As Patrick Irvine put it:[50]

"[W]ealth began to be generally diffused over the country; and .... by investments in kind, and money acquired by manufacture and commerce, the beneficial influence of the system of entailing has been much more widely extended. Since that period the increase in wealth, both of foreign and domestic acquisition has naturally tended to increase the number of persons whose inclinations lead them to follow the example of the nobles and old established families in fixing an hereditary succession to the properties acquired by them."

And this emulation had clearly been carried to ludicrous lengths. In 1814 Sir John Sinclair published a "General Report of the Agricultural State and Political Circumstances of Scotland", containing a table giving the valued rent of every estate held under entail at that time.[51] Entailed estates, like the rest of the land were allocated into one of three classes:

(a) estates with a valued rent in excess of £2,000 Scots each,[52]

(b) estates with a valued rent of between £500 and £2,000 Scots, and

(c) estates with a valued rent of less than £500 Scots.

While the occasions are few, the Report nonetheless shows several examples of the entailed land in the latter class including such ludicrous "estates" as lodgings in Edinburgh, part of a tenement in Forfar, and a field in the Haughs of Clyde.

The practice of making new entails seems to have reached its climax around 1850. Thereafter [53] the entries on the Register relate increasingly to resettlements, first by the reinvestment on strict entail of the proceeds of entailed lands compulsorily acquired by rail- way companies and others, and then as part of the general process of disentail followed by a resettlement on strict entail. From about 1875 onwards[53] even this falls off until by 1914 the rate of settlements by way of strict entail is very small.

(b) Family Preservation

The second of the three principal factors involved in the creation of perpetuities is really the negative aspect of the dynastic ambition already dis-

---

[49] Note that this table refers only to deeds relating to the *entailing* of land, disentails having been excluded. A full statement of disentail can be found in Appendix II to the Ph.D. thesis 'Perpetuities in Scots Law' to be found in Edinburgh University Library.

[50] at p.51.

[51] As indeed it gave the rental value of all other land. It transpired that about 30% of all the estates in Scotland (in terms of rental value) were entailed.

[52] £100 Scots = £8.6.8 sterling.

[53] See Appendix I of the Ph.D. Thesis (note 40 above).

cussed, for the dynast would wish to preserve an already established family just as much as a nouveau riche would wish to establish one.

On the domestic side the danger came from the increasing relaxation of the restraints imposed by the feudal system. As Professor Monteath has observed:[54]

"The cohesive form of the feudal system in its heyday afforded a substantial guarantee that the feu would not go out of the vassal's family, but the gradually amplified conception of ownership in the vassal tended to clash with a human sentiment manifested early in our history, being the desire of perpetuating the name wealth and influence of a family on the basis of ancestral holding of land, at one time the only kind of property viewed as respectable and indicating a stake in the country."

As we shall see this 'amplified conception of ownership' manifested itself in a greater and ultimately complete freedom of alienation[55] which effectively meant the possibility of the land through which the family had become established being disposed of elsewhere with the likely diminution in status and fortune that would go with it.

This alienation might occur in three ways. In the first place there might be a simple deviation from the line of heirs; this would in fact be creating a new settlement. Secondly the land might be sold and thirdly it might be loaded with debt and apprised by the creditors.

The fee tail in England provided implicit prohibitions of the first two and rendered any such debts unenforceable as against the land itself. In Scotland the strict entail provided protection by explicit clauses in the charter. A good example of this is the *Stormont Case*[56] which concerned the entail of the Lordship of Scone and which recited, 'That it should not be lawful for any of the heirs of entail to violate or dissolve the said tailzie, to dispose or wadset the said estate, or any part thereof, or to do any deed whereby the same may be evicted or comprised from them.' This clause was fenced with a resolutive clause declaring that in the event of contravention by any heir, that heir should forfeit his right to the estate which would then devolve on the next substitute.

The Earl of Annandale, being an heir of entail, contracted debts which were secured on the lordship. On his death his creditors sought to apprise the lordship whereupon the next heir, the Viscount Stormont, sought to prevent this by bringing an action of declarator to have it found that the late Earl had, by his action in contracting debt, contravened the prohibition and thereupon lost his right to the estate, which in turn would have rendered the action of the creditors null, so that he could take the lands free from the debts.

It was held that the declarator would be granted, so that the diligence of the creditors failed.

This general result seems in turn to have had two principal effects. In the first place it provided a means whereby creditors who were less than properly vigilant[57] could be defrauded by heirs of entail; and this in turn meant that

---

[54] "Heritable Rights" in Introduction to Scottish Legal History; Stair Soc. vol. 10 at p.178.
[55] See Chapters II and III for a discussion of this in relation to England and Scotland respectively.
[56] *Creditors of the Earl of Annandale* v *Viscount Stormont* (1662) M. 13994-6.
[57] One of the objects of the Act of 1685 was to protect creditors by the creation of a Register of Entails wherein had to be registered all valid entails. An entry would therefore be open to inspection by a prospective creditor who could then take action accordingly.

borrowing on the security of entailed property became less attractive, so that funds for improvements to the settled estate dried up.[58]

(c) Protection from Forfeiture

In *Sir Anthony Mildmay's Case*[59] Coke pours the following vituperations on perpetuities. He says:[60]

"That all these perpetuities were against the reason and policy of the common law; for at common law all inheritances were fee simple, as Littleton saith lib. i Cap. Estate-tail; and the reason thereof was, that neither lords should be defeated of their escheats, wards, etc. nor the farmers or purchasers lose their estates or leases, or be evicted by the heirs of the grantors or lessors, nor such infinite occasions of troubles, contentions and suits arise. But the true policy and rule of the common law in this point was in effect overthrown by the Statute de Donis Conditionalibus made anno 13 Ed. I which established a general perpetuity by Act of Parliament, for all who had or would make it, by force whereof all the possessions of England were in effect entailed accordingly, which was the occasion and cause of the said and divers other mischiefs. And the same was attempted and endeavoured to be remedied at divers Parliaments and divers bills were exhibited accordingly (which I have seen) but they were all on one pretence or another rejected. But the truth was that the Lords and Commons knowing that their estates tail were not to be forfeited for felony or treason; as their estates of inheritance were before the said Act (and chiefly in the time of H.3 in the barons war), and finding that they were not answerable for the debts and encumbrances of their ancestors, nor did the sales, alienations or leases of their ancestors bind them for the lands which were entailed to their ancestors, they always rejected such bills."

This second defensive factor is known to have played a significant part in both England and Scotland.

In England the idea that an estate tail was not forfeitable for treason came from the common law and was apparently accepted in a case in 1341.[61] The justification for it seems to be in the growing notion of inalienability attached to the entailed fee, that the tenant in tail could not do any act whereby the interests of his heirs and those entitled in remainder or reversion would be prejudiced[62] and that this applied also to acts against the Crown. Whether this justification would have stood the test of time is open to question but the issue became academic in 1352 when the Statute of Treasons confirmed what was thought to be the common law rule. Accordingly while Acts of Attainder were passed against individuals forfeiting their property the effect came to be that as far as entailed lands were concerned, the forfeiture lasted only during the lifetime of the person attainted, so that the lands were recoverable by his heirs and the entail continued.[63]

The entail however was not the only way land was sought to be protected. Another method, which proliferated during the troubles of the fifteenth century

---

[58] See below, Chapter III.
[59] 1606 4 Co. Rep. f.40a.
[60] *ibid*. at ff.40a; 40b. Compare with this Blackstone Comm. vol ii p.117.
[61] Y.B. 14 Ed. III (Rolls Series) at p.314.
[62] See per Stonore C.J. in (1331) Y.B. 4 Edw. III Tri. pl.4 and per Grene arquendo in (1346) Y.B. 20 Ed. III (Rolls Series) ii 202.
  "You see plainly how he has confessed that J. was issue in tail whose deed is as much restrained by the statute as the deed of the tenant in tail himself."
[63] See the study of Professor Bellamy in 'The Law of Treason in England in the Later Middle Ages' (1970 Cambridge) esp. at pp.191-7.

was the conveyance to feoffees to hold to the use of the grantor.[64] It has been suggested by Walter Ross[65] that this practice found its way to Scotland and that the origin of the trust in Scotland stems from such conveyances. However, as has been pointed out elsewhere,[66] there is no evidence of any kind that trusts were in use in Scotland in the fifteenth century and indeed do not appear in the reports until the early seventeenth. If Ross is right the gap of one and a half centuries is mystifying. It seems much more likely that Ross was in fact drawing from contemporary English material and assuming that a similar situation existed in Scotland.

The true use of the perpetual settlement in Scotland as a means of preventing the forfeiture of estates begins with the entail. Indeed, in spite of the assertion in the preamble that the object of the statute is the protection of creditors, it is a strongly held view that the true purpose of the Entail Act of 1685 was to secure a means whereby land could not be forfeited even for treason. Thus, Laing writes:[67]

"Amidst the new treasons which the Parliament created, and the numerous attainders which it pronounced, an act of an opposite tendency was passed, to authorise the perpetual entail of lands. That the Scots should have remained so long ignorant, or have availed themselves at such a late period of a feudal institution, which other nations were desirous to explode, are circumstances sufficient to excite our attention and surprise. The statute of entails was evaded in England before the Scots had begun to study or improve their laws; and the early sovereigns of the Stuart family would never have consented to a device adopted to perpetuate a feudal aristocracy, which it was the uniform policy of their house to depress. But the nobility at present were no longer the objects of jealousy or fear. The estates were required to confirm the sentences of Jerviswood, Argyle and Porterfield; to ratify the opinions of the Court of Session, that it was treason not to reveal the demand of contributions for traitors, nor to abjure the treasonable declaration of the fanatics; to approve the practice of the Justiciary Court in proceeding to trial and convictions the day after the citation was given; and the nobility were secretly alarmed at the retrospective treasons which they were employed to create. From these they perceived that the declation of new laws and of new crimes was lodged entirely in the breast of the judge; and from the numerous attainders which they were required to pronounce, they felt with terror that their lives were exposed to the mercy, and their estates to the rapacity, of the Crown. To preserve their estates from forfeiture, and their families from ruin, it would appear that they sought an indirect expedient to elude the iniquitous laws and corrupt practices which they were too dependent to reject or to resist. Entails had already been introduced in a few instances, but were reprobated as repugnant to the genius of the laws. Corruption of blood, which obstructs the course of succession, was a penalty never incurred as a consequence of attainder, unless it were inflicted by an act of *dishabilitation*;[68] and the estates relying secretly on the maxim that nothing more could be forfeited than the person attainted was entitled to alienate, passed an act by which lands might be entailed to perpetuity, and the rights of an endless series of heirs, be reduced almost to an usufructurary interest during their lives. Under the pretext of securing their estates from alienation or debts, the nobility undoubtedly expected to preserve their families, in the event of attainder, from the forfeiture of more than the liferent interest or escheat of an heir. The commissioner consented to the act, to perpetuate his own acquisitions to his family; and from the tyranny of James, entails were introduced into Scotland when the rigour of the feudal system had almost expired."

[64] *ibid.* Note also the speech of Bacon in Chudleigh's Case *supra* where the usage of conveying land to Feoffees to Uses is attacked.
[65] Lectures on the Law of Scotland (1792) at pp.242/243.
[66] 1974 Jur. Rev. 196.
[67] "History of Scotland" (1800) vol. 4; bk. 9; p.166.

The background of fear explicit in Laing's statement would seem accurately to represent the contemporary situation. The tremendous length of the list of those named as having suffered forfeiture in the Act of 4th July 1690 'rescinding the forfeitures and fines passed since 1665,' would seem amply to confirm this. If there exist doubts about the overall validity of Laing's opinion, it would seem that they stem from the closeness with which his account follows the English medieval position, especially with regard to the conceptual justification of the effectiveness of the entail as a protector of family estates. Again, as with Ross earlier,[69] the suspicion raised is that English sources have been translated into a Scottish context; or perhaps in this case that Laing is telescoping two pieces of legislation. This latter view derives from the fact that in 1690[70] an Act was passed 'for security of the creditors, vassals, and heirs of entail of persons forfeited'. After reciting that it is a grievance, to be remedied in that "such rights as are not in a man's power to alienate by consent should not be confiscate by his Cryme," and after dealing with vassals and creditors the Act then turns to entails and the Act of 1685 providing:

". . . . that no aires of entails in infeftments or other deeds affected with prohibitive or irritant clauses in case of contravention of the provisions therein mentioned shall be prejudged by the forfaulture of his predecessor but only insofar as the partie forfaulted had liberty to contract debt or affect the lands of others be the quality of the right and infeftment . . . . provyding the Right of Tailzie be registrate conform to the Act of Parliament of 1685."

However this may be, it would appear, even if Laing is completely accurate, the Act of 1685 failed to provide the necessary protection, for if it had the provisions of 1690 would have been unnecessary.

Of these three factors above discussed this last was of only a temporary relevance. In England estates tail became alienable after the judgements in *Taltaram's Case* 1472[71] had indicated that it would be possible to bar the claims of remaindermen and reversioners by means of a collusive common recovery with double voucher to warranty.[72] In Scotland the inviolability of entailed estates was of even shorter duration, a statute of 7 Anne, c. 20 enacting "that all persons convicted or attainted of high treason, or misprision of high treason in Scotland, shall be subject and liable to the same corruption of blood, pains, penalties, and forfeitures, with persons convicted of these crimes in England."

The Effects of Perpetuities on Beneficiaries

"[A] perpetual family settlement is made by a remote ancestor, who cluld not anticipate the various changes which may occur in the course of time and progress of society. The power of regulating succession after death according to the exigencies and circumstances of a family, is one of the most interesting exercises of parental affection and duty. But the family settlement of the entailed proprietor is made for him

---

[68] See Bellamy *supra* at p.192.
[69] In connection with trusts, see above.
[70] Act of 1690 c. 104 (A.P.S. vol. vii, p.225).
[71] (1472) Y.B. 12 Ed. IV Mich. f.14 pl.16; f.19 pl.35. Y.B. 13 Ed. IV Mich. f.1 pl.1. There is a tradition, given prominence by Pigott in his 'Common Recoveries' (1739) that the litigation in this case was instigated by Edward IV in an attempt to achieve the alienability of entailed estates in order that the lands of those participating in the Lancastrian uprising of 1471 could be forfeited to the Crown.
[72] See below Chapter II.

before his birth; and the deed of his ancestor, which inconveniently restricted his natural right of possession during his life, deprives him of the civil right of a power of distribution of his property after death . . . ."[73]

This quotation from Patrick Irvine's essay captures the essential paradox of the perpetual settlement. On the one hand the dynast creating the perpetuity is intending that the benefit of such a settlement be passed on through the ages. Yet at the same time he is prescribing that those who do benefit shall forfeit their own rights of disposition in respect of the property subject to the settlement.

Discussed in terms of abstract concepts such as rights of property, the question has a degree of unreality as far as those subject to the perpetuity are concerned. For, in a settlement designed to protect them and their families, this restriction of rights would no doubt be accepted without question if the benefits from the settlement were sufficiently obvious and sufficiently large. Yet it is these benefits which have been felt consistently to have been either insufficient, or irrelevant or else productive of other evils.

That they were insufficient is evidenced by the persistent complaints of entailed proprietors in Scotland of impoverishment. The point was that in such settlements only the income would be available to satisfy the needs of those who were supposed to benefit. There could be no resort to capital, for this would be dissipating the estate and infringing the perpetuity. Accordingly, as the income from the estate would be fixed at the time of the settlement, calls on it, for example to provide an education for members of the family, would mean that there would be that much less to meet other needs.

An economist would argue that income could be increased by improvements to both the estate and in the methods of running it. But the improvements themselves would cost money, money which properly should be derived from capital. But capital could not be forthcoming from the estate because this was inviolable. Nor, in fact would much be obtainable on credit because the estate, being inviolable, would not be available as security for a creditor. Accordingly as expenses increased with the increase in families and inflation generally, it would become less practicable to reserve a portion of current income to meet future expenditure for improvements. This in turn would mean at best no increase, but often, in actuality, a decrease, in income because of the running down of the estate and the lack of means with which such a trend could be corrected.

There were, of course, some who defended this. Sir George Mackenzie, for example said:[74]

[73] Observations on the Inexpediency of the Law of Entail in Scotland, at p.82.
[74] Pleadings in the Stormont Case *supra*.
   This seems to epitomise the other chief complaint about perpetuities which perhaps owed as much to the generation gap as to anything else, namely that the perpetual settlement tended to be disruptive of the family unit by promoting discord between father and son. Bacon (Works vol. vii at pp.634/635) put it this way:
   "Though I reverence the laws of my country, yet I observe one defect in them; and that is, there is no footstep there of the reverend postestas patria which was so commended in ancient times . . . This only yet remains: if the father has any patrimony and the son be disobedient, he may disinherit him; if he will not deserve his blessing he shall not have his living. But this device of perpetuities has taken this power from the father likewise; and has tied and made subject (as the proverb is) the parents to their cradle, and so notwithstanding he has the curse of his father yet he shall have the land of his grandfather."

"Discourage not (my Lords) such as love to be frugal, because they hope their estates may remain with their posterity. Encourage not such as resolve to shake loose by their prodigality what was established by their wise predecessors. By favouring the creditors' defences, you will but gratify the prodigality of heirs or the laziness of creditors; whereas by sustaining my client's pursuit you will perpetuate noble families and bound the luxury of those who are to succeed.'

But during the next century and a half these sentiments became less and less popular as it became more and more difficult to live adequately within the restrictive confines of the perpetuity. To meet some of the objections remedial legislation was passed in 1770[75] permitting the entailed proprietor to charge the substitute heirs with the bulk of money expended for the purpose of improving the estate, and in 1824[76] permitting a similar device to be utilised so as to make provision for other members of the family. But these were little more than palliatives and the plight of entailed proprietors continued to be acute until power to disentail was granted in 1848.[77]

Perhaps the most eloquent of the many cris de coeur of this period is that of Patrick Irvine which is written with such obvious feeling that it needs neither comment nor explanation.[78]

"The injurious consequences arising from entails are so generally known and appreciated, as to require no recapitulation. In all important transactions for loans of money upon heritable security the persons proposing to advance it consult the records; and the entailed proprietor cannot obtain a loan. But in the ordinary affairs of life the possession of property naturally lends to personal credit, without much investigation, which to a certain extent, and in many instances of daily occurrence cannot be refused, unless in cases of notorious extravagance. Hence upon the death of entailed proprietors losses frequently arise.

With the exception of some instances in which property is preserved under bad management to the worthy descendant of an extravagant ancestor entails are injurious to individuals. The benefits which arise from such occasional exceptions will not bear a comparison with the evils arising in numerous instances from the succession devolving upon a remote heir, leaving the nearest relatives of the previous heir in possession unprovided for and unprotected. Human wisdom cannot anticipate events so as to appreciate duly, and to regulate the rights and interests of posterity with discriminating foresight for any period of long duration. The rules according to which justice is administered, and all the public acts of the country are subject to alteration according to the changes produced by time and circumstances. The uncontrolled power and dominion of individuals over property should not be of unlimited duration. How many entailers would have rejected the order of succession pointed out by them, and the restrictions contained in their deeds, if they could have anticipated the intervening course of events, and the situation of their posterity.

The entailed proprietor labours under grievous hardships. Upon his succession he is probably burdened with provisions to brothers and sisters, which, however inadequate for their suitable education and support, he may not have the means to pay without the aid of friends. The prosecution of his own plans of life is obstructed by his limited credit. It is expected that he will live suitably to the rental of the estate, of which he is nominally the proprietor, but really only the liferenter. If prudent he is surrounded by difficulties in providing for a family, and improving his estate:—and if extravagant, his creditors may be under the necessity of attaching his rents. He

---

[75] Act of 10 Geo. III c. 51. (The Montgomery Act.)
[76] Act of 5 Geo. IV c. 87. (The Aberdeen Act.)
[77] Act of 11th and 12th Vict. c. 36. The Entail Amendment Act (known as the Rutherfurd Act).
[78] Considerations on the Inexpediency of the Law of Entail in Scotland at pp.78-80.

cannot borrow money in the ordinary way of loan to supply his wants. His early expectatons of succession and station in society naturally lead to a mode of living and habits by which such debts are contracted as his limited credit can command, arising rather from the situation in which he is placed than from the general extravagance ascribed .... to entailed proprietors. He cannot command money to improve his property, however much it may be susceptible of it, unless by encroaching upon his means of granting provisions to a family."

The Attitude of the Courts to Perpetuities

Given that similar factors were present in both Scotland and England with regard to the creation of perpetuities and with regard to their effects it is perhaps surprising that the attitudes of the respective courts were so markedly different. The English attitude is summed up by Lord Nottingham in the *Duke of Norfolk's Case* in the following statement:[79]

"The great matter objected to is, it is against all the rules of law and tends to a perpetuity. If it tends to a perpetuity there needs no more to be said, for the law has so long laboured against perpetuities, that it is an undeniable reason against any settlement, if it can be found to tend to a perpetuity."

In Scotland the tendency has been to describe the attitude of the law as being precisely the opposite. Thus in *Muir's Trustees* v *Williams*[80] Lord Cooper opined:

"Now as I understand it, the English rule against perpetuities is a rule or series of rules, of great antiquity and high artificiality, slowly evolved by the English courts without legislative aid. The Scottish counterpart is a relatively modern statutory innovation. The traditional English attitude towards anything 'tending' to a perpetuity us one of pronounced dislike. The attitude of the common law of Scotland is one of indifference and even of benevolence. In *Strathmore* v *Strathmore's Trustees*,[81] Lord Chancellor Brougham said:[82] 'In Scotland the law, instead of discouraging perpetuities, gives them all manner of encouragement'; and in *Suttie* v [*Suttie's Trustees*][83] Lord President Boyle referred to this statement with approval, and added;[84] 'It is manifest that our law by no means views [perpetuities] with the abhorrence in which they are held both in the language of the English authorities and in the decisions of the courts of that country. The case of *McNair in* 1791[85] unquestionably evinces that the law of Scotland rests on principles of an opposite nature.' But it is not merely in background and origin that the two systems differ. A superficial similarity conceals a fundamental difference in the content and effect of the laws of the two countries."

This dictum is typical of so many modern rationalisations[86] of the attitude adopted by the common law to perpetuities, perhaps induced by some fear of

---

[79] (1682) 3 Ch. Cas at p.31.
[80] 1942 S.C. 5 at pp.11/12.
[81] (1831) 5 W. & S. 170.
[82] *ibid.* at p.193.
[83] (1846) 18 Jur 442.
[84] *ibid.* at p.445.
[85] Bell's Cases at p.546.
[86] See especially J. M. Halliday 'The Tragedy of Sasine' (1965) 10. Jur. Rev. (N.S.) at pp. 105/106.

"Again the sacred English doctrine against perpetuities (which vexes Scottish lawyers not at all) has resulted in such comic clauses as that which specifies the endurance of a trust for a period ending upon the expiry of a stated number of years after the death of the survivor of the descendants of His late Majesty King George the Fifth alive at the execution of the deed."

'the sinister influence of the English rule against perpetuities'[87] being introduced into Scots law. In point of fact it is generally agreed that some doubt existed until as late as 1846[88] as to the legality of private trusts in perpetuity. Put at its highest, the attitude of the common law seems to have been one of indifference in which the 'benevolence' referred to by Lord Cooper is difficult to find. Put at less than its highest it is possible to discover what could be taken as flirtations with some kind of a perpetuity principle at various times prior to the *Suttie* decision.

If one looks at the strict entail and examines the attitude of the Court of Session to the object of their reluctant approval[89] one scarcely finds a picture of benevolence, or even of indifference.[90] As early as 1677 in *Rothes* v *Melville*[91] Fountainhall, speaking of the clauses fencing the prohibitions, could say that "the President in his system has declared himself no friend of these clauses". And Stair was equally hostile. He wrote:[92]

"Clauses de non aliendo or non contrahendo debitum are most unfavourable and inconvenient, especially when absolute: for first commerce is thereby hindered, which is the common interest of mankind; secondly the natural obligations of providing wives and children are thereby hindered which cannot lawfully be omitted; thirdly it is unreasonable so to clog estates descending from predecessors left us whereby they have the shadow of an estate . . . ."

Erskine writing in 1773 was of the same opinion. He said:[93]

"As to which it may be promised that though such entails appear to have been first brought into use as far back as Hope's time yet they were generally accounted not only contrary to good conscience, as they cut off the right of lineal heir . . . . but also inconsistent with the genius of our law as they sunk the property of land estates and created a perpetuity of liferents."

Indeed this approach was reflected in the courts where a strict approach was adopted so that the entail was 'interpreted with rigour'.[94] As a result the reports are full of cases where the courts have reduced an entail because a formality has not been complied with, or because on its 'true' construction a particular clause contains the possibility of a loophole. This is further confirmed by the note in the fourth edition of Stair's Institutions, published in 1824. The note reads:[95]

"We now proceed to the construction of entails. That has always been accounted stricti iuris . . . .

But, though the principle of strict interpretation be applicable to entails, yet a very marked difference in viewing this subject has lately been introduced. The principle entertained during at least the last half of the late century, and some years of this, was that entails, being calculated to put land extra commercium were to be considered as public evils which ought to be got rid of, or softened on every occasion in which the

---

[87] Per Lord Romer in *Muir's Tees* v *Williams* 1943 *S.C.* (*HL*) *at p.*58 mocking the attitude of certain members of the court below.
[88] *Suttie* v *Suttie's Trustees supra.*
[89] In *Creditors of the Earl of Annandale* v *Viscount Stormont* (1662) M 13994.
[90] For a detailed discussion of the decisions on the construction of clauses in entailed settlements see below Chapter III.
[91] (1677) 3 Bro. Supp. at p.170.
[92] Book II. Tit. III. 58.
[93] Book II. Tit. VIII. 25.
[94] *Duke of Queensberry* v *Earl of Wemyss* (1807) *M. Tailzie App.* Part I 44.
[95] At p. 271.

language could liberally allow it, however contrary the construction might be to the manifest intention of the entailer.[96]"

It had long been established that a straightforward perpetuity of liferents might fall foul of the feudal principle that a fee must not be in pendente.[97] As we have seen, Erskine was of the opinion that the use of the strict entail was simply a way of achieving this via the back door and that accordingly entails were to be deprecated.[98]

But the change came with the increasing use of the trust as a means of settling property, for the vesting of the fee in trustees overcame such objections as this.

And it was, of course, in connection with trust dispositions that Lord Cooper's remarks were made. But even here, as late as 1846, it could be seriously and strenuously argued that a trust should be reduced because it tended to perpetuity,[99] and if one examines the judgements in decided cases, again one finds dissatisfaction and hostility to the idea of perpetual settlements.

Thus in *McNair* v *McNair*[100] which is really the first case on this topic reported in any detail, the court was divided over what policy to adopt and eventually came down in favour of the limitation in question by a majority.[101] In that case there were clear statements against permitting perpetual trusts. Thus Lord Swinton stated that he had always been against perpetuities and Lord President Campbell was much troubled by the point. He said:[102]

"Trust settlements are usual with us and admit of being easily extricated when granted for certain reasonable and temporary purposes, such as payments of debts and securing provisions to wives and children . . . . [The] object of the deed was to secure the capital of the granter's fortune to his children and their descendents and that this trust should be perpetual. What is this but an entail in a new form?'

The question came up again in *Strathmore* v *Strathmore's Trustees*[103] where Lord Brougham delivered his classic statement that the law of Scotland gave perpetuities 'all manner of encouragement'. It should be pointed out that this appears very much to have been an ipse dixit for certainly there were no cases prior to this in which the attitude of the law had been expressed in a positive

---

[96] Citing *Roxburghe* v *Bellenden Ker* (1808) M. App (*Tailzie*) 18; on remit from H.L.; F.C. 17th June 1813 and 2 Dow 151. Also *Roxburghe* v *Don alias Wauchope* (1734) 1 Cr & St 126. See further, Chapter III.
[97] See below, Chapter III, footnote 241.
[98] For a detailed discussion of the perpetuities aspect of the liferent rules see Chapter IV.
[99] In the *Suttie Case, supra*.
[100] This case is reported in three places. That in Morrison's Dictionary M. 16210 is the least satisfactory, giving only a summary of the arguments without giving any details of the judgements. The report in Bell's cases (1790-92) at p.546 gives a good account of the arguments employed but a somewhat incomplete record of the judgements. This report is best supplemented with the note of the case in 5 W. & S. at pp.187-191 (the note is to the *Strathmore Case*).
[101] The majority and indeed the judges differ according to the reports. It appears that Lords Swinton, Campbell and Alva (not mentioned in Bell's reports) were against the trust, that Lords Monboddo and Macqueen were for it; and that Lords Eskgrove and Dunsinnan were reluctant to let it stand, but could find no valid reason to reduce it. According to the note in Wilson and Shaw's reports, Lords Henderland and Hailes were at some stage involved also. Lord Henderland was apparently in favour of the deed whereas Lord Hailes was definitely against it on the ground of perpetuity.
[102] 5 W. & S. at pp.189/190.
[103] (1831) 5 W. & S. 170.

way. While it is true that in the *McNair Case* the deed[104] had been upheld, the support it received was more on the ground of indifference to perpetuity rather than support, at least where trusts were concerned.[105] However as Lord Brougham's statement has been cited with approval in the *Suttie Case*[106] the judgement should be examined with some closeness, and when so examined it appears that Lord Brougham was not nearly so emphatic as at first sight he appears to have been.

Early on in his judgement when he referred to the decision of the Court below he said:[107]

". . . . the Court below have come to the right judgement in saying that this is not, by the law of Scotland, such a perpetuity as a man may not create with regard to the real property of which he is unlimited fiar."

If that passage is taken alone it would seem to imply that, by the law of Scotland, there did in fact (or at least there might) exist such a perpetuity as might not be created. On the other hand, without more, it could be argued that such an interpretation reads too much into the statement.

But there is more. Several cases were cited in favour of some principle against perpetuities. The first of these was the *Barholm Case*[108] which His Lordship dismissed as inextricable. The next was the *McNair Case* which was explained as not providing any authority against intelligible but perpetual trusts. The third of these was *Lord Hyndford's Case*, which does not appear to have been reported, but which was referred to in *McNair*. The Hyndford settlement apparently clearly tended to perpetuity, although its provisions were not discussed in detail. In *McNair's Case*[109] Lord President Campbell is reported to have said:

"In the late case of Lord Hyndford's settlements the court went as far as possible to sustain a trust deed where the purposes went a little beyond what has usually been thought reasonable and consistent with the powers of a proprietor with regard to the disposal of his estate after his death; but lawyers differed with regard to the validity of that deed, though temporary in its nature, and calculated for purposes which, in the case of a noble family were not thought inexpedient or unwise."

Of Lord Hyndford's settlement Lord Brougham had this to say:[110]

"That was not a deed for twenty-five years, except in one event—in the event of one of two alternatives happening; but nevertheless that deed was supported, if I am to take the statement of Lord President Campbell. He says it may be supported in so far as it was temporary, for special purposes; and what may possibly reconcile the books on this subject is that it was supported as far as regards the temporary part, and set aside only as regards the perpetuity."

Again, the view that the courts have set aside an intelligible settlement 'as regards the perpetuity' is hardly evidence of 'giving all manner of encouragement' to perpetuities.

But there is more to come. Even with this, had Lord Brougham then gone

---

[104] In England this would certainly have been void under the modern rule against perpetuities and probably under the old rule as well.
[105] See below. Chapter III.
[106] (1846) 18 Jur. 442.
[107] 5 W. & S. at p.194.
[108] *McCulloch* v *McCulloch*: Reported by Lord Elchies in his section on Tailzie, No. 48, but much more fully in the note to the Strathmore Case at 5 W. & S. pp.180-185.
[109] According to the note in 5 W. & S., at p.189/190, but not, apparently in either of the other two reports.
[110] 5 W. & S. at p.199.

ahead and treated the settlement before him as valid, notwithstanding its being perpetual nature, his classic dictum would still carry great authority. But he did not, for he went on:[111]

"Here it is not contended that the perpetuity be supported, nor is that contention necessary to support the judgement of the court below. I do not mean to say that there may not be an extremely good ground for setting aside an accumulation which is to go on for ever . . . ."

With the best will in the world it is difficult to see, in view of statements like this, how Lord Brougham's judgement can properly be made a foundation for a view that the Scots common law tended to encourage rather than discourage perpetuities. All he appears to be saying is that the settlement in front of him is neither inextricable nor bad for perpetuity. But, if so, what of his statement that Scots law gives perpetuities all manner of encouragement? It is suggested that the most appropriate comment on this is that of Lord Mackay in *Lindsay's Executors* v *Forsyth*:[112]

"The view of Scottish law on perpetuities is not very definite and I do not propose in the circumstances of this case to enter into any attempt of mine to define it . . . . Generally speaking perpetuities are not so obnoxious to the outlook of Scottish law as they are found in English law, where early statutes are construed as almost negativing all perpetuities. In the *Strathmore Case*, Lord Brougham said this:[113] 'In Scotland the law instead of discouraging perpetuities gives them all manner of encouragement, and . . . . permits you to tie up property for ever and ever.' Had it stood there, there would have been no question left. In the passage in question however, I have always thought that Lord Brougham, as he sometimes did, was using a sarcastic exaggeration."

Thus far it has been attempted to show that the common law of Scotland gave little encouragement to the creation of perpetuities. But on the other hand there is little to show that where the settlement was by way of trust it did very much to control them either. While some of the remarks of Lord Brougham quoted above could be cited in support of such a contention, the clearest indication of a possible flirtation with an anti-perpetuity policy comes from a case thirteen years later, decided by the same judges who, two years afterwards decided the *Suttie Case*.

The case was *Mason* v *Skinner*[114] and in itself was not very remarkable. Like the *Strathmore Case* it was concerned with an accumulation trust but, unlike the *Strathmore Case*, this settlement was eventually reduced by the First Division as being inextricable because it was shown that, on the basis of accountancy evidence the provisions of the settlement were unworkable. The point of interest centres around the note of the Lord Ordinary, Lord Cuninghame, to the First Division, the relevant part of which reads as follows:[115]

"Suppose the will and the schedule to have been validly executed as writs, the enquiry on the merits, which requires no extrinsic proof would next fall to be considered, whether the deed itself is so irrational, delusive and inextricable as to be void at common law.

The relevancy of that ground of reduction cannot be doubted. It is true that the Thellusson Act does not apply to the disposition of landed property in Scotland; and in the *Strathmore Case* a trust for thirty years, and the lifetime thereafter of

---

[111] *ibid.*
[112] 1940 S.C. 568.
[113] 5 W. & S. at p.195.
[114] (1844) 16 Jur. 422.
[115] *ibid.* at p.424.

certain parties specially excluded, was sustained as founded on well-defined and not irrational purposes; but nevertheless, the law in questions of this nature, as stated by Mr. Bell in his Commentaries,[116] has been understood as incontestable, in that it is laid down that 'when the will becomes inextricable, or *when it is intended for too distant a contingency*, it will be inefficient at common law'. That doctrine was in substance acquiesced in by the Lord Chancellor (Brougham) in the *Strathmore Case*; and it is apprehended that the present case falls clearly within the rule thus announced . . . .

If this be a correct view of the import of the settlement and scheme, an estate now yielding £120 per annum and worth from £3,000 to £4,000 capital, [will be] being hoarded and withdrawn from commerce for eighty-four years . . . . Surely if any trust be void from undue accumulation and from the shadowy and remote nature of the contingent interest given to the respective beneficiaries, the present is a case of that description."

The First Division were at pains to point out that they agreed with the views of the Lord Ordinary, only Lord Fullerton adding a qualification:[117]

"I do not hold that it is incompetent to make a settlement which is to go on for ever; but then the accumulations must have a definite object. The beneficial interests must merge immediately as in the case of a charitable endowment."[118]

Now, phrased as it is, with mention of 'too distant a contingency' and the 'remote nature of the contingent interest' one could be forgiven for thinking that this passage contains the germ of a rule against remoteness[119] having similar considerations to those of Lord Nottingham's rule. By this it is not intended to suggest that the Lord Ordinary's note can be construed as suggesting that the modern English rule against perpetuities with all its various ramifications was applicable. But it does point to a problem of remoteness and it is that problem which gave rise to the English rule.

Two years later came *Suttie's Case*[120] heard by the same Lord Ordinary, Lord Cuninghame, and then by the First Division constituted by exactly the same four judges as sat in *Mason* v *Skinner*. Here the result was emphatically different, the Court rejecting any suggestion that Scots law contained a rule against perpetuities. Lord President Boyle dealt with the matter very shortly. He said:[121]

"After perusing the cases for the parties now submitted to us on the report of the Lord Ordinary, I am unable to see any sufficient reasons for sustaining any of the

---

[116] Vol. i at p.38. The relevant passage reads: 'Trustees may be invested with a power to accumulate profits for particular purposes or destinations; to sell lands and apply the price; or to realise funds and purchase estates, and their powers and duties will depend on the terms of their appointment. But wherever a will becomes inextricable, or where it is intended for too distant a contingency, it will be inefficient at common law . . . ."
[117] (1844) 16 Jur. at p. 425.
[118] Compare Parker and Mellows—The Modern Law of Trusts (1970) 2nd Ed.
"Since mediaeval times English law has been subject to the tension between two conflicting influences. Land and other property owners have desired to tie up their property indefinitely, usually for the benefit of their family, or for some institution or cause, while the courts and legislature have always felt that it is in the interests of the nation as a whole that wealth should circulate freely and not be inalienable. The result has been a compromise. Property may be tied up indefinitely for a purpose which the law wishes to advance, namely a charity. Otherwise property may be tied up, but only for a comparatively short period."
[119] Compare with Lord Nottingham's view in *The Duke of Norfolk's Case*—see note 34 above—'especially if they be not of remote or long consideration'.
[120] (1846) 18 Jur. 442.
[121] *ibid*. at p. 445.

conclusions of this action, at least in hoc statu. The elaborate discussion in the case for the pursuer, and by which it is endeavoured to get the better of the distinction between the law of England and Scotland with regard to perpetuities, however ingenious it is, does not appear to me to be at all successful as it is manifest that our law by no means views them with the abhorrence in which they are held both in the language of the English authorities and in the decisions of the Courts of that country."

This approach was echoed by the three other members of the Court, only Lord Mackenzie showing the slightest doubt, and then not on the correctness of the Lord President's statement of the law. He said:[122]

"Nor is the duration of trusts restricted by law. There are numerous instances in the cases of mortifications, and of trusts for the foundation and maintenance of schools and hospitals, and for other charitable purposes, which are so constituted as to be calculated to exist to perpetuity: but though these trusts have given rise to much litigation, they have never been challenged on the ground of illegality because they were to endure to perpetuity. Whether such trusts are consistent with the interests of the public might indeed give rise to a shrewd question of political economy; and it might, as a question of political economy, be argued, that such trusts to perpetuity ought not to be sustained, unless it were made out to the satisfaction of high judicial authority that there was a high and permanent utility in putting funds extra commercium. We have no statute, no law, however to prevent the creation of such trusts; and though the abstract question as to the policy of permitting them may be a curious speculative question, it does not fall within our consideration."

Of *Mason* v *Skinner*[123] counsel against the settlement made much, but while the Lord Ordinary felt it might have some relevance, the First Division were not impressed, feeling that that case was authority only on the point of inextricability and that no question of inextricability arose in the case before them. They were thus free to enunciate the broad principle that perpetual settlements as such were not abhorrent to the law of Scotland.

Conclusion

In this chapter we have traced the meaning of perpetuities and the origins of perpetual settlements in Scotland and in both cases there has been found to be a close connection between ideas and situations prevalent in England and those in Scotland. Yet in spite of this the Scottish courts took up a decidedly different position in relation to perpetuities from that taken up in England. It is with the reasons for this difference that the next two chapters are concerned. The suggestion is that the reasons are largely historical and that as a result of examining the development of perpetual settlements in Scotland and referring back to the relevant developments in the south, an understanding of the Scottish common law position can be obtained.

[122] *ibid.*
[123] (1844) 16 Jur. 422.

CHAPTER II

PERPETUITIES IN ENGLISH LAW

As perpetual settlements constitute the very antithesis of free alienation, it would seem reasonable to assume that they would be found only where the system of property-holding was such that it failed to embody the restrictions found in such settlements. Accordingly it is to the rules of alienation that enquiries must first be directed in order to discover the origin of perpetuities.

Alienation

The nature of the feudal grant was originally very much against the idea of freedom of alienation. In the feudal context a "grant was not just an act of creation, an event which left the creature having an independent existence. The grantor could reach out into the future because he and his heirs would always be there controlling the grant."[1] It is important to emphasise this aspect of control, for the feudal grant would normally entitle the feudal lord not only to service or rent from the grantee but would also bring him within the ambit of his jurisdictional powers as well. The feudal grant, then, far from being simply the conveyance of a parcel of land using feudal conveyancing forms was originally the means whereby a political and social, as well as a legal and economic, relationship came into being. It was the breakdown of this control, the erosion of the political and social elements of the relationship, that brought about freedom of alienation.

In England this erosion occurred early in her history, and although some of the trappings remained until 1660[2] the process was effectively complete by 1290 at the latest. Indeed it is known that by the middle of the thirteenth century freedom of alienation by subinfeudation had been achieved in fact and was both supportable and supported in law. There was a case in the King's Court in 1225[3] from which it would appear that, if the consent of the feudal lord was needed at all, it could only have been as a formality in the completion of the grantee's title. In addition, judgements in cases decided in the fourteenth[4] and fifteenth centuries[5] acknowledge the existence of a general freedom of alienation during the reign of Henry III. By the time of Bracton's treatise, written between 1250 and 1258, this state of affairs had come under attack, for Bracton's work contains an attempted justification of the freedom to subinfeudate in that while it might 'damnum' (economic loss), it caused no 'injuria' (injury to legal rights), even in cases where the vassal subinfeudated without reservation of services.

This whole process culminated in the passing of the Statute Quia Emptores[6]

---

[1] Milsom, Historical Foundations of the Common Law (London 1969) at p.140.
[2] Tenures Abolition Act 1660.
[3] Bracton's Note Book No. 1034.
[4] See esp. (1346) Lib. Ass. f.73 ann. 20 pl. 17; (1352) Lib. Ass. f.124 ann. 26 pl. 37; (1355) Lib. Ass. f.160 ann. 24 pl. 19.
[5] See (1412) Y.B. 14 Hen. IV f.4 (Mich. pl. 6).
[6] 1290 18 Edw. I.

which, while limiting the method of alienation to substitution, confirmed that such alienations might be made without restriction.

It would appear that the legal instrument as a result of whose use freedom of alienation was achieved was the feudal warranty, which had earlier played a significant part in establishing the principle of heredity. The essential point was that in any grant of land, whether by substitution of subinfeudation, the grantor would normally warrant the title of the grantee, either expressly or by necessary implication. Thus where A made a grant 'to B and his heirs', A put himself under an obligation to warrant B's title, an obligation, the burden of which passed to A's heirs, just as the benefit of it passed to B's heirs, on death. The result was an obligation to warrant which effectively prevented A's heirs from claiming the land for themselves. It is not known exactly when this development occurred, but in the case in 1225, referred to above, the principle was upheld. By the time of Bracton the principle had been rationalised so that it had become a principle of substantive law that the words 'and his heirs' in a grant or conveyance gave no interest to the individual heirs, but rather defined as inheritable the character of the interest granted. Thus the position was arrived at whereby a grant 'to B and his heirs' gave an interest that was inheritable; if it was inheritable, it was a fee; and if it was a fee it was alienable.

From the thirteenth century, then, there was first a practice, then a rule, and ultimately a tradition of general freedom of alienation in English law, a tradition which destroyed the inviolability of the entail after 1472[7] and which provided the background against which the great perpetuity cases of the late sixteenth and seventeenth centuries were decided.[8]

But although it was the imaginative use of the feudal warranty which brought about the change in the nature of the interest granted, nonetheless it seems clear that there must have existed pressures which stimulated the creative use of this conveyancing tool, and further, pressures that did not exist in Scotland, for although Scots feudal law possessed (and in its developed form continues to possess until modern times[9]) the feudal warranty, there is no evidence to suggest that it was used in this way. Certainly the same result was not achieved.

The most immediate of these pressures would almost certainly have been a commercial one, a demand for land by those who did not have it, but who had made substantial fortunes elsewhere, either in trade[10] or in foreign wars or on crusades. The process is described by Lord Kames in the following terms:[11]

"In times only of peace, security and plenty, do men dream of distant futurity, and of perpetuating their estates in their families. The feudal law lost ground universally in times of peace. It was a violent and unnatural system, which could not be long supported in contradiction to love of independency and property, the most steady and industrious of all the human appetites. After a regular government was introduced in Britain, which made the arts of peace prevail, all men equally conspired to overthrow

---

[7] *Taltarum's Case* (1472) Y.BB. 12 Edw. IV Mich. f.14, pl. 16; f.19, pl. 25; 13 Edw. IV Mich. f.1. pl. 1.
[8] For a detailed account see Holdsworth—History of English Law vol. III. Milsom Ch. 6 and 7.
[9] In the doctrine of warrandice.
[10] See Sandford—Entails (2nd Ed.) at p.30; Dalrymple at pp.155; 160-161.
[11] History of the Law of Property published in 'Historical Law Trusts' (1761) vol. i at pp. 129/130.

the feudal system. The vassal was willing to purchase independency with his money; and the superior, who had no longer any occasion for military tenants, disposed of his land to better advantage . . . . By this time the strict principles of the feudal law were vanished, and scarce anything left but the figure only. Land, now restored to commerce, was, generally speaking, in the hands of purchasers who had paid a valuable consideration; and consequently, instead of being beneficiary, as formerly, was now become patrimonial. The property being thus transferred from the superior to the vassal, the vassal's power of alienation was a necessary consequence."

But here again it is unlikely that commercial pressures alone would have been sufficient. Indeed Kames suggests that the change came with a change in the nature of the feudal system, specifically, when its reality had vanished, leaving only its framework of rules behind. The modern view[12] is that in England this change came with the ending of true seignorial control over the fee; and the ending of true seignorial control appears to have resulted from the expansion of jurisdiction and influence of the Royal Courts at the expense of the baronial jurisdictions.

Whether this was the ultimate objective of the exercise is doubtful. It is probable this was simply one facet—possibly even a side-effect—of the centralisation policies of the early Plantagenets, designed to achieve a concentration of power and wealth in the Crown.[13] Inevitably this would involve the courts as they were political and administrative instruments and sources of revenue as well as tribunals for the dispensation of justice,[14] and expansion of royal jurisdiction and power would generally be at the expense of that of the baronage.

Certainly by Bracton's time the emphasis had moved from questions of jurisdiction and control to issues of finance, reflecting, perhaps, the fear that the erosion of the political value of seignorial rights was becoming also an erosion of their economic value as well, a fear that is apparent in the protests in the Petition of the Barons in 1257[15], in the early mortmain legislation of 1259[16] culminating in two measures of Edward I; the first was the Statute de Viris Religiosis[17] which prohibited the acquisition of land by the Church or ecclesiastical bodies except by royal licence, and the second was Quia Emptores[18] itself by which the economic benefits of lordship were preserved in return for the last vestiges of seignorial control of the fee.

---

[12] See Milsom—ch. 6 and 7.
[13] See F. Jouen des Longrais—'Henry II and his Justiciars—had they a political plan in their reforms about seisin?' (1962).
[14] As demonstrated, for example, in a recent study of the Royal Courts under John and Henry III, 'The King and his Courts' by R. V. Turner (Cornell 1968). Thus at p.200.
"John seems to have been guided by self-interest in the supervision of his courts; in some cases his motives were financial gain through the offering of favors, in others his motives were political advantage . . . ."
and at p.277.
". . . . Although Henry III was perhaps less vigorous than John in his supervision, the Royal Courts could still be made to serve as instruments of royal policy and the Judges could still feel his personal will. The justices continued to be careful to protect the king's rights in cases touching his possessions and they could still hand down judgements that must have been politically inspired."
[15] 1257 c. 27.
[16] The Provisions of Westminster 43 Hen. III c. 14.
[17] 1279, 7 Edw. I.
[18] 1290, 18 Edw. I.

Commenting on Quia Emptores, Milsom graphically describes this change. He writes:[19]

"The statute epitomises in a few lines the changes of a century and more by which great social forces had been channelled into technical rules about property. Consider its opening words: 'Forasmuch as purchasers of lands and tenements of the fees of great men and other lords have many times heretofore entered into their fees, to the prejudice of the lords . . . .' These may be compared with a passage in an ordinance made just thirty years earlier by the county court of Chester: '. . . . that none shall make grant to anyone in the fee of another, nor shall anyone presume by grant to enter the fee of another, without first securing the consent of the chief lord of the fee . . . .'[20] This is the language of lordship as power, with the chief lord of the fee able to control the holdings within it; and although the concept was still living the reality was dead. The county court of Chester was fighting against history; and by the date of its ordinance there was probably general agreement elsewhere that a lord could not prevent any alienation by his tenant, who had become in our language an owner of property. If he granted it away by subinfeudation, there was economic damage to the lord. If he granted it away by substituting the grantee for himself an immediate tenant of the lord, there was of course even more direct damage of the same nature if the grantee was an undying church; and this is why mortmain continued to be a problem after Quia Emptores. But the more obvious and invariable damage of a substitution is to the feudal relationship: the lord cannot even control who is to be his immediate tenant, let alone who is to have subordinate interests within his fee. All this is admitted by Quia Emptores which expressly empowers tenants to alienate at their own free will so long as they do it by substituting their grantees for themselves. The feudal realities are recognised as dead, and the economic realities are saved."

Precisely how seignorial control was reduced to a mere shell will probably never be known, but two principal instruments appear to have been the Assizes of Novel Disseisin and Mort D'Ancestor, both being possessory remedies provided by Henry II.

Novel Disseisin was provided in 1166 by the Assize of Clarendon as a summary remedy to enable the tenant put out of his holding to get back in again. Within the living feudal system in which it was conceived (as opposed to the formall shell it subsequently became), Novel Disseisin appears to have been directed against abuses of seignorial authority. Defences were available, the most common plea in the early cases being that of 'proper seignorial action'. But in the context of twelfth and early thirteenth century justice, to avail oneself of this defence would involve great inconvenience and expense. In purely economic terms it would often not be worth the trouble for a lord to challenge the claim even of a bad tenant. With this lack of willingness to exercise seignorial rights within the fee against his own tenants actual seignorial control begins to diminish. Eventually the lord's form of action against the fee, distraint per feodum, died altogether, leaving distress of chattels as the last vestige of seignorial control.

The next stage is the reluctance to fulfil his feudal duties of protection towards his own tenants in cases where they have been turned out of their holdings by some wrongdoer acting under some pretext of right. This development is scarcely surprising; after all, what lord is going to embark upon protracted and expensive litigation for someone else when it had become too burdensome to embark upon a similar course on his own behalf. This would

---

[19] Historical Foundations of the Common Law at pp.98/99.
[20] 1260. Cited in T. F. T. Plucknett—"The Legislation of Edward I" (Oxford 1949) at p.108.

account for the extension of the Assize to cover third parties and for a still further diminution of control within the lord's own fee.

The Assize of Northampton of 1176 made provision for a second possessory remedy—Mort D'Ancestor. This went much further than Novel Disseisin into the substance of the land law itself, for it made inroads into the sacred process of giving seisin and its requirements of a proper grant in a proper form. Thenceforth an heir to real property was deemed to have the seisin of his ancestor's holding without the prerequisite of having to go through the feudal motions which could be gone through later in order to complete the title. Thenceforth the feudal lord could not even resume seisin on the death of a tenant even for the purpose of giving it to the heir.

During the later twelfth and thirteenth centuries Mort D'Ancestor and Novel Disseisin were supplemented by the Writs of Entry, bringing more matters within the scope of the Royal Courts. With these the transfer of jurisdictions became virtually complete.

As has been mentioned these jurisdictional powers of the feudal lord were of considerable political significance, and indeed, from a political standpoint, were probably the most important that he possessed. The suggestion is that it was the strangulation of these powers by the possessory assizes by transferring the forum for such actions from local to national level that changed the underlying nature of English feudalism. With the political and jurisdictional powers being eroded away, what was left was a collection of rights with an economic value, or a nuisance value that could be turned to economic advantage. As Milsom puts it:[21]

"Lordship, of course, lingers on for centuries, a truncated and economic affair, a mere shadow. But the world in which land is now dealt with, and in which disputes now arise is a flat world; equal deals with equal over mere pieces of property and disputes over these as over anything else are for the ordinary courts."

Entails

The introduction of the entail into English law can be seen essentially as a reaction to the completeness of the process as a result of which land had become freely alienable. It can be regarded as a defensive measure[22] to deal with the effects of free alienation on family estates and has been so regarded by most commentators on feudal law. Thus in his 'Feudal Property'[23] Dalrymple writes of the origins of the entail:

---

[21] Milsom at p.124. This point is extravagantly amplified at pp.99/100 in which the overstated analogy with a modern investor nonetheless contains more than a germ of truth. It reads:
"the fee simple has become an estate, 'and his heirs' magic words to create it, and this estate, this ownership has become an article of commerce. The feudal services are income, the incidents are capital gains and land and lordship are being sold for money .... Just as the grantor in mortmain was usually a benefactor who harmed his lord incidentally, so the grantor for nominal services was usually a vendor who chose to sell for a capital sum in money rather than for a perpetual income of real value. That the choice was made because the capital payment was 'tax-free' whereas the valuable service would enrich the lord during minorities and the like, is of course very likely; and this may be reflected in the large number of freehold rents in, for example, the City of London, where incidents had never played any part. We should think, not in terms of the modern tax-planner, but of the vendor's solicitor advising on the merits of alternative modes of sale."

[22] See above, Chapter I.

[23] (London 1757) at pp.155/156.

"After the feudal law had been for some time on the decline, it was again, notwithstanding the general bent of men against it, in some degree revived by the bent of particular persons.

It was obvious to the ancient nobles that the allowing [of] land to come so much into commerce tended to weaken them; by the prodigality of some and the misfortunes of others of their own body, their lands, they saw, were continually shifting, into the hands of people who had formerly been little better than their slaves. In order to prevent such consequences they invented the artifice of entails, which took particular estates out of commerce, and with regard to those estates, revived the spirit of the feudal law."

However, although the origin of the entail can be regarded in such general terms, in fact the particular measure introduced in the Statute of Westminster II[24] was almost certainly a reaction to a development in the more limited field of the family settlement.

It will have been noticed that in one sense the very early feudal grants were themselves settlements in that they attempted to reach out into the future and control the succession under the grant. But more akin to modern ideas of settlement was the grant in liberum maritagium. The origin of this type of grant is uncertain but it was probably in a custom observed in Normandy prior to the Conquest under which a father could make provision for his children by way of gift free from all services. As this gift would normally be by way of subinfeudation it would create the relationship of lord and vassal between the donor and donee and would entitle the grantor, in the normal course to rights and services.

The essential point about this type of gift was that it was treated as being provisional. The freedom from services applied because the gift was in law incomplete and retained its incomplete character until the entry of the third heir. Upon the occurrence of this event services became exigible and the grant took on the character of an ordinary fee.

This incompleteness had several effects, stemming from the absence of homage until the entry of the third heir. One was that the comprehensive feudal warranty, imported by homage, was absent. Technically therefore, until the entry of the third heir, the donees were holding in the name of the donor and in any action affecting their right to the land the donor had to be joined as a party. Most importantly, on the failure of heirs to the marriage the land reverted automatically to the donor.

Around the year 1200[25] gifts in liberum maritagium began to be supplemented by those to the donee and the heirs of his body or to a husband and wife and the heirs of their bodies. There are plenty of examples from the reigns of Richard I and John and such gifts became increasingly frequent during the reign of Henry III. As an example one can cite a charter of 1252 by which Henry III himself granted land to his 'brother Richard to hold to him and his heirs begotten of his wife Sanchia' with an express provision that the land was to revert on the failure of such heirs, to the king and his heirs.[26]

At the time such gifts were beginning to become common (i.e. around 1200) the right to alienate without the lord's consent had not yet been fully accepted

---

[24] de Donis Conditionalibus (Stat. Westminster II c. 1) 13 Edw. I c. 1.
[25] See Pollock & Maitland—History of English Law vol ii at p.16.
[26] Placit. Abbrev. 145.

by the King's Court, and it seems that when the third heir actually entered, did homage and obtained the fee, as this fee was of an ordinary character under the general law, although it might have become heritable among the heirs general, it was not freely alienable. What happened was simply that the donor's right of reversion shrank to an escheat on the failure of the heirs general. Thus when freedom of alienation came some years later it affected these grants as well as ordinary grants in fee simple. But it affected them in a peculiar way with the result that they appear to have been interpreted as 'conditional gifts'. Thus a gift to 'A and the heirs of his body' was construed in such a way that as soon as A had a child, he acquired a full alienable fee. Indeed the courts went further. If A alienated before having a child this would not be treated as making the transaction void; instead it was to be construed as giving the alience an estate which would be good so long as A or his issue survived.[27] Again it is not known precisely how this development came about but the most plausible explanation seems to be that of Maitland who wrote:[28]

"When men were making their first attempts to devise these restricted gifts they seem to have not infrequently adopted a form of words which might reasonably be construed as the creation of a 'conditional fee'. In the first years of the [thirteenth] century a gift 'to A and his heirs, if he shall have an heir of the body,' seems to have been almost as common as the gift 'to A and the heirs of his body'. At first, little difference could be seen between these two forms. In either case the donor, with no precedents before him might well suppose that he had shown an intention that the land should descend to the issue, if any, of A, but to no other heirs. But without doing much violence to the former of these clauses . . . . [it could be construed as] 'to A and his heirs upon condition that he shall have a child born to him'. If A then has a child the condition is fulfilled for good and all; A is holding the land simply to himself and his heirs. A mode of interpretation established for one form of gift may then have extended itself to the other."

Not surprisingly this doctrine was not popular among the donors since it would run directly counter to their intentions. As these donors would usually be members of the baronage it is hardly surprising that grievances as to this principle operated by the King's Court were to be found in their formulated expressions of dissatisfaction.[29]

At last in 1285 Edward I made a concession to the feudalists in the form of the Statute de Donis Conditionalibus[30] which enacted:

"That the will of the giver according to the form in the deed of gift, manifestly expressed shall be from henceforth observed; so that they to whom the land was given under such condition, shall have no power to aliene the land so given, but that it shall remain unto the issue of them to whom it was given after their death, or shall revert unto the giver or his heirs if issue fail either by an absolute default of issue, or after the birth of issue, by its subsequent extinction . . . ."

Then follow clauses dealing with the detailed application of the Statute to particular cases.

It will be seen from this that on a literal interpretation of the Statute it clearly did not create an inalienable fee. Those bound were apparently only the

---

[27] In modern English legal parlance the interest of such an alienee would be said to constitute a 'base fee'.
[28] Pollock and Maitland vol. ii at p.18.
[29] In the Petition of the Barons *supra*.
[30] 13 Edw. I c. 1.

donees. It followed therefore that, on this interpretation, the Statute itself imposed no restraint upon alienation by the issue. Accordingly, then, the Statute, so construed, would make little more than a dent in the accepted policy of free alienation and would scarcely have 'revived the spirit of the feudal law' as Dalrymple put it.

But there was a difficulty with that interpretation, a difficulty of concept. If the issue of the first donee took by descent, as they appeared to do, since the donee's interest had been limited by the Statute, must not their interest be limited too? Should not they, therefore, be subject to the same restraints on alienation as the donee? The point was raised in 1311[31] where a case of formedon in descender came before Bereford C.J. It was admitted that the claimant's father, who was the donee's son, had gained seisin, and it was argued that the restriction on alienation applied only to the donee and that therefore the father was entitled to alienate. Bereford C.J. admitted that this was the legal effect of the statute but stated that:[32]

". . . . he who made the statute meant to bind the issue in fee tail as well as the feoffees until the tail had reached the fourth degree[33] and it was only through negligence that he omitted to insert express words to that effect in the statute; therefore we shall not debate this writ."

As one commentator has remarked:[34]

"Thus the vituperations so often showered on de Donis—not least by Scots—are not justified by the Act. They should be directed against the judges long supposed to have defeated the wicked ends of the statute by their predilection for freedom of alienation . . . . But this . . . . influence towards individualism , . . . was alien to the dynastically minded feudal English baronage to which Bereford and his brethren belonged. De Donis as eventually interpreted is clear evidence of the great strength attaching to the tradition that land belongs to, and must be preserved for, the family in all its succeeding generations. The judges were only giving legal effect to a popular sentiment of their day."

In point of fact this would seem to be overstating the position for Bereford C.J.'s exposition was not unanimously followed. While there are dicta[35] from the 1330's onwards suggesting inalienability as an inherent characteristic of the entail there was nonetheless a case in 1344[36] in which the question of the duration of the entail was inconclusively discussed, but in which the suggestion was put forward that it would not last even for four degrees. However during the remainder of the century the feeling for inalienability gradually prevailed so that in a case in 1410[37] it was stated as a settled principle that 'after the fourth degree frank marriage becomes formedon'; In other words that so long as there were heirs of the prescribed class the entail would continue.

The doubts raised as to duration were perhaps a symptom of or an attempt

---

[31] Y.B. 5 Edw. II (Selden Soc. vol. 31) at p.117.
[32] *ibid.*
[33] Clearly under the influence of the maritagium.
[34] Farran—The Principles of Scots and English Land Law (Edinburgh 1958) at p.143.
[35] See esp. per Stonore C.J. in (1331) Y.B. 4 Edw. III Tri. pl. 4; cited Y.B. 5 Edw. II (Selden Soc. xxvii note 2) as follows: "Lestatut restraint le poar le issue en la tail daliener en prejudice de celuy en le reversion per expresse parol: donque a plus fort home atteindra son poar restraint en prejudice de la tail."
[36] Y.B. 18 and 19 Edw. III 201.
[37] Y.B. 12 Hen. IV 9.

to get around the consequences of, inalienability, and as early as 1306[38] attempts were made by using the feudal warranty to bar the heirs in tail. This attempt however was rendered unsuccessful by reason of the Court's extending the provisions of the Statute of Gloucester 1278 to cover the case.[39] Further attempts were made during the course of the fourteenth century with variants on this theme, but were largely unsuccessful.

Of more utility was the 'fine' which was in essence an action commenced by writ by which lands might either be demanded or charged, which was compromised by leave of the court, the claim of the plaintiff being acknowledged by the defendant. According to the common law the title conferred by a fine was a bar to the claims of all those who, not being under a disability, did not prosecute their claims within a year and a day. Although this rule was abrogated in 1361[40] it was restored in 1484[41] with the adjustment that the period was extended to five years and that in addition there had to be a 'proclammation' of the fine. This was supplemented by the Statute of Fines of 1536[42] which enacted that all fines, levied with proclamations, whether before or after the Act, of any hereditament entailed to the tenant or his ancestors should immediately after the fine be deemed to be a sufficient bar for ever against someone claiming the land by force only of the entail. In other words by the fine it became possible more effectively than could be done with the warranty to bar the issue in tail.

Given that since *Taltarum's Case* in 1472[43] it had become possible by means of a collusive common recovery with double voucher to warranty[44] to bar the interests of anyone entitled in remainder or reversion, after 1540 a procedure arose whereby the fine and the recovery were used in conjunction so as effectively to bar the claims of anyone entitled under the entail.

Perpetual Settlements

We have seen that while land subject to an entail was inalienable, nevertheless the entail itself was not absolutely indestructible. The development of perpetual settlements was essentially a reaction to the practice, or even the possibility, of destroying the entail and so making the land alienable. In Chapter I we examined the various meanings given to the term 'perpetuity' and saw how these were derived from the devices used. What now fall to be considered are the ideas employed in these devices and the ultimate development of a rule against perpetuities.

---

[38] Y.B. 33-35 Edw. I (Rolls Series) at p.387.
[39] 6 Edw. I c. 3. The Statute of Gloucester had dealt with the case of a husband's alienating his wife's land with warranty, whether during her lifetime or as tenant by curtesy after her death. Their son was to be barred to the extent that he had 'assetz by descent' from his father. The maritagium would have been common ground between the two statutes and it would have been but a small step to go from one to the other. The result was that the heirs came to be barred only to the extent of their 'assetz by descent'.
[40] by the Statute of Non-Claim 1361 stat. 34 Edw. III c. 16.
[41] Stat. I Ric. III c. 7. This was repealed and reenacted by Henry VII in 1489 stat. 4 Hen. VII c. 24, such enactment being known as the First Statute of Fines.
[42] Stat. 28 Hen. VIII c. 36 (The Second Statute of Fines).
[43] Y.BB. 12 Edw. IV Mich. f.14 pl. 16; f.19 pl. 25; 13 Edw. IV Mich. f.1. pl. 1.
[44] For a description of this see Simpson. 'An Introduction to the History of Land Law' (Oxford 1961) at pp.118-129.

Conditions

The imposition of conditions in the grant was not surprisingly the first of the ideas tried; not surprisingly, because although the feudal realities were gone feudal conveyancing forms were still in use in England (and indeed were to remain so for some centuries yet) and the imposition of conditions in the grant was essentially a feudal idea.

What was sought to be guarded against was the barring of the entail by warranty by which the heir in tail was barred to the extent of his assets by descent. Further if the warranty could be vouched by the other interests created by the entailer, the remainder or the reversion, then the voucher would complete the bar thus permitting a complete alienation in fee simple. In idea, it will be seen that this marshalling together of the beneficial interests under the settlement is exactly the same as that used in modern times to break or vary trust settlements by deeds of arrangement using the principle in *Saunders* v *Vautier*.[45] However, just as in modern settlements it was necessary for those interested to be sui juris and for them to agree, so in those early entails agreement had to be obtained so that the appropriate vouchers could be effected.

But however difficult this may have been actually to effect it is clear that by the last quarter of the fourteenth century it was sufficiently well known to stimulate a reaction. This is known because of the discussion of the settlement of Rickhill J. to be found in Littleton.[46] Rickhill's settlement operated to convey lands to his first, second and third sons successively in tail, "and because he would that none of his sons should alien or make warranty to bar or hurt the others that should be in remainder, etc., he causeth an indenture to be made to this affect, viz. that the lands and tenements were given to his eldest son upon such condition, that if the eldest son alien in fee, or in fee tail, etc., or if any of his sons alien, etc., that then their estate should cease or be void and that then the same lands and tenements immediately should remain to the second son, and to the heirs of his body begotten et sic ultra, the remainder to his other sons, and livery of seisin was made accordingly."[47]

Littleton's view was that such a settlement was bad, but interestingly not on any broad ground of public policy that was to be employed later; instead his objections were on purely technical grounds, and further were not directly against the imposition of the conditions, but only against their consequences. Thus it was pointed out that if the eldest son did alienate the fee simple would, as a result of the alienation, vest in the alienee, the reversion would be discontinued and the remainder would necessarily fail because it would have no estate of freehold to support it.[48] This, in later cases, was rationalised so as to become a rule that the contingent remainder was invalid because of the repugnancy of the condition to the nature of the estate granted. Thus in *Colthirst* v *Bejushin*, Montague C.J. said:[49]

"[A] condition unlawful or impossible is of no effect to gain anything by the doing of it in our law.... If a gift in tail is made upon condition that, if the donee alien, it

---

[45] (1841) 4 Beav. 115.
[46] Tenures. paras. 720-723.
[47] *ibid.* at para. 720.
[48] *ibid.* at para. 722.
[49] (1551) 3 Plowd. 21 at 34-35.

shall remain to another, this is repugnant, for when he has alienated to a stranger, it is contrary to the alienation to remain over."

Furthermore, Littleton went on to attack its invalidity on the basis that it infringed the rule that the benefit of a condition or right of entry could be limited only to the donor.[50] Accordingly then, although the condition might be good as far as enforcement by the reversioner was concerned where it was coupled with a remainder, as it would be in all perpetuities, it was bad and incapable of enforcement by the remainderman.[51]

Although there was apparently a similar attempt along the same lines a few years later[52] the idea was seemingly laid to rest until the middle of the sixteenth century when it was pressed into service to combat attempted alienations of entailed land by fine and recovery. There was however one significant development. This was that the condition was to operate, not so much on the alienations themselves but on attempts to alienate, the point being that a condition of forfeiture on suffering a recovery by itself would be useless, for by then the damage would have been done. The two leading cases in which the imposition of conditions was tried were *Corbet's Case*[53] and *Mildmay's Case*[54] where the limitations were substantially the same. Basically they amounted to a conveyance to A for life, thereafter to B in tail male and in default to the use of A's heirs in tail male with remainders over. The prohibition was in the following terms, that if B "or any of his heirs male of his body should be resolved and determine, or advisedly should attempt, or procure any act or thing concerning any alienation of or for the said manor, etc., by which any estate tail before limited should be undone, barred or determined, or by which the same should not come, remain and be in manner and form as is limited in the same indenture; that then after that, and before any such act done . . . . the uses and estates to him limited who should do so, etc. should cease only in respect, and having regard to such person so attempting, in the same manner quality degree and condition as if such person so attempting was naturally dead and not otherwise. And that then immediately, in all such cases, the uses of the said manor should be to persons to whom the uses should come by intent of the same indenture, as if such person so attempting were naturally dead."

This forfeiture clause was held bad for a number of reasons, but principally it was said to be contrary to law and repugnant to the nature of the estate granted to make it cease as to the tenant in tail but keep it substiting as to the issue. The report reads:[55]

"It was resolved that it was impossible and repugnant that an estate tail should cease as if the tenant in tail were dead (had he issue or no), for an estate tail cannot cease so long as it continues; but here his interest was to continue the estate tail, and to cease it in respect to the party offending only, and not as to any other, which is impossible and repugnant and against law; for every limitation or condition ought to defeat the whole estate, and not to defeat part of the estate."

---

[50] *ibid.* at para. 723.
[51] See below, at *Contingent Remainders*.
[52] In the settlement of Thirning C.J. during the reign of Henry IV. The exact date is unknown.
[53] (1599-1600) 1 Co. Rep. 836.
[54] (1606) 6 Co. Rep. 40a. Two other and earlier but unreported cases were cited as having similar limitations. These were *Germin* v *Aiscot* (1595) and *Cholmley* v *Humble* (1595).
[55] *Mildmay's Case* at f.40b. See also *Corbet's Case* at ff.85b, 86a.

The final development was that found in *Mary Portington's Case*[56] and emulated in the Scottish strict entails. Here the condition was framed so as to operate on the doing of any act which prevented the lands from descending as provided in the settlement, with the result that the estate of the perpetrator should cease "as if he or she were dead without an heir of his or her body." On this Fearne commented:[57]

"In the former cases the proviso was repugnant to a rule of law, as being confined to the avoiding only part of the estate tail, viz. so far only as respected tenant in tail himself, still leaving it good as to his issue; and also involved something contradictory and absurd in itself, being to determine the estate tail, as if tenant in tail were dead; which in fact does not determine the estate tail. Whereas the case of Mary Portington steered clear of these objections; the proviso there enuring to defeat the whole estate tail; and to determine the estate tail as if tenant in tail were dead without heirs of his body; which really is a determination of the estate tail."

In this case the conveyancing technicalities of Littleton and the conceptual difficulties that stemmed from them were insufficient by themselves to invalidate the condition. Indeed there was a line of authority going back to 1572[58] which supported it. So the court were faced with a choice; they could decide the matter purely on the technical merits of the condition, in which case it would have to be upheld; or they could reject it moving on to the broader, general rule of policy against restrictions on alienation. They chose the latter, overturning any previous authority to the contrary, thus in effect ending the attempts to create perpetuities by imposing direct fetters on alienation in the grant.

Contingent Remainders

Conditions went hand in hand with remainders, and it was in connection with these contingent remainders that the common law made perhaps its most striking contribution to the perpetuity problem.

(*a*) Origins and Validity

If a feudal lord granted an estate in possession to a grantee by subinfeudation, when that estate[59] ended the land would "come back" or "revert" to him. Even after the abolition of transfer by subinfeudation this position was still intact where the grant was of an estate of less than fee simple and on its termination there would still be a reverter to the grantor.

In the purely feudal relationship the reversioner would be the seigneur whose right would amount to a seigneury derived from the existence of tenure between the parties. After the demise of subinfeudination the reverter, while no longer derived from the concept of tenure would still exist as a superior estate for the reversioner would have the highest of all estates, the fee simple absolute. A reversion then, was what was left in the grantor when a grant was made which

---

[56] (1614) 10 Co. Rep. f.35*b*.
[57] Contingent Remainders (9th Ed. at p.259).
[58] The first was *Scholastica's Case* (1572) *Plowd.* 708 which permitted the proviso to take effect, not as a condition but as a limitation, the point being that a condition ultimately required re-entry by the grantor whereas a limitation operated simply to determine the estate. This was followed in *Rudhall* v *Milward* (1586) *Moo.* 212 and there are dicta in *Corbet's Case* (1599-1600) 1 Co. Rep. f.83*b* at f.86*b* supporting it.
[59] Referred to in both reports and treaties as 'the particular estate'.

did not dispose of the grantor's interest completely, in most cases, the fee simple.

Where, however, an inferior estate was granted but the residue, instead of being retained, was also granted out then, in the hands of the grantee, that interest was known as a 'remainder' because it stayed away or 'remained'[60] from the grantor.

Remainders, although scarcely younger than reverters seem to have had more difficulty in finding their niche in the common law scheme of things. The problem was that under the common law, those who took did so either as heirs by inheritance or as purchasers.[61] If a remainderman was to take, it ought to have been as purchaser since he clearly was no one's heir. But if he took as purchaser the fee should vest in him from the date of the grant.[62] Yet it clearly did not, for it vested in the life tenant who had seisin and who performed the feudal services.

During the thirteenth century the courts had no solution to this problem. What happened earlier is unknown, although the answer probably lies in the fact of seignorial control: the grantor would be the lord who would, in a sense, constitute the law that would control the grant, and the remainderman would in effect be relying on the lord's promise to obtain seisin.[63]

As the law developed and seignorial control faded the position of the remainderman became less and less secure since, not being an heir, he had none of the heir's remedies open to him. Bracton stated that there was a writ designed for the remainderman and promised that later in his treatise its form would be given[64] but in fact neglected to do so. He referred to the remainderman as a 'quasi-heir' who took by substitution according to the form of the gift and certainly after de Donis[65] that is precisely how he was treated.

Where the remainder was contingent another, and, in the feudal context, more real and practical problem, presented itself, for, where the remainder in fee was contingent, to whom would the lord look for his services?

In the earliest examples, which the problem was recognised it was not considered as fatal to the grant. Thus in 1309 there was a fine which was reported thus:[65]

"B grants the tenements to Robert and renders them to him in his court, to have and to hold to Robert for his whole life, of the chief lord of the fee; and after the decease of Robert the tenements are to remain to C and the heirs of his body begotten, to hold of the chief lord of the fee; and if C die without heirs of his body the tenements are to remain to the right heirs of Robert to hold of the chief lord of the fee.

Bereford J. asked who was to do homage."

---

[60] From the Latin 'remanere'.
[61] Hence the distinction in medieval English conveyancing between words of limitation, referring to inheritance, and words of purchase. The significance was that on the entry of someone taking by inheritance feudal incidents would be exigible whereas in the case of entry by a purchaser they would not.
[62] As in the Scottish feudal law of liferent and fee where the liferent is regarded in orthodox doctrine as a mere servitude on the fee.
[63] See Milsom at p.161 citing Bracton (see note 64) concerning a case in 1220 where remainder was described as a 'conventio'.
[64] Bracton pl. 86.
[65] Y.B. 2 & C Edw. II Selden Soc. vol. 19 at p.4. The first case in which the validity of a contingent remainder was upheld appears to be (1304) Y.B. 32 & 33 Edw. I (Rolls series) at p.329.

In other words the position seemed to be that if arrangements could be made covering the question of services the court would not invalidate the gift. However, whatever arrangement might be made, it must not destroy the right of the lord to have some certain tenant all of the time who would be responsible for the services.

The next development comes from a case in 1336[66] from which two principles emerged. The first was that remainders to persons not in esse at the time of the gift were bad. This would naturally follow from the need for some certain tenant to be responsible for the services. The second was that a remainder, which though contingent at first, had vested would be upheld. Decisions from 1336 onwards[67] developed this theme and it became the general rule that where a contingent remainder became vested in the course of circumstances, that was enough. So in a case in 1388[68] the remainderman died after satisfying the contingency, but before the life tenant. The plaintiff prayed to be received as his right heir. It was held that he could be, since the interest of the remainderman had vested before his death.

During most of the fourteenth and throughout the fifteenth centuries, then, the courts were willing to recognise remainders to the right heirs of a living person in cases where that person died before the remainder fell in. The difficulties with seisin and feudal services were avoided in part by the device of giving seisin to the particular tenant, which seisin was held to enure for the benefit of the remainderman. This doctrine however had the important corollary that the remainder was dependant upon the life estate and that the destruction of the life estate would involve as a consequence the destruction of the remainder too. This was eventually confirmed in the case of *Colthirst* v *Bejushin* in 1551[69] where the experience of the common lawyers in connection with conditions was linked with the rules developed in connection with remainders. After this case the position can be summarised in the following propositions.

(1) The remainder could not be subject to any condition that was illegal or impossible.
(2) The right left the grantor at the moment of grant and was carried by the estate precedent. The remainder had therefore to vest not later that the ending of estate.
(3) However, the remainder had not to be repugnant to the estate precedent and could not cut it short. It might therefore vest before the termination of the precedent estate, but gave no right to possession until that estate had ended.

(*b*) The Weakness of the Contingent Remainder

Although the settlement of the validity of contingent remainders opened, in theory at least, great new possibilities for the creators of perpetuities by postponing the vesting of the fee until a remote date, nonetheless such

---

[66] Y.B. Edw. III Michs. No. 8.
[67] *ibid.*; see also Y.B. 11 Hen. IV. 74 no. 14; Y.B. 9 Hen. VI 23 no. 19.
[68] Y.B. 11 Ric. II (Ames Foundation volume) at pp. 283-288.
[69] Plowd. 21.

remainders contained inherent weaknesses. These came as Holdsworth has said:[70]

".... firstly [from] the rules regulating the limitation of remainders; and secondly [from] the common law principles as to seisin and disseisin, and as to merger. The rules regulating the limitations of remainders rendered a contingent remainder liable to fail irrespective of the wish of any of the parties to a settlement. The legal principles regulating seisin and disseisin and merger put it into the power of one or more of the parties to the settlements to destroy the contingent remainder limited by that settlement. A contingent remainder was therefore a very precarious interest."

(i) It will be remembered that one of the rules confirmed in *Colthirst* v *Bejushin*, although originating much earlier, dictated that, to be valid, a contingent remainder had to vest during, or at the latest on, the termination of the precedent estate. This in itself derives from the old feudal rule that there must never be an abeyance of seisin; that permission for the vesting of a freehold estate in futuro would bring this about.

In fact this requirement, no matter how extravagant the theoretical possibilities of contingent remainders, severely restricted their usefulness as instruments in creating perpetuities. The point is that as, since Quia Emptores 1290, a contingent remainder could not be limited to take effect after a fee simple. If it was to be valid at all, it would have to be limited so as to take effect after a life estate or an estate tail. If it was limited to take effect after a life estate, it had to vest within the duration of that life.[71] As a limitation in favour of an unborn person must be contingent it would follow that for it to be valid it would have to vest during an existent life. Accordingly settlors could not confidently reach further into the future than the ending of lives already in being.

But the Elizabethan courts went further. In *Chudleigh's Case*[72] Popham C.J. enunciated the principle:

"If a feoffment be made to the use of A for life, and after to the use of every person who should be his heir, one after another for the term of the life of every such heir only, in this case if the limitation should be good, the inheritance should be in nobody: but this limitation is merely void, for the limitation of a use to have a perpetual freehold is not agreeable with the rule of law in estates in possession."

This, it will be seen, is no more than an enunciation of the old rule clothed in anti-perpetuity language. But it gave rise to the particular rule preventing such a perpetual freehold by contingent remainder known as the rule in *Perrot's Case*.[73] This was that while an estate might be limited to a person for life, with remainder to his unborn son for life, all further contingent limitations after that life estate were void.

(ii) Because a contingent remainder did not of itself give an estate in the land but only a possibility of an estate, if the precedent estate on which it depended ceased before the contingency had been satisfied and the estate vested, then the contingent remainder would fall also. In *Chudleigh's Case*[74] Coke enunciated the principle:

---

[70] History of English Law vol. vii at p.104.
[71] If it had been limited to take effect after an estate tail, it would of course have been liable to destruction on the barring of the entail.
[72] (1589-95) 1 Co. Rep. f.120a at f.138a.
[73] (1595) Moo. 368.
[74] (1589-95) 1 Co. Rep. f.120a at f.135b.

"By the feoffment of the tenants for life their estate was determined and title of entry given for the forfeiture, and then those in the futuro remainder were not in esse to take it; for this reason those remainders in futuro, by this matter ex post facto were utterly destroyed and made void; and there is no difference when the estate of the tenant for life determines by the death or the tenant for life and when it determines in right by his forfeiture, for in both cases entry is given to him in the next remainder, and then if he cannot take the land when the particular estate determines, the remainder is void."

Accordingly, where, for example, there was a variation of the settlement by which the precedent estate merged with another and subsequent estate, thus ceasing to have a separate existence, any contingent remainder dependant on that estate would fall. In *Purefoy* v *Rogers*[75], for example, land was settled on A for life with remainder to her son, if she should have one. The reversioner in fee, before the birth of the son, conveyed his reversion to A. It was held that this conveyance had the effect of merging A's life estate in the fee simple and that accordingly, as the contingency had not been satisfied, the remainder was destroyed.

Similarly, if the remainder was limited to follow an estate tail, if the entail was barred effectively then the contingent remainder dependant on it would fall.

In the latter half of the seventeenth century this particular form of destruction began to be countered by the devices of limiting, after the life estate, an estate to trustees and their heirs, during the life of the tenant for life, in case his estate should be determined by forfeiture or otherwise in his lifetime, in trust for him and to preserve the contingent remainders. The efficacy of this whole device depended upon the remainder to the trustees being vested so that there could be no possibility of an abeyance of seisin. It should perhaps be emphasised that this device did no more than save the remainder from destruction by the tenant for life. It did not validate any remainder which would otherwise have been invalid. Accordingly had the life estate determined naturally and the contingency had not been satisfied the remainder would still have failed for, in such a case, there would be no one to take the fee, the trust having ended.

Executory Interests and Trusts

It will have been realised from the above that the rules relating to conditions and contingent remainders kept the perpetuity problem in check as regards the interests they covered. Their great defect was the comparatively limited field that they did cover. While the rules of common law governing future interests were being refined and re-refined, shortly after the Statute of Uses 1535[76] and the Statute of Wills 1540[77] it became realised that the restrictions of the common law rules could be avoided by creating contingent remainders or their equivalents by way of use. The process has been graphically described by Milsom in the following passage:[78]

"The matter is usually put in this way. At common law settlements of land had to obey certain rules, especially those governing contingent remainders. A remainder

---

[75] (1671) 2 Wms. Saunders 380.
[76] Stat. 27 Hen. VIII c. 10.
[77] Stat. 32 Hen. VIII c. 1.
[78] Milson at p.196.

had always to be supported by a prior estate and had to take effect as soon as that prior estate came to an end; this was because there had always to be somebody seised. But equally a remainder could not intervene and cut short the prior estate; and this was to prevent conditions being used to create indestructible settlements. Then it is said that in equity before the Statute of Uses, with a fee simple continuously in the hands of the feoffees and continuously obeying the law, interests could be made to spring, that is to break the first of these rules, or to shift, to break the second. Then lastly it is said that when the Statute of Uses brought such interests in the law, it was decided after hesitation that they should retain the plastic quality they had enjoyed in equity and not in general be subjected to the rigid legal rules. The undoubted result was a new and distinct class of legal future interests, springing and shifting uses. They were brought into being by a conveyance expressed as granting the land to feoffees to uses; and the uses, being at once exposed like magic ink to the rays of the Statute, were transmuted into legal interests."

However, while ultimately being treated differently from legal contingent remainders, these executory interests nonetheless posed exactly the same problem. By either, or by a combination of both, the vesting of the fee could be postponed far into the future. The most reasonable course would have been to bring these executory interests within the common law rules relating to contingent remainders. And indeed at one point it looked as though this approach might prevail. In *Chudleigh's Case*[79] Coke adopted this line of argument suggesting that the intention of the framers of the Statute was to revive the ancient common law and that it therefore followed that the courts should construe such interests as were allowed to exist in accordance with the principles of the common law. In his judgement in the case Popham C.J. acceded to this argument and laid it down as a principle of law that:[80]

"uses invented and limited in a new manner not agreeable to the ancient common laws of the land . . . . are utterly extirpated and extinguished by this Act . . . . Further there is no difference at this day between estates conveyed in use and estates conveyed in possession, for the estate and limitation of an use ought to be known to the common law and governed and directed by the rules thereof."

But unfortunately this principle was never consistently applied and throughout the seventeenth century was eroded until it ended up as a parody of its origin in what became known as the rule in *Purefoy* v *Rogers*,[81] that when a contingency is limited to depend on an estate of freehold which is capable of supporting a remainder, it shall never be construed to be an executory interest but rather as a contingent remainder.

Other equally ineffectual remedies were tried such as the rule in *Brent's Case*,[82] itself an unintentional parody of the common law rules whereby contingent remainders could be destroyed by the rules of seisin. Here the executory interest could be destroyed by the joint action of the feoffees to uses and the beneficiaries. Indeed the fact that this rule provided a means of destroying perpetual settlements based on executory interests was often thought to be sufficient until the decision in *Pells* v *Brown* in 1620[83] in which an innocuous shifting use threw up the principle that an executory interest was not only valid but could be indestructible as well. As has been remarked:[84]

[79] (1589-95) 1 Co. Rep. f.120a.
[80] *ibid*. at f.138a.
[81] (1671) 2 Wms. Saunders 380.
[82] (1575) Dyer 339(b).
[83] (1620) Cro. Jac. 590.
[84] Milsom at p.203.

"This was a momentous decision. Not only did it finally reject the argument that the legal remainder rules would apply and, in effect, prevent the existence of executory interests. It also finally held such interests to be indestructible by any means except by the act of their owners. There was of course no perpetuity sought in the case itself, because the gift over was to operate, if at all, upon the dropping of an existing life; but the mischief was pressed in argument, and subordinated to the hardship of allowing destructibility.

Perhaps this was the better choice. There had been much perversity in results reached by reason over the entail and over contingent remainders, allowing the extravagant creation of settlements and countering the mischief by allowing their capricious destruction. The alternative mode of control to which the courts were now driven, was to impose some initial limit upon the reach of settlers beyond which their dispositions would just be ineffective. Although undertaken by judges, this was an essentially legislative process motivated by policy rather than logic."

The result was great uncertainty as to what was and what was not permitted. Eventually in the *Duke of Norfolk's Case* in 1681[85] there was propounded what has become the modern rule against perpetuities. Lord Nottingham's main thesis was that the time at which executory interest must vest was the sole point to be regarded. Accordingly if it must vest, if at all, either during or after a life in being it would be good irrespective of the nature of the estate that preceded it.

Although the basis of the rule had now been stated as remoteness, Lord Nottingham had not settled the utmost length of time at which a future interest could be made to vest. The *Duke of Norfolk's Case* settled only that it was valid after a life or lives in being. The question as to whether it could be limited to vest at any more remote date was deliberately left open and it was eventually settled during the eighteenth century as being a life or lives in being plus twenty-one years plus the period of gestation where the beneficiary was en ventre sa mère. A variant of a straight period of twenty-one years, depending on neither lives in being nor minorities was also introduced during this period.

Any lingering doubts were set at rest by the House of Lords in *Cadell* v *Palmer*[86] in 1832.

Rules against Perpetuities

Although the rules against perpetuities developed by the English courts can be traced back to basic feudal doctrines perhaps the most significant development came in the Elizabethan era with the courts ceasing to negative perpetuities because they conflicted with technical rules and positively using those legal rules to defeat perpetuities. With the adoption of a positive approach the policy element came to the fore until, as in *Mary Portington's Case*[87] even technical perfection was insufficient.

Reasons for the Adoption of a Policy against Perpetuities

The classic articulations of the evils of perpetual settlements come from *Chudleigh's Case*[88], from the argument of Bacon[89] and the judgement of

---

[85] (1681) 3 Ch. Cas. 1.
[86] (1832) 1 Cl. and Fin. 372.
[87] (1614) 10 Co. Rep. f.35*b*.
[88] (1589-95) 1 Co. Rep. f.120*a*.
[89] Works vol. vii (Spedding ed.) pp.632-635.

Popham C.J.[90] Indeed these statements provided the foundation for a Bill introduced into the House of Lords in 1597[91] designed to abolish perpetuities.

It will be remembered that much of the argument in Chudleigh's Case was concerned with the position of contingent uses, and the discussion of perpetuities is conducted against that background. Bacon indeed founded his argument on the preamble to the Statute of Uses[92] and began by detailing the mischiefs attributed to uses there. He then turned to perpetuities specifically arguing that they were contrary to public policy, to humanity, to the discipline of families and to clearness and certainty in the law. As to public policy:[93]

"We should consider the perils imminent in the present estate; who see in this time the desperate humours of divers men in devising treason and conspiracies,—who being such men, that in the course of their ambition or other furious apprehensions, they make very small or no account of their proper lives; if to the common desire and sweetness of life the natural regard for their posterity be not adjoined, the bridle, I doubt, will be too weak; for when they see that whatever comes of themselves, yet their posterity shall not be overthrown, they will be made more audacious to attempt such matters. And another reason of State may be added . . . . and that is the peril which necessarily grows to any state, if the greatness of man's possessions be in discontented races; the which must necessarily follow if, notwithstanding the attainder of the father, the son shall succeed to his line and estate."

As to humanity:[94]

"A man is taken prisoner in war. Life and liberty are more precious than land or goods. For his ransom it is necessary for him to sell. If then he be shackled in such conveyances, he is as much captive to his conveyances as to his enemy, and so must die in misery to make his son and heir after him to live in jollity. Some young heir when he first comes to the float of his living outcompasseth himself in expenses; yet perhaps in good time reclaims himself, and has a desire to recover his estates; but has no readier way than to sell a parcel to free himself from the biting and consuming interest. But now he cannot redeem himself with his proper means, and though he be reclaimed in mind, yet can he not remedy his estate."

As to family discipline:[95]

"Though I reverence the laws of my country, yet I observe one defect in them, and that is, there is no footstep there of the reverend potestas patria which was so commended in ancient times . . . . This only yet remains: if the father has any patrimony and the son be disobedient, he may disinherit him; if he will not deserve his blessing he shall not have his living. But this device of perpetuities has taken this power from the father likewise; and has tied and made subject (as the proverb is) the parents to their cradle, and so notwithstanding he has the curse of his father, yet he shall have the land of his grandfather."

As to the state of the law:[96]

"If this clause which is put in perpetuities be considered, that is to say, that the land shall remain upon forfeiture to him who is next in limitation, as if the other committing the forfeiture were dead, it is not possible for the most learned judge to answer the questions. For there will be heirs without death, the which is a thing prodigious in our law and is a common highway to many subtle questions."

Popham C.J.'s attack is concentrated more on the mischiefs to the family. Thus he said:[97]

---

[90] 1 Co. Rep. at ff.138a-140a.
[91] Calendared in third Rep. Hist. MSS. Com. 10. See Holdsworth (1919) 35 L.Q.R. at p.258.
[92] 1535 Stat. 27 Hen. VIII c. 10.
[93] at p.633-634.
[94] *ibid.* at p.634.
[95] *ibid.* at p.634-635.
[96] *ibid.* at p.635.
[97] 1 Co. Rep. at ff.138b-139a.

". . . . the said construction did tend to the subversion of noble and great families and to the disinherison of their heirs, so that no land subject to such perpetuities could continue four descents; for if he, who is restrained and bound with the provisos of perpetuities, should sell any part of the land for payments of any debts or legacies, or, if he be taken prisoner in the war, for his ransom, or for the preferment of his younger sons, or for the advancement of his daughters in marriage, or for any cause, or upon any necessity whatsoever he would forfeit his estate;[98] also when the eldest son knows he shall have the lands and possessions of his father, whether he will or no, it makes the son become dissolute and disobedient, so that he will not depend upon the government of his father, but refuse to be ruled and directed by him. It would likewise occasion variance and discord in the same blood, and in effect tear the bowels of nature, for it would stir up the son (upon every supposition of breach of the provisos) to put his father out of the land; from whence great suits and troubles would arise, to the wasting and subversion of the families; and so of the brother and brother, and of the cousin and cousin; and he who hath such perpetuity ought always to have a counsellor at law at his elbow, for he cannot do any act concerning his land, but his son, who is next to the land, watches for a forfeiture . . . . Also, if the wives of such persons become incontinent, and have issue by other men than by their husbands, this adulterous generation shall inherit the husband's lands whether they will or no; and this would be a great occasion for women to offend, when they know their issues shall inherit."

As to the state of the law Popham C.J. was more specific than Bacon,[99] first as to the proprietor, then as to any purchaser and finally as to any lessee.

"Also he who hath an estate subject to such perpetuity, if he hath two several farms, out of which two several rents have been reserved, and peradventure where the several usual rents amount but to 40s per ann. and he joins both in one lease for life, and reserves one rent of four marks per ann. it is a forfeiture of his estate: for upon this lease the usual and accustomed rent is not reserved; so in many other cases if he do not observe the precise form of the power which is given him it will amount to a forfeiture of his estate; and within two or three descents the provisos and limitations will not be so fresh in memory that every gentleman can, in every lease which he shall make, follow the precise form of the provisos . . . . Also no purchaser would be sure of his purchase without an Act of Parliament; and where, at the common law, if he had purchased the land bona fide without notice of the use, he had been free of the use, he will now be in a worse case, for by the construction which hath been made has lands shall be subject to these future uses.

Also farmers and lessees cannot have any certain and full assurance, for suppose a feoffment in fee to be made to the use of one for life, and after to the use of another in tail, with remainder over, with power to the lessee for life to make leases so that he reserves the accustomed rent payable to all those who shall have the reversion; if the tenant for life makes leases according to his power, the lessees derive their interest out of the first feoffment, how then can the reservation of the rent be good, and how can his heir, or he in the remainder come at it? and if a proviso be added in the original assurance, that the lessee shall pay the rent, then forasmuch as it is no rent, it ought to be paid without demand, and if he do not pay it, his interest shall immediately cease by the limitation of the use . . . ."

And lastly there was the economic argument:[99]

"And many other inconveniences would ensue upon such a construction in maintenance of these perpetuities: and so men who overreach the providence of God and covet to establish their lands in their blood by these ways are in truth thereby the cause and the wasting and subversion of their homes . . . .

Also the King and other lords will lose their wards, escheats and other profits of their seigniories; for if the said case before put of a perpetual freehold should be main-

---

[98] Compare Patrick Irvine W.S. writing in 1827; Chapter I, Supra.
[99] 1 Co. Rep. at f.139a.

tained, that no heir shall have but an estate for life, and that the inheritance shall be in nobody, what escheat or ward or heriot or other profit will accrue to the king or other lords?"

These factors then, political, social, economic and legal were the foundation of the anti-perpetuity policy that ultimately resulted in the modern law of perpetuities. That these views were genuinely held is beyond doubt. That they were consistently held is more questionable. The point was that the monied classes, and particularly the common lawyers, many of whom made large fortunes out of their legal practice, would often hold a split view, depending on whether they were in the market for land or were seeking to establish their house. Hence many of the arguments used above have a double edge to them and, looked at from a distance of four hundred years, appear somewhat unconvincing. Of much more relevance would appear to be the economic consequences of taking and keeping land out of commerce which were stressed two hundred years later when the problem became acute in Scotland. However it must be remembered that the debates took place in different ages; economic theory had at this time not yet reached the mercantalist stage and socially and politically the period, though post-feudal, still had many of the forms and folk-memories of the feudal past, and it is these that would seem to have shaped the English perpetuity policy.

The Relationship between the Rules

Although the Elizabethan courts took the step of formulating and articulating an anti-perpetuity policy the instruments used to implement it were still, by and large, those that were available to Littleton. They were the technical rules governing seisin and the limitation of estates consequent upon that and they were pressed into service with some success.

Although not specifically aimed in that direction, these rules nonetheless had the effect of controlling dispositions which were unduly remote and indeed produced a shorter period of vesting than the modern rule. At the same time the influences of these old rules can clearly be seen, especially in the early stages, on the development of the modern rule. But there were undoubted differences. Whatever its effect on remoteness the old rules operated on the limitation itself; the period of vesting was a very secondary matter. In the modern rule the period of vesting is all.

Furthermore the old rules were concerned with factual situations, and not hypotheses. If a contingent remainder did not vest before the termination of the particular estate it was void; but one had to wait and see. It was perhaps this aspect which caused Holdsworth to comment:[100]

"They were inadequate in their contents because they were, for the most part, merely negative. They condemned certain sorts of limitations, or rendered them liable to destruction in certain ways; but they gave no information to landowners what limitations were valid. They laid down no positive rule for their guidance. What was wanted was a rule which was both positive and negative—a rule which would tell owners of property both what settlements they might, and what they might not, make."

In a sense the modern rule satisfied this criticism. One feature of it is the

---

[100] History of English Law vol. vii p.195.

requirement that one must be able to tell at the inception of the settlement whether the limitation is good or bad—if it may possibly vest outside the perpetuity period it will be bad.[101]

The principal difference between the two sets of rules, though, related to the types of property they were designed to cover, for the old rules were meant to cover legal contingent remainders in land, but little else. The modern rule was meant to cover other interests and in other property. Eventually, throughout the nineteenth century contingent remainders were equated with executory interests and in 1925[102] the two were completely assimilated, the varieties of future interest being reduced to one and controlled by one rule—the modern rule.

One result of this has been, perhaps, that although family settlements were still made, a resettlement took place every generation, keeping within the perpetuity rules in fact, but achieving the desired object all the same.

The Effect of the English Law of Perpetuities in Scotland

The reaction that is most apparent in the more modern judgements of the Scottish courts in cases involving points with a possible perpetuity connection is one of nervousness, perhaps induced by the fear that 'the sinister influence of the English rule against perpetuities'[103] might be brought to bear on Scottish rules and doctrines. Accordingly suggestions of the possible relevance of English decisions with a perpetuity connection have frequently been met with a comprehensive assertion to the contrary. Thus in *Muir's Trustees* v *Williams*[104] Lord Justice-Clerk Cooper said:[105]

"Now as I understand it, the English rule against perpetuities is a rule, or series of rules, of great antiquity and high artificiality, slowly evolved by the English courts without legislative aid. The Scottish counterpart is a relatively modern statutory innovation . . . .

. . . . But it is not merely in background and in origin that the two systems differ. A superficial similarity conceals a difference in content and effect of the laws of the two countries and that difference seems to me to be very material to the present controversy. The basic English principle, as laid down in the leading standard works . . . . is that every attempted disposition of land or goods is void unless at the time when the instrument creating it takes effect, one can say that it must take effect, if it takes effect at all, within a life or lives then in being plus twenty-one years and nine months. It will be noted:

(*a*) that this rule operates as a limitation upon the power to make certain kinds of disposition of property; and

(*b*) that the infringing disposition is void ab initio. The Scottish statutory counterpart . . . . proceeds upon the totally different principle of imposing no bar of illegality and no penalty of nullity, but merely prescribing the conditions upon which an interest intended to be a liferent will or may be transformed into a fee. It follows naturally enough that an English court should approach the question ab ante . . . . But the

---

[101] However this aspect of the modern rule was consistently criticised (see for example Morris & Leach—The Rule against Perpetuities, 2nd ed. 1962) as being inflexible and as producing capricious and absurd results. Accordingly in 1964 the Perpetuities and Accumulations Act introduced a 'wait and see' principle for dispositions infringing the rule and taking effect after the coming into operation of the Act, 15th July 1964.

[102] Law of Property Act 1925 s. 161 for instruments taking effect after 1st January 1926.

[103] Per Lord Romer in *Muir's Trustees* v *Williams* 1943 S.C. (HL) 47 at p.58.

[104] 1942 S.C. 5.

[105] *ibid.* at p.11, 12.

appropriate Scottish approach . . . . is ex post facto with an inquiry directed solely to the question whether the events prescribed by the statute have in fact occurred."

Pausing there for a moment it is apparent that Lord Cooper was either unaware of, or else chose to ignore, the fact that English law developed two rules against perpetuities, and that while his statement is perfectly accurate with regard to the modern rule; the old rule has much more affinity with the Scottish rules. The point, which the Scottish courts have ignored is that their own perpetuity provisions were originally essentially of an anti-avoidance nature, designed to prevent the evasion of the provisions of the Rutherfurd Act[106] by a conveyance of land to trustees for a succession of limited interests. This device which was designed to get over difficulties caused by the feudal rule that a fee might not be in pendente; and it will be remembered that it was this principle that was one of the basic elements of the 'old rule'.

However there is little doubt that Lord Cooper is correct in stating that the Scottish rules owe nothing to the 'modern rule against perpetuities'. It would therefore seem reasonable to assume that English cases cited as authoritative by counsel which contain connections with the 'modern rule' would be dealt with on the basis that the perpetuity point was irrelevant to the question before them. But instead the courts in Scotland have tended to go much further and to regard the perpetuity connection, not as irrelevant in itself, but as a ground for rejecting the relevance of the case altogether. Thus, for example, in *Muir's Trustees* a rule of construction relating to powers of appointment had been developed in England and it was sought to apply that rule to a power under a Scottish trust. While the construction was not inconsistent with the principles of Scots law, it was nevertheless sought to be excluded by the Court of Session on the basis of its having been derived from the rule against perpetuities. On appeal to the House of Lords[107] the decision of the Scottish court was reversed on the facts, it being shown that the rule of construction was of general application in several branches of English law, of which the modern rule against perpetuities was one.

However the substance of the Court of Session's decision seemed to be left intact, its being accepted that principles of law or rules of construction founded on "the specialties of the English rule against perpetuities" would not be applicable.

There are several points that arise from this approach. In the first place it would seem mistaken to reject a perfectly viable rule of law which could be of general application simply because at some point in its evolution it became part of, or indeed had its origin in the modern rule. The fact of the acceptance of the particular principle would scarcely imply acceptance of, and still less the importation of the modern rule against perpetuities.

In the second place the approach would seem to be self defeating, for to ascertain whether a particular principle had its origin in the rules against perpetuities it would be necessary to delve into the history of both the principle and the English perpetuity rules. To go to such lengths simply to exclude what might prove to be a perfectly useful principle is absurd.

---

[106] Entail Amendment (Scotland) Act 1848, 11 & 12 Vict. c. 36.
[107] 1943 S.C. (HL) 47.

In the third place it is possible to envisage a situation where legislation would render this approach inappropriate. For example the Accumulations Act 1800 was passed as a direct result of a consequence arising from the modern rule. In this, or indeed in any analogous case it would seem essential that the perpetuity background be taken into account.

The specific difficulty in *Muir's* case arose from the suggestion made in general terms that English learning was relevant in dealing with questions under the Scottish perpetuity rules. The suggestion came from Lord Sands in *Stewart's Trustees* v *Whitelaw* in the following terms:[108]

"But in view of the statutory origin of the rules we are applying, [English] authority may perhaps be regarded as standing in a peculiar position. An analogous question might have arisen in Scotland under the Thellusson Act, but it did not arise. It arose in England and was decided in favour of [solution A]. As regards legislation against the creation of 'perpetuities' the question could not have arisen until the passing of the recent legislation[109] with which we are here concerned. The rule, however, that, in regard to laws against perpetuities analogous to those struck at by the Scottish Acts [solution A is to be adopted] has been established in England. Now, although the Acts here in question apply to Scotland only, they are Acts of the Imperial Parliament. If it is to be taken that the English Courts, the only courts which had adjudicated on the matter had, as regards both the Thellusson Act[110] and perpetuities recognised [a particular rule] may not perhaps there be room for argument that the legislature, in framing the Scottish Acts, had this judicial interpretation of such provision in view, there being nothing in this interpretation repugnant to any established principle of Scottish law."

This may be regarded going to the other extreme and, not surprisingly, was rejected by Lord Cooper.[111] Its difficulty is that it is equating specific legislation covering a particular problem, such as the Thellusson Act, which applied to both jurisdictions, with other legislation which, while directed towards the same end, adopts a different means of achieving it from that in England. To accept Lord Sands' proposition is, therefore, accepting that something approaching a common general aim is enough. Similar objections (from the opposite standpoint) can therefore be levelled against this view as can be levelled against the Cooper approach. Does it entail the acceptance of an inconvenient principle of law or construction provided such principle is not contrary to any established principle of Scots law? Does it not also entail, albeit to a lesser degree, any enquiry into the principle's origins.

With respect, the present writer feels that the middle view that, except in possibly special cases such as a Thellusson Act situation, the fact of a principle's association with the English rule against perpetuities should be treated as irrelevant. If it is desired to accept or reject a principle it should be done on its merits and not dealt with on the basis of possible contamination or enrichment because of its association with the English perpetuity rule.

Apart from accumulations[112] the English rule against perpetuities (that is the modern rule) would appear to have little effect on the substantive rules of Scots law, although, surprisingly, it is not without effect in practice, specifically in connection with drafting trust deeds for unit trust schemes.

[108] 1926 S.C. 701 at p.719.
[109] Trusts (Scotland) Act 1921 s. 9; 11 and 12 Geo. V c. 58.
[110] The Accumulations Act 1800; 39 & 40 Geo. III c. 9.
[111] 1942 S.C. at p. 13.
[112] See below Chapter V.

Unit trusts originated in London in 1868, the trust form which had been used for centuries as a means of holding family and institutional wealth, being adapted for use as a medium for investment.[113] The form of the first unit trusts was such that a provision was included for their termination within twenty years, so as to avoid any possible invalidity for perpetuity. Yet though Scots law has no rules against remoteness, and while unit trust schemes could not infringe the statutory perpetuity rule, nevertheless the form of trust deeds adopted by Scottish unit trust managers still provides for the traditional termination on the original English model, a practice unnecessary even in England now.[114]

---

[113] See R. Burgess—'The Development of the Managed Investment Fund' (1973) 18 Journal of the Law Society of Scotland at pp.277 et seq; and 321 et seq.

[114] See Pennington 'The Investor and the Law' (London 1967). See also the judgement of Wynn-Parry J. in *Re AEG Unit Trust (Managers) Ltd.'s Trust Deed* [1957] Ch. 415 where it was held that the accumulation rules had no application to unit trusts which provided for the accumulation of income.

Chapter III

PERPETUITIES IN SCOTS LAW

English Law and Scots Law

A study of the evolution of perpetuities and perpetuity rules in Scotland provides a marked contrast to what happened in England, not only in terms of what was done but also as to why and how it was done. Perpetuity law would appear to be one of those areas in which the individual styles of English and Scots law contrast most clearly.

Perhaps the most significant characteristic of the Scottish law of landholding has been its gradual evolution, gradual, that is, not only in terms of time but also in terms of principle; only the context has changed, and in Scotland even that has changed slowly. The whole process looks pedestrian when compared with the more flamboyant developments that occurred in the South.

This flamboyance in England seems to have come from two sources. In the first place it came from legislation making tremendous changes in the substantive law of landholding. It may be asked what legislation in Scotland prior to 1747 made such a shattering impact on the prior law and on subsequent conveyancing practice as Quia Emptores, The Statutes of Fines, the Statutes of Uses and Wills, and what statute in Scotland had such an effect on the theory of landownership as de Donis Conditionalibus? In Scotland legislative intervention tended to be of the type that made detailed amendments to existing principle while leaving that principle intact. The various statutes of the fifteenth, sixteenth and seventeenth centuries concerned with the registration[1] of deeds of title exemplify this; even the Entail Act 1685 was passed in confirmation of and to give statutory force to a development which (on one view at least) the common law had reached by itself.

One reason for this may well be the use that was made of legislative amendments to landholding. In England all the great pillars of the land law were essentially politically or financially motivated (or both). As we have seen, de Donis was a concession to the feudal baronage, Quia Emptores an instrument for preserving seignorial revenues; The Statutes of Fines had their origins in the Wars of the Roses and the Statute of Uses must be the prime example of legislative interference with substantive legal principle for financial ends. In Scotland the amendments seem to have been more in the nature of law reform measures, pure and simple. Whatever the political background, even the Entail Act 1685 can be viewed in this light. Hence Scots law gives the impression of a smooth, slow, and gradual evolution, in almost complete contrast to the English position.

Equally important seems to have been the skill and imagination of the mediaeval English conveyancers, which had seemingly no counterpart in mediaeval Scotland.

---

[1] Act of 1469 c. 27; Act of 1503 c. 89; Act of 1555 c. 46; Act 31st July 1599 (Act Anent the Register of Seasings, Reversions, etc.); Act of 1617 c. 16 (Anent Registration of Reversions, Seasings and other writs); Act of 1693 c. 13 (Act concerning the Preference of Real Rights).

While Scottish legal historians write of "skilled conveyancers"[2] there seem to have been few attempts to see how far feudal concepts could be pushed in the manner and on the scale that there were in England. Certainly the developments utilising the potentialities of the feudal warranty which played so important a part in achieving freedom of alienation in England were apparently absent from Scottish usage. Perhaps this is explained by—or perhaps it explains—Lord Cooper's assertion that:[3]

".... the Scottish lawyers, nearly all of whom were then ecclesiastics, would view with instinctive distaste the later trend of English developments, and particularly the empirical effort to contrive a new tool for every new job, to use that tool only for that job, and to circumvent occasional obstacles by legal fictions. The Scottish aim would rather be to use the smallest possible number of tools for the largest possible number of jobs, to abstract the general from the particular and to avoid excessive technicality and needless elaborations."

But these differences are perhaps only illustrative of the greater divergence of Scots law from English law and its establishment as a separate system. To quote Lord Cooper again:[4]

"For a large part of the period the borrowing from England, or at least from Norman law, was slavish, and most of the English remedies and expedients appear one by one in Scotland, though only after a time lag of many years accounted for by the slow penetration to the North of the system which was being rapidly developed under the lawyers of Henry II and his successors in the South. It would seem however that it was only the English master patents that were thus infringed. Thus Scotland appropriated such notable inventions as the writs of right, mortancester and novel disseisin, but soon imparted to them national characteristics and never pursued to any distance the developments and refinements to which these remedies were subjected in England . . . .

For over a hundred years Scotland was well content to follow in England's wake and to appropriate and apply the best of the system which Glanvill described. But the age of Bracton succeeded the age of Glanvill in England, and the Justices of Henry III and Edward I, having at their disposal large and growing volumes of juristic material on which to work, pursued with enthusiasm the task of refining and elaborating the law. The relative simplicity of Norman law rapidly became overlaid with innumerable technicalities . . . .

Before this process had been carried very far Scotland dropped out of the race. For one thing the task of following the English lead was an impossible one under the conditions which then prevailed. With neither law reports, nor digests, nor up-to-date textbooks, and with a system of communications which separated Edinburgh from Westminster by an interval of weeks, Scotland had no chance of maintaining close contact with London, and most of the English provinces must have been completely detached from the remoter districts of Scotland. The divergence of the two legal systems would thus have been inevitable . . . .

By the time of Bruce the divergence of the two legal systems was clearly visible in the rejection of new English ideas, in the modification of ideas already borrowed from England, and in a general effort towards greater simplicity and flexibility. The extent of the divergence and the recognition by England are shown by two notable instances. There is an English record in 1305 of a litigation relating to the wardship of the insane in which it was specifically averred that Scots law was different from English and a remit was made to ascertain what Scots law on the subject was. In the same year, when Edward I assumed that he was free to impose a new legal system on Scotland, his

---

[2] per G. C. H. Paton "The Dark Age 1329-1532" in Introduction to Scottish Legal History Stair Soc. vol. 20 at p.22.
[3] David I to Bruce; *ibid.* at p.15.
[4] *ibid.* at pp.10, 14, 15.

first step was to initiate, before a mixed Anglo-Scottish advisory council, an investigation into the law of Scotland."

Alienation

Nowhere is this divergence more apparent than in the development of the law governing the alienation of land in Scotland; nowhere is the slow plod of evolution more evident and the contrast with the style and nature of developments in England more evident than here. Of the use of the warranty, of its implications there is little or nothing except, of course, its normal insertion in charters. Certainly there is no evidence of any creative use of feudal principle to achieve relative freedom of alienation as there was in England.

Of course there is a tremendous difficulty in that there is comparatively little early evidence, owing in part to the Scottish records having been transported by Edward I to England, and in part to the political anarchy which existed in Scotland from the death of Bruce for much of the succeeding two and a half centuries, factors which scarcely made for the preservation of much legal material.

There is one view, however, to the effect that after the Wars of Independence Scotland tended to take its law from the England of the pre-war era. Thus C. D'Olivier Farran writes:[5]

"Feudal Scotland's land law was, and feudal it had to remain, for the whole social and economic life of the Scots was . . . . irrevocably based on a feudal organisation of society. Barred from following English developments by new-found national pride, and yet unable to revolutionise itself on civilian lines, Scots land law had little choice but to remain in its pre-Edwardian state, borrowing at a later date much terminology and some conceptions from the old feudal laws of the continent, but in the main preserving the earlier structure of English land law, which in that country was undergoing, and was to undergo through the centuries, some very considerable changes."

It will be seen at once that this view runs directly counter to what may be considered as the classical Scots view that Bractonian technicalities were shunned in preference to the more purely feudal doctrines of Glanvil, and indeed sounds strange when considering on the one hand the fact of freedom of alienation in the England of Henry III and, on the other, the emphasis on the rights of the superior to be found in Balfour and Craig, and the fact that there existed legal restraints on alienating land held in ward until 1747.[6] Furthermore (although this is not fatal to his thesis) Farran apparently rejects what would seem to be the most promising line of support.

This comes from the statements of some commentators that a Scottish counterpart of the English statute Quia Emptores was enacted by the Scottish Parliament during the reign of Robert I.[7] If the statute was genuine, which is doubtful, it would seem inexplicable that its provisions could be or would be imposed on a baronage that had been a pillar of support during the Wars of Independence taking away, as they did, the power to control who should be their vassals, unless this power had, as in England, already effectively gone. But if this view is right, it remains to be explained how the feudal system reasserted itself. An explanation was suggested by Ross, who put it down to

---

[5] The Principles of Scots and English Land Law (Edinburgh 1958) at p.78.
[6] 20 Geo. II. c. 58.
[7] Stat. Rob. I c. 25.

politics, and in particular the rise of the power and influence of the nobility at the expense of the Crown. He wrote:[8]

". . . . a statute was made in England in the reign of Edward I . . . . which takes its title from the initial words, 'Qu[i]a Emptores Terrarum'. It is unnecessary to give the tenor of the English act, because it was afterwards transplanted into Scotland verbatim, by statute of our Robert Bruce about the year 1325 . . . .

Our own writers upon this subject have supposed that the statute of Robert was never executed [i.e. implemented] in Scotland; it is certain, however, that it was executed during the remainder of that century; and it is the genuine source of our precepts of sasine and obligements to infeft a me et de superiore meo. The vassals, by the act, could only alienate their lands to be held of their immediate superiors; and consequently a man could only infeft a purchaser a se et de superiore suo, otherwise the sale was null upon the statute. The superiors, however, refused to obey upon their part, and claimed a power of confirming the infeftment. In short the nobility at last took advantage of that part of the statute which strengthened their own interest, and refused to comply with the other, which favoured the vassal. Thus the very law which gives complete relief to the body of the people in England, rendered the condition of the same rank in Scotland worse than ever. So completely was the act of Robert I neglected by superiors that, in the reign of Robert III in the year 1400,[9] an act passed, declaring, that 'if the tenant anaillied his land without licence of the overlord, in that case the overlord might recognosce them'. Robert III was a weak and unfortunate Prince: His nobility got the ascendence, and trampled both upon him and upon the people. After this period it was that the aristocracy continued to gain strength. At last our connection with the French became very close, and our lawyers and courts had recourse to the written feudal law upon every occasion. They adopted its rigours and the subtleties of its commentators, whose inferences always tended to increase the power, and swell the pride of the haughty nobility and great Crown vassals."

This explanation however, while it may fit the political facts, scarcely corresponds with actuality, many grants by way of subinfeudation having been found which were effected during the fourteenth century. Still more surprising is the fact that not one case appears to have been presented to the courts in which the supposed statute was relied on. Furthermore, had there been any translation of the statute to Scotland, one would have expected Craig to have commented on it. But Craig is silent on the matter, as is Stair and the other institutional writers. Ross's point, too, about the origin of grants in Scotland a me et de superiore meo would also seem not to follow from his premise. Such a grant would indeed be a substitution, but it would not have been necessary for the statute to have been passed for such a substitution to have been effected. Such dispositions, with the superior's consent, were perfectly in accord with feudal principle.

As for Farran's main thesis, the difficulty is his reluctance to produce anything in support of it. There are, it is true, comparisons drawn between Glanvil and the Regiam Majestitem, unsurprisingly in view of the fact that the latter was very largely a transcription of the former, with detailed local amendments, and his principal examples, the quantum of land that might be alienated and the existence of conquest in early English as well as in Scots law, both come from

---

[8] Lectures on the Law of Scotland (1798) vol. II at pp.257/258. Other exponents of the genuineness of the statute have been, notably Sandford (Entails at p.32) and Lord Kames, who, in his "Statute Law of Scotland" (Edinburgh & London 1757) devoted several pages (pp.350, 432-436) to it, coming to essentially the same conclusion as Ross.

[9] Act of 1400 c. 19, section 4.

the Glanvilian age and had disappeared by Bracton's time.[10] If therefore Farran's description is taken as referring to the pre-Bractonian period of pre-Edwardian England he is no doubt correct. But it unfortunately cannot be so taken, for he then goes on to discuss the Bractonian view of gifts in liberum maritagium as conditional gifts and assumes that this development applied in Scotland as well. Having stated the mechanics of these conditional grants he goes on:[11]

"English and Scots law advanced thus far together—we may assume. There is a scribal interpolation in some M.SS of the Regiam which shows that Bracton's text probably circulated in Scotland. Even if it did not, the ideas put forward by Bracton would be those of all civilians, which the early Scots Judges, being mostly churchmen, tended to be. Certainly Bracton's view that the donee in tail acquires an indefeasible interest as soon as the condition is fulfilled, corresponds pretty closely to the conclusions of the classical Scots law. There is thus a direct chain of continuity between the views of Bracton and those of modern Scotland. But Bracton's view is very far removed from that of the developed English law on this subject. This is yet another instance of the tendency for Scotland to preserve the pre-Edward I English law."

Now, the only fact offered as evidence for this fantastic speculative non-sequitur is the existence of a scribal interpolation in some manuscripts of the Regiam Majestatem.[12] No date is given for this interpolation or even the nature of it. All the scholars tell us is that it shows traces of Bractonian influence, although there is no indication as to any acceptance of Bractonian doctrines. Farran then turns to clerical judges, but seems to assume they occupied the important positions they did in the pre-Reformation Court of Session, completely ignoring the decentralised, fragmented and by general consent, unsatisfactory system of administering justice in mediaeval Scotland; in short he appears to be attaching an importance to civilian training that was not obviously in a position to influence the weight of legal development to the extent suggested. But then, dubious as these points are, to use them in conjunction with the fact that the classical Scots law bore some resemblances to Bractonian doctrine to produce the conclusion that there existed "a direct chain of continuity" from one to the other savours more of fantasy than of fact and of wishful thinking rather than logical or historical deduction.

If, then, the Farran view can be discarded, we are thrown back on Glanvilian feudal principle and what opens up before us is the long, slow and very gradual amplification of the rights of the vassal into something approaching ownership, a process which, as in England, seems to have coincided with the erosion of seignorial control over the fee.

The Control of the Feudal Superior

We saw when examining the achievement of free alienation of land in England that such freedom came with the ending of true seignorial control over the fee with the result that the lord's interest changed from the exercise of his political power and influence to the preservation of the economic value of the seigneury. We suggested that this change came about as a result of the strangulation of the lord's local jurisdictional powers by the operation of the possessary assizes of

---

[10] See Farran at p.137.
[11] ibid. at p. 141.
[12] Lord Cooper—Regiam Majestatem (Stair Society vol. XI) at p.44.

novel disseisin and mort d'ancestor, and in turn that the provision of these remedies might have been part of the centralisation policies of the early Plantagenets.

In Scotland the political climate was vastly different. Whereas by the time of Edward I the power struggle between Crown and baronage was largely over, in Scotland it had hardly begun. And when it did begin the results were dramatically different. Instead of an increasing centralisation of power in the Crown, a combination of circumstances such as intermittent civil war, the capture and detention of the king by the English, and most importantly the successive minorities of the Stewarts made for a period of two and a half centuries during which—with the exception of short intervals of "strong" government—effective power was with the baronage. As one legal historian has remarked of this period:[13]

"The 14th, 15th and 16th centuries witnessed continuous political strife and economic troubles, recurrent national war, internal rebellion and internecine feuds. The feudalism on which the government and the legal system had been based moved in the 15th century to a position where the central authority was weak and strong barons siezed control in the outlying regions and got from a weak government powers it was unable to exercise. There developed a situation whereby the support of the less powerful by the more powerful magnates could defy the King and the Government. These long continued wars, disturbances, disorders and political confusions were not compatible with the development of private law. They weakened the strength of the government, broke down the law and slowed down the progress of social life by which law lives and develops. They prohibited the normal development of legal institutions and indeed were all but destructive of the legal institutions we have."

It is hardly surprising, then, that in this climate the emphasis should be placed on the rights and might of the superiors rather than on their vassals, and that such rights and powers should flourish rather than be stifled. Insofar as there was a political force in operation comparable to that in England it operated in precisely the opposite direction not inducing or promoting freedom of alienation but postponing it.

At the same time the Scottish counterparts of novel disseisin and mort d'ancestor had no effect on the local jurisdictional powers of superiors comparable to that produced in England. In part this can no doubt be explained by the lack of a political dimension on the part of the Scottish Crown's use of them, although in the case of the brieve of Novel Disseisin as constituted by statute of Alexander II[14] the fact that a target is the feudal superior is even more apparent than in the English assize, the relevant part of the statute reading:

". . . . gif ony man plenzies to the king or til his Justice that *his lord* or any othir man his disseysit hym wranguisly and wythoutin ingment of ony thing the quhilk he was befor vestyt and sesyt and fyndis borowys to folow his plagnt the Justice or the Schireff throu the Kyngis commandment sal ger it be knawin throu leil men and worthy of the cuntre gif the man that plenzies sayis suth. And if it be fundin suth be the said assyse the Justice or the schireff sal restor hym til his landis and the disseysour sal be in the Kingis amercyment. And gif it be knowin that the playntiff sayis fals he sal be in the kyngis amercyment of 10 libres."

As for the brieve of mortancestor, which was originally indistinguishable from its English counterpart, this rapidly changed its character, the emphasis

---

[13] G. Campbell H. Paton. "Introduction to Scottish Legal History" (Stair Soc. vol. 20) at p.18.
[14] (1230) Stat. Alex II c. 7. A.P.S. vol. i at p.400.

changing from getting out an intruder to declaring the title of the heir to succeed.

But the essential point must surely be that the object of the Scottish brieves was simply to provide a remedy: the background of transference of actions from local to national courts was just not there, if only because there were no national courts of the centralised type set up by Henry II in England.[15] And it was this lack of transference that was the important point, for the existence of a powerful local jurisdiction under little or no central control could be and was an instrument of power and influence in the hands of its proprietor. Indeed as late as 1747[16] this fact was expressly recognised in the statute of that year abolishing heritable jurisdictions, one reason for which being that it was felt that their existence was a significant factor in the marshalling of support for the cause of the Pretender in 1745, and that with abolition such influence would cease.

But pressure for a different system of administering justice grew, largely because the local courts were unsatisfactory judicial instruments, showing little consistency and inspiring little confidence. As has been said:[17]

"The administration of justice was, however, too much in the hands of the judges ordinary—the local and franchise courts. Particularly in the latter part of the fourteenth century and till at least 1424, these came to be more and more unpopular. Not only were they corrupt and inefficient but they became virtually independent without supervision following their own interpretation of law and giving decisions of interest only to the litigants. It is not surprising that there was little, if any, public confidence in them. Various unhappy and unsuccessful expedients were vainly resorted to in an attempt to secure law and order. The dislike of local courts led dissatisfied litigants to seek their remedies at Parliament and Council causing continual congestion of business there .... Despite the lack of redress in the feudal courts there was no true system of royal justice in operation and Parliament and Council did not apparently—were reluctant to—adopt a critical attitude towards the feudal courts."

This reluctance is perhaps understandable. Feudal courts were part of the very fabric of the feudal system and it was on this system that society and government in Scotland were based. By its very nature it would be decentralised and its continued acceptance as the framework of local government is evident into the sixteenth century.

"The continued acceptance of feudalism as the framework of local government is evident in the creation of new baronies. During James IV's reign the pages of the register of the great seal are spattered with creations of baronies—a cursory examination reveals more than eighty. Nor had their function changed from that of the twelfth century: when lands near the Great Glen were conferred upon John Grant of Freuchie in 1509 they were incorporated into a barony (to be held in feu farm) so that good rule might be established among the inhabitants and 'to make those obedient to the laws who formerly were undaunted and disobedient'."[18]

The great leap forward came with the establishment of the Court of Session in 1532; and it came for two reasons. In the first place it was the first

---

[15] The two brieves were in fact reconstituted in the 1318 Parliament, A.P.S. i p.110 c. 13 (novel disseisin) and A.P.S. i p.112 (mortancestor). In their reconstituted form they survived until the establishment of the Court of Session—See McKechnie, Judicial Process upon Brieves 1219-1532 (Glasgow 1956).

[16] Stat. 20 Geo. II c. 43.

[17] G. Campbell H. Paton at p.20.

[18] See Ranald Nicholson—"Feudal Developments in late Mediaeval Scotland" [1973] Jur. Rev. 1. The grant quoted is from Registrum Magni Sigilli vol. II No. 3390.

centralised supreme court in Scotland; it had supervisory jurisdiction over the feudal courts which must necessarily have caused a diminution in the independence and importance of these feudal courts and jurisdictions. But it also accelerated the process of regarding land as an item of commerce.

Ross regards this process as having begun as a result of the Diligence Act 1469[19] which provided the means (by way of legal fiction) whereby dispositions in substitution could be effected without the consent of the feudal superior. The Act directed the Sheriff of the Shire where a debtor had lands, to value and assign to the creditor property to the amount of the debt due to him, the debtor's superior being thereupon directed to receive the creditor upon payment of one year's rent. If the superior proved reluctant, the King's Chancery would issue a brieve to the creditor giving him a right to enter. According to Ross the enforcement machinery was seized upon by imaginative conveyancers so that land could be alienated at the will of the vassal with the result that:[20]

"The commerce of lands grew by these precautions more common and the superiors came to do with facility what the law would compel them to perform if unwilling. The security of purchasers increased as the public registers rose to perfection; and a greater confidence in civil business naturally took the place of the more ancient jealousy and apprehension. In consequence of this alteration the price was either immediately paid or a separate bond granted for it.... The purchaser had little more to do than pay the price. All the obligement necessary in the business was on the side of the seller...."

However, the evidence—such as it is—does not entirely support Ross's conclusion. Between 1478 and 1487 only seventeen transactions are recorded in the Registrum Magni Sigilli in which apprising was applied.[21] Again in the twenty years 1468-1488 only sixty sales of land (that is sales at the rate of three per year) received confirmation under the great seal.[22] Admittedly the transactions recorded are only those in which the Crown was involved, but nevertheless they hardly give the impression of a flourishing market in land.

It seems more likely, in point of fact, that the upsurge came with the rise of the feu farm which came into prominence after the Acts of 1504 permitting first the King[23] and then his subjects[24] to feu out land provided there was no diminution in rental, grassum and other duties.

---

[19] Act of 1469 c. 12; A.P.S. ii p.96.
"*Item* to eschew the great hardship and destruction on the King's subjects (?) and inhabitants of their lord's lands thrown on them by force of the brieve of distress that where any sums are due to be obtained by virtue of the said brieve upon the lord of the ground, that the goods and cattle of the poor, mean inhabitants of the ground are taken and distrained against for their lord's debts ... And if the sum obtained by the brieve of distress exceeds the amount of the maill by official sale, they shall go against the goods ....

If he has no goods or lands within the said shire the creditor shall go to the King and bring certification of the Sheriff how much he wants recovered by the brieve of distress [and cannot get].

.... If the debtor has no moveable goods, only his land, the Sheriff before whom the said sum is to be recovered by the brieve of distress shall sell the land to the satisfaction of the debt and pay the creditors so that the inhabitants of the land may not be hurt or grieved for their lord's debts."

Originally this applied only to apprisings but by the Adjudications Act 1672 (c. 19) was brought within the scope of adjudications.
[20] Vol. ii at p.270.
[21] Ranald Nicholson op. cit. at p.12.
[22] *ibid.* at p.9.
[23] Act of 1504 c. 30. A.P.S. vol. ii at p.244.
[24] Act of 1504 c. 36. A.P.S. vol. ii at p.253.

Grants in feu farm were not new, having been made by the Church on a small scale in the fourteenth century and on an equally small scale by the Crown to the more important royal burghs. By the middle of the fifteenth century its characteristics had become more or less settled, the holder of the feu being exempt from the normal feudal casualties of wardship and relief, yet at the same time having an interest which was heritable and secure so long as he and his heirs paid the required feuduty. In return for these advantages the grantee was required to pay a lump sum on receipt of his feu-charter and the feuduty was likely to be fixed at a figure in excess of the former annualrent of the land.[25]

Certainly during the reign of James III feu garm grants were rare, as they were during James IV's reign up to the Acts of 1504. Thereafter they increased rapidly and "a generous process set in of converting royal tenants into feuars .... feu farm became the almost universal tenure of small parcels of land and a very usual tenure even of larger estates granted by the crown"[26], the Registrum Magni Sigilli showing one hundred and seventeen grants from the Crown in feu, the vast body of them having been effected after 1504.

It would seem then that the upsurge of commercial activity in land comes largely from the sixteenth century, and that activity was, in the main, transacted by feuing and subfeuing rather than by substitution. But even in the case of substitutions, the evidence of the Registrum indicates that they were far more plentiful during the reign of James IV, two hundred and ninety voluntary sales having been confirmed, together with one hundred and nineteen apprisings, in both cases the transactions becoming more frequent towards the end of the reign, and furthermore there are indications, especially in the latter category, of the ultimate acquirer's being an investor.[27]

Now the role of the newly established Court of Session in this process was twofold. In the first place there is the traditional view that half the judges on the bench were to be prelates (until the Reformation) who would have had a civilian training which was supposed to produce a leaning towards alienation.[28] But perhaps the second aspect of the foundation of the Court is more important and was stimulated by the trend towards viewing land as a commercial investment instead of the basis of a sacred relationship. As Irvine Smith has put it:[29]

---

[25] Grants in feu farm were not, as is frequently stated, peculiar to Scotland alone. cf. Nicholson at p.3 and references cited there (note 9). In fact feu farm tenure was common in England prior to 1290, although Quia Emptores effectively made further grants impossible. At the present day there are a few fee farm grants in Ireland made "non obstante Quia Emptores". See J. C. W. Wylie, "Fee Farm Grants—Montrose Continued" (1972) 23 N.I.L.Q. 285.

[26] per Aeneas J. G. Mackay, "The Exchequer Rolls of Scotland" vol. xiii at 119-120.

[27] See generally Ranald Nicholson op. cit. at p.10 (voluntary sales) at p.13 (apprisings) and at p.16, "About half of the recorded cases show that the apprised lands went to the original creditor. The other half show that they went to a person distinct from either creditor of debtor, who may be regarded as an investor in land."
  See also at p.9. "Another development which has attracted less attention than feuing was the growth of an open market in land doubtless apparently stimulated by the use of wadsets, under which the lands that were sold to the wadsetter might revert to the seller on payment of a stipulated sum. In November 1469 Parliament implicitly recognised the validity of wadsets and sought to circumvent fraud by stipulating that reversions be recorded in the register."

[28] See esp. Farran op. cit.

[29] "Introduction to Scottish Legal History" (Stair Soc. vol. 20) at p.32.

"In the course of the sixteenth century the traditional view of landholding underwent a radical change. Feudal relationships became less sacrosanct and land increasingly [became] the subject of commercial investment. This change, which is apparent in the early years of the sixteenth century, was greatly accelerated by the alienation of the Church lands in the period between 1532 and 1560—at first in an attempt by the Church to obtain ready money with which to pay the Great Tax imposed in 1532 to uphold the College of Justice; and latterly in an attempt by the prelates to save to themselves or their kin, something of the Church property from what they saw to be the impending disaster of the Reformation."

Legal Restraint on Alienation

Given the diminution in importance and influence of the feudal jurisdictions by the establishment of the Court of Session and the gradual change in the underlying views about landholding in the sixteenth century it might have been expected that the feudal realities would have faded away as they did in England. But in fact this was not the case; the feudal past held on tenaciously, and this can be observed in the pages of the legal writers of the period, Balfour, whose 'Practicks' were produced about 1579 and Craig, whose 'Jus Feudale' was written in 1608, although not published until 1652. The contrast between them and Bracton is marked. If one reads Bracton one reads the words of an advocate of alienation in an age of economic rights; if one reads Balfour and Craig one still sees the trappings of genuine feudal power.

(*a*) *Wardholding*

Where land was still held in ward the legal restraints on alienation tended to be strong. Much time and space[30] has been spent on ascertaining the general position with regard to alienation in the early feudal period and whether consideration of it should start by assuming absolute freedom to alienate on to which restraints were gradually imposed, or whether consideration should start at the other extreme of assuming the fee to have been absolutely inalienable with the gradual increase in the powers of the vassal as against his superior. Probably neither is correct in that each assumes the existence of proprietorial rights and concepts which were not defined or formulated until much later. Thus, with Pollock and Maitland:[31]

". . . . we must start, not from the absolute inalienability of 'the fief', nor from the absolute alienability of the 'fee simple', but from something much less satisfactory, an indeterminate right of the lord to prevent alienations which would seriously impair his interests."

The first attempt to define this position is the attempt made in a statute, reputed to be of William the Lion which provides.[32]

"Nullus liber homo potest dare, vel vendere alicui plus de terra sua, quam de residuo terrae possit fieri domino feudi servitium ei debitum; et quod pertinent ad feudum;

2. Et si qui oppositum fecerit, si vocetur forisfactum ad curiam ea de causa, omittet id quod tenet, nisi Domini superioris ad hoc habuerit benevolentiam aut confirmationem."

It is interesting to note that this provision is found also in the Magnae

---

[30] See esp. Coke 2nd Inst. 65; Blackstone Com. ii 71-2.
[31] History of English Law vol. i at p.344.
[32] Leg. Gul. c. 31. The authenticity of this provision as being of William the Lion has been doubted (see Farran at p.138), although it is cited in some of the late cases on recognition.

Cartae of 1217 and 1225 granted by Henry III in England to the effect that 'No free man shall henceforth give or sell so much of his land that the residue shall be insufficient to support the service due in respect of the fee'. In England this provision had little or no effect and was certainly not observed by the time of Bracton. But in Scotland the provision was refined so as to prohibit alienating more than one half of the fief without the consent of the superior and continued in existence until the abolition of wardholding.

This rule also seems to have been the foundation of two other mediaeval statutory provisions, the first in 1347 being an Act for the 'Recognition of lands halden of strangers"[33] which provides:
"Gif anie man analeis his heill heretage or tenement quhilk he halds of the King in chief' or the maist part, without special licence (consent, or confirmation) the samin lands sall be taken in the King's hands and sall be recognosced be him."

In an Act of 1400[34] which seems to be an early attempt to codify the law of recognition the right of superiors generally to recognosce is confirmed. The Act provides:
"These are the just and lauchful cases to recognosce lands be the law of this land, be the overlord, against his tenant or vassal.
. . . . 4. The fourt, gif the tenant analeis his lands without licence of his overlord, in that case the overlord (may recognosce them and thereafter) let them to borgh to his tenant."

Two things are noteworthy about this latter provision. In the first place there is nothing in the statute to limit recognition to lands held in ward, yet nonetheless by feudal principle it did not extend to non-military holdings. Perhaps it was taken as axiomatic in view of the distinction which appertained at that time between noble fiefs and base or socoge fiefs. In the latter alienation (especially by subinfeudation) was unrestricted.[34a]

In the second place there is no mention of any restriction on the superior's power to recognosce. Thus if only one-tenth of the fee were alienated, on a strict construction of the provision, recognition would still lie. However by the time of Balfour it would appear that recognition only lay where the alienation was of more than half the holding. Thus Balfour writes:[35]

"vi. The overlord may recognosce all the haill the landis, gif the samin be annalzeit be the tenant without licence of the overlord: And in this case the overlord is not oblist to let them to the borgh. Rob. III c.21.

Item. Gif ony fre tenant or vassal, quha haldis his landis be service of ward and relief immediately of ane superior, sell or annalzie, all or haill the said landis, with their pertinentis, or maist part thereof, without licence, consent or confirmation of his overlord or his predecessor, to be halden of him, and the aires of his superioris; all and haill the said landis, als weill annalzeit as not annalzeit, with their pertinentis, may be recognoscit and ressavit in the superioris landis and baith the properties and possession of the samin sould pertain to him to be disponit at his pleasour in all time to cum. 12 Jan 1501. *The King contra William Douglas;* 20 Novemb. 1509 *The King contra Alexander Stratoun;* 12 Jan. 1509 *Tuiching the landis of Glenclone;* 13 Julij 1536 *The King contra David Boswell* i.b.c. 117.

---

[33] 6th November 1347, David II c. 34.
[34] Act of 1400 c. 19.
[34a] Grants in feu farm were still very rare at this time.
[35] Practicks at p.483 under the title "Anent recognition of landis in superiouris handis".

Bot if the leist part of the landis be annalzeit be the tenant without consent of his superior, it is not leasum to the superior to recognosce the saidis landis, or any part thereof by reassoun of the said alienation. 11 Decemb. 1506. *The King contra John Lord Maxwell.* And it is to wit that the landis may be recognoscit be the superior for alienation of annualrentis furth of the seissin, extending to all and haill the profits of the maist part of the saidis landis. 16 Mart. 1569 *David Balfour contra David Balfour*."

It is apparent that this restriction extended to all transactions concerning land in ward which could be held to constitute alienations. Dispositions were clearly caught[36], as, by extension, were wadsets.[37] And so were most subinfeudations. Surprisingly there seems to have been considerable learned agonising over this question. Craig, indeed, expresses considerable doubt over the conflicting feudal sources[38] and fails to reach a satisfactory conclusion. In point of fact in Scotland the reality, rather than the feudal theory[39] seems to have been adhered to in that as a general principle subinfeudations of land held in ward were considered alienations and as such inferred recognition. However if the subinfeudation consisted of a grant in feu-farm, then provided the requirements of sufficiency of feu-duty were complied with the superior would be unable to recognosce.[40] The reason for this in spite of attempts by Stair and Craig to find an explanation within the bounds of feudal principle, seems to be based in the statutory provisions permitting grants in feu-farm.

However although wardholding and its restrictive influence remained until 1747[41] its practical importance became less and less with the growth of grants in feu-farm. Nonetheless the power of recognition remained capable of creating mischief and cases continued to come before the Court of Session until shortly before abolition.[42]

(b) The Superior's Consent

The other principal restraint was the requisite of the superior's consent. In most cases this was not necessary for the actual disposition (where the land was not held in ward) unless the grant contained conditions reserving the right of consent to an alienation either a me or de me, which was backed up by an irritant clause;[43] but rather that in the case of a grant a me de superiore meo the superior's confirmation of the infeftment was necessary for the grantee to obtain a complete title.

As we have seen the procedure under the Act of 1469 c.12 provided a means whereby this obstacle could be overcome. However this device, useful as it was, was not wholly satisfactory, especially if the purchaser required a quick transfer, for there were any number of formal obstructions that could be employed by a recalcitrant superior. Nor too, was this method cheap. The statutory

---

[36] *Sir James Hall of Dunglas* v *John Gow* Jan 13/14 1725 M. 13395 in which land held in ward by a bride was disponed to her husband and his heirs, infeftment being taken thereon.
[37] See. *King's Advocate* v *Creditors of Cromarty* 1683 M. 13393; *Earl of Aberdeen* v ———March 1683 M. 13394; *Ker* v *Law* June 1687 M. 13395.
[38] III.3.22 Clyde translation at p.965/966.
[39] As in Bracton, see above Chapter II.
[40] See Stair; II.11.13.
[41] Stat. 20 Geo. II c. 50.
[42] See note 36 above.
[43] See Craig cited above at note 38.

bribe of one year's rent could be quite considerable and to overcome these inconveniences the device of a disposition a me vel de me was introduced. There is no clear evidence as to the precise time this device was introduced but it would seem to have been around 1560.[44]

Originally the device operated on the basis of there being two separate charters or dispositions; one of these would be an ordinary feu or blench charter that would be used in the case of a sub-feu, the second charter would be the same except that it would contain an obligation to infeft a me upon the same terms and conditions as the disponer had himself held the land. At first there were separate precepts of sasine granted, one for each charter. These were later combined into one precept in such a way that it was impossible to know whether the grantee held a me or de me.

The point was that possible recalcitrance on the part of the superior would now be irrelevant for even if confirmation of the infeftment a me was not forthcoming the grantee still had infeftment de me of the disponer who was left with an economically worthless though legally existant mid-superiority.

When the grantee found it expedient or imperative to enter with the true superior, he produced his charter a me with the ambiguous but equally appropriate precept of sasine and had these confirmed. Having done this the de me charter lost its importance and simply disappeared.

This mode of disposition proved so effective that in the course fo time the two separate charters were dispensed with, to be replaced by one disposition which contained an obligation to infeft by two separate infeftments, one de me to be held of the disponer, and the other a me of the true superior. In its final form this device continued until rendered obsolete by the Conveyancing (Scotland) Act 1874.

The Reaction

Apart from a few spheres of ever decreasing importance, by the time of the setting up of the Register of Sasines, by and large there was complete freedom of alienation in Scotland either by subinfeudation or, using the a me vel de me procedure, by substitution. With the establishemnt of an effective registration system purchasers of land could be secure in their purchase.

From another point of view this development was disastrous for it meant that land could no longer be certain of retention within the family, and the growth of extravagance, and borrowing to finance it during the early seventeenth century[45] would make for even greater fluidity in the situation. The time was ripe for a reaction. As Dalrymple rather picturesquely put it:[46]

"As long as the great part of the lands in the country were unalienable beyond a half; as long as there was not a sufficient commerce to cover a considerable fluctuation of land property; and even when land came into commerce, as long as the great families were powerful enough to defy the law, and laugh at execution by apprising used against

---

[44] Monteath—'Heritable Rights' in Introduction to Scottish Legal History at p.162, suggests the second half of the 16th century as its time of origin. Girvan suggests its origin as coming from Stat. 1540 c. 105 (concerning fraudulent alienations).
[45] See Irvine Smith—Introduction to Scottish Legal History at p.33.
[46] Feudal Property at p.161/162.

their estates there was no need of entails. In the highlands of Scotland to this day entails are far less frequent than in the low-countries.

But when arts and commerce introduced luxury, when the alienation of land property became more frequent and when the voice of the laws was heard through the land, then people to secure their families introduced entails."

The precise date of this reaction is unknown. Certainly the entailed settlement of earliest date that came to be entered into the Register of Entails, the Roxburghe entail, was made in February 1648. However there is evidence to suggest that this was not the first. Thus Fountainhall, in his report of *Rothes* v *Melville*[47] gives the following information:

"The first of them are within these sixty or seventy years. What was first in Scotland was the laird of Calderwood's Tailzie of his lands, advised by Sir Thomas Hope; then there was one Duncan's; then there was Thomas Moodie's as to the lands of Sauchtonhall; then the Viscount of Stormont's as to the estate of Annandale, and many since . . . ."

Entails

Whereas in England entails constituted the starting point for the development of devices to create and rules to prevent perpetuities, in Scotland the position was different, for the entail itself, until the mid-nineteenth century was sufficient, without more, to create an effective perpetuity. Indeed in the Scottish legal literature dealing with entails in the eighteenth and nineteenth centuries the terms 'perpetuity' and 'strict entail' are largely synonymous. When other varieties of perpetual settlement arose they did so, not because of any weakness in the entail but rather because the law of entail applied only to land, and accordingly the new forms of wealth that appeared during the nineteenth century necessitated the development of other types of perpetual settlement.

Just as in England the approach of the courts to these settlements tended to be founded on their earlier treatment of entails. Thus in *McNair* v *McNair*[48] the view was propounded that as the common law had accepted as valid one type of perpetuity in the strict entail it should accept other types of perpetual settlement provided they did not fall foul of any substantive rule of law.

However this raises in an acute form the problem of the origin of the entail in Scots law; for if the above view is correct then there is foundation for the opinion that the later decisions approving perpetual settlements were in accordance with the established principles of the common law. The question of the origin of the Scots entail has been the subject of much discussion which has centred around two points: first, as to whether entails were imported from another system or whether they were purely Scots in origin, and second as to whether they were in fact recognised as valid by the common law or whether their validity depended on the force of the Entail Act 1685.

Origins—External Influences?

(*a*) *Roman Law*

Of modern writers only Professor T. B. Smith has favoured the view that Roman law was the source of the entail in Scotland.[48a] Discussing the origin

---
[47] (1677) Bro. Supp. 168 at p.170.
[48] (1791) Bell's Cas. 546 per Lord Justice-Clerk Macqueen.
[48a] "Trusts and Fiduciary Relationships in the Law of Scotland" in his "Studies Critical and Comparative" (1962).

of the Scots law trust he treats the entail as "a 'trustlike' institution dividing ownership and administration and designed to perpetuate family succession."[49] Specifically Professor Smith believes the origin of the entail to be in the fidei-commissum, basing himself largely on a passage in Bankton which points to the similarities between Scots entails and Roman fidei-commissa as showing that the one was derived from the other. The passage reads:[50]

"There is no doubt but our tailies, even those with strict irritant clauses, are founded in the civil law: their fides-commisses resembled them greatly; for by these, the estate, subject to the same, could not be sold otherwise than for the testator's debt, and the burthen of the fidei-commis followed it to all singular successors. But a prohibition by the testator upon the heir to alienate without showing in whose favour it was so ordered, is void, as of the nature only of a counsil [sic] or simple command which infers no burthen on the right; and cannot abate or infringe the power inherent in every proprietor to dispose of his own, where no other person is vested with any interest in the subject. However a fidei-commis, to be restored to another, if the heir died without issue, without a prohibition to contract debt thereon is effectual; and a simple prohibition in behalf of certain heirs is on that fidei-commis implying that the subject must be saved to them. And this will hold for certain with us viz. that an absolute fee or fee simple, being conveyed to any person and his heirs whatsoever, he could not be limited in the exercise of his property by any prohibition to contract debt or alien the subject: whereas in a tailzie, such clause has its effect, as shall appear afterwards, being always in favour of the subsequent heirs of entail. And as by the civil law, an estate may be left in testament under a strict prohibition to alien the same which shall have effect to bar all conveyance of the subject or burthening it in prejudice of the fidei-comissary heir: so with us an estate may be conveyed with strict prohibition upon the disponee as much as on any of the heirs of entail."

The fidei-commission owed their origin to the peculiar forms required for drawing up wills and to the rules which rendered certain persons incapable of succession. The original mechanism was a conveyance of the relevant property to a nominal heir who would then be bound to convey it to the intended beneficiary. Originally fidei-commissa were without legal effect[51] and it was not until Augustus granted a personal action to the fidei-commissarius that there existed any legal means of enforcement.[52] Indeed it was not until Justinian's time that a real action was allowed to the haeres fidei-commissarius when the distinctions between legata and fidei-commissa were abolished permitting both to be enforced by the actio hypothecaria and by the rei vindicatio.[53] These reforms had a significant effect on the rights of the parties, restraining the heir in possession from exercising ordinary proprietorial rights over the property, the words of the "trust" being strictly construed.

Whatever their original purpose fidei-commissa came to be drafted in such a way as to prevent the heir from alienating the property or encumbering the succession, and obliging him to transmit it to his children under similar limitations. Whereas the ordinary mode of completing was in the form:

"Titius heares esto, eundem vero rogo, ut haereditatem Sempronio restituat,"[54]

---

[49] *ibid.* at p. 205. It should perhaps be mentioned that the present writer dissents from Professor Smith's views on the origin of the Scots law trust. See "Some Thoughts on the Origin of the Trust in Scots Law" [1974] Jur. Rev. 196.
[50] Institute Vol. I p. 582 para. 135.
[51] Cicero, de Finibus lib. ii.
[52] Inst. lib. ii tit. 23.
[53] By a rescript. See lib. ii, tit. 23, 7; Codex lib. vi, tit. 43, 1.
[54] Inst. lib. ii, tit. 23.

when it was desired to impose restraints on alienation and so create an effectual substitution, the form used was:

"Rogo haeradem, ne haereditatem alienet, sed familiae relinquat."[55]

or

"Rogo haeradem, ut testamento suo, Seium haeradem faciat."[56]

Where the substitutions were intended to pertuate the family of the donor[57] a form came to be used which is much closer to the form used to create the strict entail in Scotland for not only was there a prohibition of alienation by sale or otherwise but there were also clauses designed to prevent the heir's borrowing money on the security of the entrusted land. To back up these there were clauses declaring any acts done in contravention of the prohibitions null and void, as in the following:[58]

"Volo meas aedes non vendi ab haeredibus meis, neque foenerari super eas, sed manere eas firmas simplices meis filiis et nepolibus universum tempus. Si autem aliquis eorum voluerit vendere partem suam, vel foenerari super eam, potestatem habeat vendere cohaeredi suo, et foenerari ab eo; si autem aliquis praeter haec fecerit, erit quod obligatur inutile atque irritum."

Accordingly, then, property subject to these settlements had become effectively entailed by Justinian's time. But, having ensured their validity, Justinian's law then sought to restrict their effect, for in a case where the deed declared that the heir succeeding in virtue of it should have no power to sell or alienate in any way, it was decreed that these limitations should last no longer than four generations including that of the grantor.[59]

It will be seen at once that there are striking similarities between the concepts employed in the late fidei-commissum and the strict entail, each providing for the settled property to be held absolutely by a series of successive substitutes subject to the restrictions imposed in the grant. In neither Scots nor Roman law is there any idea that the proprietor of property so settled had a limited interest in the sense that an entailed proprietor under English law had. Equally there are similarities as to the form of words used to settle the property, both the Roman fidei-commissum and the Scots entail containing prohibitive and irritant clauses.

But there are also important differences; in the first place the fidei-commissum contained no express prohibition against altering the line of succession—this seems to have been implied; in the second place the fidei-commissum lacked the resolutive clause providing for forfeiture in the event of a breach or attempted breach of the prohibitions, a clause whose inclusion was vital to the efficacy of the entail in Scotland.

Further, there was a difference in scope of the two institutions, for the Scots entail was restricted to land, whereas any property in Roman law could be made the subject of a fidei-commissum.

---

[55] Dig. lib. xxxi 1. 69. 3.
[56] Heineccii Inst. 668.
[57] If the object of the settlement was to perpetuate the name and family of the grantor the form was:
"Neque per venditionem, neque damnationem, neque per mutationem, neque quocunque, tandem titulo in alium transferant, rejiciantve aut eam domum, seu praescripta, e meo nomine et mea familia alienent"—Novellae 159 tit. 42 Praefatio.
[58] Dig. lib. xxxi.
[59] Novellae 159 c. 2 & 3.

Bankton's view, it is suggested, is essentially that of the comparativist, seeing the Scots entail in a general European context and having affinity to other substitutionary settlements in other countries. Thus he writes:[60]

"Some of these strict entails tend to infer a perpetuity of the estate subject thereto which no doubt is an inconveniency; but at the same time such settlements were allowed by the civil law, tho' the emperor Justinian at last made a kind of temperament in this case viz. that unless the will of the testator was very express, the fidei-commissary settlement should not endure beyond the fourth generation. And still such perpetuities are in use in many countries, particularly in Holland and elsewhere, but in France they cannot be extended beyond the fourth generation."

With respect, Bankton seems to be making the mistake of so many Scots comparativists, of assuming that, because there exist similarities, it necessarily follows that the later institution was derived from the former. As we have seen there are differences as well as similarities, and these differences would seem to be dictated by the requirements of Scots feudal law. The point is that the context of such settlements in Scotland was exclusively feudal. It is just possible that the principle of fidei-commissary settlements was introduced into this context and adapted to meet feudal requirements as Bankton seems to be suggesting. But the probabilities are slight for the fidei-commissum was never received into Scotland, principally because the existing feudal laws had thrown up an institution in the trust[61] which largely did the work that the fidei-commissum did in Roman law.

It is perhaps significant that no other writer of institutional status, from Craig down to McLaren has suggested in dealing with entails that they have Roman origins and indeed most have placed the origin elsewhere. It is suggested therefore that Bankton's view is to be treated as more of a rationalisation and that the true source of the strict entail is in the feudal law.

(b) French Law

It might perhaps have been expected that, had anyone claimed Roman origins for the entail it would have been Stair. But instead Stair suggested France as the origin. He wrote:[62]

"Heirs, by the course of law, are called heirs of line as befalling the line of succession appointed and known in law. All other heirs do cross or cut that line and therefore are called heirs of tailzie, from the French word tailzer, to cut; whence Craig conceiveth that tailzied succession hath been first denominated amongst the French and Normans, and whence being brought into England by the Norman Conquest, both in custom and in name, hath been derived to us; yet it is liker to have come to us immediately from France, with which we kept greater intercourse than with England, of old; and our tailzies, at least to heirs male, are ancienter than the English, which begun but from the famous law, called the second Statute of Westminster, in the reign of Edward the First of that name of the Norman line."

Discussing this, Professor T. B. Smith treats the French connection within the framework of fidei-commissary substitutions, pointing out that, although substitutions in perpetuity had at one time been permitted in France, from 1560 such destinations were limited to two degrees by the Ordonnance of Orleans,

---

[60] *supra* at para. 147.
[61] See "Some Thoughts on the Origin of the Trust in Scots Law" [1974] Jur. Rev. 196.
[62] 3.4.33.

while the Ordonnance of Moulins 1566 provided for the insertion of the deed in a public register on pain of its being null.[63]

However this misses the point of Stair's comment, for he was not writing of fidei-commissary substitutions but of feudal grants.

The principal difficulty with Stair's view is that it is unclear whether he was referring to entails having the nature of perpetuities or to something less; in either case his statement displays innacuracy. One would, for instance, hardly think he was writing of the strict entail since its efficacy was not sanctioned until 1662 at the earliest.[64] If he were, then clearly this could not be "ancienter" than the entails of English law. Yet if he was referring to something less, such as a grant in favour of someone's "heirs male" this would clearly not be sufficient to restrict the alienability of the fee, in which case his comparison with English entails under the Statute de Donis Conditionalibus is inappropriate for it did (as construed by the courts) provide for the inalienability of the entailed fee. And further, as we have seen, simple destinations in favour of a grantee and his male heirs were common in England long before de Donis.[65]

But perhaps such criticism is overly pedantic. Stair's basic point seems to be that entails in Scotland had a feudal origin and that insofar as feudalism can be traced back ultimately to France the ultimate origin of Scots entails must lie there. This basic point, as regards the feudal origins of the entail, at least, seems unobjectionable.

(c) *English Law*

Whereas support for a Roman or French origin is small among Scottish commentators there exists a great weight of opinion in favour of the view that entails in Scotland were received from English law. Thus Craig categorically states that "it was introduced into our country from England which received it from the Normans".[66] Mackenzie, reputedly the draftsman of the Entail Act 1685, follows Craig in the belief that "our tailzies proceed immediately from the English entails".[67] And as we have seen, Stair appeared to consider England as a possible alternative to France as the true source. Sandford, the author of the leading treatise on the Law of Entail in Scotland, also favours England as the source although his views differ somewhat from those of Craig and Mackenzie.[68] Most recently, Farran, in his historical study of the development of land laws in England and Scotland, has also come down in favour of a substantial English influence in the development of the Scots entail.[69]

The difficulty with Craig's view, and indeed of all those who found themselves on him, is that he does not appear to consider the entail per se, either in Scotland or in England, as a perpetuity. While he states that:[70]

---

[63] Studies Critical and Comparative *supra* at p.204.
[64] In *Creditors of the Earl of Annandale* v *Viscount Stormont* 1662 M. 13994-6.
[65] See Chapter II above; at pp.44 et seq.
[66] Ius Feudale II.16.1. Clyde Translation at p.697.
[67] On Tailzies at p.484.
[68] Entails, Chapter I.
[69] "The Principles of Scots and English Land Law" at pp.144-149.
[70] Ius Feudale II.16.12; Clyde Translation at p.704.

"Tailzies are more familiar in Scotland than in any other country, for the reason that the pride of our old families and the wish to perpetuate their high position makes succession in the male line preferable . . . ."

it seems that the "perpetuation" is to come from the ordinary operation of the rules of primogeniture rather than from any restriction on alienation in the grant, for in his view the only effect of entailing land in Scotland was to alter the line succession. Thus he writes:[71]

"We say that a feu is tailzied not only when the legal line of succession (direct or collateral) is broken, but also when the heirs of the legal line are made the subject of restriction or selection—either as regards the persons favoured or as regards the order of their succession—and in short, whenever there is any interference with the order of succession in a simple feu such as to cause the estate to be diverted from the ordinary course of succession and to devolve upon persons other than those who would naturally succeed and so to become open to the superior on the failure of the chosen heirs."

And again that:[72]

"There is thus no difficulty in defining a tailzied feu as one in which the legal order of succession is excluded and the property is destined to a series of substituted heirs named in the tenor of the investiture. This does not make the tailzied feu any less feudal in quality than the title to a simple feu. Indeed paying strict regard to the principles of the Feudal Law, we might say that a tailzied feu is essentially identical with what was known in the general feudal law as a simple feu."

With regard to entails in England, he writes:[73]

"It was accordingly determined and enacted by all the estates assembled in parliament at Westminster that the owner of any feu (ancestral or novel) in which he was duly vested, should be allowed to name the heirs, both institute and substitute, to whom the fee should transmit at his death and to attach to their rights of succession such conditions and limitations—both as to the order of succession and the persons who should succeed—as he chose, provided always that the heirs named were sound in body and in mind[74] and the superior had given his consent."

But even on his own restricted terms, leaving aside for the moment the question of alienability, Craig's basis of derivation, his construction of de Donis, is woefully inaccurate. In the first place holders of land in fee in England did not at this time need the consent of the superior to alienate[75] either in tail or in fee simple.

More importantly there was never the complete freedom with regard to the selection of heirs that Craig implies for de Donis operated only on three types of gift,[76] namely those:

(*a*) to husband and wife and the heirs of their bodies, with a reversion expressly reserved,

(*b*) in frankmarriage,

(*c*) in the form "to A and the heirs of his body".

In any of these cases the only classes of heirs to come within the statute were heirs of the body. Nor indeed could the conditions as to the succession men-

---

[71] *ibid.* II.16.15; Clyde translation at p.706/7.
[72] *ibid.* II.16.3; Clyde translation at p.698.
[73] *ibid.* II.16.4; Clyde translation at p.699.
[74] Farran doubts the accuracy of Clyde's translation on this particular point, although it seems to matter little to the general critique of Craig's statement. Farran *supra* at p.145.
[75] Certainly not by subinfeudation in 1285, or by substitution after 1290. See Chapter II above.
[76] In the preamble.

tioned by Craig alter this very much, their relevance seemingly being only that they were the means of creating a limitation in special tail.[77]

Perhaps the greatest fault with Craig's conception of the English fee tail is his failure to recognise that it was something different—and had been so regarded from an early date—from the fee simple or simple feu. By the time Craig wrote his treatise[77a] this difference had been rationalised and developed into the doctrine of estates, and specifically that the "tail" now referred not simply to a line of heirs "cut from" the general line but indicated that the fee tail was a special type of fee which was cut up and partitioned among the various parties to the entail. As Plucknett has put it:[78]

"In Coke's thought, to carve an entail was analogous to carving a joint—a certain amount is cut off, and a certain amount is left; adding them together we have exactly one fee simple."

One probable reason for Craig's failure to grasp the point about the entail might be that at the time of his writing the entail had acquired the characteristic of being barrable by the conjunct use of the fine and recovery[79] and indeed his work contains a complex commentary on this procedure.[80]

For him, the perpetuity aspect stemmed from the imposition of conditions on the fee tail restricting the holder's right to alienate. He writes:[81]

"A distinction is closely observed in England between grants in fee simple and grants in tail (whether general or special). In a fee simple grant the condition against alienation is held invalid on the ground that every man is entitled to the free disposal of his own property: but in a grant in tail (whether general or special) the condition is sustained and alienation is forbidden and, moreover, the superior is entitled in the event of contravention to claim the estate as having reverted to him. This distinction is justified on the ground that while a grantee in fee simple must have absolute power of disposal, the same reasoning does not apply to a grantee in tail who may properly be restrained from alienation in order to [facilitate] the carrying out of the intention of the grantor which would otherwise be liable to be defeated."

At first glance—ignoring the inaccuracies concerning feudal superiors in England—it might seem that Craig was rationalising the feature of inalienability that characterised the classic English entail into conditional terms and that he really did understand the different natures of the fee simple and the fee tail. Admittedly this would be mistaken for there were in reality no such conditions, the entail achieving its inalienable character by virtue of the operation of de Donis on the words of grant in the feoffment: put simply, if the appropriate words of grant were employed then the disposition was in fee tail and consequently inalienable. But even so it would seem to be intellectually possible to rationalise this in terms of conditions of grant and to explain that a condition restraining alienation was responsible for the pereptuity.

But later in the same paragraph Craig makes clear that this is not his understanding for he cites in connection with Rickhill's settlement[82] with its grants

---

[77] As he himself appears to recognise. See Craig I.11.26. Clyde translation at p.193/194.
[77a] 1608, although it was not published until 1652.
[78] Concise History of the Common Law 5th Ed. at p.557. The first occasion on which this rationale was used was in *Willion* v *Berkley* (1562) Plowd. 225 at p.251.
[79] See above Chapter II.
[80] II.5.6. Clyde translation at p.445/446.
[81] II.5.5. Clyde translation at p.444/445.
[82] *ibid.* Clyde translation at p.445.

became standard in Scotland, were examined by the English courts in *Scholastica's Case*[89] and latterly in *Mary Portington's Case*[90] where the limitations in the settlement almost exactly corresponded with those approved nearly fifty years later in the *Stormont Case*.[91]

Sandford too appears to favour this view, feeling that if English influence was effective at all it was in the imposition and formulation of the fencing clauses. Thus he wrote:[92]

"In the time of Craig it appears that the entail with an irritant clause was not known: but if the system was, as he states, introduced from England, it is not surprising that, after this device had been attempted in the testamentary deeds of that country, in the reign of Queen Elizabeth, the same form should be adopted here."

Sandford's general approach however is that Scots law produced its own entail, that the institution was not imported, although the conveyancing device whereby that institution achieved its effectiveness might have come from England. And certainly as we have seen, the two institutions were markedly different in concept. As Lord Blackburn said in a nineteenth century appeal to the House of Lords:[93]

"In England it is an estate of limited inheritance: in Scotland it is an estate of absolute inheritance with restrictions which practically cut it down."

What would probably be of more relevance, then, would be to trace the origins and development of the entail within Scotland and to show how these external influences operated.

Origins—Scots Feudal Law

In contrast to the well-known development of the English entail from its origins in grants in liberum maritagium through conditional fees, the origins of the entail in Scotland are much more obscure. Indeed, in spite of references to entails in Balfour, a case could be made out showing that they were simply a seventeenth century variation on ordinary feus.

As we have seen, most of the commentators on the subject resolved this question simply by assuming that the institution was derived from a legal system outside Scotland, but, as we have sought to show, external factors would seem to have operated more as influences rather than as sources.

The most recent theory—that of Farran—seeks to connect Scots entails with grants in liberum maritagium and to show in consequence that both English and Scottish entails shared the same feudal root, whatever their subsequent development.

The justification for this view is based on two grounds: the first, that grants in liberum maritagium existed in Scotland just as they did in England; and the second, that somehow the English statute de Donis wielded a peculiar influence over subsequent developments in Scotland and that this influence provided the connecting link with the entails of the seventeenth century.

As to the first point, it is undoubtedly true that grants in liberum maritagium

---

[89] (1572) Plowd. 408.
[90] (1614) 10 Co. Rep. F.356.
[91] (1662) M. 13994-6.
[92] Entails at p.36.
[93] In *Earl of Zetland* v *Lord Advocate* (1878) 3 App. Cas. 505 at p.526.

in tail fenced around with resolutive clauses and describes how the courts held such clauses invalid. He then concludes:[83]

"In the law of England necessity is held to justify alienation *even in the case of an entail containing a prohibition against alienation* on the ground that a man must have more regard for himself than for his heirs."

Clearly Craig cannot be referring to the ordinary characteristic of inalienability conferred by the operation of de Donis[84], for if he were, there would be no need for the phrase "even in the case of an entail, etc." Equally clearly this passage demonstrates Craig's apparent view that the law of England contained entails without such prohibition and which were alienable.

This can however be reconciled with the contemporary situation by visualising Craig telescoping the developments of three hundred years and equating the alienation possibilities of the ordinary entail of his time with those of a fee simple and concluding in effect that a fee tail was but a species of simple feu. This, for him, would, as the passage quoted above shows,[85] enable him to fit such grants into the mainstream of feudal theory and link them up with the tailzied feus that were appearing in Scotland.

It must by now be apparent that Craig's derivation is without much foundation, but it may well be that Craig's exposition of the elements of the English entail came to have a significant effect on developments in Scotland, for it may help explain Mackenzie's adoption of it,[86] which also at first sight, seems inexplicable.

This difficulty comes from the more advanced state of the entail concept in Scotland in Mackenzie's time. Whereas in Craig's Scotland, tailzies were little more than simple destinations, by Mackenzie's time they had taken on the aspect of perpetuities, as the following passage from his treatise on "Tailies" shows:[87]

"The great Design of Tailies being to perpetuate the succession of the Maker, they ordinarily insert clauses disabling the Persons institute and substitute to dispone which are called pacta de non aliendo and by this clause it is ordinarily provided that the Persons institute and substitute shall do no fact or deed which may prejudge the succession of the heirs of Tailie or that it should not be lawful to them to dispone or wadset any of the lands so tailied, or do any deed whereby the lands may be evicted or apprised from them without the consent of all persons contained in the Tailie."

Given, then, this intimate knowledge of the mechanics of the tailzie it seems inconceivable that Mackenzie did not appreciate that the English entail operated on entirely different principles, that it operated through the words of grant creating a special type of fee and not by placing restrictive conditions on the grant of an ordinary fee. But if the framework of exposition was Craig's, as exemplified by his description of Rickhill's settlement, then the difficulty disappears, for, in this event, what Mackenzie is referring to is the "perpetuity", which, it will be remembered, was a settlement comprising one or more grants successively in tail backed up by the appropriate fencing clauses.[88] Indeed, clauses of an exactly similar type, in almost exactly similar terms to those which

---

[83] II.5.7. Clyde translation at p.447.
[84] As interpreted by the early fourteenth century English courts—See above Chapter II.
[85] See above at note 71.
[86] "Tailies" in collected works Vol. II at p.454.
[87] at p.487.
[88] See above at Chapter I at p.2 et seq.

were made in Scotland. Extant charters[94] provide examples dating from the early years of the thirteenth century. Grants seem to have been fairly common during the thirteenth and fourteenth centuries but seem to die out thereafter. The present writer has been unable to trace any fifteenth century grants in liberum maritagium.

The second limb of Farran's thesis however, is much more tenuous. It is based on a passage from Craig's discussion of de Donis, in the context, it will be remembered, of English, and not of Scots law. This passage has been discussed above[95] but for the sake of clarity will be repeated here. It reads:[96]

"It was accordingly determined and enacted . . . that the owner of any feu (ancestral or novel) in which he was duly vested, should be allowed to name the heirs, both institute and substitute to whom the fee should transmit at his death and to attach to their rights of succession such conditions and limitations—both as to the order of limitation and the persons who should succeed as he chose, provided always that the heirs named were sound in body and mind and the superior had given his consent."

After a quibble over the precise accuracy of the Clyde translation[97] Farran then proceeds to detail the errors embodied in this statement relating to the degree of freedom of selection of heirs, to the degree of imposing conditions, to the requirement of the superior's consent and to Craig's lack of comprehension of the effect of the doctrine of estates. He then goes on:[98]

"It is submitted that although Craig's remarks are therefore very inaccurate as an account of what de Donis actually said or effected in English law, the summary that he gives of its provisions affords some guidance as to the course of events in Scotland. We have no records to guide us as to the development of Scots law at such an early stage but it seems not unreasonable to surmise that the step by which the maritagium limited to three generations became the entail in aeternum was caused by Scots lawyers of the fourteenth century misunderstanding the effect of a revolutionary statute. Possibly no authoritative text of the Act found its way to Edinburgh, but only some non-legal traveller's report and that about fifty years after its passing. Support for this supposition is derived from the fact that no mention is made of the lacuna in the Act by which only the original donee was bound. This was not filled by the English judges until the thirteen-forties. Wars had then caused a long break in ordinary relations between the two countries. These wars raged on and off from about 1292 to 1346. During them Scotland had no time to think of law, but when peace came the Scots may well have wished to catch up with the times. It is significant that the wars covered the period between the passing of de Donis and the final fixing of its meaning by the English courts."

This whole passage seems to indicate Farran's obliviousness to the fact that Craig was not a fourteenth century lawyer and that he wrote over three centuries after de Donis. There is no reason whatever why Craig's views should be antedated in this way or even treated as indicative of fourteenth century Scottish legal thought. Further, there is no possible justification for the assumption Farran makes that because Craig got his English law wrong, that wrong interpretation was a general Scottish one and so for believing that the English statute had any influence in Scotland.

---

[94] See, for example, the many reproduced in the publications of the Scottish History Society, e.g. Highland Papers.
[95] See above; 'External Influences—English Law.'
[96] Craig: II.16.4. Clyde's translation at p.699.
[97] See above at note 74.
[98] Principles of Scots and English Land Law at pp.146/147.

The truth of the matter would appear to be that the maritagium did not, as Farran suggests, become the entail but rather that it simply faded out of use. The reasons can only be guessed at. Possibly the re-emphasis of baronial power and the greater cohesiveness this would give to the feudal system as a whole was sufficient to ensure that land remained within the family unit and that the restraints and benefits given by maritagium grants were unnecessary. In any event the suggestion that the entail in Scotland was derived from the maritagium seems to be wrong.

It is submitted that the origin of the entail in Scotland is to be found in political events. A feature almost peculiarly Scottish has been the number of occasions on which the succession to the Crown has been settled and resettled to take account of various contingencies. The first Act of Settlement was that of Alexander III in 1284 providing for the succession of the Maid of Norway. This was followed by three more such Acts in the fourteenth century, two of them relating to the succession to Robert I and a third, in 1373 providing for the succession to Robert III. These were essentially public acts, sanctioned and variable only by Parliament.

A similar, indeed, corresponding procedure was adopted in the case of certain of the King's great vassals. Thus in 1342 Parliament passed an Act providing for the succession to the Earldom of Douglas and sanctioned the settlement in 1370 concerning the Earldom of Ross. In both of these cases the succession departed from ordinary feudal rules, limiting the right to succeed to specified heirs and their descendants, and, in the case of the Ross settlement, to specified heirs and their legitimate male descendants, and was already by 1389 being described as "tailzied". Almost certainly the prestige of the houses involved became associated with the specialties in the destinations for in the last years of the fourteenth and early years of the fifteenth centuries grants were made to important families such as the Crichtons, Livingstons, Homes and Hepburns bearing destinations to the heirs male of the line subject to conditions resembling a modern name and arms clause.[99]

However these grants continued to be special cases. The proliferation of tailzied grants seems to have come from the changes that took place during the fifteenth and early sixteenth centuries with the rise in popularity and frequency of grants in feu farm.[100] A prominent feature of this process was the redefinition of the rights of the parties, particularly where land was held of the Crown; where estates formerly held on whatever conditions of service (most usually military service) were surrendered up and regranted for a capital sum and an increased rent in return for the lifting of certain feudal incidents of the old tenures. In most cases these regrants would be in such terms that the general line of heirs would inherit after the feuar's death. In others it seems that the Crown

---

[99] The Acts governing the royal succession are to be found in A.P.S. i at pp.424 (1284); 464 (1315); 549 (1373). The text of the Act of 1326 appears to have been lost during the seventeenth century.

The Douglas settlement is referred to in proceedings in Parliament on 7th April 1389; A.P.S. i. 557-8. The Ross settlement is contained in A.P.S. i. 537-538.

For the grants to the Crichtons and others see R.M.S. ii. 1045, 1064, 1191, 1214, 1534, 1595. See generally Nicholson "Scotland in the Later Middle Ages" (Edinburgh 1974).

[100] See generally Ranald Nicholson [1973] Jur. Rev. 1 et seq.

or other superior was induced to regrant on terms such that the general line of inheritance was departed from or "cut". The essential nature of the grant would be the same, the rights and duties of the parties similar to, if not identical with, those where the orthodox line of inheritance had been adopted. The point is then that these original tailzies were no more than simple feus with a special line of succession. Hence this would explain Craig's[101], Balfour's[102], Hope's[103], Stair's[104] and their successors' treatment of the entail in terms almost exclusively of succession, ignoring any possible perpetuity element because such an element simply did not exist.

To repeat Craig's definition:[105]

"There is no difficulty in defining a tailzied feu as one in which the legal order of succession is excluded and the property is destined to a series of substituted heirs named in the tenor of the investiture. This does not make the tailzied feu any less feudal in quality than the title to a simple feu. Indeed, paying strict regard to the principles of Feudal Law, we might say that a tailzied feu is eventually identical with what was known in the general feudal law as a simple feu."

Developments to 1685

If entails were originally merely a species of simple feu, then they could be made subject to any of the restrictions that would be imposed in a simple feu by means of conditions in the grant. The efficacy of these restrictions depended primarily on consent: the grantee was bound because he had bound himself; his heirs would be bound by their acceptance of the succession. As Lord Kames put it:[106]

"It is plain that every single heir who accepts the succession is bound by this prohibition so far as he can be bound by his own consent. His very acceptance of the deed, vouched by his serving heir and taking possession, subjects him in common justice to the prohibition: for no man is permitted to take the benefit of a deed without fulfilling the provisions and burdens imposed on him in the deed."

As we have already seen[107] land could be alienated in one of three ways: it could be given away gratuitously, it could be sold or it could be apprised[108] for debt. The conditions of grant, therefore, that would have to be imposed to prevent alienation would need to restrict, if not entirely prohibit, the activities of feuars in respect of these. The problem was whether conditions embodying these restrictions would be valid. Although Balfour is silent on what conditions might be validly imposed Craig gives several examples of conditions valid and invalid[108] but displays considerable uncertainty with regard to those purporting to restrict or prohibit alienation. He writes:[109]

"Coming to our law, I may say that in my opinion the condition against alienation is of no force or effect in the case of any infeftment (whatever the manner of holding may be) if conceived in favour of one, his heirs and assignees."

---

[101] Ius Feudale II.16.
[102] Practicks pp.173-175.
[103] Major Practicks III. 9. (Stair Soc. vol. 3 at pp.183/184).
[104] III.4.33.
[105] II.16.3. Clyde translation at p.698.
[106] Historical Law Tracts at p.133.
[107] See above; 'The Control of the Feudal Superior.'
[108] II.5. Clyde translation at p.441 et seq.
[109] II.5.7. Clyde translation at p.446.

But he qualifies this by indicating that his reason is the technical one of the inclusion of "assignees" was apparently the then modern practice and which, not unnaturally, were considered as importing a right to alienate. He goes on:[110]

"It would be otherwise in a military feu which did not include assignees. In titles of ancient date the references to assignees are few and far between and I would suspect the inclusion of them in feudal grants is invented to legalise what would otherwise be illegal."

In other words Craig would seem to be suggesting that in accordance with pure feudal principle conditions restraining alienation would be unnecessary since alienation (at least without the superior's consent) would probably be illegal anyway. If this is correct then it would seem that a condition to reinforce this principle would be valid, unless, of course, it was inconsistent with the terms of the grant.

By the time of Stair[111] and Mackenzie the problem was being discussed in terms of principle rather than of the technical words contained in conveyances and the point of principle was now quite clearly that a grant in fee conferred also the right to alienate, so that any prohibition on alienation would be inconsistent with the character of the fee, or as Mackenzie put it, "inconsistent with the nature of property and dominion".[112]

But at the same time Stair felt that a restriction or limited prohibition might be treated differently. Thus, for example, a prohibition against alienation without the consent of the superior or other person might be considered valid. The reasoning behind this distinction would appear to be that restrictions on how the right to alienate is used do not conflict with the essential nature of that right whereas an absolute prohibition does. Lord Kames articulated the point in this way:[113]

"Though none of the powers of property can be annihilated by will or consent, a proprietor however may, by will or consent, limit himself in the exercise of his property, for the benefit of others. Such limitations are effectual in law and are at the same time perfectly consistent with absolute property. If a man be put in chains, or shut up in a dungeon, his property, in a legal sense is as entire as ever; though at present he is deprived of the use or enjoyment of the subjects which belong to him. In like manner a civil obligation may restrain a proprietor from the free use of his own subject: but such restraint limits not his right to the subject more than restraint by walls or chains."

There appears to be only one known example of a condition de non aliendo in a charter before the seventeenth century although its validity had never been pronounced upon by either courts or commentators prior to 1685.[114] Indeed up to the passing of the Entail Act the question of the validity of prohibitions de non aliendo et non contrahendo debitum only came before the courts once, in the case of *Creditors of the Earl of Annandale* v *Viscount Stormont* in 1662.[115]

---

[110] *ibid.*; Clyde translation at p.447.
[111] II.3.58.
[112] Institutions III.8.
[113] Historical Law Tracts at p.121.
[114] In a charter dated 1489 Adv. Lib. MS.34.2.1. Indeed no writer since 1685 appears to have commented on its validity either, all being content to follow Dalrymple in recording its existence and singularity. In fact if the distinction between limited and absolute prohibitions held any validity it would appear to operate against the condition in the charter which is in absolute terms. On the other hand, given the limited rights of alienation at this time, its utility is somewhat doubtful.
[115] 1662 M. 13994-6.

The case concerned the entail of the lordship of Scone which contained the declaration that it should not be lawful for any of the heirs of entail to violate or dissolve it, to dispone or wadset the entailed estate "or do any deed whereby the same may be evicted or comprised from them without the special consent of all the persons contained in the tailzie or their heirs if of full age".

The Earl of Annandale, having succeeded to the estate, contracted debts which were secured on the estate in contravention of the prohibition. On his death the creditors apprised the estate. As the prohibition was fenced with a resolutive clause the next heir, Viscount Stormont, brought an action of declarator to have it found that on contravening the prohibitions the Earl had lost his right to the estate, that accordingly the diligence of the creditors was incompetent and that he was therefore entitled to enter onto the lands free from the Earl's debts.

For the creditors the question of the validity of the prohibitions was naturally of prime importance and they pleaded that the prohibitions were null and void as being inconsistent with the nature of property which gave to every proprietor in fee the free exercise of his rights; as the Earl had been vested in fee no such prohibitions could affect their claims.

The court rejected the claims of the creditors, feeling that these clauses were not contrary to law as they were found in many feudal grants and were indeed implied by law in the case of wardholding.

However while the prohibition in this case was not held to be bad the decision of the court is not without difficulty as to its applicability to other prohibitions against alienation. The point is that the prohibition here was not absolute and so could be reconciled, in theory, with feudal principle on the basis that it did not take away the proprietor's right of property in the estate but merely prescribed conditions as to its use. Indeed what limited support the case received from Stair[116] appears to be on the basis of this distinction between limited restraint and absolute prohibition. But on the other hand the case appears to have been argued, with regard to the prohibitions, on more general lines and Sir George Mackenzie, counsel for Viscount Stormont, presented a long argument on the desirability of restraints against alienation generally in the case of entailed estates.[117] Certainly the Act of 1685 envisaged no such distinctions and absolute prohibitions were perfectly acceptable thereunder. But whether this was an innovation made by the Act, or simply a confirmation of existing law is uncertain. That it confirmed existing practice however is not in doubt for both limited and absolute restraints in respect of pre-statute entails appear to have been approved on registration thereafter.

Yet even if the *Stormont Case* were to be read as sanctioning absolute prohibitions, it was evident that the use of prohibitory clauses alone would not be effective to ensure that the entailed land was not alienated. The reason was that while the prohibitions might declare what might not be done, they did not prescribe what was to happen if the proprietor acted in contravention of them. While they might take away the *right* of the proprietor to alienate or contract debt, as proprietor he none the less still had the *power* to alienate or secure his

[116] II.3.58.
[117] Pleadings by Sir George Mackenzie. Second Pleading at p.28.

debts on the entailed land if he so chose. Unlike the position of those entitled under an entail in England, successors to an entailed proprietor in Scotland had no interest in the land as such. The most they could be said to have was a spes successionis, which was never sufficient to give any rights in rem against the entailed estate. Put at its highest, the prohibition was treated as imposing an obligation on the proprietor, the benefit of which amounted to a personal right giving rise, at most, to an action for damages. As Lord Kames put it:[118]

"Admitting then that the heir is bound by his acceptance, let us enquire whether this consent be effectual to fulfil the purposes of the entail. He sells the estate notwithstanding the prohibition; will not the purchaser be secure, leaving to the heirs of entail an action against the vendor for damages? This has been doubted for the following reason, that a purchaser who buys from an heir of entail, in whom it is a breach of duty to sell, concurs thereby with his author in doing what is unjust. But this argument applies not against a bona fide purchaser ignorant of the restraint; and therefore he must be secure. Or to put yet a simpler case let us suppose the estate is adjudged for payment of debt. It is necessity and not choice that makes a creditor proceed to legal execution; and even supposing him to be in the knowledge of the restraint there can be no justice in his taking the benefit of the law to make his claim effectual. Hence it is plain that a prohibition cannot alone have the effect to secure the estate against the debts and deeds of the tenant in tail."

The solution, generally attributed to Sir Thomas Hope who is supposed to have discovered it in England while acting as King's Advocate,[119] was the use of irritant and resolutive clauses to fence round the prohibitions. As Hope himself put it[120] "either to make the party contractor of the debt to incur the loss and tinsel of his right in favour of the next in tailzie, or to declare all deeds done in prejudice of the tailzie, by bond, contract, infeftment or comprising, to be null of the law".[121]

Again it was in the *Stormont Case*[115] that the only pre-statute testing of the validity of the fencing clauses occurred. Here the prohibition was coupled with a resolutive clause in terms that: "if any of the said persons or their heirs should contravene the said provision, that they should lose their right and title to the said infeftment, and of all the lands and others therein contained ipso facto; and the said charter and infeftment with all right and title thereof, should be null and expire and their right should accresce and belong to the next heir of tailzie who is immediately provided to succeed the failing contravener".

For the creditors it was pleaded that the resolutive clause had no foundation in law and that in any event it could not operate so as to annul their rights. In the event however the court rejected this plea and granted the declarator sought. It did so however on a rather strange and technical ground. It was found that the prohibitive and resolutive clauses were contained in the instru-

---

[118] Historical Law Tracts at p.133/134; even this doctrine of the personal rights of substitutes was abolished during the first half of the nineteenth century.
[119] See e.g. Farran at p.161; Sandford at p.36.
[120] Minor Practicks 143.
[121] In fact, put in this form (i.e. of alternatives) this does raise a doubt as to the supposed derivation of this device from that used in *Mary Portington's Case* (1610) 10 Co. Rep. F.35b, the point being that in Mary Portington the irritant and resolutive clauses were applied in tandem and not, as Hope appears to think effectual, in the alternative. However, it may be that Hope was simply adopting the component parts to Scottish conditions. In any event the use of the two clauses in tandem became common practice very soon after the introduction of the device in Scotland.

ment of sasine which had been duly entered in the Register. As such, it was said, the prohibitions had been effectively published so that the creditors should be treated as having notice of them and accordingly should be bound by them (thus, in effect, going contrary to the proposition advanced by Lord Kames, supra). From the report it is difficult to ascertain whether the nature and validity of resolutive clauses were discussed at all; the judgement merely seems to assume that they were valid.[122]

The theory on which the resolutive clause was supposed to operate was comparatively simple. It was founded on the undoubted right of the entailer to impose conditions on those heirs he had appointed to succeed and as a consequence he would have the power to forfeit or "resolve" the rights of those heirs on such conditions as he chose. Accordingly on taking infeftment of the settled property the heirs of entail, being bound by its conditions, must lose their rights to the estate if the conditions were contravened. However the theory had the further elaboration that, with the forfeiture of the contravener's right, his acts of contravention must fall also as being the deeds of someone who was no longer owner of the estate.

Certainly the court's acceptance of Viscount Stormont's plea to enter free of the Earl of Annandale's debts necessarily involved acceptance of this last step in the reasoning, but, even allowing the efficacy of a forfeiture clause under the general law, there would appear to be a number of objections to this result.

In the first place the forfeiture would appear to come too late. If the resolution of the contravener's right is conditioned to operate as a consequence of an act of contravention then clearly that act of contravention must precede the forfeiture. As it must so precede the forfeiture it must operate at a time when the proprietor still had the power (if not the right) to dispone; and any exercise of that power would still confer a good title on a purchaser or creditor.[123] But even if the forfeiture is conditioned to take effect on the occurrence of an act of contravention it would seem that the same objections would apply. As Lord Kames has articulated it at length:[124]

"The consent here is obviously conditional, 'I shall abandon if I transgress or contravene any of the prohibitions'. Therefore, from the nature of the thing, there can be no abandon till there first be an act of contravention. This is not less clear than that the crime must precede the punishment. Where then is the security that arises from a resolutive clause? A tenant in tail agrees to sell by the lump; a disposition is made out —nothing wanting but the subscription: the disponer takes a pen in his hand, and begins to write his name. During this act there is not abandon nor forfeiture, because as yet there is no alienation. Let it be so, that the forfeiture takes place upon the last stroke of the pen; but then the alienation is also completed by the same stroke; and the land is gone past redemption. The defect is still more palpable, if possible, in the case of contracting debt. No man can subsist without contracting debt more or less; and no lawyer has been found so chimerical as to assert, that the contracting debt singly will produce a forfeiture. All agree that the debtor's right is forfeited no sooner than when the debt is secured on the land by adjudication. But what avails the forfeiture after the debt is made real and secured upon the land."

It will be remembered that the same problem was faced by the framers of English perpetuities and the attempted solution there was to condition the

---

[122] Institutions of the Law of Scotland III.8.
[123] Although not apparently a gratuitous alienee—see below at p. 142.
[124] Historical Law Tracts at pp.135/136.

forfeiture to take effect on an attempt to contravene, although this was held to be invalid for uncertainty.[125]

There is the further point that, whatever view be taken of his rights under the entail, the proprietor still held the feudal title to his land in spite of his acts of contravention, and this would remain with him until the appropriate judgement or act of infeftment of the next heir had deprived him of it. In short the conveyancing mechanics rendered it impossible for a proprietor to be deprived of his feudal title simply by an act of contravention. Whatever the entail might say, his powers would not be impaired by such contravention but would become voidable at the instance of the heir next entitled. But this being so, the power would remain in the proprietor until such time as action were taken to divest him of it. To quote Lord Kames again:[126]

"It is a rule of law that has never been called into question, that consent alone without delivery cannot transfer property. Nay, it is universally admitted that consent alone cannot even have the effect to divest the consenter of his property till another be invested; or, which comes to the same, that one infeftment cannot be taken away but by another. If so, what avails a resolutive clause more than one is simply prohibitary? Suppose the consent to abandon, which at first was conditional, is now purified by an act of contravention, the tenant in tail is indeed laid open to have his right voided and the land taken from him; but he still remains proprietor, and his infeftment stands good till the next heir be infeft; or at least till the next heir obtain a decree declaring the forfeiture. Before such process be commenced every debt contracted by the tenant in tail, and every disposition granted by him, must be effectual, being deeds of a man, who, at the time of executing, was proprietor."

This defect in the resolutive clause was sought to be remedied by coupling it with an irritant clause nullifying, or purporting to nullify, the acts of the proprietor in contravention of the prohibition. Even though, therefore, the forfeiture might come too late, if the contravening acts of the proprietor were in the meantime nullified might not such a clause be sufficient to plug that gap?

The only objection to this is that until forfeiture the proprietor still held the fee and would therefore still have the power to dispone or burden with debt the entailed estate. An irritant clause would certainly avoid any conveyance or bond, as far as the proprietor was concerned, but it is a much more dubious proposition to hold that it would affect the rights of purchasers or creditors derived from (what was for them) a validly executed instrument. Indeed (with regard to the resolutive clause) the creditors in the Stormont case put this point. The court, however overrode this objection on the basis that the creditors had notice of the restraints as, being contained in the instruments of sasine which had been duly registered, having been effectively published; this being so, having notice of them, the creditors were to be treated as dealing subject to them, with the result that their interests would be postponed to those under the entail.

There was no direct authority for this approach. Instead the court treated the published restraints as equivalent to published interdictions, and on this analogy the court rested its decision.

As with so many aspects of the *Stormont* case, difficulties are presented by the poor quality of the reports, but nevertheless, it would seem that the only point on which the analogy holds good is that both instruments of sasine and inter-

---

[125] *Mildmay's Case* (1606) 6 Co. Rep. f.40a at ff.42a; 42b.
[126] Historical Law Tracts at pp.136/137.

dictions were required to be recorded. As to the substance of the comparison there seems to be little common ground. An interdiction was essentially a public thing; it was a common law writ, prohibiting the proprietor from selling or entering into transactions affecting his land without the consent of those responsible for the interdiction. The purpose was to provide a legal restraint on the activities of those who, because of their personal inadequacies might be induced to fritter away their inheritance. It was notified to the public by a solemn act of publication, after which those who still dealt with an interdicted proprietor became just as subject to the interdiction as the proprietor, their activities in respect of the relevant property being liable to be set aside. After publication the interdiction was then recorded in the Register of Sasines. It is to be emphasised that the recording itself had no effect on existing legal rights and remedies; the effect was derived from the publication.

On the other hand the context to which the court sought to apply the analogy of the interdiction lacked the necessary element of publication and by so doing the court was ascribing to the action of registration a consequence which (at this time at any rate) it did not have, namely that of altering the nature of the rights of those governed by the document registered.

However, notwithstanding the technical objections to the court's action, it must be admitted that this approach did solve a number of problems emanating from the difficulty as to whether irritant or resolutive clauses could be said to operate not only against the heirs of entail but also against third parties. The point was that an interdiction operated not only against the proprietor but also against those who dealt with him. If this were to be applied to entails it would get over the problem as to whether an entailer could prescribe the consequences not only of his heirs' acts, but also those of such persons who might deal with his heirs.

Whatever the objections to the *Stormont* decision there is no doubt that it was acted upon by landed proprietors. Shaw's Index of Entails indicates that nineteen entails were executed between the date of the decision and the passing of the Act of 1685. This figure, however, represents only those entails which satisfied the requirements laid down by the Act itself; it takes no account of those entails executed with only two clauses on the Stormont model which did not satisfy the Act. As to this latter category the number can only be guessed at. Lord Kames on the one hand suggests that many such were executed.[127] Other commentators have doubted this[128] suggesting the low figure in Shaw as being indicative of the lack of faith in the correctness and durability of the decision. Of contemporary writers, Mackenzie, while supporting the validity of entails, nevertheless felt that a statute was needed to secure them. He wrote:[129]

"If the maker of a taillie designed that the taillied lands should not be alienable even for onerous causes then he adjects to the pactum de non aliendo, a clause irritant and resolutive, declaring all deeds done contrary to and in prejudice of the taillie to be null and void; and in that case all posterior alienations, even for onerous causes,

---

[127] *ibid.* at p.132.
[128] e.g. Patrick Irving at p.32.
[129] Institutions III.8.

will be reducible.... And because such clauses prejudge creditors and commerce very much, and seem to be inconsistent with the nature of property and dominion, therefore an Act of Parliament was necessary for securing them."

The Act of 1685[130]

The Act of 1685 made provision for the regulation of the law of entail in the following terms:

"Our Sovereign Lord, with advice and consent of his estates in Parliament, statutes and declares, That it shall be lawful to his Majesty's subjects to tailzie their lands and estates and to substitute heirs in their tailzies, with such provisions and conditions as they shall think fit, and to affect the said tailzies with irritant and resolutive clauses, whereby it shall not be lawful to the heirs of tailzie to sell, annailzie or dispone the said lands or any part thereof, or contract debt or do any deed whereby the samen may be apprised, adjudged or evicted from the other substitutes in the tailzie, or the succession frustrate or interrupted, declaring all such deeds to be in themselves null and void, and that the next heir of tailzie may, immediately upon contravention, pursue declarators thereof and serve himself heir to him who died last infeft in the fee, and did not contravene, without necessity any ways to represent the contravener; it is always declared, that such tailzies only shall be allowed, in which the presaid irritant and resolutive clauses are insert in the procuratories of resignation, charters, precepts and instruments of sasine; and the original tailzie once produced before the Lords of Session judicially, who are hereby ordained to interpose their authority thereto; and that a record be made in a particular register book to be kept for that effect, wherein shall be recorded the names of the maker of tailzie, and of the heirs of tailzie, and the general designations of the lordships and baronies, and the provisions and conditions contained in the tailzie with the foresaid irritant and resolution clauses sub-joined thereto, to remain in the said register ad perpetuam rei memoriam; and for which record there shall be paid to the clerk of register and his deputies the same dues as is paid for the registration of sasines; and which provisions and irritant clauses shall be repeated in all the subsequent conveyances of the said tailzied estate, to any of the heirs of tailzie; and being so insert, his Majesty, with advice and consent aforesaid, declares the same to be real and effectual, not only against the contraveners and their heirs, but also against their creditors comprizers, adjudgers and other singular successors whatsoever, whether by legal or conventional titles. It is always hereby declared, that if the said provisions and irritant clauses shall not be repeated in the rights and conveyances, whereby any of the heirs of tailzie shall brook or enjoy the tailzied estate, the said omission shall import a contravention of the irritant and resolutive clauses against the person and his heirs who shall omit to insert the same whereby the said estate shall, ipso facto, fall, accresce and be devolved to the next heir of tailzie, but shall not militate against creditors and other singular successors, who shall happen to have contracted bona fide with the person who stood infeft in the said estate, without the said irritant and resolutive clauses in the body of his right; and it is further declared, that nothing in this act shall prejudge his Majesty as to confiscations or other fines, as to the punishment of crimes, or his Majesty or any other lawful superior, of the casualties of superiority which may arise to them out of the tailzied estate, but these fines shall import no contravention of the irritant clause."

The Act therefore made provision for the legality of settlements by way of entail, provided that the deed of entail contained certain specified clauses and provided that the procedure for production before the Court of Session, and recording in the newly set-up Register of Entails was followed. It disposed of the difficulties apparent at common law regarding the effects of a contravention of the prohibitions on the irritant and resolutive clause as to the heir of entail in possession, as to the heir next entitled and as to the rights of third parties in

---

[130] Act of 1685 c. 22.

the entailed estate. What the Act did not do however was to define its relationship with the common law. The problem therefore which presented itself was as to its precise effect; did it provide a new code which was to apply exclusively to entailed settlements or did it merely provide a facility which did not impinge upon or abrogate common law principles so that those principles operate as an alternative; and did it relate to all entails or only to those created after the passing of the Act?

(*a*) *Defective Entails and the Common Law*

As might be expected, since the Act made no provision for pre-1685 entails, it was their status that was to present many of the early problems. The problems, however, were not so much substantive, as the form of settlement sanctioned by the Act was essentially that of the developed settlements already used, but were more concerned with the conveyancing technicalities. Thus in *Viscount Garnock v Heirs of Entail*,[131] on the death of the institute the estate had been transferred to the heir, but without repeating the prohibitions and fencing clauses in his service and instrument of sasine. Instead these documents had attempted to incorporate by reference the various provisions of the original charter and infeftment. When it was subsequently sought to sell the entailed estate for the payment of debts the heirs objected that such an act was contrary to the provisions of the entail. The creditors however pleaded that this lack of repetition took the entail outside the scope of the Act with the result that the estate could be sold. To this the heirs pleaded that the Act of 1685 was not made retrospective and as such did not apply to entails made prior to that date, so that the issue should be decided on the basis of the common law which they felt, rightly or wrongly, would assist them. The Court found:

"That the act 1685 regulates the transmissions of tailzies made before the said act as well as those made since; and that the general reference in the sasine is not sufficient to interpel creditors, according to the act 1685."

The Court was less decisive with regard to the requirement for the registration of pre-statute settlements. In *Cant v Borthwick*[132] a pre-statute entail which was perfect in all other respects was sought to be reduced on the basis of its lack of registration. It was held that as the Act was not retrospective it was unnecessary for pre-statute settlements to be registered. No reason seems to have been offered as to why, if it was not retrospective as regards registration, the Act should have been treated as retrospective with regard to the formalities of a transmission document a year before. Possibly the answer lies in the fact that even under the common law the documents in the *Garnock Case* would have been regarded as inadequate publication of the restraints. Certainly in the next case, that of *Creditors of Hepburn*[133] the adequacy of the publication seems to have been the decisive factor. Here an unrecorded deed was upheld as its restrictions and limitations had been engrossed in the registered instrument of sasine and as such had in reality been effectively published. The decision reads:

"That as the tailzie was executed and completed by infeftment prior to the act 1685 there was no necessity for recording it in the register of tailzies appointed by the act."

[131] 28th July 1725, M. 15596.
[132] 27th December 1726, M. 15554.
[133] 34d February 1738, M. 15567.

These decisions however were reversed some years later in *Lord Kinnaird* v *Hunter*[134] after which it became settled principle that, whether the entail was made either before or after the Act, to come within its provisions, it had to be registered.

Although in these cases it seems to have been assumed that, insofar as it went, the Act superseded the principles of the common law, especially in view of the statement in the Act that "such tailzies only shall be allowed, in which the foresaid irritant and resolutive clauses are insert", it was nevertheless still sought to argue that the Act merely provided a facility, which did not exclude the possibility of an entail being valid and effectual at common law. Thus in *Hamilton* v *McDowall*[135] counsel sought to show that an entail which was defective in terms of the Act still might be valid on the basis of the decision in the *Stormont Case*.[136] This, however, met with very little sympathy, Lord Meadowbank dismissing it as follows:[137]

"My Lords, it seems seriously to be suggested that entails are not founded on statute only, but have an existence at common law. I don't blame a party for attempting anything that may seem to him to have the remote possibility of aiding his cause; but I must say, that a more desperate attempt I never saw in any case; and sure I am that it will not impose, I do not say on any lawyer, but on any person even moderately skilled in the rudiments of the Law. My Lords, I am not speaking from my own authority; I speak the unanimous judgement of this Court, while Lord Justice-Clerk Miller and Lord Braxfield sat on the bench. It was the uninamous opinion of the Court, in the case of *Agnew of Sheuchan*[138] that the case of *Stormont* was wrongly decided, and that entails had not a foot to stand upon but the statute 1685. They are the mere creation of statute."

Yet while an entailed settlement that was in some measure deficient in terms of the Act could not derive its efficacy from the common law, it did not follow that its provisions were wholly without effect. If, for example, the defect was in complying with one of the requirements of the Act as to form or procedure, but where the prohibitions and the fencing clauses were perfect it seems inconceivable that they should not have been given effect to insofar as the common law could give effect to them. The point is that while the irritant and resolutive clauses without the statutory backing would have been insufficient to preserve the inviolability of the entailed estate, they should nevertheless still have been operative inter haeredes so that a contravening entailed proprietor could still be faced with an action of declarator to have it found that his right had been forfeited by virtue of the resolutive clause and that the next heir was entitled to be infeft. The point seems almost to be without direct judicial authority. There is however the case of *Ross* v *Drummond*[139] in which an action of irritancy had been brought against the heir of entail in possession for alleged acts contravening the prohibitions. The entail had not been registered and so was outwith the protection of the Act of 1685. Most of the discussion, both by counsel and by members of the court concerned the effect of the action on the status of the

---

[134] 26th November 1761, M. 15611; see also *Earl of Roseberry* v *Baird* 22nd June 1765 M. 15616.
[135] 3rd March 1815 F.C.
[136] 26th February 1662 M. 13994.
[137] 3rd March 1815 F.C. at p.326.
[138] *Stewart* v *Vans Agnew*, 3rd March 1784 M. 15435.
[139] 9th February 1836.

creditors of the estate, and, unsurprisingly it was found that their rights were unaffected. But the court then went on to grant a declarator confirming the forfeiture of the contravening heir in pursuance of the resolutive clause.

Where the defect which excluded the Act was not one of mere formality, but was rather a matter of the perfection of the fencing clauses the position might have been different, depending on whether the defect was contained in or comprised the omission of the irritant clause. It is difficult however to see what precise effect this would have, for a clause which ineffectually declared acts of contravention null would scarcely cause any repercussions on the interests under the settlement. The resolutive clause would still be available to effect the forfeiture of the contravener's interest and the position would seem to be much the same as if the defect was one of formality.

If the defect was in the resolutive clause then not even the right to forfeit the contravener's interest would be open to the following heirs. All that would be left would be the force of the prohibitions, such as they were.

Now, although, as we have seen, the clauses of prohibition could not, of themselves, protect the settled property, nevertheless it was felt for a considerable period of time that they might be effectual to protect the interests under the settlement.[140] The basis of this view was the theory that, while creating no real right, the prohibitions created a personal right in favour of the heirs. As Sandford explains:[141]

"This prohibitory clause may be conceived either in general terms, declaring that the heirs of entail shall do no act or deed by which the course of the succession may be altered or innovated, or the lands affected; or it may declare that it shall not be lawful to any of the heirs of entail to contract debt, alienate the property, or alter the destination. By such clauses the rights of the heir in possession, and of the substitutes are materially affected; the former cannot grant any gratuitous deed by which the substitutes can be disappointed of the succession; and the latter have a right of credit in their favour, which entitles them to claim performance of the obligation conceived in their favour and to set aside any gratuitous deed done to their prejudice. By taking up the succession under the burden of the condition annexed to it, the heir in possession binds himself to implement it, and the substitutes are creditors to that effect."

Thus, if an entailed proprietor could be restrained from alienating gratuitously, and although he still might alienate for onerous causes, if such consideration as he received must necessarily be held under, or invested in subjects to be held under, the entail then a perpetuity of sorts would still exist, for although the settled property itself might change, the interests under the settlement would continue so long as there were substitutes to satisfy the destination. The right of the substitute heirs to reduce gratuitous alienations in contravention of the prohibitions was established early in the case of the *Earl of Callendar v Lord John Hamilton*,[142] although the correctness of the decision has often been doubted since it appears to have been based on the provisions of the Bankruptcy Act 1621[143] in spite of the fact that it was not found in that case

---

[140] Provided of course that there was still some property left subject to the settlement. In many cases the question would be purely academic since the power of alienation or contracting debt would have been exercised with regard to the entire estate.
[141] *supra* at p.101.
[142] January 27, 1687 M. 15476.
[143] Act of 1621 c. 18.

that there had been an insolvency. Nevertheless the jus crediti of the heirs was held sufficient eight years later in *Wallace*[144], in 1695, to reduce a gratuitous deed of alienation and by the middle of the eighteenth century the principle was beyond doubt.[145]

The second limb of the process, the securing of the sums raised and their investment for the benefit of the heirs of entail took a little longer to establish. It began in 1728 in *Lord Strathnaver* v *Duke of Douglas*[146] where debts had been contracted on the security of the entailed estate in contravention of the prohibitory clause. The court, while agreeing that an entailed proprietor subject only to clauses of prohibition held the estate in fee, and that the powers that went with such a holding, including those of burdening the estates with debt or alienating them for an onerous cause were unaffected,[147] held that he was nevertheless obliged to fulfil the condition under which he had accepted the estate. If, therefore, he acted in breach of such conditions he was bound to make reparation to those heirs following for the injury he had done to them.

This principle was applied in *Gordon Cumming* v *Gordon* in 1761[148] where the entailed proprietor of the estate of Pitlurg sought a declarator that he was entitled to sell the estate in contravention of the prohibitions in the entail and to dispose of the price at his pleasure. The Court found in the following terms:

". . . . [T]he pursuer is laid under a prohibition of selling or alienating the estate to the prejudice of the substitute heirs of tailzie; and therefore that however safe an onerous purchaser might be, the pursuer, by a voluntary sale of the lands, would contravene the entail and be subjected to an action of reparation and damages, at the instance of the substitute heirs of tailzie."

Up till this point the issue had been discussed by the courts in terms only of the availability of an action for reparation and damages, and indeed the commentators acquiesced in this view.[149] But in the same year as the Pitlurg case the court went further. In *Young* v *Young*[150] the entailed estate was sold contrary to the prohibition. In an action brought at the instance of the substitute heir it was held that although the purchaser's right to the estate was unimpeachable, the purchase price must be reinvested and resettled in terms of the entail because the prohibition had been breached and a liability for reparation in damages thus arose in favour of those thereby prejudiced.

However there does not appear to have been another case directly on this point for fifty years, until *Lockharts* v *Stewart Denham*[151] came before the court in 1811. Here again the contravention consisted of a sale in breach of the prohibition. Again the court, while finding that the proprietor had the power to sell, declared that, having done so, he was obliged to invest the proceeds. The court articulated its decision in the following terms:

"[T]he simple prohibition did give a jus crediti to the substitutes though they were merely personal creditors; that they no doubt had not the benefit of the statute, as they would have had if the entail had been complete, which would have made them

---

[144] February 8, 1695 4 Bro. Supp. 65.
[145] *Ure* v *Earl of Crawfurd* July 1, 1756 M. 4315.
[146] February 2nd 1728, M. 15373.
[147] Established in *Young* v *Bothwells*; December 7, 1705 M. 15482.
[148] July 29th, 1761, M. 15513.
[149] See esp. Lord Kames cited above at note 118.
[150] November 13th 1761 5 Bro. Supp. 884.
[151] June 8th 1811 F.C.

real creditors, and might be disappointed if the heir in possession spent the whole, or if it was carried off from them by his creditors; but that so long as any part of the price remained they were entitled to insist on its being secured in terms of the entail."[152]

Up to this point, then, it seemed that while a settlement containing a simple prohibition (or one fenced with defective irritant or resolutive clauses) would not ensure the perpetual retention of the entailed land subject to the entailer's prescribed destination, it would nevertheless provide a settlement under which the interests created thereunder might continue in perpetuity. The principle was, in the words of Sandford:[153]

". . . . that the substitutes in a deed of entail, which only contained a prohibitory clause, or which, contained prohibitions not sufficiently fenced by the irritant and resolutive clauses, in terms of the statute 1685, were entitled to demand fulfilment of what was held to be an obligation upon the heir in possession to transmit the estate to them according to the intention of the maker of the deed in their favour; or to demand reparation for its breach, by the investment of the sum received as the price of the estate, in the purchase of other estates, to be limited to the same uses as the original property. It was considered, that as the obligation imposed by the deed was not real, but merely personal upon the heir, it did not give the substitutes a jus vindicandi over the property itself, so as to interfere with the power of disposal which possession of the fee gave; but that the personal obligation deprived the heir of the right, though not of the legal power to alienate and rendered him liable to an action to enforce implement of the obligation, or remedy the wrong he may have committed."

The *Stewart Denham Case* however was appealed to the House of Lords, inconclusively as it turned out, for while doubts were expressed as to the correctness of the principles on which it had been decided and while it was remitted to the Court of Session for their further deliberations, the parties decided to proceed no further.

There the matter rested until 1830 when the House of Lords was called to pronounce upon three alienations of land settled under defective entails and in particular as to whether the price received should be reinvested, or paid out and apportioned between the substitute heirs, or retained by the disponer. In the first two *Stewart* v *Fullarton*[154] concerning the lands of Ascog and *Bruce* v *Bruce*[155] concerning the lands of Tillicoultry the entire line of cases decided by the Court of Session which gave rise to the above principle was brought into question, as was the very basis of the principle, the existence of an enforceable obligation in favour of the substitute heirs. Their Lordships denied the existence of such an enforceable obligation, at least in so far as it was supposed to give the substitute heirs a jus crediti on the price. It was held that as prohibitions in a deed of entail could not be the foundation of inhibitory diligence and as they did not take away from the proprietor his power to contravene the prohibitions for onerous causes, the alleged obligation simply did not exist. This being so, there could be no insistence that the price derived from the sale of property settled under a defective entail be reinvested under the terms of the entail, nor could there be reparation for the substitute heirs.

The third case was slightly different. While the Ascog entail contained no resolutive clause and that in the Tillicoultry entail was found to be defective,

---

[152] Followed in *Campbell* v *Earl of Breadalbane* 12th June 1812.
[153] at p.108.
[154] July 16, 1830, 4 W. & S. 196.
[155] July 16, 1830, 4 W. & S. 240.

the deficiency in the Queensberry entail of the lands of Tinwald[156] was merely formal in that the entail had not been registered in accordance with the Act. In this case, while the same principle, that there was no enforceable obligation under which the proceeds should be invested, was applied, the substitute heirs were not left entirely helpless, being able to apply for a declarator of irritancy in order to forfeit the heir's right to the estate, this, of course, being as a result of the resolutive clause.

With these three decisions the House of Lords effectively prevented the creation of a type of perpetual settlement by way of the defective entail rules.[157] However, in doing so they created a further difficulty as to whether this left the prohibitions completely redundant or whether they still had a use, and specifically whether they still conferred on substitute heirs the right to reduce a deed purporting to make a gratuitous alienation. The difficulty arose from the doctrine of the Scottish courts that this right derived from the obligation created by the existence of the prohibition in the deed of entail. If however this obligation no longer existed, as it did not according to the House of Lords, how could the substitute heirs still retain their right? Subsequent judicial pronouncements provide little assistance, simply asserting, as they do, that prohibitory clauses remained sufficient to prevent gratuitous alienations.[158] Perhaps the answer lies in the fact that the three decisions of July 16th 1830 were embodiments of the rules of strict interpolation that were applied to entailed settlements; that in accordance with these rules, as the Act of 1685 did not apply, the substitute heirs must look to the provisions of the deed of entail itself for their rights and that there were no provisions for reinvestment in their favour in the deed; but that the right to reduce gratuitous deeds needed no implication of any extraneous matter or idea with the result that its survival would not conflict with the rules of strict interpretation.[159]

(b) *Effective Entails*

While the Act of 1685 was designed to give protection for entailed property it nevertheless occurred that, even when all the requirements of the Act had been met, so that it operated with full force, it was not sufficient, without more, to prevent the entailed estate from being alienated. To fill this gap the common law had to be pressed into service.

The point was that the Act was expressed as operating against "heirs of entail". Accordingly where the proprietor of an entailed estate could not be so described the question arose as to whether he was bound by the prohibitions. The difficulty arose in two situations: first, where the entailer directly disponed the estate to X and then substituted to him a number of other persons as heirs of tailzie, and secondly where the proprietor entailed his estate on himself.

The earliest cases concerned situations of the first type. In the first of them,

---

[156] *Marquis of Queensberry* v *Executors of Duke of Queensberry* July 16, 1830 4 W. & S. 254.
[157] For a discussion of the policy aspects and a detailed examination of the judgment of the House of Lords in these three cases see below, The Judicial Approach to Entails.
[158] See per Lord Moncrieff in *Lockhart* v *Lockhart* 1841; per Lord Brougham in *Cathcart* v *Cathcart* (1831) 5 W. & S. 315 at p.344.
[159] See below, at p.149 et seq.

Willison v *Willison*[160] the institute put forward what was to become the standard plea, that although the settlement was within the Act of 1685 the prohibitions were directed against the heirs of entail and therefore, not being within such description, they did not apply to him. The court however found that the prohibitions were applicable to him.

In *Hay* v *Erskine Balfour*,[161] the court decided the other way, finding that the institute "was not restricted from contracting debts, he being the disponee, and the restriction only laid on the heirs of tailzie".

The question went for decision to the House of Lords in *Edmonstone of Duntreath* v *Edmonstone*[162] where the prohibitions were directed against the heirs of entail without specific mention of the institute. The Court of Session held, as a matter of construction, that "the purchaser is comprehended under the description and designation of heir of entail [and] is thereby subjected to the restrictions and limitations of the said entail". The House of Lords however, acting upon the principle that entailed settlements were res odiosae and so required a strict interpretation, reversed this, holding that if the institute was to be bound it was for the entailer specifically to bind him by directing the prohibitions against him. Where there was no such specific direction, it would not be implied by the courts. Thus the judgement declares:

"That the appellant, being fiar or disponee, and not an heir of entail, ought not by implication from other parts of the deed of entail to be construed within the prohibitory, irritant and resolutive clauses, laid only upon the heirs of tailzie."

This principle was applied to the second class of cases where the question concerned the entailer's being bound by the prohibitions of the settlement. The issue here was not so much the entailed proprietor's right to dispone as whether the entailer's creditors could proceed against the estate (of which the entailer was still proprietor under the deed of entail).

Again the point was that the Act of 1685 was stated to be operative only against "heirs of entail" and that the entailer was clearly not one of these. But there was also the point that to permit such restrictions to apply, either by an extension of the statute or by operation of the common law, would provide a means whereby the entailer's debts might be evaded as a result of the settlement.

On the first point there was no difficulty. The statute would not be extended to cover the position of the entailer. Thus in *Dickson* v *Cunningham*[163] the report reads:

"The statute 1685, authorising settlements of that sort [i.e. entails] related, it is observed, to the case of heirs alone, whose interest might, according to the forms therein prescribed, be limited or modified by the deed of the ancestor, from whose gift they derived the estate. But the case of the proprietor himself was left to the consideration of the common law."

But as to the second point there was much uncertainty. Again there was the undoubted rule that without the prohibitions being directed specifically against the entailer they would not apply. Whether one could accept the other half of this proposition, that if they were so effectively directed, then the entailed estate would be safe was more doubtful, for this would mean going against an estab-

---

[160] February 26th, 1726 M. 15458.
[161] February, 14th, 1758 M. 4406; M. 15461.
[162] November 24th, 1769 M. 4409 (H.L. judgment delivered in 1771).

lished rule of law. As Lord Robertson said in the case of *Agnew of Sheuchan*:[164]

"It is clear in the law of Scotland, and runs through the whole system, that the whole estate of every debtor is liable to be affected by the diligence of his creditor; and it is impossible that any man can have in his own person the fee of an estate, continue in it, and at the same time by any deed or operation of his own prevent the attachment of it by his creditors."

In *Dickson* v *Cunningham*[163] it was held that where the entail was gratuitous then even though the prohibitions might be directed against the entailer they would not be effectual to bar his creditors from proceeding against the settled estate. The case concerned the entail of the estate of Kilbucho which was settled on the entailer and his nominated substitutes, the prohibitions being directed against both. After the settlement, however, the entailer contracted a number of debts and felt obliged to sell a portion of the entailed estate to satisfy them. The substitutes then brought an action to nullify the validity of the sale. The report reads:

"The Lords considered the entail to be altogether ineffectual in a question with the creditors of the entailer .... The maker of the entail in question might have restricted his right to mere liferent; or by executing a bond of interdiction, he might have precluded his burdening of the lands unless for onerous or rational causes. These however were the only methods by which the order of succession marked out by him could be secured against his future contractions the general rule being undoubted, 'That no man can, by any device, withdraw his estate from being liable for his debts'."

Two years later came the case of *Stewart* v *Vans Agnew*[164] where the entail was not gratuitous and which was found not to have been made with the intention of defrauding the entailer's creditors. Here, unlike the situation in Dickson's case the debts related to periods both before and after the settlement. The original action was brought by the trustees for the creditors against the son of the original entailer who was apparently anxious that the debts of his father should be paid and was agreeable to there being recourse to the entailed estate to satisfy them if this were possible. In the first action it was unanimously held that recourse could be had to the settled estate. To quote Lord Braxfield, with whom the other members of the court agreed:[164]

"No fraud here: the entail must subsist, but as not to affect creditors. All debts contracted before recording infeftment must be good. This provided by the statute 1685, and this agreeable to the principles of the feudal law of Scotland. A personal deed of entail cannot qualify a right in a person by charter and seisin; but I incline to go further. Prior to the statute 1685 entails were in use, but doubted how far by common law a proprietor could lay such extraordinary burdens. The statute 1685 interposed to prevent such questions, it lays burdens on the heirs of tailzie; but nothing in the statute which says that a man may tie up his own hands, possess the estate and yet secure it from creditors; that is contrary to the nature of property; and it would have been unlawful[?] in the legislature to do so. A different case when the maker of the entail puts the fee in the heir and reserves only a liferent. No difference that here a mutual entail; that good among the persons contracting with him; but still the debts will be good quoad the creditors."

The defender, however, died in 1809, to be succeeded by his son as substitute heir. In 1812 this son lodged an appeal to the House of Lords who, on hearing it, remitted the case to the Court of Session for reconsideration.[165] The Court

---

[163] March 10th 1786 M. 15534; affirmed by H.L. 1831 5 W. & S. (App. Cas.) 693.
[164] 3rd March 1784 M. 15435.
[165] 3rd March 1784 M. 15435.

of Session duly reconsidered the case[166] but unanimously came down in favour of their earlier decision. The case was then re-appealed to the House of Lords who upset the decision of the Scottish court, drawing a distinction between debts incurred prior to the settlement and those incurred afterwards, and holding that only the former were capable of founding diligence against the entailed estate. As to the point that an entailer could not disable himself from satisfying his debtors by reason of the entail, Lord Eldon, L.C. said:[167]

"My Lords, when we come to look at the reasoning why he cannot do it against himself, it is said that statute enables him to do it, as against heirs of entail. To which it was answered, it is true that statute was made to remove doubts, and to enable good and valid entails against heirs of tailzie; but still that statute could not alter what the law was with relation to provisions as to others than the heirs of entail; and this has been repeatedly observed in this House, in the case of Duntreath,[168] and a variety of other cases with which all your Lordships must be familiar, that an institute, for instance, is not an heir of tailzie; that the description of an institute is nowhere to be found in the act of 1685; and yet you have very few questions whether the institute is not bound, if you only bind the heirs of entail. The description frequently is, 'John, such a one, and the other heirs of tailzie', where John, such a one, was an institute. It is said that you cannot imply, from these words, that he was an heir of tailzie meant to be fettered, because he was not an heir of tailzie. In the case of Duntreath, it will be in your Lordships' recollection, that expressions of that kind are to be found in various places, 'the institute' naming him, and the other heirs of tailzie; but when you come to look at the resolutive, irritant and prohibitory clauses, they are only on the heirs of tailzie; and though that man was called one of the heirs of tailzie, by the reference to the others as 'the other heirs of tailzie,' and though it is said that you cannot, by implification, fetter the man, but that he must be expressly named, yet if you find, as you have done over and over again, that if the institute is expressly named, he is as much bound as the heirs of tailzie; there does not appear to me to be, in that case, any difference between the institute and the succeeding heirs of tailzie. If your Lordships will look at what is found in Stair, in Hope, and in Mackenzie, it appears to me that the maker of the entail himself may be bound, it is said clearly he may be, if the deed of tailzie is an onerous deed. It is very true that after these cases, your Lordships will not hastily decide, that if the deed was not an onerous deed, he could bind himself; but if it be an onerous deed, made on sufficient consideration, notwithstanding all the reasoning I have seen, it does appear to me to be quite sufficient to support the obligations entered into. I say such a deed will bind him if he sells the estate for money, and money constitutes the consideration. What is this in truth, if you come to analyze it, but a sale according to the expression to be found in it . . . . and the question is whether this is not in effect the same thing, considering the nature of the contract and the other obligation which arises out of the consideration.

I do confess, after considering the arguments, I have a very strong conviction that, independently of the statute 1685, such a deed as this—recollect my Lords, I do not say a gratuitous deed;—but such a deed as this, proceeding on onerous consideration, and valuable consideration, not a mere mutual entail, but proceeding likewise on money considerations, is competent to bind him."

The essence of the decision therefore was the fact of onerous consideration, a fact which effectively made the competition one between two equally innocent parties, both of which had provided consideration for their claims, unlike the case of *Dickson* v *Cunningham*[163] where no consideration had been provided for the settlement. Thereafter the decision proceeded on the grounds of notice and

---

[166] June 2nd 1818.
[167] In *Agnew* v *Earl of Stair* (1822) 1 Shaw's App. Cas. at p.355.
[168] 1786 M. 15534.

priority of time. As the entail effectively published the restraints, so all creditors dealing with the entailed proprietor must be deemed to deal with knowledge of them; however during the period before these restraints came into being the interests of the creditors must prevail, the restraints being incapable of acting retrospectively.

It can scarcely be doubted that the Act of 1685 made provision for the creation of the first effective private perpetuities in Scots Law. While it did so by making use of, and giving legal authority to, ideas and devices developed by the common law, it became clear during the century and a half after the Act that the common law itself would not have achieved the same effectiveness.

That a perpetuity of interests under the settlement could have been achieved at common law is probable; that it was not was the result of the rules of interpretation which were applied by the courts to entailed settlements generally. It is with these rules of interpretation that we now concern ourselves.

The Judicial Approach to Entails

It will be remembered from our look at entails in English law that their effectiveness was broken by the courts as a result of a device, or combination of devices, suggested in part by the judgements in *Taltarum's Case*.[169] In Scotland the suggestion that the Court of Session might follow this example was not without support, and indeed was the subject of invitations to the House of Lords to break the stranglehold that the practice of entailing was acquiring on the Scottish land economy.[170] However these suggestions and invitations met with little success, not so much because of any attachment to the entail system but rather because the nature of the judicial function had become more restrictively defined, so that, while decisions might mitigate its effects, the courts would not openly abrogate the statute itself.

It will be remembered that the Act of 1685 prescribed to the court a role in establishing the validity of entails in that the original entail should be "produced before the Lords of Session judicially, who are hereby ordained to interpone their authority thereto". It has been suggested that the court "could have used this requirement to prevent 'perpetuities', had [it] wished to do so".[171] No doubt, on one interpretation the court could have acted in this way. But the tenor of this part of the Act casts the court's function as an administrative one and indeed the requirement became (if it was ever anything else) simply a procedural step whereby a petition was to be presented to the court prior to registration. Whether this shows, as has been suggested,[171] that Scottish judges were less antagonistic towards entails than their English counterparts is, perhaps, open to question. It would seem that, if it shows anything at all, it is rather the more modern view of the court's position in relation to legislative enactments. As Lord Eldon said:[172]

"In England, too, the legislature had endeavoured to protect the entails of estates. The English mode of barring the issue and remaindermen was only a fiction of law;

---

[169] (1472) YBB. 12 Edw. IV Mich. f.14, p.1.16; f.19 p.1.25; 13 Edw. IV Mich. f.1. p.1.1.
[170] See below; 'The Legislative Approach to Entails.'
[171] Farran at pp.164/165.
[172] *The Case of the Roxburghe Feus* 1813 2 Dow at p.208.

and it has often occurred to me as a very great singularity, with respect to the judicial and legislative powers, that it should have been permitted judicially to destroy these entails. But if the English statute protecting entails had been passed only about a century ago, it might be doubted whether the legislature would have permitted the exercise of such a stretch of power by the judges."

And again six years later:[173]

".... the power of the judges in this respect may be doubted. Upon that subject, as it applies to English law, I have formed an opinion which leads me to think that the judges of this age in England would not have been permitted to get rid of the statute of English entails as judges of that age did, soon after the passing of the statute de donis."

Indeed Scottish judges seem to have been scarcely more enamoured of entails than do their English counterparts, but their line of attack came to be concentrated on the interpretation of the provisions of the entail. As Sandford put it:[174]

"In Scotland, although judges were impressed with an unfavourable idea of their nature, and foresaw their probable effect upon the agricultural and commercial improvement of the country, they could not evade or overturn the special words of the statute. They knew, however, that every lawyer considered their introduction to be an encroachment on the common law of the land. They were aware that our highest authorities had declared them to be res odiosae znd to require a strict interpretation; and accordingly, by refusing to bind the heir in possession, where the maker of the entail had not done it; and by granting him, in such circumstances, the full powers of a proprietor and fiar, uithout any reference to the presumed intention of the entailer, they, in some degree, lessened the evils of the system."

Surprisingly, perhaps, the rules of strict interpretation derive, not only from pre-Statute days, but from the days before restrictive clauses began to be inserted in entailed grants.

The first indication that the law tended to frown upon tailzied destinations is to be found in Craig who writes:[175]

"Tailzies are more familiar in Scotland than in any other country for the reason that the pride of our old families and the wish to perpetuate their high position makes succession in the male line preferable to succession through females. But notwithstanding the sentiments and desires of a large number of our nobility in favour of tailzies they are regarded in our law as odious and receive the strictest construction. Always if there is doubt they are interpreted in accordance with the legal rules of succession."

Craig unfortunately is not explicit as to why this should be, stating only that "both conscience (which must always prevail) and the law of the land are opposed to them".[176] He then proceeds to doubt both these justifications in the light of what he conceives to be the law of his time. Indeed, at first sight, it does seem somewhat odd that grants, whose only deviation from the norm was their special destination, should be treated in this way. The cases of the period provide no real indication and by the time of Stair, ideas had become more sophisticated and concerned the effect of the restrictions on the right of property.[177] But as we have seen these ideas of property can have had less force

---

[173] *The Case of the Queensberry Leases* 1819 1 Bligh at p.423.
[174] Entails at p.39.
[175] Ius Feudale II.16.12; Clyde translation at p.704.
[176] *ibid.*; Clyde translation at pp.704/705.
[177] Institutions: IV.18.6 and 7.

in Craig's time and certainly would not have been a justification for this treatment of what Craig describes as a species of simple feu.[178]

It is suggested that the answer lies in the remains of the feudal idea of a grant of land being to and for the family, and of the consequence of this in the form of rights, either moral or legal, in the heirs to have the land descend to them. Certainly an evacuation was likely to be seen as depriving the heirs of their birthright and therefore against good conscience. Indeed this point seems to have been embodied in a statute of James IV[179] declaring that it was "Against justice and good conscience for superiors to receive resignations in prejudice of righteous heirs".

However by the time of Balfour the effect of this statute on tailzied grants must be considered doubtful for he expressly states that grants of tailzie are quite legal and not hurtful to the King's soul,[180] presumably because in most of such cases the immediate heir of line and the heir of tailzie would be the same person, with the result that objections would only be forthcoming from the remoter heirs of line whose hopes of succession would be thereby dashed.

The only institutional authority who elaborates Craig's point is Bankton[181] whose views seem broadly to support the position taken above. He writes;[182]

"Tailies are to be strictly interpreted, because restriction of property is unfavourable. Hence of old, tailzies of all kinds, whereby the course of lineal succession was altered were esteemed so odious that we have an express statute declaring it 'Against justice and good conscience....'[179] Heirs of line, or heirs at law are so termed because the succession descends to them by right of blood and provision of law and therefore they are still called Right Heirs; for this reason our Kings, at their majority always revoked such tailies and resignations from heirs general to heirs male. Heirs at law are heirs general because they succeed by a universal representation, and are primarily liable to the ancestor's debts; but then there is a just exception in one of these statutes as to a man's conquest for as the act bears,[183] it is not against conscience, that one who acquires right to lands to take it to such heirs as he pleases, whereas in estates descending from ancestors, the heirs in the investiture, especially if likewise heirs by right of blood, were deemed to have a kind of established claim of succession which it was thought the present fiar ought not to deprive them of."

If, then, strict interpretation of grants deviating from the norm was the established rule before the restrictive clauses were introduced it is not surprising that it should be continued when the obvious dangers to commerce in land were perceived. However, while the early rules related to the description of the heirs who were to succeed, the practice of strict interpretation was extended to cover the entail as a whole, and specifically the prohibitions and the clauses fencing them.[184] Indeed in the report of a case in 1677[185] there is the comment that "the President in his system has declared himself no friend of these clauses". It was however during the eighteenth and nineteenth centuries that the ramifications of this approach became apparent.

---

[178] Ius Feudale II.16.3; Clyde translation at p.698.
[179] Act of 1493 c. 50.
[180] Practicks at p.173.
[181] Erskine also mentions (but does not discuss) the statute. Inst. III.8.25.
[182] II.3.14.9 (vol. i at p.587/588).
[183] Act of 1587 c. 31. See also Craig, cited above at note 175 for discussion of his statute.
[184] See Sandford at pp.71-101 for a detailed discussion.
[185] *Rothes* v *Melville*: Fountainhall's report in 3 Bro. Supp. 168 at 170.

The basic theme running throughout the cases is one of absence of help: the law would not step in to rectify an omission or a defect; if a deed of entail was defective, it fell; if the statutory procedure had not been complied with in the minutest detail, the entail would be ineffectual against third parties. It meant that there was no room for intendment or implication from the surrounding circumstances. Accordingly therefore if one of the prohibitions had been omitted, for whatever reason, the entail would be and, so far as the court was concerned, would remain defective as regards that prohibition. Thus for example in the case of *Heirs of Campbell* v *Wightman*[186] the entail did not expressly prohibit sale, although it was clear from the tenor of the rest of the deed that such a prohibition had been intended. The Court of Session, however, was not impressed and refused to make the necessary implication; similarly in *Stewart* v *Home*[187] and *Brown* v *Countess of Dalhousie*[188] where the absent prohibitions were those relating to contracting debt and altering the order of succession respectively. The principle was stated by Sandford in the following terms:[189]

"[W]here an omission does occur, the jealousy with which the common law views restraints on property affords the presumption that the entailer did not intend to bind the heirs in that respect. This presumption cannot be overturned by the argument that, if not restricted in the exercise of the power left, the entail may be completely destroyed, and the intention of the maker of the deed wholly frustrated. The favour of the law for freedom of property does not admit of this consideration and the effect of the omission cannot be allowed to weigh, when determining to what extent the prohibitions apply."

And exactly the same approach would apply where the defect was in one of the fencing clauses. Thus in *Sharpe* v *Sharpe*[190] the defect consisted of an omission in the irritant clause which was clearly the result of a clerical error. The Lord Ordinary was prepared to sanction the insertion of remedial words, as was the Inner House, but the House of Lords emphatically reaffirmed the old principle, Lord Brougham stating the positions with absolute clarity. He said:[191]

"The law is that in order to make the tailzie effectual, not only to prohibit and resolve, that is, forfeit in the contravener, but also declare null the thing done in contravention, there must be a declaration of nullity, sometimes called irritancy; but that word is also used for the clauses of forfeiture, and sometimes it is used to designate both the fencing clauses together. But a nullity must in some way be declared, and it must be declared in precise and distinct terms; and although not in one set technical phrase, yet it must be declared with such precision that you read it as in the deed and do not merely gather it by intendment. Nor have you any right whatever to say that the nullity exists because things are stated which imply a nullity, or things which would follow from that nullity having been declared. Thus observe the other kinds of prohibition: it would not be a valid prohibition to sell annailzie or dispone, were an entail to forbid 'making any title to any disponee' and yet no one so tied up could effectually sell. So it is clearly not a prohibition to sell if you only prohibit altering the order of succession, or doing anything whereby the estate may be adjudged or evicted; and yet an estate may be adjudged or evicted by the purchaser, if it be sold;

---

[186] June 17th 1746, M. 15505.
[187] July 8th 1789 M. 15535.
[188] May 25th 1803 M. App. No. 19.
[189] at p. 259.
[190] 1835, 1 S. & M. App. Cas. 594.
[191] *ibid.* at p.622/623.

and if it be sold the order of succession is altered with a vengeance. So here, if the acts of deeds done be null, it will follow that they cannot burden the estate or affect the succeeding heirs of tailzie. But this is not the same thing as declaring acts or deeds in themselves; it is a declaration that certain things shall not have any effect against the estate or the heirs of tailzie; it is different from a declaration that those things shall be in themselves null and void."

So also, although an entail might contain fencing clauses perfect in themselves it had to be clear that they applied to all the prohibitions. Thus in *Kempt* v *Watt*[192] the tailzie failed to provide for the irritation of the debts and deeds, and so, in spite of its containing a declaration that creditors should not have any power to adjudge for debt or to evict the estate in pursuance of such debts, the court held this to be insufficient.

The point about this rule of strict interpretation is that it placed the burden directly upon the entailer; it did not operate so as to prevent him achieving his object, but it provided simply that if he was to do so it would be without the assistance of the court; he must do it himself. This approach underlined the decisions of the House of Lords on the Ascog[193] and Tillicoultry entails[194] and in the case of the Queensberry leases[195] where the entails were found to be defective and where, although it was admitted that the settled estates could be sold, it was sought to have it found that the proceeds should be applied for the purposes of the entail. The basis of these decisions was that without the force of the Act of 1685 the rights and obligations of the parties, insofar as the purported to detract from the ordinary right of the proprietor, must be founded upon the provisions of the deed of entail. The intentions of the entailers were largely irrelevant for clearly they had desired that the entailed estate should be secured to all the heirs covered by the respective destination and had failed to effect this by the one and only means available. Accordingly, looking to the deeds of entail, and seeing that there were no provisions therein for reinvestment the court would not imply such provisions. The proprietors therefore had not only the power to sell the settled estate, but also the right to retain the proceeds.

The same point, that the entailer must look to himself to secure his ends, is illustrated also by the *Duntreath Case*[196] where the House of Lords found that an entail properly constituted in accordance with the provisions of the Act of 1685 was still insufficient to secure the inviolability of the settlement where the prohibitions had been directed only against the heirs of entail and not against the institute. It was underlined when the House of Lords founded on the Duntreath decision as authority for approving the inviolability of a settlement on the entailer and substitute heirs where the entailer's rights of alienation and contracting debt had been expressly dealt with.[197]

---

[192] January 28th 1779 M. 15528.
[193] *Stewart* v *Fullarton* (1830) 4 W. & S. 196.
[194] *Bruce* v *Bruce* (1830) 4 W. & S. 240.
[195] *Marquis of Queensberry* v *Exors. of Duke of Queensberry* (1830) 4 W. & S. 254.
[196] *Edmonstone* v *Edmondstone* November 24th 1769 (Ct. of Sess.) 1771 (H.L.) M. 4409.
[197] *Agnew* v *Earl of Stair* (1822) 1 Shaw's App. Cas. 333.

Applying this rule as they did[198] the courts in Scotland could scarcely be said to have aided or facilitated the maintaining of perpetuities by way of entail. And yet at the same time it is a difficult question as to whether their treatment of entails amounted to a general anti-perpetuity policy; certainly aspects of this treatment could be said to have formed the basis of such a policy.

In the first place there are statements suggesting that such a policy did actually exist. Thus Dalrymple in discussing the effects of the Act of 1685 and the courts' attitude to it states that although justification could be found for the reduction of the entails in *Baillie* v *Carmichael*[199] and *Heirs of Campbell* v *Wightman*[200] the real reason was disapproval of entails generally. And in the case of the *Roxburghe feus*[201] Lord Eldon also felt that he could trace the influence of an anti-perpetuity policy in the Duntreath decision. He said:

"It has been said that an heir of entail was an absolute proprietor except in so far as he was fettered; and in the *Duntreath* case it had been decided that fetters were not to be implied; though perhaps then the English policy in regard to entails weighed a little in the judgement."

But there is more than mere opinion. Hope[202] and Mackenzie,[203] who wrote shortly after the passing of the Act of 1685, had expressed the view that the prohibitions of an entailed settlement might be rendered effectual by use of an inhibition. Clearly, if this view were correct then it might be possible to achieve inalienability even if the deed did not comply with the requirements of the Act. In the late eighteenth century this question was put to the test in two cases, *Bryson* v *Chapman*[204] and *Lord Ankerville* v *Sanders*.[205] In both cases the entails contained the standard prohibitions but no effective fencing clauses and the proprietors were therefore able to sell. The question arose because of the reluctance of the purchaser to make payment. Accordingly the purchaser applied to the court to have the vendor's charge for payment, which was affecting

---

[198] There was however criticism of the rule in appeals to the House of Lords in which English Chancery lawyers, notably Lords Thurlow, Loughborough and Eldon who favoured a policy in which the intention of the entailer should be respected and, where possible, given effect to, participated. This gave rise to a line of cases based on what became known as the "fair play rule" described by Lord Corehouse in *Speid* v *Speid* February 21st 1837 FC 505 at p.572/3 in the following terms:

"The opposite maxim is that the entailer's intentions are entitled, as it is commonly expressed, to fair play, relying on which they have been supported even in the case of real ambiguity; for example the colloquial has been preferred to the technical sense of a term; or of two technical senses, that which is rare and unfrequent to that which is in general use; or a phrase has been limited or extended to give effect to apparent intention."

In this case the irritant clause was defective with the result that if the rules of strict interpretation were followed the court would have to find for the pursuer: if however the "fair play" rule were adopted the court would have to find for the defender. The Lord Ordinary (Lord Corehouse) stated the effect of the two rules and decided their facts but made no decision. The Inner House expressed great difficulty as to the conflicting strains of authority but took comfort from the decision of the House of Lords in *Sharpe* v *Sharpe*, pronounced a little over a year earlier, reaffirming the old rule of strict interpretation. After this decision the validity of the strict interpretation rule was never again in doubt.

[199] July 11th 1734 M. 15500.
[200] June 17th 1746 M. 15505.
[201] (1813) X Dow. at p.210.
[202] Minor Practicks paras. 364; 365.
[203] Institutions III.8.16.
[204] January 22nd 1760 M. 15511.
[205] August 8th 1787 M. 7010.

the land, removed on the ground that an inhibition raised by the substitutes had barred the power of sale and was effectual against him as a third party. The court however was not impressed holding that the inhibition could not affect a purchaser. There is, in addition, a third, unnamed, case, mentioned by *Lord Hailes*[206] where it was held that "inhibition was inept and unavailing" in a situation where a landed proprietor had bound himself not to sell or dispone certain lands, nor contract debt or do anything whereby the lands might be burdened.

The point was that had inhibition been effectual in these cases a new series of perpetuity by way of entail, not sanctioned by the Act, would have been possible, in contravention of the very provisions of the Act which had excluded the effectuality of all entails not approved therein.

Parallel reasoning can also be applied to the principles enunciated by the House of Lords in the Ascog case; had the alleged duty of re-investment been upheld, a form of perpetuity would have been created whereby the interests of those under the entail would have continued in the new capital which would have become the subject of the settlement. But again, the courts' approach was that, there were procedures for permitting reinvestment where the settlement was by way of trust, that as the settlement in question was by way of entail and not by way of trust, such reinvestment could not be permitted in the absence of a special direction in the deed.

Both these examples can of course be explained on grounds other than the courts' implementation of an anti-perpetuity policy. In the cases on inhibition there was the provision of the Act and in the investment cases the powers were clearly absent. Nevertheless, in dealing with settlements outwith the Act (and specifically those cases in which the inhibition issue was raised), the House of Lords can scarcely have been unaware of the perpetuity implications of their decisions, and Lord Wynford, at least, was prepared to justify his opinion on the broad grounds of the anti-perpetuity policy of the law.[207]

"It is the policy of the law to prevent the accumulation of property, and perpetuating the possession of it in families. Acting on that policy the legislature had said that an estate shall not be entailed but in a particular manner. No man can bind himself, either by an implied or expressed promise, not to sell his estate, unless the promise be in the form and accompanied by the sanctions specified by the law."

The Legislative Approach to Entails

While the activities of the courts were concentrated on ensuring that the Act was strictly complied with and in so doing providing some kind of check on the establishment and maintenance of entailed setltements, there were never any serious attempts to get rid of them judicially, a course, which, in any event, was confirmed as impossible after the House of Lords' judgement in the *Roxburghe Case*.[208] If, therefore, entails were to be abolished, or at least their consequences mitigated, it was clear from a fairly early date that legislation would have to be the instrument.

We have seen that in the reign of Queen Anne legislation[209] was passed put-

---

[206] Lord Hailes Decisions at p.1030.
[207] 1830 4 W. & S. at p.236.
[208] 1813 2 Dow. 149-230 (esp. per Lord Eldon at p.210).
[209] Stat. 7 Anne c. 20.

ting entails in Scotland on the same footing as those in England as regards forfeiture for treason. Further changes inspired by political considerations came with the abolition of the heritable jurisdictions in 1747[210], several of which had been entailed. The import, however, of this latter statute was clearly small as far as entails were concerned for, out of the compensation fund set up by the Act, only five claims by substitute heirs were received.[211]

But, in marked contrast to that which appertained in England two centuries earlier, the opposition to entails was based largely on economic grounds, and specifically on the effects of putting land extra commercium. Indeed this ground seems to have weighed considerably (although clearly not decisively) with the Court of Session in the *Stormont Case*,[212] for, in addition to the remarks of Stair,[213] the Pleadings of Sir George Mackenzie reveal his arguments for upholding the settlement on policy grounds. He said:[214]

"To the second difficulty, hearing, that these clauses are destructive of commerce, it is answered, that the liberty of disposing upon our own as we think fit doth more nearly concern us than the liberty of commerce, especially in this kingdom wh'ch stands more by ancient families than by merchants. And, therefore, seeing that these clauses tend necessarily to perpetuate families, and the other doth only tend to the better being of trade, we ought to prefer the pursuit to the defence. And to what purpose shall we gain an estate by commerce, as is alleged, more than inhibitions or interdictions; and it is easier to read a charter than to try the registers. And England and Spain which are more interested in commerce than we, have, by allowing such clauses, evidently declared that they think them not absolutely inconsistent with commerce. But the truth is, real rights are not the foundations of commerce, for commerce is maintained upon the stock of personal trust, and the main thing which traffickers rely upon is the personal trust which is among them and not the consideration of any real right."

When, however, during the next century, experience of the working of the entail system was to hand, the picture was very different from that portrayed in Mackenzie's argument. Of the effects on the beneficiaries subject to those settlements mention has already been made.[215] On the broader economic effects much has been said and written, particularly in the Debate in the Faculty of Advocates on the Law of Entail in 1764 and in the many pages of evidence to the Select Committees set up by the Commons in 1828[216] to look into the law of entail in Scotland generally and by the Lords in 1845[217] to look at specific improvements that might be permitted to entailed proprietors who lacked appropriate powers under the settlement. Indeed the first remedial statute, passed in 1770[218] justified the reform which followed on the following statement from the preamble:

"And whereas many taillies and estates in Scotland, made as well before as after passing the said Act [i.e. of 1685], do contain clauses limiting the heirs of entail from granting tickets or leases of a longer endurance than their own times, or for a small number of years only, whereby the cultivation of land in that part of the kingdom is

---

[210] Stat. 20 Geo. II c. 43.
[211] Act of Sederunt, 15th June 1748.
[212] (1662) M. 13994.
[213] II.3.58.
[214] Pleadings of Sir George MacKenzie: Second Pleading p.28.
[215] Chapter I above.
[216] See Reports of Commissioners 1828 vol. vii; 1829 vol. iii.
[217] See Reports of Commissioners 1845 vol. xii.
[218] 10 Geo. III c. 51 (The Montgomery Act).

greatly obstructed, and much mischief arises to the public, and which must daily increase so long as the law allowing such entails subsists, if some remedy be not provided: Wherefore to prevent a mischief and inconveniency so hurtful to the public, be it enacted . . . ."

Specifically these mischiefs arose from the effects of the fetters put on the proprietor, the inability to raise capital to finance necessary improvements, the consequent deterioration in the efficient management of, and income return from, the estate, leading in turn to the deterioration of the agricultural economy of Scotland. The evidence before the Committee in 1828 brings this out in detail, not only as to the effect of entails themselves, but as to the lack of effectiveness produced by the remedial statutes of 1770 and 1824.[218] Perhaps the best reasoned statement to be presented to the Committee which presents succinctly the relevant points of objection is that of James Glassford.[220]

"The disadvantages of Entail settlements when carried to an extent such as that supported by the Scotch law, are twofold: either affecting the public at large, or affecting more particularly the entailed proprietors themselves.

The system confers upon individuals a disproportionate and almost unlimited power over the most important possessions and rights of a succeeding generation, not only after the individual who constitutes the entail has long ceased to have any interest in the matter, but for a period of time to which the utmost human wisdom is unable to reach; so that instead of continuing to be a prudent and wise arrangement, and which the same person would, if alive, have carried into effect, it may become directly the reverse, and be one which, if he had existed under these new circumstances, the entailer himself would have revoked or rectified. In this respect it may be as injurious as if the legislature of one age could tie up the hands of succeeding legislatures, for a century or a longer period, from altering a statutory enactment which was perhaps expedient when it passed, but has become inexpedient or mischievous. The interests of society require therefore that there should be some limit, and that not placed at a very remote distance where the power of individuals to legislate even for their own family and posterity, and still more for successors to their property who may be strangers to them as to any ties of relationship or natural interest, ought to cease; that is to say ought not to be supported by special statutory enactment. According to the present Scottish law of Entail the wisdom of an individual is raised above the wisdom as well as the interest of many succeeding generations.

But in addition to this view which places the interests and feelings of the original entailer in contrast with the interests of society, and of a long and remote series of descendants or disponees, who are governed and restrained by his will, another important objection to the plan is that so far from effecting the real and substantial objects of the right of entailing, namely the prudent protection of the property from an improvident heir, and the benefit of the persons to whom the succession is thus secured, a prospective settlement of such unlimited duration often defeats much more effectively those very objects, and produces great evils, and for a long series of time.

The benefit of entails as supporting a hereditary aristocracy is now left out of consideration. The expediency of legislative interference for such a purpose is at best questionable; and if well founded, it would scarcely apply to a system which supports all such deeds, however limited the extent of the property, and under whatever conditions imposed; besides that, the real advantages sought for even in this respect come to be also in great measure counteracted and defeated by those changes in the circumstances of society which counteract and defeat the more private and substantial objects which the individual had in view. The same remarks therefore apply to both.

In alluding briefly to some of the inconveniences which have been produced both to society and to the individuals concerned, by the system of strict Scottish Entail, it is not necessary to draw a marked line of separation between them. The community

[219] 5 Geo. IV c. 87 (The Aberdeen Act).
[220] Second Report on Scotch Entails; Evidence thereto at pp. 41-3.

and the individuals holding their property under such settlements suffer nearly from the same causes; and there is scarcely any entail of long endurance which does not produce injury to both.

1st. The commerce and transmission of land is obstructed by these settlements, and may be so to a great extent and over large districts of territory. In a commercial and trading country the disdavantages are obvious. The entailer who wishes to establish and continue a family may in the exercise of this power find some motive for his industrous exertions. But the stimulus, even to this extent, terminates with himself. The incentive is by the same act taken away from his heirs in the line of succession, and a contrary influence, that of indolence or indifference is substituted.

2nd. The improvement of such estates by advanced methods of culture and the progress of invention is discouraged and rendered difficult through the restraints placed on the proprietor, by his limited means, and the limited interest which he has in making such ameliorations.

3rd. Not only is improvement retarded, but a system of mismanagement may be perpetuated. For individuals making Entails may do so under very imprudent and unwise conditions, not indeed for the purpose of wasting the estate, but through some narrow policy of an opposite kind, or perhaps under the influence of some wrong bias or partial law, or from mere caprice, which thus comes to be upheld by the sanction of the law.

4th. One great rule and principle of the Scotch law itself is violated by the system; more important perhaps than any advantage which society at large can derive from the power of entailing, namely the right which at common law in Scotland, the creditor has to obtain payment of his just debts from the property of every description belonging to his debtor. The Entailer himself indeed is not so protected but the succeeding heirs under a strict entail are exempt from the operation of the common law, so far as the estate itself . . . . is concerned. It is true that the creditor has it in his power to ascertain whether a proprietor is thus fettered, and without this precaution ought not to give credit on the estate; but practically this is not an effectual safeguard, for in the ordinary transaction of life, people do not think of consulting the records before they deal with a landed proprietor. In lending large sums of money, they or those whom they employ will do so, but not in ordinary dealings even to a large amount. Nor is this an imaginary or even a rare case, but occurs every day and cannot be avoided.

5th. The evils of the system are equally or even more strongly felt by the persons immediately concerned, namely the heirs of Entail themselves, who may be and often are, put to the most serious inconvenience and without any improvidence or fault on their part, by not having the power of borrowing money, even for prudent and useful purposes and to the most moderate extent for the security of their estates. This is indeed a necessary condition for the support of the system; for otherwise if they could give a real security effectual against the property (as well as their interest in it) Entails could not be protected. But still the evil is real and great, for it is not the spendthrift only who is thus restrained, but the provident proprietor is also fettered, and it may be to the disadvantage of the estate, as well as himself personally . . . .

6th. The estate itself may, from such causes come to suffer materially as well as the present possessor, and that even permanently or for a long period of time. For the heir of Entail in possession may be without the means of laying out those sums, even in the proper management of it, which to secure future advantage for the property would be highly expedient and which, if he had the usual facilities for doing so, it would be prudent to advance. Or he may have little motive and interest to employ the means which he actually possesses. The heir of Entail, for example, on whose death the estate is to descend to a distant collateral or even to a substitute who is quite a stranger to him, has comparatively little interest in laying out large sums even on the requisite improvements—such as building farm houses, draining, planting, etc. He has an interest to take the most he can from the property, and to do the least for it. He has an inducement to commit waste by cutting more timber than he ought, and in other ways to lessen the value of the estate to subsequent heirs with whom he is unconnected. Or if he does not yield to such inducements, he may, as has been observed, find it impossible, if he does not possess separate funds sufficient for the purpose, to adopt any liberal course of management . . . .

7th. . . . . [I]t is the general objection to the strict Scotch Entails . . . . that by encouraging so much the desire of establishing a family and name in a line of male heirs, the other children of the entailer, and those of his heirs of Entail, are neglected and excluded from their proper portion of their father's fortune . . . .

In short an artificial state of property, of rights and burthens, is introduced by the system of Entails, which does not allow the changes of events, and the successive conditions of society, to have their proper issue; and by requiring frequent legislative interference disturbs and inverts the common law rights both of the holders of such property and the commonalty at large."

It will be seen that the objections to the system of entails in Scotland were based on the precepts: first, that the very concept of entail was iniquitous, impractical and unsound; and secondly, that the prohibitions of an entailed settlement had the consequence of depriving the proprietor of the means whereby the estate might be effectively managed, with the results mentioned above. While virtually no one involved was satisfied with the status quo, and virtually everyone wished to improve the lot of those subject to settlements in strict entail the course of legislative action was dominated by a dispute as to whether the system as a whole should be reconstituted or whether its basic elements should be preserved but amending legislation passed to remove specific defects.

The first initiative came in 1764 when Alexander Lockhart,[221] Dean of Faculty, put for consideration of the Faculty of Advocates, the whole question of the law of entail and whether, and, if so, how, it should be reformed. The proposal was that after due consideration the Faculty should suggest an appropriate remedy and take steps to ensure that their suggestions were implemented.[221a] By an overwhelming majority it was decided that the system of settling land should be recast. It was resolved that the Faculty should prepare Heads for a Bill to be introduced into Parliament to undertake this fundamental reform embodying the following principles:[222]

"that perpetuities should be abolished:

[A]nd that for the future, such entails containing prohibitory, irritant and resolutive clauses de non aliendo et contrahendo and other clauses of the like nature, restraining the heirs of taillie in the free enjoyment of their respective lands and estates, and placing such estates extra commercium, should be simpliciter prohibited and discharged at least for any longer period than the lives of such heirs as did exist at the date of such taillies, without prejudice still to such future entails, to the purpose and effect of establishing the line of succession, and series of heirs, and restraining said heirs from altering said line of succession by any voluntary gratuitous deed and be obliged then to carry the names, arms and titles of their respective families under the usual certification of a forfeiture and irritancy of the contravener only:

[A]nd that, in order to bring the entails already established as near to a conformity to future entails as could be consistent with the rules of law and justice, these former entails should continue in full force during the lives of such of the heirs of taillie as should be existing and in life at the date of such act of Parliament, as should be obtained for explaining and amending the law in these particulars, and that from and after the failure of all such heirs as were then existing and in life, these former entails should be

---

[221] The suggestion has been made, principally by Patrick Irvine W.S. in his evidence to the Commons Select Committee, and in his essay "Considerations on the Inexpedience of the Law of Entail in Scotland" (2nd Ed. 1827) at p.54 that the Dean of Faculty acted at the instigation of Lord Mansfield.

[221a] On the background to this proposal see Phillipson [1976] Jur. Rev. 97.

[222] The Scots Magazine, July 1764.

declared to stand precisely on the same footing with future entails, as regulated by the said act."223

223 The Heads of the Bill summarised above are set out here for the sake of completeness (reproduced from the Scots Magazine, April 1765) *"Heads for a Bill to Amend the Law concerning Tailzies in that part of Great Britain called Scotland"*. *By the Faculty of Advocates*.

  I. [This simply recites portions of the Act of 1685].
  II. Under the authority of the aforesaid act, a great part of the lands in Scotland are already subjected to such tailzies, with prohibitive, irritant and resolutive clauses restraining the heirs of tailzie to the most remote generations from alienating or incumbering the same, or any part thereof. And as such clauses and provisions are by experience to be attended with many ill consequences, both to public and private interest.
  III. For remedy thereof it is proposed that from and after the—day of—next to come in this present year—it shall not be lawful for any person or persons, proprietors of lands or heritages, in that part of Great Britain called Scotland, by any settlement disposition, bond of tailzie or any other deed to be by him or them executed, or all or part of their said lands or estates, to burden or affect the said settlement with any prohibitive, irritant or resolutive clauses, so as to limit and restrain any of the heirs of tailzie not in life at the time of making such settlement or not specially named therein, from alienating such lands in whole or in part for just and necessary causes, or for a true price or other valuable consideration paid for the same, or from granting wadsets and other real securities upon or out of the same; as from charging the same with debts, as such heir of tailzie shall think proper.
  IV. And it is hereby proposed that all such prohibitive, irritant and resolutive clauses contained in any such tailzie or settlement of date posterior to the said — days of — shall be void and of no form or effect whatsoever, with respect to such heirs as aforesaid.
  V. Provided nevertheless that it shall be lawful for and in the power of every such proprietor of lands, or estates in Scotland, by such tailzie or settlement, to impose prohibitive, irritant and resolutive clauses to their full extent as they might have done before the making of this [proposed] act, upon any heir or heirs of tailzie who shall be in life at the time of making such settlement and therein specially names; and in the case of contravention, not only to irritate and resolve the right of the heir so contravening, but also to annul the debts and other deeds of contravention, so far as the same may affect, charge of burden such tailzied lands or estate. Provided such tailzies shall be in other respects completed and perfected according to the directions of the aforesaid Act of 1685, in all points; and that the said prohibitive, irritant and resolutive clauses, shall be ingrossed in the procuratories of resignation, charters, precepts and instruments of seisin, whereby or under which any of the said heirs of tailzie shall, or may hold, or enjoy such tailzied lands or estates.
  VI. Provided always that from and after the said — day of — it shall not be lawful for any such proprietors of lands or heritages, in that part of Great Britain called Scotland, in any settlement, disposition, bond of tailzie, or other deed to be by him or them executed, of all or any part of their said lands or estates, to limit or restrain by any prohibitive, irritant or resolutive clauses, or in any other manner whatever, their heirs of tailzies from granting leases of all or any part of the lands or heritages contained in such deed of tailzie for any life or lives, not exceeding — lives, as for any term of years not exceeding — years; such leases being always granted for a rent or tack duty, not under what the lands so leased do pay or yield at the time of granting the same; or from providing the husbands or wives of such respective heirs of tailzie in such jointure or jointures, or liferent provisions as they shall think proper; the same not exceeding one-third of the free rent of such lands or estate, after deduction of other jointures and liferent provisions, and of the interest of such debts, real or personal, as shall then be chargeable on the respective estates; or from granting provisions to their children, the same not exceeding three years free rent of such lands or estate, after deduction of the interest of such debts, real or personal, as aforesaid. And all such prohibitive, irritant, and resolutive clauses contained in any such deed of tailzie or settlement to be made or executed after the — day of — shall be held void, and of no force whatever.
  VII. And in order to give all possible security to purchasers, creditors and others contracting bona fide with the person in possession of such tailzied estates, and to prevent, as far as may be, their being deceived or defrauded, it is further proposed that it be enacted that no prohibitive, irritant and resolutive clauses contained in any deed of

tailzie to be made and executed after the said — day of — shall be of force or avail against purchasers, creditors, or others contracting with the heirs of tailzie in possession of such estates, until such time as the said tailzies shall not only be recorded in the register of tailzies according to the directions of the aforesaid act of 1685, but also until such time or infeftment should be thereupon taken; and all the prohibitive, irritant and resolutive clauses be ingrossed in the instrument of seisin and the seisin recorded in the proper register.

VIII. And it is further proposed with respect to all such tailzies as shall be made and executed after the said — day of — that the contravention of any of the conditions or prohibitions therein contained, shall only operate as an irritancy or forfeiture of the right of the person contravening, and shall not affect the heirs, though descended of the body of the contravener, any law, custom or usage, or any provision in the tailzie to the contrary notwithstanding.

IX. Under the authority of the aforesaid act of 1685, many tailzies have been made containing prohibitive, irritant and resolutive clauses, which are hereby proposed to be prohibited and restrained for the future; and as it is reasonable, so far as may be consistent with the rights and interests of the several heirs of tailzie now alive and existing, to introduce and establish on uniformity and equality between the tailzies already made and those to be made after the said — day of — by reducing the limitation and restrictions of the tailzies already made within reasonable bounds; and it is proposed, that all tailzies already made and established pursuant to the directions of the act of 1685, shall subsist and stand in full force and have effect with and under the exception aftermentioned during the lives and existence of all or any of the heirs of tailzie called to the succession by any such deed of tailzie who shall be in life upon the said — day of — but that from and after the death of the longest liver of the said heirs of tailzie respectively, all prohibitive, irritant and resolutive clauses contained in any such deed of tailzie or settlement already made and established, other than those which are by this act authorised and allowed with respect to future tailzies, shall, thenceforth cease and determine and have no force or effect whatever.

X. Proposed, that notwithstanding any such prohibitive, irritant and resolutive clauses contained in any tailzies already made and established, pursuant to the directions of the said act of 1685, it shall be lawful for the respective heirs in possession, by virtue of such tailzies, to grant leases of all or any part of the lands or heritages therein contained, for any life or lives, not exceeding lives, or for any term of years not exceeding the term of years; such leases being always granted for a rent or tack-duty, not under what the lands so leased do pay or yield at the time of granting such leases, or from providing the husbands or wives of the respective heirs of tailzie in such jointure, or jointures, or liferent provisions as they shall think proper; the same not exceeding one third of the free rent of such lands or estates after deduction of other jointures and liferent provisions, and the interest of such debts, real or personal, as shall be chargeable thereupon; or from granting provisions to their children, the same not excedeing three years' free rent of such lands after deduction of the interest of such debts as aforesaid.

XI. Proposed, That where lands or estates, whether contained in tailzies already made under the said act of 1685, or to be made under the authority of this act, shall be lawfully charged with debts and incumbrances, it shall be lawful for the heirs of tailzie possessed of such lands or estates to sell by public roup or auction such parts of the said tailzied lands and estates as may be sufficient to satisfy and pay the said debts and incumbrances. Providing always that such sale shall be made only by the authority of the Court of Session upon a summons of sale against all the subsequent heirs of tailzie then in life; and that the price shall be applied by direction of the said court in payment of the said debts and defraying the expense of the said sale; and such sale so made shall not only be a sufficient security to the respective purchasers, but also shall not operate any irritancy, contravention, or forfeiture of the right of the heir who shall make such sale: anything herein contained, or in any other law or usage, or any provision in the tailzie in the century notwithstanding.

XII. That it be provided that nothing herein contained shall be contrived to repeal or alter the said act of 1685 in any of the heads, articles, clauses or provisions thereof other than those hereinbefore mentioned, but the said act shall remain in full force as to all such heads, articles, clauses or provisions concerning which no provision is made or which are not inconsistent therewith in the same way and manner as if this act had never been made.

When the Faculty deliberated on the detailed proposals put before them in August, 1764, they secured the overwhelming approval of those present, the majority being forty-three votes to four.[224] However the principles as set out by the Faculty never in fact became the subject of any Bill introduced into Parliament and the initiative seems to have been abandoned sometime in 1767.

That it was so abandoned was largely due to the efforts of Sir John Dalrymple, one of the four dissenters from the Faculty resolution. His principal objection was that the measures suggested were inappropriate. He wrote:[225]

"Men who were to consider the total dissolution of entails in Scotland, as it regarded their country might perhaps foresee with pain in such a step, so great a tide of land property in the market, as from the cheapness occasioned by that tide, would call the money out of trade to the purchase of land; as would render our landed men discontented and bankrupt, and our traders, what they are too apt, when they have got a little money to hasten to be little lairds, poor proud and idle: instead of wishing that more land property were brought into the market, he would perhaps wish that he had as little as the Dutch, or that the price of what we had was kept high; the former to turn our native countryman into manufacturers and merchants and the latter to put it out of their thought when they become such, to convert their circulating cash into a dead stock of land. And in general he would foresee, and in part dread many consequences which attend the innovation of every system if not at the exact period of society ripe for that innovation."

And according to Dalrymple the time was not yet ripe. That it might become ripe, he thought, was possible,[226] though unlikely, given the rules of strict interpretation employed by the courts. It is to be noticed that at no time did Dalrymple defend the existing system as not being in need of reform. Instead he preferred to adopt the second of the two approaches mentioned above, an approach which might be described as the traditional Scottish approach to amendments relating to heritable property, namely to retain the system basically intact but to make detailed amendments to remedy the deficiencies apparent therein. These were seen principally as lack of powers available to the entailed proprietor whereby he might raise the necessary finance to undertake necessary improvements and promote the efficient management of the estate. In addition, though, Dalrymple recognised the hardship to those dependents of an heir of entail who would not benefit under the settlement and suggested that provision might be allowed for them.

It was this policy of palliative measures, while substantially retaining the entail principle intact, that was adopted in the Act of 1770[227] and indeed in all the subsequent legislation down to the Entail Amendment Act of 1848[228].

The provisions of the Montgomery Act were concerned with extending the powers of the entailed proprietor in three ways: in the first place his powers of leasing were enlarged; secondly he was authorised to expend money for the benefit of the settled estate by way of improvements; and thirdly he was given the right of excambion so that he might exchange limited portions of the estate

---

[224] The Scots Magazine, March 1765.
[225] Feudal Property at pp.183/184.
[226] Dalrymple felt that the time would only be ripe when most of the land in Scotland had been put under entail. At the time of his writing the amount was only 20%. This point was seized on by the anti-entail faction of the 1820's, notably Patrick Irvine and George Selkrig.
[227] Statute 10 Geo. III c. 51 (The Montgomery Act).
[228] Statute 11 & 12 Vict. c. 36 (The Rutherford Act).

for other land. The powers of leasing and of excambion were extended further by the Rosebery Act in 1836[229] but were still restricted. These limitations were removed in 1848 when the Rutherfurd Act gave the entailed proprietor powers whereby he might lease or excamb the whole or any part of the settled estate under the authority of the Court of Session, provided that the consents of appropriate substitute heirs were obtained.[230]

As to improvements, the Montgomery Act applied the principle that the personal resources of the entailed proprietor, expended for the improvement of the estate, conferred benefits on the substitute heirs who should therefore be treated as being under an obligation to the improver. The Act laid down a complex procedure whereby the entailed proprietor was to be treated as a creditor for three quarters of the amount expended; however the debt was not charged to the estate as such, but rather to the substitute heirs. This principle was found in practice to be unsound and caused resentment among the substitutes. It was accordingly replaced by a rule under which the improver charged three-quarters of his expenditure against the estate and was given an annual rent charge to be paid out of the rents of the estate during the remainder of his life and for twenty-five years thereafter.[231]

Limited powers of feuing, and of granting land on long lease had been given in the amending Act of 1840,[232] although these powers were given only for special purposes. The Rutherfurd Act swept away the restrictions, allowing a general power of feuing, providing, as always, that the requisite consents were obtained.[233]

The other half of the Dalrymple programme, the establishment of means whereby family provision might be made, was introduced in the Aberdeen Act of 1824[234] which attempted to achieve this by permitting the entailed proprietor to infeft his or her spouse with an annuity not exceeding one-third of the free rents.[235] In addition power was given for a fund to be set up to finance portions for those younger children who would not succeed to the estate, such portions to be exigible from each succeeding heir.[236] The Aberdeen Act was repealed in 1848 insofar as it was stated as being inapplicable to any tailzie executed on or after 1st August 1848. Thereafter the principle was that the estate was to be made liable to provision for younger children, either by charging the income of the estate or by permitting sales of entailed land to finance these portions.[237]

The legislative provisions, then, down to 1848 can be seen as leaving intact, the fundamentals of the entail and were indeed clearly meant to supplement those which might have been provided by the creator of the settlement, the statutes almost invariably providing that the provisions therein were not to operate so as to cut down any special powers given to the proprietor in the deed

---

[229] Statute 6 & 7 Will. IV c. 62; see also Stat. 1 & 2 Vict. c. 70 where the powers to grant tacks and to excamb were further increased.
[230] Section 4 (leasing); section 5 (exemption).
[231] Sections 13-19.
[232] Statute 3 & 4 Vict. c. 48.
[233] Sections 3, 4 & 6.
[234] Statute 5 Geo. IV c. 87.
[235] Sections 1-3.
[236] Section 4.
[237] Statute 11 & 12 Vict. c. 36 section 12.

of entail itself. These, of course, would be perfectly valid provided they were not inconsistent with the fundamentals of the entail.[238]

The great change that came in 1848 was not in the extension of these powers but was in the fundamental nature of the Scots entail.

Reconstitution and Restriction

Although reconstitution did not come effectively until 1848 there were two other significant attempts between the death of the Faculty of Advocates' initiative in 1767 and the introduction of the Entail Amendment Bill. The first of these has already been alluded to—the Commons Select Committee of 1828 which recommended fundamental changes in the nature of the entail. A Bill was drawn up and presented to Parliament in 1829 but was found to be defective.[239]

A further Select Committee reported in 1833 again favouring radical reform, resolving:[240]

"That considering the great extent of land in Scotland now held under the fetters of strict Entail, and the serious evils arising therefrom, both to individuals and to the public at large which must continue to exist and to increase if provision be not made to modify the principle of perpetuity in all such cases; it is highly important that a measure should be devised by which the principles to be established for the regulation of the future settlement of land, shall be let in upon existing Entails at the earliest period at which this object can be effected with a due regard to the rights and interests of individuals."

A Bill was drafted and sent to Edinburgh for comments from the Lords of Session. These again showed the proposed provisions to be defective, chiefly, it may be said, in that they could be avoided with ease.[241] Also criticised was the fact that the terminology of the Bill was that of English law and not Scots law, a fact which was hardly surprising since the stated and accepted aim of

---

[238] See *Baird* v *Baird* (1844) 6 D 643 esp. at pp. 650, 651 per Lord Justice-Clerk Hope and at p.655 per Lord Moncrieff.
[239] Parliamentary Papers 1828 (198) (404) vol. vii; 1829 (102) vol. iii.
[240] *ibid*. 1833 (109) vol. xvi.
[241] Reply of the Lords of Session on the Entails (Scotland) Bill 1835; Parliamentary Papers 1835 (163) xlvi. "Thus the entailer may settle his estate on a series of persons, for example, his children and their issue successively in liferent, for the liferent use of each allenarly, and to a 3rd party and to his heirs whatsoever in fee. As the law of Scotland stands it does not appear that there is anything to prevent a series of liferents of this nature being effectual and the power of each liferenter, though not the same as that of a Scottish Heir of Tailzie or an English tenant in tail, will greatly resemble both insofar as the Use of the Subject is concerned, and that for an indefinite period.

Thus also the estate may be settled on a series of Heirs with a Clause of Devolution of the Fee whenever the Heir in Possession attains the age of 21 years (or if he has attained that age before the succession opens to him) in favour of the next substitute being a Minor under condition that the substitute from whom the estate has just passed, shall retain the rents during his life and with the Power of Management or such other powers as the entailer chooses to confer on him.

Thus also a man may entail his land on a series of persons all in life at the date of the Entail, expressly including the heirs of each substitute; a settlement competent by the law of Scotland, though it is believed to be otherwise by the law of England, but with a power to each, as he comes into possession, to burden to the amount of the rents, or to any other amount in favour of the issue successively, or in favour of any other line of Persons he may select. If the Series is numerous, the Entail must continue till the last life drops, which may not be for a century."

the reform was to remodel the Scots entail in the image of the English.

Fundamental reform came eventually in 1848. The Bill was unopposed and incorporated anti-avoidance measures to deal with the devices suggested by the Lords of Session and others, such as the possible use of successive leases, liferents and trusts to create a perpetuity.

The Act changed the whole basis of constitution of entails. No longer was the creator of an entailed settlement required to spell out the prohibitions and the consequences of contravening them; prohibitive, irritant and resolutive clauses were to be implied in future entails, provided that there was present a clause directing registration.[242] With regard to existing entails, if it was found that they were defective in some way, they would cease to be valid even inter haeredes; if a deed of entail was defective in one respect it was to be treated as wholly defective.[243]

We have seen the extensions of the powers of feuing, of leasing, of excambion and of family provision. In addition, powers to sell the estate and to charge it with debts, subject to the appropriate consents being obtained, were also given.[224] But perhaps the most important feature of these extended powers was the reversal of effect of the House of Lords decisions in the Ascog, Tillicoultry and Tinwald cases,[245] in that for the future any capital money produced had to be expended for the purposes of the entail; specifically, after paying off debts, expenses, etc. it was to be used (if in excess of £200) for the purchase of additional lands to be entailed under the original entail.[246] In other words, while the Act prevented such a perpetuity as might render the land inalienable, it might still be possible to create a perpetuity of beneficial interests in that no proprietor could hold the settled estate in such a way that he could realise the estate and treat the proceeds as his own. It transformed, by these measures, an entailed settlement into a kind of quasi-trust with the entailed proprietor a sort of quasi-trustee, with powers of fiduciary nature to enable him to deal with the subject of the settlement for the benefit of those entitled thereunder. Thus, in this sense, what can be seen as the culmination of the Dalrymple doctrine effected this change.

But the Act went much further. Its avowed purpose was to assimilate the Scots law of entail to the English law of entail as far as possible. Under English law the possibility of perpetuity was prevented by the right of the tenant in tail in possession to disentail, a right which, since 1833,[247] had been rendered easier to exercise with the abolition of the old fine and recovery procedure and its replacement with a new species of conveyance whereby entailed land might be transferred free from the settlement. This right to disentail was now given to heirs of entail in possession in Scotland. The provisions of the 1848 Act in effect permitted any heir of entail born after the passing of the Act and, in the case of post-statute entails, born after the creation of the entail, to disentail without any consents, provided he was sui juris and in possession.

---

[242] 11th & 12th Vict. c. 36 section 39.
[243] *ibid.* section 43.
[244] *ibid.* section 4.
[245] See above at notes 154-156.
[246] 11th & 12th Vict. c. 36 section 26.
[247] Fines and Recoveries Act, 1833.

Consents were needed however for disentailment by heirs of tailzie born before the passing of the Act, except where they were unnamed and where there were no substitute heirs in existence. The consents, where needed, were those of the next three substitutes (or of all the substitutes in existence if three or less).[248] In addition creditors of the heir of tailzie in possession were permitted to force a disentailment in certain cases of insolvency.[249]

The 1848 Act, then, permitted the breaking of the settlement itself; no longer would it be possible for a landowner to ensure by his own deed that his estates were retained in the family. If they were to be so retained his heirs would be responsible for such retention.

In England landowners had come to terms with this problem by the device of settlement and resettlement whereby the tenant in possession usually managed to secure that his son enjoyed only a limited interest which prevented him from disposing of the estate during his lifetime.[250] In Scotland the same device was resorted to and brought forth the complaint that, whatever might be the theoretical possibilities of the Rutherfurd Act, in fact, land was scarcely more marketable after than before its passing, and that agricultural development had not noticeably improved as a result of the new freedom given by the Act.

A principal proponent of this view was John (afterwards Lord) McLaren who, in a paper published in 1869, articulated the point. He wrote:[251]

"The Act of Lord Rutherfurd (passed in 1848) was intended to limit the duration of entails. It was a very important step in that direction; and it has this merit, that it removed one great obstacle to future legislation, by doing away with the vested interests of expectant heirs to a very large extent. But without wishing to detract from the merits of this excellent legislative measure, I may say that I do not believe it will accomplish the object which its author is understood to have had in view—the gradual extinction of entails: and for this reason, that its provisions are merely permissive, and they can only be put in force by the heirs of entail themselves—that is, by the parties who are most strongly interested in maintaining the system. According to Lord Rutherfurd's Act, an heir born after 1st August, 1848, on coming into possession of the estate, and being of full age, may disentail the estate. But as the law stands, he may immediately re entail it, either upon the same or upon a different series of heirs: and the new entail, on being recorded, will be binding until the estate shall come into the possession of an heir born after its date, that is for at least two generations. It will be binding, not only against the maker and his successors but against creditors whose rights are subsequent to it in date. No doubt the power of disentailing will be largely used for the purpose of paying off or securing family provisions; but there is just as little doubt that, as soon as these objects are accomplished, the estate will be re entailed[252] and very little entailed land will find its way into the market. The effect of Lord Rutherfurd's Act, when it comes into full operation, is to place the law of entail on the same footing as that in England; and the practice, in England has been to resettle the property after getting as much money as is required secured upon it. The effect of such a system upon the cultivation of the soil is even worse than that of a system of strict entail.[253] Under

---

[248] 11th & 12th Vict. c. 36 sections 1-3.
[249] *ibid.* sections 25; 30.
[250] For a full description of the process of settlement and resettlement see Cheshire—The Modern Law of Real Property (11th Ed. 1972) pp.70-82.
[251] "Papers of the Scottish Law Amendment Society on the Law of Entail" (1869) 13 Journal of Jurisprudence 436 at pp. 440-441.
[252] Compare this with the English position. See Cheshire cited above at note 250.
[253] For a detailed amplification of this point with regard to settled estates in England, dealing with the agricultural position and that arising out of the Industrial Revolution see Sir Arthur Underhill "A Century of Law Reform" at pp.284 et seq.

the old law an heir of entail succeeding to an improvident proprietor, took the property unencumbered, and might, if so disposed, expend part of his revenues on its improvement. Under the new law he will take it heavily mortgaged, deprived of the means of improving the land, and without power of bringing it onto the market except by purchasing the consents of the next three heirs of entail."

Legilsation during the remainder of the century did little to attack this practice. The basic traditional approach of Scottish conveyancing legislation reasserted itself and the amending legislation, the Entail Amendment (Scotland) Acts of 1853,[254] 1868,[255] 1875,[256] 1878[257] and the Entail (Scotland) Act of 1882,[258] was largely concerned only with detailed amendments to procedure, with assimilating the consent rules of pre- and post- 1848 entails, and with the general amplification of the removal of restraints on, the exercise of management powers.

A similar programme of piecemeal reform was undertaken in England and, after 1848, an attempt was made to keep the laws of England and Scotland with regard to settled estates in step with each other. However, just as in Scotland prior to 1848, it became increasingly felt that piecemeal detailed reforms were insufficient. As Cheshire relates:[259]

"About this time an agitation sprang up for the total abolition of life estates and the restriction of grants to the creation of a fee simple, the argument being that settlements, beside making conveyances difficult and costly, deprived a father of a much needed power of control over his eldest son, and prevented the estate from being thrown on the market when its poverty made such a course desirable. For better or worse the argument did not prevail. It was realised that settlements enabled a fair and reasonable provision to be made for all the members of a family, and therefore, while the general features of the time honoured system were retained, a plan was evolved to prevent settled land from becoming an inert mass through lack of caiptal or of adequate powers of management."

This plan was embodied in the Settled Land Act of 1882 whose principles were carried forward in modified form into the Settled Land Act 1925, which forms the basis of the present English law of landed settlements.

In Scotland the same agitation was apparent and similar pleas for restrictions on the employment of liferents and entails in settlements were heard. Thus McLaren writes:[260]

"It does not appear to me that the principle of Lord Rutherfurd's Act admits of any further extension. The utmost that could be done in that direction would be to make the entail come to an end of itself when the estate came into the possession of an heir born after the date of the settlement, instead of giving the heir a mere power to disentail. But this does not meet the real difficulty, which, as I have explained, arises from the power of re-entailing the estate, which power will, of course, exist as long as entails are permitted, even for a limited period. It humbly appears to me, therefore, that there is only one way by which is by depriving the landowner of the power which he at present possesses of settling his estates upon a series of heirs in succession to each other. Here, however, it is necessary to pause for the purpose of considering how far it is possible or desirable to set a limit to the creation of life-interests. In the Act to which I have referred, clauses were inserted restricting the operation of liferents and estates

---

[254] Statute 16 & 17 Vict. c. 94.
[255] *ibid.* 31 & 32 Vict. c. 84.
[256] *ibid.* 38 & 39 Vict. c. 61.
[257] *ibid.* 41 & 42 Vict. c. 28.
[258] *ibid.* 45 & 46 Vict. c. 53.
[259] The Modern Law of Real Property (11th Ed.) at pp.77/78.
[260] (1869) 13 Journal of Jurisprudence at pp.441-442.

in trust within the same limits as were assigned to entails. It was obvious that a series of liferent rights was only a particular way of making an entail, and all the arguments that can be used against the system of entails established by the Scottish statute, apply equally to entails in the form of liferents. On the other hand, a simple liferent right is a convenient mode of making a family provision, where the intention is to give the legatee an annuity with the benefit of real security. In all, or almost all, systems of jurisprudence, liferent provisions to widows have been respected by the law. In such cases the fee or capital is usually given to the children: and the different members of the testator's family are thus provided for in a manner that is felt to be just and convenient. To some extent the same considerations apply to the case of liferent provisions to married daughters, where the fee is given to the children. As a general rule however I should say that the system of giving only a liferent to children and the fee to grandchildren, was neither consonant to reason, nor beneficial in practice. But the legislator, who looks to general results, and recognises the impossibility of providing for particular cases, will give the preference to a mode of succession which, subject only to the widow's annuity, provides for the children of the family by an immediate division of the inheritance. In the case of succession to land the admitted inconveniences which result from the policy of tying up estates for periods measured by the duration of life are such as to outweigh any advantages that may be supposed to accrue from it. My own opinion is therefore against the admissibility of liferents of heritable estate, except in favour of widows . . . . and that in all cases land, which was the subject of inheritance, ought to descend in fee simple to the objects of the disposition. If this should be thought too great a step in advance to be immediately taken, it would at least be desirable to prohibit the creation of liferents in succession. Where two persons are appointed to take life-interests, the one after the other, the person named as the second liferentor, if he survive the first, ought to take the estate in fee simple. The same rule ought to apply to existing entails. Any person taking under the entail after the institute (or first taker) should be held to take as under a simple destination, and should, without executing any instrument of disentail, or obtaining the authority of the Court, be entitled to sell or burden the estate, or alter the succession at his pleasure."

However, unlike the position in England, where the reforms effectively created a statutory trust under which the land was to be held and managed for the benefit of all those entitled under the settlement, the reformers had become convinced abolitionists, feeling that the factors which had prevailed in England (namely the facility for family provision) could be adequately met by other means. Accordingly the power to re-entail was eventually taken away by the Entail (Scotland) Act of 1914[261] which prohibited the future creation of entailed settlements.

Yet the reforms did not go much further; certainly they did not attempt to abolish liferents; still less did they attempt to abolish entails per se. The hope of Dalrymple, and of Rutherfurd, however, seemed at last in sight. The entail would now wither away with the passage of time.[262] And as the twentieth

---

[261] Statute 4 & 5 Geo. V section 2.

[262] Although no longer presenting a perpetuity problem the precise extent to which this withering away has progressed is uncertain.

In 1958 Professor Monteath, in his Chapter on "Heritable Rights" in the Stair Society's "Introduction to Scottish Legal History" (vol. 20) expressed the view (at p.177) that there must be well over 1000 entails in existence. In an attempt to verify and bring this figure up to date the present writer spent many days in Register House working through the volumes that constitute the Register of Entails. It soon became clear, however, that it was impossible to arrive at any meaningful, still less, accurate figure either for 1958 or 1975.

It is unfortunate that Professor Monteath does not provide any basis for his assertion; still less does he give any indication as to what factors he took into account. If the figure

century progressed the increasing burden of capital taxation would give it every encouragement to do so.[262a]

Perpetual Settlements

Unlike the position in England, as we have seen, the courts were not able effectively to break the entail in Scotland, and accordingly therefore the growth of other types of perpetual settlement in Scotland can scarcely be attributed, as it can in England, to attempts by settlers simply to secure the inalienability of the subjects settled.

Instead, in Scotland the growth of other types of perpetual settlement seems to have been influenced by two factors; first, by the limitations of the entailed settlement, and secondly, by any increasing awareness that the interposition of a trust between the subjects and the beneficiaries could overcome most of these limitations.

This is not to say that there could not be and were not perpetual settlements created outwith the trust framework: indeed as the evidence of the Lords of Session showed, effects similar to those achieved with an entail could be obtained by a series of successive liferents, provided the fee could be vested effectively in someone during the period of the subsistence of the liferents, or by a series of defeasible fees coupled with income provisions for those defeated.[263] But these types of settlement suffered from precisely the same defects as the strict entail.

---

[262] *continued*

of 1000+ represents a judgement drawn from his personal experience of dealing with entails, it clearly is incapable of being checked.

If however it is based on an examination of the Register, not only is the figure itself surprising, but even more so is the supposition that a meaningful figure could be obtained from this source for, in the first place, the Register does not contain a complete record of property which was subjected to entailed settlement. Many settlements were made, whose deeds were recorded in the Books of Council and Session, but which do not appear in the Register of Tailsies (and which would accordingly not be within the protection of the Act of 1685).

But even confining calculations to those based on entries in the Register, one has to proceed with great care. The first pitfall is that not only lands per se were capable of entailment, but in fact any feudal right or document connected therewith. Accordingly within the folios of the Register one may find entails of salmon fishings, superiorities, right to appoint livings, one may come across Bonds of Provision, Agreements, Decreets of Declarator, Deeds of Restriction, Deeds of Instruction, Additional Obligements and such like. A simple count, therefore, with a subtraction of disentails, revocations and renunciations (which would, in fact, produce a figure well in excess of 1600) is highly misleading. Even a more careful sifting, relating subsequent registrations to existing entails where appropriate, while doubtless producing a less inaccurate picture is still highly unsatisfactory.

The reason is that, especially prior to 1848, many entails were broken privately, either by the Heir of Entail's managing to discover some defect in the deed or formal requirements, or by an enforced sale, brought about by the necessity to satisfy the entailer's debts which would be recoverable out of the estate, provided they were incurred prior to registration. An inspection of the Register will show how very many entails remained unregistered for years after the execution of the deed. Accordingly therefore it is really impossible to derive a meaningful figure from the Register representing the number of entails in existence. A statement of the transactions entered on the Register from its inception is contained in the Appendices to the Thesis on which this Volume is based and is to be found in Edinburgh University Library.

[262a] See below, Chapter VI.

[263] See above at note 241.

The limitations were really of two kinds. In the first place, after some hesitation,[264] it was held that the Act of 1685 only applied to subjects which were capable of being feudalised,[265] with the result that moveables could not be entailed[266] nor indeed could some heritable rights such as those obtained under an assignation of a lease.[267] Accordingly, then, if it was desired to settle moveable property or a combination of moveables and heritage the entail would be inappropriate.[266] The easiest, if not the only, way to get round this difficulty was to use the trust.

The second limitation comes from the very nature of the entail, from its emphatic assertion of the principle of primogeniture, from the fact that it operated step by step, with substitute succeeding substitute. In the absence of express provisions in the deed it was impossible until the Aberdeen Act[268] to secure portions for dependents, and even here this had to be achieved without violating the principle of the proprietor's right to the whole of the fee. It was possible to make provision for younger children by creating separate settlements in their favour, but if one wished to provide for grandchildren per stirpes the strict entail was a cumbersome way of doing it; if one wished to go further, it was virtually impossible. The interposition of a trust however alleviated these problems. Thus in *McNair* v *McNair*[269] Robert McNair was proprietor of some houses in Glasgow, some land in the neighbourhood thereof and moveable property. He conveyed the whole lot to his son and his heirs whomsoever successively (as set out in the deed) as trustees to give effect to the following purposes:

(a) to pay the settler's debts;
(b) to make payment of certain provisions to his widow, daughter, sons, etc.;
(c) to make payment of certain sums to the descendants of the testator on their attaining the age of 25 years, for all time coming; and
(d) for each succeeding trustee to be entitled to 5% of the rents and profits during his trusteeship, the provision, again, to operate for all time coming.

By a supplementary deed of trust, executed a few months before his death, it was provided that any surplus income was to be accumulated and distributed every seven years among his children and descendants in such proportions as were allocated under the settlement.

The Court, albeit with some hesitation and reluctance, upheld the validity of these provisions, provisions which, irrespective of the inclusion of moveable property, could scarcely have been achieved by way of strict entail.

A third feature of the early perpetual trust settlement in Scotland was the way it could be used more effectively, and comprehend more than an ordinary strict entail, providing for a form of accumulation trust.

---

[264] For examples of furniture and money entailed see Appendix I to the Thesis 'Perpetuities in Scots Law' to be found in Edinburgh University Library.
[265] *Dalyell* v *Dalyell* 17th Jan. 1810 F.C.; *Howdens* v *Rocheid* 1869 7 M. (H.L.) and cases cited there.
[266] *Baillie* v *Grant* 1859 21 D. 838.
[267] *Earl Dalhousie* v *Ramsay-Maule* 1782 M. 10963.
[268] Statute 5 Geo. IV c. 87.
[269] (1791) Bell's Cas. 547; See also note to 5 W. & S. 187.

It had always been possible (and entails were frequently found embodying this principle) for an entailer to direct that surplus income from the estate should be used for the purchase of additional lands which were to be entailed on the terms and condition of the original settlement. In the *Barholm Case, McCullogh* v *McCullogh and others*,[270] this idea was extended to a remarkable degree. The facts are extremely complex and concern five distinct settlements:

Settlement No. 1: A strict entail of the estates of Barholm and Peble.

Settlement No. 2: A deed of trust whereby all debts owing to the settler, all money (heritable and moveable), rents, arrears of rents and more particularly the rents from his whole estate for 60 years, from the first term preceding the death of the survivor of the settler and his wife for the following purposes:

(a) the payment of his, and his wife's, debts and funeral expenses.

(b) the purchase of lands in the neighbourhood of Barholm and to add such purchases to the entail in Settlement No. 1.

(c) the purchase of other lands in favour of the second son of his grandson, John McCullogh and the heirs whatsoever of his body, with remainders over and a clause of return.

(d) for effecting similar purchases for the third, son of the said John McCullogh with remainders over and a clause of return.

(e) for effecting similar purchases for the fourth, fifth and other sons of the said John McCullogh with destinations over and a clause of return.

(f) for ensuring that all lands so purchased were settled under strict entail with substantially the same provisions and conditions as Settlement No. 1 provided that the trustees should not denude of the purchases until such time as the younger great grandchildren should be married and that, in the meantime the rents from such purchases should be added to the trust fund for the making of further purchases.

(g) that if any funds remained after these purchases, they should be applied in such a way that like purchases of land should be made for the behoof of the settler's great great grandchildren, and that such purchases also were to be settled in the form of strict entails with substantially the same provisions and conditions as in Settlement No. 1.

---

[270] Nov. 28, 5 W. & S. 180. Note that this was the first Barholm Case. After the settlement here was broken a further action followed on the original entail, see *Gordon* v *Dewar* 25th January 1771 M. 15579.

Settlement No. 3: This consisted of a second Deed of Trust whereby there were transferred to the trustees the entire rents from his Barholm and Peble estate together with other landed subjects on similar though not identical trusts to those of Settlement No. 2. It was however an essential part of this trust that the rents be settled on strict entail.

Settlement No. 4: This consisted of a resettlement of Barholm on the settler and his wife in liferent and then to the said John McCullogh in strict entail in accordance with the provisions of Settlement No. 1.

Settlement No. 5: This consisted of a deathbed settlement of recently acquired lands on the terms of Settlement No. 4.

It will be seen that by the joint operation of these settlements the settler had attempted to tie up not only the property (which is the case with an ordinary strict entail and which was quite permissible), but also the income from the estate for a long period after his death. For the pursuer, the son, John McCullogh, it was argued that [271] the law would not permit such "preposterous provisions, locking up estates for ages, securing from them the best possible advantage to his family and leaving his immediate descendants in poverty and ignorance" and further that:[271]

"If a settlement having such an object be sustained there is no point where you can stop. Ingenious conveyancers will speedily devise clauses whereby not merely property, but the first fruits of that property may be locked up for generations."

The Court reduced the settlements which provided for the locking up of the rents and profits on the basis that the provisions contained therein were contradictory and irrational, and therefore inextricable.

Having seen, then, the factors which brought about a widening of the perpetuity concept beyond the limits of the strict entail it remains to consider how and why the courts upheld the validity of perpetual trust settlements, and how they could be impeached.

Legality

The case which is regarded as establishing the principle of perpetuity in Scots law is that of *McNair* v *McNair*,[272] confirmed, as it was in *Suttie* v *Suttie's Trustees*.[273] An examination of these two decisions reveals that the perpetual trust settlements there were upheld by analogy with entails and with mortifications.

(a) The Analogy with Entails

At first sight it seems strange that a perpetual trust settlement should be upheld on the basis of an analogy with entails. We have, after all, seen how the courts have generally applied a rule of strict interpretation to entails, and how in the case of *Bryson* v *Chapman*[274] it had been held that the interests of the sub-

---

[271] 5 W. & S. (Note) at p.184.
[272] Bell's Cas. 542; 5 W. & S. at p.187.
[273] (1846) 18 Jur. 442.
[274] 22nd January 1760 M. 15511.

stitute heirs under an entail, which were said to arise from the prohibitions, were not capable of founding inhibitory diligence, so that the inalienability of property entailed otherwise than in accordance with the requirements of the Act of 1685 could not be secured by other means. In view, therefore, of the courts' policy with regard to entails, that question arises as to how it was that a settlement which, it was admitted, was "an entail in a new from" came to be sanctioned?

Certainly this fact caused considerable discomfort among some members of the court in *McNair*. Thus Lord President Campbell felt:[275]

"The appointing each succeeding heir to be a trustee, and to be liable in a certain distribution among the descendants progressively at their age of 25 in all time coming .... would, if sanctioned by this Court lay the foundation for a new species of entail not hitherto recognised in the law of Scotland, and therefore of dangerous example, being wild and extravagant in its nature ....

In the answers it is said the object of this deed was to secure the capital of the grantor's fortune to his children and their descendants, and that this trust should be perpetual. What is this but an entail in a new form, viz. that of a trust deed vested in the heirs themselves for the behoof of themselves and those interested in the succession, in among whom the rents and produce are to be divided in all time coming, not for the preservation of the family by having one representative succeeding another in a certain order, and enjoying successively the whole benefit of the estate, but by a partition of the rents among all the members of the family, and still carrying the succession to the remotest generation."

But the trust was nevertheless upheld and there appear to have been two facets of the entail that were considered relevant: first, that although the trust gave no power of sale to the trustees, the property was not rendered inalienable. To quote Lord President Campbell again:[276]

"The case of a perpetual trust in the individual owner of an estate, himself and his heirs forever succeeding to that estate, declaring the right to be vested in them indefeasibly for certain ends and purposes is a novelty both in law and practice. The mere name of a trust cannot tie up their hands, for if they succeed to the fee of the estate, they must have the power of disposal . . . ."

The second is perhaps more important and derives from the rule that even under a defective entail the obligations under which the proprietor took the property, while clearly not valid against third parties who had provided consideration, might yet be valid inter haeredes. Indeed we have seen that, given the necessary prohibitions, the entailed proprietor could be prevented from alienating gratuitously, and that prior to the decisions in the *Ascog, Tillicoultry* and *Tinwald* cases[277] the substitute heirs were considered as having a jus crediti enforcible against the proprietor to repair any loss suffered as a result of acts in breach of the obligations. It will be remembered that the *McNair* case was decided during this period, and indeed Lord President Campbell refers to this principle specifically.[278]

If, therefore, the courts were prepared to sanction schemes whereby, although the subject of a defective entail might be alienated for value, the proceeds of such alienations had to be reinvested for the benefit of those entitled under the entail—which, like the McNair trust, might go on for ever—why should they

[275] 5 W. & S. at p.189/190.
[276] *ibid*. at p.190.
[277] 14th July 1830, 4 W. & S. 196; 240; & 256 respectively.
[278] 5 W. & S. at p.189.

not sanction a scheme whereby the subjects of a trust settlement might equally be alienated, but where the beneficiaries under the trust had a jus crediti enforcible against the trustees in similar fashion. It has been remarked above that the effect of the pre 1830 cases on defective entails was to create a sort of quasi-trust; if such a quasi-trust could countenance its beneficiaries continuing to perpetuity, why should not a genuine trust also?

It would seem, then, that in 1791 when the *McNair Case* was decided the application of the entail analogy to uphold a perpetual trust settlement was not unreasonable. But it will be remembered that this right to compel reinvestment of the funds produced by an alienation for value was negatived by the House of Lords and the cases applying it treated as wrongly decided. Can it be said, then, that the *McNair Case* was overruled also, and that the application of the *McNair* principle in *Suttie's Case*[279] in 1846 was wrong?

The answer would appear to be that the decisions in the *Ascog* and associated cases left the *McNair* decision untouched in that they in no way impeached the principle that beneficiaries having a jus crediti might compel reparation (whether by way of reinvestment or otherwise) for every loss incurred in breach of the obligation owed to them. What was decided was that the substitute heirs under a defective entail had no such jus crediti enforcible against the heir in possession for alienations made for onerous causes. Where, therefore, the jus crediti was present—as it was in the trustee-beneficiary relationship—it would continue to be enforcible.

(b) The Analogy with Mortifications

The second strand of authority used by the court in *McNair* and *Suttie* was that of mortifications and public trusts.

Originally mortifications were feudal or feudal-type grants of land in favour of the Church or some ecclesiastical body in return for nominal services, usually that prayers be said, or masses be read for the donor after his death, for ever. They were the Scottish equivalent of the grants in Frankalmoign of English law.[280] Unlike the position in England however these grants were not made subject to the restrictive and effective mortmain legislation, introduced originally in the last years of Henry III, emphatically reinforced by Edward I and continued into the nineteenth century.[281] The original reason for this legislation was the economic damage caused by these grants to the interests of the seigneurs. The point was that grants in favour of the Church as an undying corporation would yeild no incidents, and with such nominal services would tend to eliminate any income yield; further, such a grant would almost invariably withdraw the subject land from commerce because of the restrictions on alienation imposed on ecclesiastical bodies by the Canon Law. In account of this, then, land so granted was regarded as having been placed under a "dead hand" (mort-main).

---

[279] (1846) 18 Jur. 442.
[280] See Craig I, 11. 20 & 21; Clyde translation at p.189/190.
[281] See above Chapter II. There was a Scottish mortmain Act passed in 1391 restricting such grants without royal licence—A.P.S. i. 577. But its effect appears to have been negligible

That Scotland was without such legislation would seem to be due principally to the more powerful position of the feudal superior under Scots law as compared with an English seigneur. Accordingly, the requirement of the superior's consent, which lasted in Scotland for several centuries after it had disappeared in England,[282] was felt to be sufficient.

Almost all of the institutional writers have made some mention of mortifications,[283] but perhaps, for our purposes the most relevant treatment is that of Erskine, who wrote:—[284]

"Feudal subjects granted in donations to churches, monasteries or other corporations, for religious, charitable or public uses, or said to be given in mortmain, or, in our law—style, to be mortified, either because all casualties must necessarily be lost to the proprietor, where the vassal is a corporation, which never dies, or because the property of those subjects is made over to a dead hand, which cannot, contrary to the donor's intention transfer it to another . . . .

The purposes for which the lands had been given to the Church in the times of Popery were, after the Reformation, accounted superstitions, and therefore [such lands were] declared to belong to the Crown by the act of annexation, 1587 c. 29, so that now the only lands which continue mortified to the Church are the manses and glebes of parochial ministers which by that statute are appropriated to the use of the reformed clergy. But moritfications may still be granted in favour of hospitals, either for the subsistence of the aged and infirm, or for the maintenance and education of indigent children, or in favour of universities or other public lawful societies, to be holden either in blench or in feu farm."

In their original form, then, the grants had the features of being perpetual and of rendering the subjects inalienable. In their more modern form these two features of perpetuity have continued; indeed any grants to the perpetual use of a school, college, hospital, for the relief of the poor and such like can be said to be mortified.

Although such grants might still be made direct to the appropriate corporation it became increasingly common during the seventeenth and eighteenth centuries to effect the grants by way of trust. And indeed in the case of one mortification of property in Edinburgh a private Act of Parliament was obtained to confer the legal status of a trust upon it.[285] Accordingly therefore at the time of the *McNair Case* there could be cited several examples[286] of trusts intended and designed to exist and operate in perpetuity, and it was to these that counsel turned. Thus the report sets out the point in the argument of counsel for the defenders:[287]

"The question therefore is whether a proprietor can vest his estate in a series of trustees, though it may happen that the trust may be perpetual? A trust of this nature is not reprobated by law; and in fact, many such exist in this country. Thus the management and revenue of Watson's and Heriot's hospitals are vested in trustees by a perpetual trust."

---

[282] See above; 'Alienation'.
[283] See Craig I. 10.35; II. 3.35; Clyde translation at pp. 168/169 & 419 respectively. Stair, II. 3.39 & 40; II. 4.20 & 67; II. 12.18. Bankton Vol. I at pp.558-561; Vol. II at pp.8-10; 46.
[284] Erskine II. 4.10 & 11.
[285] The Craigcrook Mortification.
[286] *City of Edinburgh* v *Binny* 1694 M. 9107; *Perth Hospital* v *Campbell* 1724 M. 5729; *Merchant Co. & Trades of Edinburgh* v *Governors of Heriot's Hospital* 1765 M. 5750.
[287] Bell's Cas. at p.550.

The question for the court was, therefore, whether they would extend the principle of perpetuity which applied to such public trusts to private trusts. Counsel for the pursuer attempted to draw a distinction between public and private trusts, but could find no principle of law on which to base such a distinction. The most he could say was that it would raise inconvenience. Accordingly the court accepted the analogy. As Lord Eskgrove said:[288]

"This deed might have been effectively conceived to a body corporate, with directions to employ the fund in paying provisions to all eternity: it must be equally valid when it is directed to the heir as trustee; and the heir entering under that deed must act in conformity with it."

And when in *Suttie* the same question was raised, Lord Mackenzie confirmed this approach. He said:[289]

". . . . it is the tendency of our law to supporting trusts; and this opinion receives the strongest sanction from the common practice. Nor is the duration of such trusts restricted by law. There are numerous instances in the case of mortifications, and of trusts for the foundation and maintenance of schools and hospitals and for othe; charitable purposes, which are so constituted as to be calculated to exist to perpetuity- but though such trusts have given rise to much litigation, they have never been chalr lenged on the ground of illegality because they were to endure to perpetuity."

Illegality

While the *McNair* and *Suttie Cases* established the principle that a settlement would not be invalid merely because it tended to perpetuity, nevertheless perpetuity could be a relevant factor in the court's deciding to reduce a deed. In these cases counsel employed a second line of attack; even if the settlement might not be set aside solely because it tended to perpetuity, might that settlement not be rendered inextricable by virtue of the perpetuity factor?

In the perpetuity cases decided on the common law rules the head of inextricability was used in three senses: first, that the settlement was unintelligible or contradictory; secondly, that its purpose was absurd; and thirdly that it was unworkable.

(a) Unintelligibility

The first settlement in which this ground was relied upon was that of the Barholm estates. As we saw, the complex accumulation trusts were ultimately reduced as being inextricable. While Lord Elchies'[290] report rests the decision on another head of inextricability, when the case came to be cited as authoritative in the *Strathmore Case*,[291] Lord Brougham appeared to prefer to accept the decision on the basis of the settlements' unintelligibility. He said:[292]

". . . . the decision in the Barholm case very possibly might have been different if the court had seen a plain, consistent and distinct intention on the part of the maker of the deeds, such as they plainly, clearly and consistently perceive to have existed in the mind of the maker of Lord Strathmore's deeds . . . . but when I find the settlement there [i.e. in Barholm] mixed up with such a mass of clauses, impossible to be construed that very nonsense of itself constitutes a material specialty, and prevents the case from applying as an authority to another case where no such specialty exists, but where a

---

[288] *ibid.* at p.553.
[289] (1846) 18 Jur. at p. 445.
[290] Elch. "Tailye" No. 48.
[291] (1831) 5 W. & S. 170.
[292] *ibid.* at pp. 195/196.

clear, consistent and intelligible sense is seen operating from the beginning to the end of a very short and single conveyance."

Whether one agrees with Lord Brougham or not on the intelligibility of the Barholm settlements it would seem that the factor of perpetuity here is irrelevant, the matter being solely one of construction.

(b) Absurdity

While it is clear that the court will not look sympathetically on any absurd or irrational disposition, it would seem that the fact that the disposition tends to perpetuity will add on additional edge to the court's attitude. The position was explained by Lord Campbell in *Jeffries* v *Alexander* in the following terms:[293]

"A man has a natural right to enjoy his property during his life, and to leave it to his children at his death, but the liberty to determine how his property shall be enjoyed in saecula saeculorum when he, who was the owner of it, is in his grave, and to destine it in perpetuity to any purposes however fantastical, useless or ludicrous, so that they cannot be said to be directly contrary to religion or morality is a right and liberty which, I think, cannot be claimed by any natural or divine law, and which I think, ought by human law to be strictly watched and regulated."

From Lord Elchies' report it would appear that the Barholm settlements were reduced on the ground of absurdity,[294] although quite why they were felt to be absurd is not made clear. Perhaps the best example of a settlement being reduced on this ground is the case of *Mason* v *Skinner*,[295] another accumulation trust, but one in which there appeared to be no purpose at all behind the provisions, the accumulation of wealth seemingly being felt to be an end in itself, such accumulation to continue in perpetuity. As Lord Fullerton said:[296]

"I do not hold that it is incompetent to make a settlement that is to last for ever; but then accumulation must have a definite object. The beneficial interests must merge immediately as in the case of a charitable endowment. Here not only is the fund to continue for ever, but the accumulations also are to continue for ever, and, without any definite object, making it impossible for any court to carry the testators intentions into effect. It is in fact a mere emulous accumulation."

Accordingly, then, a perpetual accumulation, with no purpose, or at least no intelligible purpose would be reducible as inextricable whereas a temporary one would not. In the latter case at the end of the accumulation period the property and accumulations must vest in someone (even if they merely revert back to the settler or his heirs); in the case of a perpetual accumulation however it would appear that all possibility of benefit is absent.

(c) Impracticability

The third type of case where perpetual settlements have been reduced as inextricable is where the intention to benefit is clear but where the implementation of the settler's purpose is impracticable. Here again the factor of perpetuity

---

[293] (1860) 8 H.L.C. 594 at p.648.
[294] Elch. "Tailye" No. 48—"This was a question of reducing two most ridiculous entails and trust rights whereby, excepting small aliments to the heir, the rents were to be applied for many years in purchasing other estates and [settling] them in the same manner. We all agreed to reduce the whole deeds."
[295] (1844) 16 Jur. 422.
[296] *ibid.* at p.425.

was relevant in that while it might be expedient to carry out the settler's trust for a temporary period, it would not be expedient to do so in perpetuity. Perhaps the best example of this is *McNair* v *McNair*[297] where, it will be remembered the court in 1791 refused to find that the settlement was inextricable and accordingly upheld it. However approximately twenty years later the same settlement was found to be unworkable and so was reduced.[298] Again, in *Mason* v *Skinner*[299] the trust, on accountancy evidence, was found to be unworkable, as well as pointless, and so was reduced.

Accordingly then, as with absurdity, the impracticality of carrying out a trust in perpetuity may constitute a good ground for setting it aside. However, here the perpetuity factor cannot stand alone; it must be read with and seen in the light of the other provisions of the deed.

Perpetuities and Perpetuity Rules

By 1846, then, the common law of Scotland had hesitatingly adopted the principle that settlements might subsist for the satisfaction of beneficial interests in perpetuity. In a sense this was still a subsidiary rule in a subsidiary branch of the law of settled estates. The principal type of settlement was still the entail and would continue to be until 1914. It was only then, when the means of resettlement were removed that conscious attempts achieve the same result were made in a spirit resembling that of the Elizabethan settlers in England. The files of some of the older Edinburgh firms detail attempts to create entails by various means, chiefly by types of successive liferent settlements. But by this time it was too late. The Entail Amendment Acts of 1848[300] and 1868[301] had imposed restrictions to counter such devices. From the middle of the nineteenth century, then, Scotland had a rule against perpetuities; and it is with this that Chapter IV is concerned.

---

[297] 1791 Bell's Cas. 542.
[298] Unreported, but referred to by Lord Cuninghame in *Mason* v *Skinner* at p.424. It is believed that the reduction took place sometime between 1811 & 1815.
[299] (1844) 16 Jur. 422.
[300] Statute 11 & 12 Vict. c. 36.
[301] Statute 31 & 32 Vict. c. 84.

CHAPTER IV

PERPETUITY RULES IN SCOTLAND

"The law against perpetuities in Scotland is entirely of statutory origin, the earliest provision being contained in the Entail Amendment (Scotland) Act 1848[1], sections 47 and 48, which related only to heritage. Provisions relating to moveable and personal estate on lines analogous to section 48 of that Act was made by section 17 of the Entail Amendment (Scotland) Act 1868.[2] This section was repealed and replaced by Section 9 of the Trusts (Scotland) Act 1921.[3]"[4]

While Lord Thankerton's statement has been partially superseded by events in that, with regard to liferent interests created after 25th November 1968, section 48 of the 1848 Act and section 9 of the Act of 1921 are no longer applicable, having been replaced by section 18 of the Law Reform (Miscellaneous Provisions) (Scotland) Act 1968,[5] the substance of it, that specific rules aimed at preventing perpetuities are creatures of statute, is undoubtedly corrent.

If criticism can be levelled at the statement, it must be on the basis that it does not present a complete picture in that it ignores the existence and operation of certain common law rules which, although not specifically designed for the purpose, nevertheless had the effect of defeating the tendency to perpetuity of certain types of settlement.

It will be remembered that in English law there existed certain rules which operated to limit the creation of contingent remainders and which were subsequently used to frustrate the effectiveness of perpetuities employing contingent remainders. The basic premise from which these rules were derived was the unacceptability of allowing a fee to be in pendente, or, as it was frequently expressed, the abhorrence of an abeyance of seisin.[6] Substantially the same premise obtained in Scotland too, although the emphasis was more on the pendent fee itself than on abeyance of sasine. As Farran observed:[7]

"[T]he whole English doctrine of escheat was based on the principle that if at any time the lord of the fee is left without a tenant, or one capable of holding land, the fee ceases to exist and the land belongs to the lord. The same principle was known in Scotland in theory. 'The superior is at all times entitled to have a vassal.'[8] But because of the different rules as to escheat the same consequences did not flow from it.

.... [W]hat English law abhors is a vacuum in the seisin, not in the fee simple, and the tenant for life is sufficiently seised .... It should [however] be noted at once that in the Scots view the rule has nothing particularly to do with sasine. Many occasions exist when there is no one with sasine of the land. Thus on every death in Scotland there was no one seised of the land (in the Scots sense) until the heir had made up his titles and received formal sasine from the superior, which might not occur for many years. Moreover the feudal casualty of non-entry only gave the superior a temporary right to enter on the lands in the interregnum, but he came in just because there was an abeyance of his vassal's sasine. What is not allowed to be in abeyance,

---

[1] Statute 11 and 12 Vict. c. 36.
[2] *ibid*. 31 and 32 Vict. c. 84.
[3] *ibid*. 11 and 12 Geo. V. c. 58.
[4] per Lord Thankerton in *Muir's Trustees* v *Williams* 1943 S.C. (HL) 47 at p. 51.
[5] Statute 1968 c. 70.
[6] See above Chapter II.
[7] Principles of Scots and English Land Law at pp. 219, 220 and 225.
[8] citing Bell, Principles at para. 1711.

then, in Scotland, is not the sasine, but the dominium . . . . The point is that there should never be a res without a dominus rather than that land should not lie without someone's being seised of it."

As we have seen, the English approach developed out of an attempt to safeguard the economic benefits of lordship by the device of giving seisin to the tenant for life which was then treated as enuring for the benefit of those interests which were in remainder.[9] Those interests would be in futuro in law as well as in fact and would be dependent for their existence on the validity and subsistence of the prior life estate. The "ownership", therefore, of land which was the subject of a destination involving one or more life interests would in a very real sense be divided.[10] In order that this division might not prejudice the lord's interest, as we have seen, there had to be someone in existence who would satisfy the vassal's obligations. In the case of contingent remainders this problem was met by avoiding any interest which did not vest in time. If, therefore, the contingency was satisfied in time the services were secured; if it was not, then the remainder was declared void so that the land reverted to the original grantor to whom the lord could now look for his services.

But even assuming the contingency to have been fulfilled there was the further problem of the remainderman's status on the death of the life tenant. On the one hand if he entered by virtue only of the destination it would seem that he should enter as purchaser since a life tenancy was not an inheritable estate. Accordingly, although he took as successor to the life tenant, the remainderman could hardly be said to be taking as his heir. But if he entered as purchaser the lord would lose his reliefs exigible on the entry of his vassal's heir.

While Bracton had designated the remainderman as a "quasi-heir who takes by substitution according to the form of the gift"[11] the question did not come before the courts for decision until the mid-fourteenth century. The first meaningful reference is in a case in 1350[12] in which, in the course of discussion, Willoughby J. observed that, "according to some people, when the fee is limited to the right heirs of a certain person, then the fee is in the ancestor". In 1366 a case arose[13] from which it transpired that land had been given to J for life, with remainder in tail to his eldest son, with remainder in fee to the right heirs of J. After the death of J, and on the extinction of the entail, R, the second son of J

---

[9] See Chapter II above.
[10] In contrast to the position in Scotland where liferents are, in theory at least, treated more as servitudes on the fee. Thus in *Studd* v *Studd's Trustees* (1880) 8 R 249 Lord Justice-Clerk Moncrieff explained (at p. 268): " . . . . a devise to a tenant for life and after his death to the use of another in tail male with remainders over is not equivalent to, but is entirely discrepant from a Scotch disposition to A in liferent and to B in fee. The difference is vital. A disposition to A in liferent and B in fee makes B the immediate proprietor under burden of the liferent and unless he is limited by the fetters of a strict entail he may sell, etc. . . . . although only under burden of the liferent. . . . . But a devise of real estate in England to A as tenant for life and then to B as tenant in tail male is . . . a gift in which the interest of the tenant in tail commences only when that of the tenant for life terminates and in which the validity of the grant for life is essential to support the grant in remainder. There is no fee in existence in the sense that we use the term other than the right for life while the tenant for life lives; although the interest in expectancy vests, and must vest, from the date of the grant."
[11] Bracton at ff. 68b, 69.
[12] YB.24 Edw. III 70 no. 79.
[13] YB.40 Edw. III f.9 no. 18.

entered as right heir, whereupon the seigneur, the provost of Beverley distrained for relief, which would be due if R had entered as heir, but not as purchaser. Thorpe C.J. said:

"You have pleaded that you ought not to have to pay relief since you are in as purchaser, being the first in whom the remainder takes effect according to the words of the deed. But you are in as heir to your father . . . . and the remainder was not entailed to you by your proper name but under the description of heir."

The report continues:

"And so it was awarded by all the justices that the lord should have return of the distress."

This case then is a clear precedent for the rule in *Shelley's case*[14] that a grant to A for life, with remainder to his heirs gave the fee to A, with the attendant result that the interest of the heirs was reduced to no more than a spes successionis, and that A could alienate. Furthermore where the remainder had been contingent, this principle carried the bonus of overcoming any conceptual difficulty as to abeyance of seisin; the fee was once and for all in A.

It was this self-same rule which operated in Scotland as a check on destinations tending to perpetuity. As Professor Wood put it:[15]

"Where heritable property is, by a deed, to take immediate effect, or granted by a third party, conveyed directly to a parent in liferent and his children unnamed in fee, notwithstanding the word liferent, the fee is in the parent with full right of disposal. The children have only a hope of succeeding. The ground of this principle is strictly feudal. The feudal idea was that a feu—a fee—could not be vacant, could not be in a person who did not yet exist. This doctrine has been said to be 'a triumph of legal subtlety over the intention of the maker of the deed'.[16] There is an analogous rule in England, where, in certain circumstances, what is nominally a life interest in real estate becomes truly a fee. This is called the rule in *Shelley's case.*"

The Common Law Rule

Surprisingly, perhaps, the rule is not discussed in depth by the institutional writers, most being content with a mere mention. Erskine, however, devotes a paragraph to it in an attempt to show that it had no foundation. He writes:[17]

"It is a rule almost universally received by our lawyers till towards the beginning of this century that Dominium non potest esse in pedenti, 'Property cannot float in an uncertainty, but must at every period of time be vested in some person or another.'[18] Lord Dirleton is the only writer of the last century who speaks doubtfully about it.[19] But it appears to have no foundation either in nature or in law. Many things are, ex sua natura, fit subjects of property, which nevertheless have no proprietor; those for example which the proprietor abandons with a design to be no longer owner of them, or waste lands of which no person hath yet seized the possession. In like manner, where the fee or property of any subject is granted to children yet to be procreated, and the bare liferent to the father and mother, the property of that subject must of necessity be pendant till the existence of a child.[20] And as by the Roman law all estates in haereditate jacente of persons deceased were without proper owners, so by ours, the fee is upon the death of all fiars in pedenti till the next heir shall make up his titles. The

---

[14] (1581) 1 Co. Rep. f.88b. See Challis—Real Property (3rd Ed.) at p. 154; Holdsworth H.E.L. vol. iii p. 107.
[15] Lectures on Conveyancing (1903) at p. 312.
[16] per Lord Ardmillan in *Cumstie* v *Cumstie's Trustees* 1880 3 R. at p. 927.
[17] II.1.4.
[18] citing Stair III.5.50 and Mackenzie h.t. 30.
[19] v. Fiar, Nos. 9 and 10.
[20] citing Steuart—Answers to Dirleton's Questions and Doubts on the Law of Scotland—Fiar.

necessity imposed by the law upon an heir to enter in order to establish the fee in his person is a demonstration that he is not fiar till he be entered."[21]

This view has been almost universally doubted and the difficulties raised by Erskine would seem to be difficulties more of semantics than substance. As Professor Bell points out:[22]

"The principle on which this [rule] rests is, that the superior on the one hand, and the vassal on the other, must have someone to fill the feudal place of vassal and superior; and that creditors shall be able to know with whom the right of property is. The fee, therefore, is not in pendente merely because of the death of the proprietor; for the creditors of the ancestor can affect it as in haereditate jacente, and the heir or anyone in his right, can take it, while in the feudal relation of superior and vassal the remedy is open to either. It is in pendente only when there is no one in whom it can be vested."[23]

The objection, then, is not to a gap in ownership per se, but to an unfillable gap, or one which cannot, by the nature of its creation, be filled for a considerable time, thus destroying the powers of property for its duration. Accordingly, abandonment of subjects, where the law permits this,[24] would not create a pendant fee so as to destroy the powers of property for any acquirer would be entitled to sell, dispone or otherwise deal with the subjects without restriction.

By definition, the second of Erskine's examples is inappropriate: pendency implies that the subjects were at one time owned. Waste lands, therefore, that have never been owned, would scarcely qualify.

The only objection of substance would seem to be the third one, the example of the settlement of property on parents in liferent and children in fee, and it was with this very situation that the common law attempted to deal.

The first case in which the issue came before the court was that of *Creditors of Robert Frog* v *His Children*[25] which concerned a disposition to A in liferent and to the heirs of his body nascituri in fee, which failing to B in liferent and the heirs of his body in fee, which failing to C. A contracted debts which he charged on the estate. The issue before the court was whether he had the fee; if he had, then the creditors could pursue diligence against the estate; if not, then the creditors were lost. The arguments revolved around the construction of the precise words of the destination and the fact that, if a construction limiting A's right to a liferent were allowed, the result would be that the fee would be in nobody. This, it was argued was contrary to the maxim of feudal law that a fee may not be in pendente but must be settled on some person in existence at the time of the disposition, "the reason for which maxim is, that it would be inconsistent with common sense to suppose a property without a proprietor; and if the contrary doctrine took place many absurdities would follow. Thus if the dominium directum were allowed to be pendant, the vassal could not be

---

[21] In support of his view Erskine cites two cases, *Douglas* v *Douglas and Drummond* 1724 M 12910 and *Gibson* v *Arbuthnot* 1726 M 11481, but in fact neither of these decisions appear to constitute authority for the propositions advanced. See Farran pp. 227/8.
[22] Principles at para. 1711.
[23] In *McIntosh* v *McIntosh* Jan. 28th 1812 F.C. Lord Meadowbank cites the notes of Lord Justice-Clerk Braxfield (Macqueen) from which it appears that the latter adopted the wide definition of pendency, at least with regard to the haereditas jacens, treating it as an exception.
[24] The feudal relationship would seem to render abandonment of feudalised land impossible, at least in the Erskine sense.
[25] 1735 M. 4262.

entered; if the dominium utile, the superior could not have a vassal; if the former proprietor had contracted debt, his creditors could not affect it, because there was no person from whom it could be adjudged; besides several others that might be mentioned".

It was held by the court that the interest of A "resolved into a right of fee" and that the estate was therefore available for the satisfaction of his debts.

Six years later, in 1741, a further case came before the court,[26] this time concerning a marriage contract settlement containing a disposition to the settler's son in liferent and to the children to be procreated by his body in fee. The court, expressly following the decision in *Frog's Creditors*, held that the fee was in the son. A note, however was appended to the report to the effect that the reason for the action being brought was that conflicting judgements had been delivered in *Frog's* case. After 1741 the validity of the rule was secure.[27]

Origins of the Rule

Given, then, the broad principle of feudal law that a fee might not be in pendente, the question arises as to why this particular rule, that a grant to A in liferent and to the heirs of his body (or some such similar destination) in fee gave the fee to A, came to be adopted to resolve the difficulty caused. The cases throw up two conflicting views, neither of which can be said to be completely satisfactory.

What might perhaps be termed the majority view is that "the rule was introduced from a legal necessity, contrary to what might have been presumed to have been the intention of the granter."[28] Thus in *Cumstie* v *Cumstie's Trustees*[29] Lord Ardmillan, reviewing the operation of the rule observed:

"Where a subject is conveyed to a father in liferent and his children nascituri in fee, and where the word 'allenarly' or some clearly equivalent word has not been used, it has been long settled that the fee is in the father, though he is termed liferenter in the deed. This has been so repeatedly decided that I need not detain you by referring to the authorities. The rule has been introduced in consequence of the feudal maxim that the fee cannot be in pendente, and that, the granter being divested, the fee can be nowhere else than in the liferenter, and thus a result not always according to the intention of the maker of the deed has been accomplished by the pressure of this nicety of feudal law."[30]

---

[26] 1741 M. 4267.
[27] It has been applied, not always consistently, for 200 years: see *Douglas* v *Ainslie* 1761 M. 4269; *Campbell* v *McNeil* 1766 M. 4287; *Porterfield* v *Graham* 1779 M. 4277; *Cuthbertson* v *Thomson & Graham* 1781 M. 4279; *Muir* v *Muir* 1786 M. 4288; *Duke of Atholl* v *Robertson* 20th Nov. 1806 F.C.; *Lindsay* v *Dott* 9th Dec. 1807 F.C(; *Maxwell* v *Gracie* (1822) 1S 509; *Dewar* v *Campbell* (1825) 1 W & S 161; *Kennedy* v *Allan* (1825) 2S 554; *Williamson* v *Cochran* (1828) 6S 1035; *Gordon* v *Mackintosh* (1841) 4D 192; affd. (1845) 4 Bell's App Cas 105; *Hutton's Trs.* v *Hutton* (1847) 9D 639; *Ferguson's Trs.* v *Hamilton* (1860) 22D 1442; affd. (1862) 24D (H.L.) 8; *Ranken and others* (1870) 8 M. 878; *Beveridge* v *Beveridge's Trs.* (1878) 5R 1116; *Williamson* v *Williamson's Trs.* (1881) 19 S.L.R. 276 (O.H.); *McClymont's Exors.* v *Osborne* (1895) 22 R 411; *Fraser's Trs.* v *Turner* (1901) 8 S.L.T. 466 (O.H.); *Mearns* v *Charles* 1926 S.L.T. 118 (O.H.); *Dalrymple's Trs.* v *Watson's Trs.* 1932 S.L.T. 480 (O.H.).
[28] per Lord Mackenzie in *Gordon* v *Mackintosh* (1841) 4 D 192 at pp. 200/201.
[29] (1876) 3 R 921 at p. 924.
[30] See also per Lord Corehouse in *Mein* v *Taylor* (1827) 5 S 779 at p. 781; Lord Brougham in *Gordon* v *Mackintosh* (1845) 4 Bell's App. Cas. 105 at p. 121; and esp. per Lord Cuninghame in *Mackellar* v *Marquis* (1840) 3 D 172.

It is to be observed that the proponents of this view are all ex post facto reviewers of the rule, seeking to justify its application in a particular case. Whether, and how seriously, this view of necessitas legis was put forward in the eighteenth century cases is virtually impossible to ascertain from the available reports. Indeed such contemporary reports as are sufficiently detailed to provide the grounds of the judgements tend to suggest the opposite view, that the rule in *Frog's Creditors* was really an implementation of the settler's intention. The difficulty, however, is that these reports are all of cases decided by one particular judge, Lord Braxfield (or Lord Justice-Clerk Macqueen as he is frequently referred to). The earliest report in which this view appears is that of *Gerran* v *Alexander*[31] which reads:

"The Lord Reporter [Lord Braxfield] observed that by many decisions it had been found that the fee was really in the parents, though the destination bore only in liferent to them, and in fee to their children: but that this was not ex necessitate as had sometimes been supposed, lest the fee should be in pendente. It was upon the presumed will of the granter, who only meant a spes successionis to be in the children; and therefore wherever there appeared to be a right of property in the children, the parents right was either limited to a mere liferent or considered as a trust fee which could be defeated."

This view was substantially repeated in *Preston* v *Wellwood* in 1791[32], in *Newlands* v *Creditors of Newlands* in 1794,[33] and in the case of *Rosehaugh*.[34] Authorities subsequent to Lord Braxfield however, while tending to base their decisions more and more on the supposed intention of the creator of the settlement have not expressed the basis of the rule in *Frog's Creditors* as being on such ground.[35] Indeed at first sight the idea seems absurd: if a destination purports to grant an interest in fee, how can it be said that those within the class to be benefited are intended only to have a spes successionis? It is true of course that a grant to A and his children in fee would confer the fee on A and only a spes on the children, but in the type of grant in question A's interest is specifically designated as a liferent: to give him the fee would surely be to go against the stated intention of the settler. Lord Braxfield's answer was reported by Lord Meadowbank in *McIntosh* v *McIntosh* as follows:[34]

"Taking then the rule that a fee cannot be in pendente, as universally applicable to cases like the present, and that the maxim uti quisque legasset, etc. ita jus esto is the general rule of law, thinks the court have put a natural construction on the grants that have been the subject of the decisions. We must construe the deed on these principles. 1*st* The donor has given away the whole from himself. 2*ndly* Must presume he knows fee cannot go to a person not existing. Then he must mean to give the fee to an existing person."

And as the only existing person involved would be the liferenter, the fee would go to him.

On the other hand an equally tenable construction would appear to be that whatever the difficulties of attempting to give the fee to a non-existent body,

---

[31] 1781 M. 4402.
[32] 1791 Bell's Cas. 191 at pp. 197/198.
[33] 1794 M. 4289; Ross Leading Cases vol. iii 634 esp. at p. 644.
[34] Referred to by Lord Meadowbank in *McIntosh* v *McIntosh* 28th Jan. 1812 F.C. where the notes of Lord Braxfield's opinion are set out in full in Lord Meadowbank's judgement.
[35] Although it has been resurrected by Wilson and Duncan in 'Trusts, Trustees and Executors' (Edinburgh 1975) at p. 62.

the mere grant of a liferent without more would seem to indicate that the powers of disposition, of sale, of burdening with debt were to be withheld from him: if this be the case how can giving him the fee be reconciled with the settler's intention? Lord Ardmillan's comment on this point would appear to be apposite. He said:[36]

"A conveyance to A and his heirs whomsoever confers on A the fee. A conveyance to A in liferent, and his children nascituri in fee has also been found to confer on A the fee. The result was effected by force of the feudal maxim of Scottish law what forbids the fee to float on poised wing till it finds a fitting settlement, and which demands that from the first the fee shall have a local habitation as well as a name.

The enforcement of this maxim by converting the liferent into a fee was not according to the intention of the maker of the deed. It was a triumph of legal subtlety over the intention of the maker of the deed and this was judicially felt and acknowledged in some of the earlier cases."

In *Preston* v *Wellwood*[37] Lord Braxfield reiterated his views but here added an extra dimension. He said:

"Though a father settling his estate in his marriage contract takes it to himself in liferent and the children of the marriage in fee, the father is construed to be fiar: 1*st* Because the fee cannot be in pendente and therefore must vest in him since there is no other in whom it can vest: 2*nd* Because there is a natural presumption that the father, though he intends to settle his estate on his child, means to retain the full property of it until his death. This has been decided often."

The idea then was a kind of "family-assets" theory; that, whatever the settlement said, it was intended that the father, as head of the family, should have full control over it. As Lord Braxfield stated, there were cases in support of this view. Thus in *Veitch* v *Robertson*[38] a husband disponed to his second wife an annualrent out of his land in liferent and to his children in fee. The question arose out of a sale by the children of the annualrent, the purchaser claiming a right superior to that of a purchaser of the land from the husband. It was held that notwithstanding the sasine given to the wife and children, the fee of the annualrent subsisted in the husband's person. Accordingly the husband's disposition of the land was not affected by the burden of the annualrent so that his purchaser took free from it. Again in *Wemyss* v *Mackintosh*[39] a sum of 2,000 marks was payable as tocher to a husband for the use of his wife and himself in liferent, and to the heirs of the marriage in fee. It was held that this disposition vested the fee in the husband and, as such, the sum was assignable and arrestable by his creditors.

The salient point about these cases, and about *Preston* v *Wellwood*, was that they all concerned settlements made by one party to a marriage in favour of the family, and as such the presumption that the husband/father should have the property of the subjects settled seems to have prevailed over the precise terms of the destination. The justification for such a course was set out by Baron David Hume:[40]

"I have said, that it is not readily to be presumed, that a person means to make over a part of his estate or funds from himself, in favour of his wife or her relations.

---

[36] In *Cumstie's* v *Cumstie's Trs.* (1876) 3 R 921 at p. 927.
[37] 1791 Bell's Cas. 191 at p. 197/198.
[38] 1630 M. 4256.
[39] 1672 M. 7257.
[40] Lectures on the Law of Scotland vol. iv at pp. 336/337 (Stair Soc vol. 17).

Now, neither is it a likely thing, that for his own lifetime he has any such intention in favour of his issue—persons who, by law and nature are dependant on him,—and who in the common case, it is equally right and salutary for him and them, that he should retain in that state of discipline and subordination. His opinion of their several deserts may happen to alter in the course of his life; his own circumstances and situation may alter; and he may have immediate occasion for the sums or subjects, on his own account, which had been invested in this joint form to himself and them. As long therefore, as there is room for construction,—and while the terms of the investiture will bear it, it shall always to understood, respecting a father who invests any part of his own funds in this sort of form, that he means to retain the fee—the power to use, spend and onerously dispose of the fund—in his own person; and to establish for his issue a right of succession merely on his death—a right which shall be subject therefore to all his debts and deeds,—and shall depand, as to the ultimate profit thereof, upon the existence of a free—an unencumbered—subject to make it good at that time."

However while there might be justification for such a construction where the settler was the parent, such considerations can hardly be given the same weight when the settlement was made by a third party.

There are two other lines of authority however for the construction of "liferent" in such a way as to give the parent the fee, which according to the words of the settlement, is apparently destined for the children.

The first is a destination in favour of the parties to a marriage in conjunct fee and liferent, and to the children of that marriage in fee. Thus in *Pearson* v *Martin*[41] under the terms of a marriage contract, subjects were payable to husband and wife in conjunct fee and liferent and to the heirs of the marriage in fee. On the death of the wife the question arose as to the location of the fee, there being no children. It was held to be vested in the husband. And again in *Creditors of Paterson & Anderson* v *Douglasses*[42] where the dispositive clause by an heiress in her marriage contract, in favour of her husband in liferent and the heirs of the marriage in fee, which failing to his heirs and assignees, reserving to herself a liferent, was found to give the fee to the husband; the basis of this decision was apparently that the obligement to infeft and procuratory of resignation were to him and her in conjunct fee and liferent and to the heirs of the marriage in fee.

But the difficulty with these cases is the inclusion of the word "fee" in the destination to the spouses which was interpreted at this time as giving the fee to the husband and a liferent to the wife on his death. Indeed this confusion and apparent contradiction is treated by Bell as the principal source of the rule in *Frog's Creditors*.[43] He writes:[44]

"Much confusion has arisen from the loose way in which the words fee and liferent have been used by conveyancers. In common language they are quite distinct: liferent importing a life interest merely: fee a full right of property in reversion after liferent. But the proper meaning of the word liferent has sometimes been confounded by a combination with the word fee, so as in some degree to lose its appropriate sense and occasionally to import a fee. This seems to have begun chiefly in destinations to 'husband and wife in conjunct fee and liferent, and children in fee', where the true meaning is that each person has a joint liferent while both live, but that each has a *possible* fee, as it is uncertain which is to survive. The same confusion of terms came to be extended

---

[41] 1665 M. 4249.
[42] 1705 M. 4259.
[43] 1735 M. 4262.
[44] "Principles of the Law of Scotland" at para. 1712.

to the case of a destination to parent and child—'to AB in liferent, and the heirs of the marriage in fee'—where the word liferent was held to confer a fee on the parent. It gradually came to be held as the technical meaning of the words 'liferent to a parent, with a fee to his children nascituri', that is to say unnamed or unborn children as a class that the word liferent meant a fee in the father."

The second line of cases is in some respects more at one with the rule in *Frog's Creditors* in that it concerns grants by third parties to parents in liferent and their children in fee; and further in that there is no mention in the destination of any possible fee to the parent. Of the old cases the nearest would appear to be *Thomsons* v *Lawson*[45] which concerned a disposition by a father, subject to the reservation of a liferent to himself to his son and his son's spouse in liferent and to the heirs of that marriage, whom failing to certain persons thereafter named. It was held that the son was fiar "by the conception of the disposition". Precisely what, in the disposition, provided this is difficult to say, but it became a principle of construction that wherever the deed contained provisions inconsistent with the nominated liferent, these would prevail. As Lord President Inglis said in *Cumstie* v *Cumstie's Trustees*:[46]

"That the law of Scotland sometimes holds what is ex figura verborum a liferent to be in legal effect a fee nobody can dispute; but I apprehend that that has never been done except in two classes of cases. The first is where the words of the deed itself make it perfectly clear that it was the intention of the maker of the deed that the liferenter should be fiar. Of that, the most obvious and familiar example is where an estate is conveyed to a person in liferent and to another in fee, but giving to the liferenter a power of disposal over, at pleasure. The liferenter then has the whole attributes of an absolute proprietor. He has beneficial enjoyment of the estate and he has the absolute power of disposal. There the law holds the liferenter to be fiar out of deference to the plain intention of the maker of the deed. The other class of cases is that which is represented by the judgement in *Frog's Creditors*."

It is noteworthy that the Lord President chose to contrast the rule in *Frog's Creditors* with this line of cases giving effect to the settler's intention. He went on to emphasise the point.

"Now that [i.e. *Frog's Creditors*] is an extremely important case, and it fixes undoubtedly that where the words used are simply to A in liferent and to his children nascituri in fee, or the heirs of his body in fee, or the issue of a marriage in fee, there the parent is the fiar . . . . It is perhaps a strong thing to hold that because the fiar was non-existent it must therefore have been the intention of the maker of the deed that the liferenter should be fiar. But the necessity of complying with what was supposed to be a rule of the feudal law induced the Court to fix that, and to settle it in such a way that the rule has never been and never can be now disturbed."

Indeed the very thing that was absent from cases such as *Frog's* was a set of provisions inconsistent with the grant of a liferent. Accordingly then this third line of authority provides little support for Lord Braxfield's view. If such a view can be supported at all it must be on the wide "family-assets" basis extending the rules of construction developed in the cases of dispositions by parents in favour of themselves in liferent, and their children in fee, and of dispositions to husband and wife in conjunct fee and liferent, and to the children in fee; but in view of the different circumstances of grants by third parties and the absence of any mention of a "fee" in the parents, to cloud the issue, the

---

[45] 1681 M. 4258.
[46] (1876) 3 R 921 at p. 941.

factors involved in cases of the *Frog* type would hardly seem to provide much support for this view of the settler's intention.

But if the intention theory is unsatisfactory, the alternative, that the rule in *Frog's Creditors* developed out of necessity to avoid the possibility of a pendant fee is hardly less so. The difficulty arises both from the necessity and from the solution. Indeed in none of the cases in which the parent's liferent was enlarged into a fee because of the rule in *Frog's Creditors* has there been any attempt to explain why it should have been felt necessary to overcome the feudal principle at all, still less why it was necessary to enlarge the liferent in order to do so.

As to the first, the alternative of declaring the grant of the fee incompetent seems not to have been seriously considered. That such grants could be so declared is hardly in dispute. To quote Lord President Inglis again:[47]

"My brother Deas says that it is not the custom of the Court, and it would be inconsistent with feudal principle, to consider what is the intention of the maker of the deed in regard to the liferenter without considering at the same time what is to become of the fee, and I am quite sensible to the importance of that observation. But what I mean is this, that I will not construe the intention of the maker of the deed in regard to the fee in any sense that is inconsistent with his plainly expressed intention as to the nature of the liferent. For example, in the present case if I could concur with my brother Lord Deas in holding that the conveyance of the fee here to the heirs whatsoever of AC is not a good conveyance of the fee to them—as is the substance and result of his opinion—I should then seek for a solution of the difficulty, *not be holding the liferenter to be fiar in contradiction of the expressed intention of the maker of the deed, but by holding that the fee was not disposed of at all*; for that a liferent may be created without disposing of the fee at all, or that a liferent might be created while an ineffectual attempt is made to dispose of the fee, I suppose, is quite a legal possibility. And therefore, if the fee is not well given in this case to the heirs whatsoever of AC, then in my humble opinion, it would remain with the granter .... and in the event of his death, it would be in his haereditas jacens."

With respect, it would seem to be the embodiment of common sense that if an interest were not properly given, it should remain with the granter. Thus, for example, if the appropriate words of grant were not used so as to convey the fee to an existing and nominated beneficiary, it would seem to be inconceivable that, had that interest have been burdened with a liferent, that liferent should be enlarged into a fee. It would remain with the granter who would hold it subject to the liferent which had been validly given. In *Falconer* v *Wright*[48] that is precisely what did happen. There a father intended to settle subjects on himself in liferent, and subject thereto for his children in fee. It was held that although the tenor of the deed indicated that he had intended to make a genuine grant in fee to his children, he had not done this effectually, with the result that the fee remained with him.

If therefore the words of the deed—conveyancing machinery—are inadequate, how much more inadequate would be an attempt to do something that was impossible, namely to grant a fee to persons not in esse at the time of the grant? If defects in a conveyance clearly intended to convey the fee prevented such a result, with the fee therefore remaining in the granter, why should not a conveyance in breach of a rule of law have the same result?

---

[47] *ibid.* at p. 942.
[48] (1824) 2S 633. The authority of this case has been doubted because of uncertainty as to the precise reasons for the decisions. The report however does give the ground above stated.

I

The only answer that has been given is that while the intended fiars were incapable of taking the fee, it had nevertheless left the granter. But this begs rather than answers the question. How, given the rule against the fee being in pendente, can a disposition effectively divest the granter without effectively vesting the subjects in the grantee? As Lord Braxfield concluded:[49]

"The donor has given away the whole from himself [but we] must presume he knows [that the] fee cannot go to a person not existing . . . . But presume that he understands the law, he must then mean to give a nominal fee for behoof of the children. Now is it not lawful for him to create merely a substantial liferent? [S]uppose a man dispone to his son for his liferent use allenarly and to provide that no fee is to be vested in him fiduciarily or otherwise, what is the consequence? The only consequence is that the fee must remain with the disponer."

Clearly then, even where the disposition apparently operated to divest the granter, if the fee did not vest immediately in the grantee, it should remain with the granter. The "difficulty" which was said to give rise to the necessitas legis would have resolved itself.

What seems to have happened is that the courts in construing the destinations before them found that they were in three parts; that the first part, the intention to divest and the steps necessary to implement that intention had been properly executed; that the grant in liferent had been properly made, thus apparently getting rid of the subjects for a lifetime; but that the third and most important part, the vesting of the fee, was impossible. Accordingly, if they were to reduce the grant in fee they would be failing to give effect to the granter's effective intention to divest himself,[49a] and thereby render ineffectual the substance of the deed, leaving only the liferent intact. In other words the intention to divest was given precedence over everything else, irrespective of the fact that there should not be an effective divesting without a corresponding vesting in the grantee.

But given the difficulty this construction would bring as to the resting place of the fee, it still does not explain why it was necessary to give it to the liferenter beneficially. Even if the liferenter were the only person living in whom the fee could have vested, why could he not have held it in a fiduciary capacity, as he was later held to do where the word "allenarly" was used to qualify the liferent grant? The answer probably lies in the nature of the "fiduciary fee" which Lord Justice-Clerk Braxfield explained in the following terms:[50]

"It may be said that there is no child, that nobody has an interest and that the fee cannot be in pendente; and it is very fine that, although entitled only to a liferent, as there is no heir existing, the father has the fee. But it is a mere caducary fee, falling to the heir of the marriage on his existence . . . . The father in such a case would be merely a trustee for his son; and a truster is not obliged to serve a trustee. He has a jus crediti under the right. The heir on his existence can bring an action of declarator of trust against the father for having him declared to be a mere trustee."[51]

The point is that while trusts had been known in some form since at least the early seventeenth century the trust concept had not been developed sufficiently in the century to 1735 for implied trusts to have been accepted, or indeed

---

[49] In the *Rosehaugh* case: see above at note 34.
[49a] See per Lord Fullerton in *Mackellar* v *Marquis* (1840) 3 D at p. 180, quoted below at p. 233.
[50] *In Preston* v *Wellwood* 1791 Bell's Cas. 191 at p. 198.
[51] See below.

perhaps, even considered. With the greater awareness of the potentialities of the trust concept and the gradual reception of English Chancery learning throughout the eighteenth century, it is perhaps unfair to criticise the courts for not applying what was at that time virtually an unknown concept.[51a]

What happened instead, it is suggested, was that the courts turned to existing precedents for a way out. And as we have seen there were three types of case where, whether rightly or wrongly, destinations in fee in favour of unborn children had been construed as giving the fee to the liferenter parent: therefore, as the courts could apparently think of nothing else to do with the fee and at the same time adhere to their view that the granter had effectively divested himself, this construction was applied in *Frog's Creditors*.[52] Lord Cuninghame's note in *Mackellar* v *Marquis* contains the essence of this.[53]

1. In the first place there never was at any period, nor is there now, any doubt that a conveyance in general and ordinary terms to a specified party (by name) in liferent, and to another party (also named) in fee, confers only a limited right of liferent on the first party, while the fee descends to the second. In cases of that description, there is no need of the qualifying term "allenarly" to limit the liferenter's right, because he is, both ex figura verborum, and in every legal point of view, a mere liferenter, as the conveyance imports.
2. In the next place, however, it appears from a history of the law and its precedents, that in the process of time, from various causes, a species of liferent came to be recognised, which was only a limited right in name, while the liferenter truly enjoyed all the rights of fee. Such was the case when the parties made resignation or took charters from the superior for new infeftment in their own favour in liferent, and to their heirs male or heirs of line in fee, reserving power to alter, burden or sell the premises. Such a title was expede to give the heirs facility in getting infeftment when the succession opened to them, and it is well-known that many of the mortis causa settlements of heritage were made in these terms. Hence liferents in a large class of cases were construed and truly constituted rights of fee.
[3]. In like manner nominal rights of liferent were considered as rights of fee, in other instances, where a supposed technical necessity existed for that construction as when dispositions or settlements were given to individuals in liferent and their children nascituri in fee. According to the view of old feudalists, no fee could continue in pendente; and as it was often difficult to find any party in whom the fee could even by fiction be held to be vested, when a right was conveyed to unmarried parties in liferent, and to their lawful children in fee, it came to be presumed in such cases that the rights of ownership were meant to be given to the disponee, though denominated a liferenter only."

The suggestion is, then, that this construction was neither necessary in strict law nor at one with the clearly expressed intention of the settler. But nonetheless, it established itself in the law of Scotland and was the means, such as it was, of frustrating certain destinations which tended to perpetuity.

Effect and Extent

The effect of the rule in *Frog's Creditors* with regard to perpetuities became apparent to the courts when the first breaches occurred. In *Newlands* v *Newland's Creditors*[54] the minority view in the Court of Session was to have nothing

---
[51a] Perhaps that is why, when the suggestion was made in *Frog's* case, it was not taken seriously.
[52] 1735 M. 4259.
[53] (1840) 3 D 172 at p. 177.
[54] 1794 M. 4289 at p. 4294.

to do with the idea of a fiduciary fee since "the notion of a fiduciary fee, in cases like this, is not only repugnant to feudal principles but highly inexpedient in itself as, if once allowed, such fees might be continued through many generations and substitutions and thus become a worse species of entail than any hitherto known . . . ."

Similar fears were voiced in *Allardice* v *Allardice*[55] in the following year, although, as in *Newlands*, the doctrine of the fiduciary fee was upheld. The essence of the comparison was that the fetters of a strict entail took away the proprietor's rights and powers relating to alienation by express provision; in the case of destinations giving the fee to those not in esse those powers went by default; that whereas in the case of a strict entail the powers of altering the succession, alienating or burdening the land with debt had to be strictly and specifically withdrawn, in the case of a simple destination those powers would not exist, let alone be taken away, unless and until someone came into existence in whom the fee would vest. Accordingly had the decision in *Frog's Creditors* been otherwise, by the simple creation of a series of successive interests in liferent, with the fee ultimately to vest in the original liferenter's remote descendents, a perpetuity just as effective as the entail could have been created without the difficulties attendant upon entailed settlements.

In the case of simple destinations, then, the rule in *Frog's Creditors* clearly operated so as to prevent such possible attempts to create perpetuities; and indeed, even where the simple destination was supplemented by a destination over in the event of the failure of the liferenter's heirs or issue the rule has been held to apply.[56] But the essential element in its application generally, as in the comparable English rule,[57] was the fact that those designated as entitled in fee were the children or heirs of the liferenter. What the rule had effectively done was to equate the destination, "to A in liferent and his heirs in fee" with the destination "to A and his heirs in fee". Where therefore this element was absent the rule should have no application. This would be important in two situations: first where the designated beneficiaries in fee were other than the children or heirs of the liferenter. Such a destination, "to A in liferent and the children of B in fee" occurred infrequently in family settlements and there have been no cases of simple destinations directly involving such limitations to come before the courts. This is probably accounted for by virtue of the fact that gifts across the direct line of descent would tend to be by way of substitution. But in such a situation it seems clear that the rule would not apply so as to vest the fee in A. As Lord Justice-Clerk Hope said in *Ramsay* v *Beveridge*:[58]

". . . . the cases . . . . relate to one, and a very peculiar class of deeds viz. of a conveyance to a parent in liferent and children nascituri or unnamed in fee. This is the class of cases in which the doctrine referred to has been applied. None of the cases are conveyances to AB in liferent and the children of CD in fee. They are to parents in liferent and *their*[59] children in fee. In the former case it has not yet been found that

---

[55] 1795 Bell's Cas. 156; per Lord President Campbell at p. 157 and Lord Eskgrove at p. 152.
[56] *Frog's Creditors* supra: See per Lord Moncrieff in *Gifford's Trustees* v *Gifford* (1903) 5 F 723 at p. 737. See also *Robertson* v *Duke of Atholl* 20th Nov. 1806 F.C.; *Gordon* v *Macintosh* (1845) 4 Bell 105.
[57] See above.
[58] (1854) 16 D 764 at p. 774.

even on the bare terms of a destination to AB in liferent and the children of CD in fee, the right of AB is a right of fee."

Ramsay v *Beveridge* was in fact an example of the second of the two situations; where the extent of the liferent in the parent did not match the extent of the fee in the children. It concerned a grant to two brothers and a sister in liferent and the children of the sister in fee. The fee was claimed by one of the brothers, seeking to apply the rule in *Frog's Creditors*. His claim was, unsurprisingly, rejected. Jord Justice-Clerk Hope set out the broad ground for this. He said:[60]

"When the deed runs in favour of a parent and his children nascituri in fee, not only the relation between those grantees but the very conception and form of the grant, enabled the court originally (in order to satisfy a legal fiction) to draw from such a fee appended to the parent's liferent ready means, apparently of enlarging the liferent of the father, and he held that the gift was truly for his benefit solely and that his children were only in spes successionis. But it would be the oddest thing in the world in my apprehension, where liferents are given to three parties in a general estate, and a destination of the whole fee exclusively to the children of one of them, to infer from that that the other two were to have a fee against these children of another party, and to hold, that because the fee is given away from the two liferents altogether to strangers, that therefore these two liferenters were to have each a fee. That certainly strikes me as a very singular course of reasoning. There is no connection between the liferents and the destination of the fee. The conclusion in law and reason is just the other way. To two grantees simple liferents are given and the fee of the whole estate generally is given to strangers, so that the dependance the one on the other in no degree subsists. If the sister whose children are called to the fee had contended that her liferent was truly a right of fee, there might have been the more semblance of similarity to the decided cases. But even in her case only the semblance of similarity—because the very fact that the destination to her children is of the fee of the whole estate and much more extensive and larger than her right of liferent, at once cuts off that connection between the liferent given and the fee, which renders the former capable, under the form and terms of the grant, of being taken in a gift of the whole estate, fee and liferent, to the parent. But as to the liferents of the two brothers, it seems to set at defiance all rules of conveyance, and every principle of construction to hold liferents given to A and B to be rights of fee, because the fee of the whole estate is specially conveyed to the children of a third and different liferenter; who shares the liferent with A and B."

The rule has also been stated as not applying in certain cases where the grant is made from one spouse to another in liferent and to the children of the marriage in fee. This conclusion comes principally from *Mackellar* v *Marquis*[61] which involved the conveyance by both spouses of the whole of the property that should belong to them at the time of their death "to and in favour of the longest liver of us in liferent, and to the children that may be procreated of our marriage equally among them in fee" with a destination over in the event of the failure of such heirs. There was a full power to alter the settlement reserved to both during the joint lives of the spouses and to the husband if he were to survive. There was no provision for alteration or revocation in the event of the wife's surviving. The husband predeceased his wife and the question then arose as to the nature of her interest. The First Division, upholding an interlocutor of Lord Cuninghame, found her interest to be restricted to a liferent. However

---

[59] My emphasis.
[60] (1854) 16 D at p. 771.
[61] (1840) 3 D 172.

the reasoning behind this decision was not unanimous. Lord Cuninghame, with whom Lord Gillies concurred, relied on the construction of the deed as a whole, feeling that, in effect, it was not to become operative until the death of one of the parties to the marriage. On the death of the husband therefore, as there were no children, the deed must be read as giving to the wife the designated liferent with the fee going to the beneficiary under the substitutionary destination.[62]

Lord Mackenzie, while also relying on the construction of the deed, felt that the wife had been given only a liferent but for a slightly different reason. He said:[63]

"The reason why the husband is held to have a fee where the liferent is given to the spouses and their children nascituri is that by a principle of our law the fee cannot be in pendente. That principle may force the fee into the husband but it cannot force the fee into the wife. I see no technical principle therefore to free the fee into the wife; and if you get rid of the technical principle and look to the whole circumstances and the fair construction of the deed, the right of the surviving wife seems to be only a liferent. I cannot think that the husband could have intended to give everything to his wife so . . . . that she should have the disposal of his estate possibly to the exclusion of his own heirs. The husband had not only a technical fee, but a power reserved to him should he be the survivor to revoke the deed and settle the estate as he chose. No such power was given to his wife and the contrast is of importance."

Lord Mackenzie then is basing his view on the old idea of the husband as head of the family having the family assets vested in him. He is somewhat unclear as to the position during the joint lives, not indicating whether he treated the deed as immediately operative or coming into effect only on the death of one spouse. But in any event, the principal factors seem to have been the absence of a power of revocation coupled with the wife's liferent and the fact that she was the wife.

Lord Fullerton's judgement, however, went further[64] in that it was based on more general grounds, propounding the principle that conveyances between spouses ousted the rule in *Frog's Creditors*.[65] He said:[66]

"It is true that if there be a conveyance from a third party to one of the spouses in liferent and his or her children nascituri in fee, the fee is held to vest in the person to whom, on the fact of the deed, nothing is given but the liferent. There was at one time great difficulty in determining in whom, in such a case, the fee was truly vested. From the supposed necessity of satisfying the theory that a fee cannot be in pendente, it was assumed that it could not be in the children unborn. In some of the cases it was argued that in such circumstances the fee remained with the disponer. But that view was excluded by the obvious consideration that as between the disponer and the disponee there could be no doubt that the deed was to take instant effect, so as at all events to divest the disponer; and the conclusion was come to that the fee must be held to be in the parent or parents, though nominally liferenters . . . . It is quite another case however when the conveyance flows, not from a third party, but from one of the married parties themselves. There, there is no room for the presumption that the deed was intended to take instant effect, but rather the reverse and accordingly the fee is held, in such circumstances, not to be in the other spouse to whom the liferent is given but to be retained in the person of the granter."

---

[62] *ibid*. at pp. 177-179 (note).
[63] *ibid*. at p. 179.
[64] His was the only judgement that was revised before insertion in the report.
[65] 1735 M. 4262.
[66] (1840) 5 D at p. 180.

His Lordship then sought to justify this principle on the basis of an early decision, *Fraser* v *Brown*[67], which concerned a disposition by an heiress of some lands to her husband in liferent and the heirs procreated or to be procreated of the marriage, whom failing to the husband and his heirs, assignees, etc. in fee subject to a reserved liferent in favour of herself. The question of the spouses' interest arose when the creditors of the husband sought to attach the lands, which they could do if he were entitled in fee. It was held however that on the true construction of the deed, the husband was entitled in liferent only.

If this decision is correct it would certainly support Lord Fullarton's view of the principle as applying irrespective of the sex of the liferenter. The difficulty is however that the report does not give the court's reasons for its decision.

With respect, it is submitted that the decision in *Mackellar* v *Marquis* can best be supported on the grounds given by the Lord Ordinary. Unlike the situation in *Frog's case* and in those decisions in which the rule in *Frog Creditors* has been applied the settlement in this case was clearly not intended to have instant effect; it was for the settlement of the spouses' affairs on death and as such would only become operative on the death of one of them. This being the case the construction of the deed should be viewed in the light of the circumstances appertaining at that point. Had there been in existence any children of the marriage the class would have been complete; there would have been no possibility of increase or indeed of the fee being in pendente at all. If there were no children in existence the substitutionary destination would come into operation (which it did). In either case the circumstances giving rise to the rule in *Frog's Creditors* would not be present. And indeed Lord Fullarton later recognised this, suggesting this as an alternative basis for his decision.[68] Where however the fee was to be given to children of a future marriage it would seem that this reasoning could hardly apply and, in the absence of anything to the contrary, that the rule in *Frog's case* would apply.[69]

Avoidance

The strength of the rule in *Frog's Creditors*[70] as a means of frustrating destinations tending to perpetuity was that it ensured that the fee went to a person in esse at the date of the coming into operation of the grant, enlarging that person's liferent so as to invest him with full powers of disposition, thereby securing the alienability of the subjects. If, however, the liferent and the fee could effectively be prevented from lodging in the same person the alienability of the subjects would in practice be destroyed for the period of the separation. The point was that while, in theory, the fiar would still have full powers to sell, burden with debt and such like, if the enjoyment of the fruits of the subjects

---

[67] 1707 M. 4529. If the view expressed above as to the true ground for the decision in *Mackellar* v *Marquis* is correct, then clearly this case is irrelevant to the issue. If not its value must still be somewhat dubious, especially as the factors taken into account by the court in construing this deed are not reported.

[68] (1840) 3 D at p. 182; But see per contra Dobie—Liferent and Fee at p. 52 et seq.

[69] This seems to be implicit in Lord Cullen's concluding remarks in *Lockhart's Trustees* v *Lockhart* 1921 SC 761 at p. 772 where the question as to conveyances between spouses was raised but not decided.

[70] 1735 M. 4262.

were postponed by reason of a succession of liferents any attempt to sell or raise money on the security of the subjects would be rendered virtually impossible as the fee would be worthless. Accordingly, therefore, if lands were disponed to A and his heirs male successively in liferent, and to B and his heirs whomsoever in fee, B being alive at the date of the grant, the subjects would have been effectively tied up for the duration of the male line of A.

The only weakness in this perpetuity would be the possibility that the fiar might alienate in favour of the liferenter in possession (who would be the only possible purchaser of his interest). Were this to happen then the liferenter would have the full rights of an unencumbered proprietor and the perpetuity would be effectively destroyed. If however this could be prevented by the imposition of some obligation on the fiars so as to secure the retention of the fee in them, the feudal requirements relating to pendant fees would have been satisfied, the rule in *Frog's Creditors* avoided and the perpetuity secured. As Lord Jeffrey remarked, the effect of the interposition of trustees in such destinations is that they "save all the difficulty, they avoid all the perplexing capes and reefs of feudal navigation by keeping the fee in their own hands".[71] That the trust could operate so as to avoid the operation of the rule in *Frog's case* on a destination was admitted towards the end of the eighteenth century, first in connection with express trusts,[72] and then, in the following year by pressing into service the trust concept in the form of the fiduciary fee doctrine.[73] Later, in the nineteenth century other implied trusts were held to be capable of excluding the rule.[74]

(a) *Express Trusts*

The first use of the trust form in this area to come before the courts was in *Seton* v *Creditors of Seton*[75], where, in pursuance of the terms of a marriage contract, a heritable bond was conveyed to trustees for the behoof of "Hugh Seton in liferent and the heirs male to be procreate of the marriage in fee". The court unanimously rejected the application of *Frog's case* to this settlement being of the opinion that "the effect and sole intention of appointing trustees was to prevent the father from being fiar. The subject (it was observed) was vested in the trustees who held the fee for the behoof of the children and the liferent only for the father. If they had paid the sum to Hugh Seton, they would, as infringing the trust, have been liable in damages to [the children]."[76]

The basis of the decision was the intention of the settler, as expressed in the terms of the deed, that the subjects were to be "held" by the trustees for the benefit of the interests nominated. Where however that intention was absent and the trust was not executory in that what was required of the trustees was a transfer or a conveyance in accordance with the destination then clearly this principle could have no effect. Just as a conveyance to trustees directing them to entail the subjects did not alter the requirements or effects of the rules of the law of

---

[71] In *Ross* v *King* (1847) 9 D 1327 at p. 1333.
[72] In *Seton* v *Creditors of Seton* 1793 M. 4219.
[73] In *Newlands* v *Creditors of Newlands* 1794 M. 4289.
[74] In *Mein* v *Taylor* (1827) 5S 780.
[75] 1793 M. 4219.
[76] *ibid.* at p. 4220.

entail for establishing entailed settlements, so a direction to trustees to pay[77] or convey[78] or divide[78a] subjects in liferent and fee would not alter the law affecting such destinations, and the rule in *Frog's Creditors* would still apply to them.[79] As Lord Mackenzie said in *Ross* v *King*:[80]

"In the first place, where a conveyance is made to a father in liferent and to issue nascituris in fee, that gives the fee to the father, the reason being that no fee can be in pendente. And suppose there were twenty interjected trustees, the rule would just be the same, if their appointment was solely to make the conveyance in the same terms."

The distinction, then, with regard to express trusts was between those "of an executorial character, merely for the purpose of payment"[81] where the general rules of law would apply, and those for the "holding and continuing administration of the estate [with regard to which] it is settled that the same strictness of construction is not to be applied, but that the intention and meaning of the testator, as expressed in the deed, is to be especially attended to".[81] As the nineteenth century progressed this "intention" was construed by the courts in the main in such a way as to avoid giving the fee to the liferenter parent. Accordingly where the deed contained an ambiguity, that ambiguity was usually resolved by such a construction. Thus, for example, in *Scott* v *Price*[82] there was a general disposition of an estate in trust for the children of X, reserving a liferent for X. It was held that the disposition of the beneficial interest in fee to the children, which was subject to certain conditions, did not enlarge the interest of the liferenter parent. In *Dennistown* v *Dalgleish*[83] the case concerned a trust settlement under which subjects were held by the trustees under which they were to be invested and secured to the named beneficiaries in liferent and their children in fee. The court upheld an interlocutor of the Lord Ordinary, Lord Jeffrey, finding that the direction to "secure" the subjects in the way designated prevented the fee from vesting in the nominated beneficiaries. In *Watson* v *Watson*[84] the trustees were directed to convey on the death of the liferenter. It was held that the intention that the fee was to go to the children had been clearly shown. Again in *Morice's Trustees* v *Yeats*[85] the trustees were directed that the subjects should be secured "for her proper liferent use and afterwards for her children in fee". This, again, was found to restrict the parent's right to that of a liferent. In *Rait* v *Arbuthnot*[86] the existence of a power given to the parent to appoint the fee among his children was held to have the same effect, and in *Gifford's Trustees* v *Gifford*[87] a declaration that the subjects were to "belong to" the child-

---

[77] See esp. *Hutton's Trustees* v *Hutton* (1847) 9 D 639; *Ferguson's Trustees* v *Hamilton* (1862) 24 D (H.L.) 8; *Beveridge* v *Beveridge's Trustees* (1878) 5 R 1116; *Fraser's Trustees* v *Turner* (O.H.) (1901) 8 S.L.T. 466.
[78] *Ranken* (1870) 8 M. 878; *Mearns* v *Charles* (O.H.) 1926 S.L.T. 118.
[78a] *Dalrymple's Trustees* v *Watson's Trustees* (O.H.) 1932 S.L.T. 480.
[79] *Hutton's Trustees* v *Hutton* supra; *Fergusons' Trustees* v *Hamilton* supra; *Beveridge's Trustees* v *Beveridge* supra; *Williamson* v *Williamson's Trustees* supra.
[80] (1847) 9 D 1327 at p. 1332.
[81] per Lord Ardmillan in *Morice's Trustees* v *Yeats* (1872) 10 S.L.R. 141 at p. 144.
[82] (1837) 15 S 916.
[83] (1838) 1 D 69.
[84] (1854) 16 D 803.
[85] (1872) 10 S.L.R. 141.
[86] (1892) 19 R 687.
[87] (1903) 5 F 723.

ren was found by a majority also to exclude the rule in *Frog's Creditors*.[88] In *Brash* v *Phillipson*[89] the instruction was to "make over" certain heritage, a phrase that would under normal circumstances imply the enlargement of the liferent. Here, however, because the will had clearly been drawn without professional advice it was held that the parent's right was restricted to a liferent. As Lord Salvesen said:[90]

"This is not a case . . . . of a testator directing trustees to convey in specified terms, but is rather the case of a man, ignorant of the forms of conveyancing who directs his trustees what he wishes done with certain properties, leaving them to take the necessary legal advice to enable them to carry out his wishes."[91]

Indeed the application of the rule in *Frog's case* seems to have been restricted to those cases of professionally drawn conveyances where the intention to "convey" was sufficiently definite for it to be presumed that the settler intended the rule to have effect. Certainly, time and again, judges have stated that they would not extend the rule's scope[92], and, with one exception, the cases seem to bear that out. The exception is *McClymont's Exors.* v *Osborne*[93] where trustees were directed to invest a portion of the residuary estate in shares in the name of a niece of the testator "she to have the interest or dividends from the same during her lifetime, for the maintenance, upbringing and education of her children, and, at her death, the principal to be divided equally among her children, except George and Thomas". It was held, as a matter of construction, that this amounted in essence to a simple destination in favour of a parent's liferent with the fee to the children, that accordingly the rule in *Frog's case* applied and that the niece was therefore entitled to the fee.

(b) Implied Trusts

There are three lines of cases in which the rule in *Frog's Creditors* has been held excluded by the implication of a trust; all involve in some degree the application of the doctrine of the fiduciary fee.

(i) The notion that the fee might be held by someone in a trustlike capacity without the setting up of an express trust was really the product of the late eighteenth century. It is apparently true that counsel in *Frog's case* put forward the idea, although seemingly with little conviction.[94] The report of *Mure* v *Mure*[95] in 1786 also contains references to arguments based on the idea of a "fiduciary fee" and, though these arguments were apparently accepted by the court their details are not known. A much more detailed discussion is to be found in *Preston* v *Wellwood*[96] five years later, a case primarily on the law of entail. Indeed the judgements suggest that, contrary to the generally accepted

---

[88] 1735 M. 4262.
[89] 1916 S.C. 271.
[90] *ibid.* at p. 276.
[91] See also *Lockhart's Trustees* v *Lockhart* 1921 S.C. 761.
[92] See per Inglis L.P. in *Cumstie* v *Cumstie's Trustees* (1876) 3 R 921 at p. 941 per Lord McLaren in *Gifford's Trustees* v *Gifford* supra at p. 730.
[93] (1995) 22 R 411.
[94] See the note in the Session Papers re *Newlands' case* by Sir Ilay Campbell reported in 3 Ross —Leading Cases at p. 651.
[95] 1786 M. 4268. Mackenzie Stuart—"Law of Trusts" (Edinburgh 1932) also cites *Lillie* v *Riddell* 1741 M. 4267, although the report does not seem to support this.
[96] 1791 Bell's Cas. 191.

view, the doctrine was well known and accepted prior to the *Newlands' case*.[97] In this case a granter disponed to himself "for his liferent use only during his lifetime and failing him by decease, to Robert, his nephew" under strict entail. The question for the court concerned the location of the fee and it was held that it remained with the disponer (Henry) until his death. Two judgements particularly suggest that the fiduciary fee doctrine, which was apparently established three years later in *Newlands' case*, was already part of the law of Scotland. First, Lord President Campbell said:[98]

"It is a rule well fixed in law that a fee cannot be in pendente, it must either be in the granter or in the disponee. This is illustrated by the first words of the settlement 'in favour and for new infeftment to be made, given and granted to myself in liferent for my liferent use only during all the days of my lifetime, and failing of me by decease, to my heirs of taillie and provision, etc.' Here there is no heir named; and it would seem that although in this case ex figura verborum the granter has merely a liferent it will in law be construed to be a fee. Perhaps the fee would only be fiduciary; but, although these words 'for liferent use allenarly' would no doubt make it a fiduciary fee, yet it would be a fee."

And then Lord Justice-Clerk Braxfield said:[99]

"Though a father settling his estate in his marriage contract takes it to himself in liferent and the children of the marriage in fee, the father is construed to be fiar. And there is good reason for it. *First:* Because the fee cannot be in pendente and therefore must vest in him since there is no other in whom it can vest. *Second:* Because there is a natural presumption that a father, though he intends to settle his estate on his child means to retain the full property of it until his death. This has been decided often.

But suppose the estate is taken to himself in liferent, "for his liferent use only", he in that case reserves no earthly power over the estate. He enjoys the rents, it is true; but he can exercise no right except that of a mere liferenter. His creditors are not entitled to carry it off. It may be said that there is no child, that nobody has an interest, and that the fee cannot be in pendente; and it is very true that, though entitled only to the liferent, as there is no heir existing, the father has the fee. But it is a mere caduciary fee, falling to the heir of the marriage on his existence. . . . . The father in such a case would be merely the trustee for his son; and a truster is not obliged to serve a trustee. He has a jus crediti under the right. The heir on his existence can bring an action of declarator of trust against the father for having him declared to be a mere trustee."

[97] 1794 M. 4289; 1798 4 Pat. 43 (H.L.); 3 Ross Leading Cases 634. These prior cases would perhaps explain Lord Justice-Clerk Braxfield's comment that the fiduciary fee doctrine was an established rule of law (3 Ross at p. 647). Indeed in the 1794 hearing of *Newlands' case*, Lord Justice-Clerk Braxfield's speech contains an exposition of the doctrine in substantially the same terms. Thus he said: (3 Ross at p. 644)

". . . . but then every man must be assumed to know that in law a fee cannot be in pendente, and therefore where a conveyance by a father to a son in liferent and children to be born in fee, no more is given to the children than a spes successionis, and the solid right of liferent and the fee is in the father, who may spend and dilapidate the subject and disappoint the children. But this is a different case. Here it is given to the son for his liferent use allenarly, which makes this a mere fruit in the father and gives the son the fee, and the father a liferent and no more. A father may make his son a trustee as well as a stranger. A trustee's debts cannot affect the trust estate, no more can the son's debts here where the estate is conveyed for his liferent use allenarly. Therefore the creditors of Newlands cannot affect this estate, nor have they reason to complain, as if they had looked into their debtor's right they must have seen that he had nothing but a liferent. It is said, where is the fee after the father's death and during the son's life, before the son has children? I have no difficulty in answering that. There was here a fiduciary or trust-fee in the son for behoof of children of the son, when they should exist. This is a mere trust, no more than a name as fee cannot be in pendente, but the moment children of the son exist, the fee is in them.'

[98] 1791 Bell's Cas. at p. 196/197.
[99] *ibid.* at p. 197/198.

If, then, the doctrine had been both articulated and applied in prior cases, what was so special about the *Newlands' case*? Perhaps the answer is that the case provided the first example of the validity of the rule being questioned and upheld[100] and of having this validity supported by the House of Lords, albeit without any great confidence. The facts of *Newlands' case* were essentially the same as those in *Frog*[101] save that grant in liferent to the parent was qualified by the phrase "for his liferent use allenarly". The competition therefore was between two established rules of construction: on the one hand the rule that a grant in liferent to the parent and in fee to his children nascituri gave the fee to the parent, and on the other that a grant in liferent allenarly was not to be construed as giving the liferenter any larger right.[102] The result is well known. As Lord Ardmillan rationalised it in *Cumstie's* v *Cumstie's Trustees*:[103]

"[The rule in *Frog's Creditors*] was the triumph of a legal subtlety over the intention of the maker of the deed and this was judicially felt and acknowledged in several of the earlier cases. But when by the use of the word 'allenarly' a liferent was restricted and limited as I have already explained, the converting of that liferent into a fee would be strikingly opposed to intention. Some remedy was required to sustain intention, to disarm subtlety and to vindicate the essential equity of law. This remedy was found. A new subtlety was evoked to redress the balance disturbed by the regretted enforcement of the former subtlety. A fiduciary fee in the person of the liferenter was recognised in order to sustain the intention—as I think the clear intention—of the deed. A liferenter declared expressly to be a life- renter allenary can never be held to be an absolute fiar. He is held to be a trustee, with only so much of the character of a fiar as is required to sustain the character of the trust."

The reasoning behind this result which is generally accepted is that of Lord Braxfield: that it was a well-known rule of law that a single grant in liferent to a parent with the fee going to the children gave the fee to the parent: that if it was genuinely intended that the parent could enjoy only a liferent something more was needed; and that the qualification of the liferent by the word "allenarly" or by some equivalent restrictive phrase ousted the interpretation adopted in *Frog's case*; that unfortunately the question of the pendent fee still remained and that this was to be solved by vesting a sort of constructive fee in the liferenter; that by employing the trust concept the legal formalities could be satisfied while at the same time giving effect to the intention of the granter.

There was an alternative approach, suggested by the speech of Lord President Campbell in *Preston* v *Wellwood*.[104] This was in effect that the rule in *Frog's Creditors* should be applied in such cases so that the fee was effectively vested in the liferenter parent; but that the inclusion of the word allenarly in the grant indicated that the fee was not to be enjoyed beneficially by the liferenter with the result that he was given a bare trust estate which was to be held for the behoof of the children. Its difficulty is that it implies the retention of the trust fee by the liferenter for the duration of his interest, whereas, at least according to the Braxfield view, the fee vested in the children on their coming into

---

[100] Sed quaere *Mure* v *Mure* supra.
[101] 1735 M. 4262.
[102] See esp. speeches of Lord Justice-Clerk Braxfield in *Preston* v *Wellwood* and *Newlands*; see also *Thomson* v *Lawson* 1681 M. 4258 cited by Lord Eskgrove and Lord Loughborough, L.C. (dubitante) in *Newlands*.
[103] (1876) 3 R 921 at p. 927.
[104] 1791 Bell's Cas. at p. 196/197. See also *Mein* v *Taylor* (1830) 4 W & S 22 (H.L.). See below at note 126.

existence.[105]

However, the perpetuity implications of the doctrine were enormous; the rule in *Frog's Creditors* could now be defeated without the interposition of an express trust, simply by the inclusion of the word "allenarly" or by some some equivalent phrase of restriction. As we have seen[106] Lord President Campbell acknowledged the existence of a perpetuity rpoblem in his dissenting judgement. But perhaps his reservations are best expressed in his note included in the Session Papers covering the *Newlands' case*. He wrote:[107]

"Besides, the argument on the other side [i.e. in favour of recognising the fiduciary fee doctrine] would be establishing a new kind of tailzied fee not yet acknowledged in the law of Scotland. A trust in a man's person for the neirs of his own body, who may never exist, cannot in its nature receive execution. If a trust or fiduciary fee may take place in the first institute, the same form may go all through the substitutes and, accordingly .... we have various substitutes all in the same terms. Every heir may be declared to be a fiduciary fiar or a liferenter allenarly for the succeeding heirs. If this clause be sufficient to qualify the right, what use is there for the Act 1686 [sic] and for clauses prohibitory, etc. We at once introduce the Statute de donis conditionalibus into the law of Scotland and the Register of Tailzies becomes useless. The case of *McNair*[108] is an alarming example."

However, unlike the situation in the *McNair case*, the perpetuity point was not taken up. Even Lord Swinton, who had expressed himself to be steadfastly against perpetuities in *McNair*, was content to accept this "new subtlety". And accordingly later in the same year in *Thomson* v *Thomson*[109] *Newlands* was expressly followed. The implications of the decision in *Newlands*, indeed, may not have been universally understood, for in *Allardice* v *Allardice* in 1795[110] expressions of regret at some of the consequences of the fiduciary fee doctrine were apparent in the judgements. Thus Lord Eskgrove remarked:[111]

"I am much alarmed by this succession of trusts. The next step will be to give the estate to the eldest son in liferent allenarly; whom failing to the heirs of his body in liferent allenarly, and so on through all the heirs of a destination, and I am afraid that there are principles in the decisions which we have pronounced that would support such a destination."

And Lord President Campbell said:[112]

"In *Newlands' case* the fee was given to the heirs nascituri; and here, failing the heirs of the body of the first son, the liferent is given to the second son and the fee to the heirs of his body. I remember in *Newlands' case* it was said that to support such deeds would be to authorise a series of liferents, and introduce a new way of making an entail. Here we have an instance of it. But you did not think that a sufficient ground for setting aside the deed . . . ."

In these two cases the acceptance of perpetual settlements created by way of an implied trust were possibly influenced by the acceptance of a principle of perpetuity in *McNair* in 1791. Yet, apart from the Lord President the apparent significance of the *McNair* decision was not mentioned in the judgements or notes to the cases, nor, apparently in the arguments.

---

[105] The view of Lord Justice-Clerk Braxfield has however been doubted in this respect. See per Lord Ardmillan in *Ferguson* v *Ferguson* (1875) 2 R 627 at p. 632.
[106] See above at p. 228.
[107] 3 Ross—Leading Cases at p. 654.
[108] 1791 Bell's Cas. 546.
[109] 1794 Bell's Cas. (Fol.) 72.
[110] 1795 Bell's Cas. 153.
[111] *ibid.* at p. 158.
[112] *ibid.* at p. 157.

Perhaps the reason for this apparent lack of connection was the point that, in spite of *Allardice* v *Allardice*, the fiduciary fee doctrine would not in fact tie up the subjects of settlements to which it was applied for more than one generation; and, indeed, if Lord Braxfield's approach [113] was correct would not tie it up even for that length of time. The essential point at issue was whether the doctrine would be confined to the same situations to which the rule in *Frog's Creditors*[114] was confined, or whether, and, if so, to what lengths, it would be expanded. In other words, if the doctrine of the fiduciary fee was to be applied only in cases of disposition to parents in liferent allenarly with the fee to go to their children nascituri, the perpetuity danger would in fact be slight, as the fee would be vested in the children at birth (that is, during the lifetime of the fiduciary fiar) and would therefore, in theory, become capable of alienation. If, on the other hand, the doctrine could be applied in situations where the destined fiars were not the children of the liferenter then the perpetuity danger would be much more acute.

The most obvious example is that feared by Lord President Campbell and Lord Eskgrove but not in fact met in *Allardice*. In that case D.A. [senior] executed a disposition in the following terms: "to R.A., my eldest son in liferent allenarly and to the lawful heirs of his body from any marriage he shall enter into, in fee, whom failing to D.A. [junior], my second son in liferent allenarly" and then in the same terms as those applicable to R.A.

R.A. took infeftment, and with a view to altering the destination, obtained precept from his superior in favour of himself in liferent and the heirs of any marriage he should enter into, which failing to Jean A., his daughter by his deceased wife, which failing to D.A. as in the original settlement.

The question was whether R.A. could do this, D.A. bringing an action for reduction. It was held that he could not, his right and title coming from the original disposition, which gave him only a liferent and a fiduciary, but not a substantial, fee. As Lord Justice-Clerk Braxfield remarked:[115]

"The only difference betwixt it and *Newlands* is that there is here a succession of liferenters; but there is nothing in that."

But the succession of liferents here related to persons in esse at the date of the disposition, and indeed there have been no cases of the court's upholding destinations through the doctrine of the fiduciary fee where the parties, with the exception of the children ultimately entitled in fee, were not in esse at the appropriate time.[116] It must be observed that the principle in *Allardice* would

---

[113] See above at note 105.
[114] 1735 M. 4262.
[115] 1795 Bell's Cas. (Fol.) at p. 158.
[116] See *Campbell* v *Duncan* 1913 1 S.L.T. 260; *Cripps' Trustees* v *Cripps* 1926 S.C. 188 where in both cases the immediate liferenter and his successor (the parent of the children in the destination) were in esse at the date of the disposition. In the former case the disposition was in favour of the grantor's daughter and her son and the survivor of them in liferent allenarly and to the heirs of the body of the son in fee with a destination over. It was held that the fiduciary fee rested with the daughter, and on her death, with her son, so, in fact, applying the *Allardice* principle directly.

In the latter case however the relevant liferenter's interest was expressly made subject to that of his mother. It was held here that his interest, though not beneficially in possession at the date of the grant, was sufficient to carry the fiduciary fee which therefore vested in him.

In both cases however the statutory provisions restricting the creation of liferents were in force so that the danger of perpetuity was in reality non-existent.

require only a small extension for this to be so, for the court there appeared to sanction the validity of treating the first liferenter (R.A.) as possible fiduciary fiar both for his brother, who was also entitled in liferent, and his brother's children, thus paving the way for the validity of an infinite number of substitutions in liferent interposed between the original liferent and the ultimate destination of the substantive fee. During the first three-quarters of the nineteenth century the validity of such an extension was viewed with some suspicion. In *Elmslie* v *Fraser*[117], Lord Fullerton expressed doubts. He said:

"Is this doctrine to be carried beyond the case of a fiduciary fee for behoof of the children of the liferenter himself? We can conceive of a disposition to A in liferent allenarly and to the children nascituri of B in fee. No doubt the fee is vested in A so as to take it out of the granter; but can it be said that A, who has no connection with the children of B is to be looked on as a trustee for them. That is a very delicate question."

But in *Cumstie* v *Cumstie's Trustees*[118] the majority of the First Division held that the doctrine applied where the fee was not limited to the liferenter's children, but to his heirs whomsoever. The dissentient, Lord Deas, held that the fiduciary fee doctrine applied only as between a liferenter and his children and not between him and his remoter issue.

On the basis of this decision therefore the perpetuity danger was confirmed, for provided the ultimate beneficiaries in fee could be brought within the description of "heirs whomsoever" the settlement would be valid, however remote their connection with the liferenter. By this time[119] however there were in existence statutory provisions applying both to heritage[120] and moveables[121] which obviated this.

(ii) A second line of cases concerning the implication of a trust in this context were decided in the nineteenth century. They are often referred to as examples of the application of the fiduciary fee doctrine, although in point of fact they have little in common with the orthodox view of that principle. The cases begin with *Mein* v *Taylor*[122] which concerned a direct conveyance of heritage to four parties under direction that the subjects should be held by them in liferent and to belong to their children in fee. The said parties were required to divide the subjects into shares, certain of which were to be held by one of them (A) in liferent "and at his decease the fee and property thereof" were to be divided among his children. The disponees, or the survivors of them, were to ensure that the shares of A's children were secured for them in liferent and their issue in fee. While these directions obviously implied fiduciary duties no legal machinery (i.e. a trust) had been set up. The court, adhering to the inter-

---

[117] (1850) 12 D 724 at p. 731.
[118] (1876) 3 R 921.
[119] Since the passing of the liferent restriction rules the principles discussed above have been elaborated in the following decisions; *Allen* v *Flint* (1886) 13 R 975; *Logan's Trs.* v *Ellis* (1890) 17 R 425; *Tristram* v *McHaffies* (1894) 22 R 121; *Colville's Trs.* v *Marinden* 1908 S.C. 911; *Devlin* v *Lowrie* 1922 S.C. 255; *Cripps Trs.* v *Cripps* 1926 S.C. 188. For discussions of the development of these principles see esp. Henderson on Vesting (2nd Ed. 1938) at pp. 392-397; Dobie—Liferent and Fee (1941) at pp. 35-44; Wilson and Dnncan on Trusts, Trustees and Executors (1975) at pp. 65-67 and cases cited there.
[120] Statute 11 and 12 Vict. c. 36 Section 48.
[121] Statute 31 and 32 Vict. c. 84 Section 17.
[122] (1827) 5 S 779 (Court of Session); (1830) 4 W & S 22 (House of Lords).

locutor of the Lord Ordinary, Lord Corehouse, held that a trust would be implied and would be considered as continuing until A's death, and that accordingly, on the principle in *Seton's Creditors*[123] A was to be treated as a mere liferenter. This decision was upheld by the House of Lords.[124]

The contrast between this case and those decided on the fiduciary fee doctrine is brought out in Lord Corehouse's note, which reads:[125]

"When a conveyance is made to one in liferent, and his children unnamed or unborn in fee, it is settled law that the fee is the parent and that the children have only a hope of succession to prevent the feudal maxim that a fee cannot be in pendente. It is perhaps to be regretted that the point was so settled because the plain intention of the maker is, in consequence, often sacrificed to a mere form of rxpression; and the feudal maxim might have been saved by supposing a fiduciary fee in the parent, as is done when the liferent is restricted by the word allenarly or only. Upon this point however it is too late to go back; but certainly the principle ought not to be extended to cases which have not yet been brought under it. In the present case the subjects are not disponed to Messrs. Taylor in liferent and their children in fee; but on the contrary, to the Messrs. Taylor in fee because the obligation to infeft is in favour of them and their heirs and assignees. The question therefore is whether the fee so given is absolute or qualified, a question to be determined by the ordinary rules of construction. It clearly appears that it is a qualified or fiduciary fee because it is granted under certain burdens and conditions. [These are then set out and explained]. But where a fiduciary fee is given to a person and it is directed that he himself shall enjoy the liferent, and still more clearly where a fiduciary fee is vested in several persons collectively and the survivor or survivors, and each of them separately is to have a liferent, such liferent must be construed as a naked usefruct in the same manner as if it had been qualified by the word allenarly.

It will be seen that Lord Corehouse recognised the difference between the case before him and the orthodox fiduciary fee doctrine: indeed he sought to apply the latter by analogy. The essential difference however is in what is granted. The doctrine of the fiduciary fee operates on a liferent; in *Mein* v *Taylor* what was conveyed was the fee itself. The decision identifies closely with the English doctrine of constructive trusts where the Courts of Equity imposed a trust on a conveyance in fee to give effect to the intentions of the disponer.[126] What the decision in *Mein* v *Taylor* does is to confirm the legal ownership of the subjects, but to restrict the powers of enjoyment, giving effect to the stated intentions of the granter by supplying by implication the required instrument. The principle was also pressed into service in *Ewan* v *Watt*[127] where the court gave effect to the beneficial interests under a trust which the trustees declined to accept so as to vest the fee in the liferenter's children irrespective of the otherwise absolute right of the parent to legitim, which if unqualified, would have been at variance with the disponer's intention. And in *Keating* v *Collins*[128] the difficulty was caused by the fact that a disposition purported to transfer moveables to the

---

[123] 1793 M. 4219.
[124] (1830) 4 W & S at p. 27.
[125] (1827) 5 S at p. 7; (1830) 4 W & S at pp. 24/25.
[126] It also identifies with the approach of Lord President Campbell in *Preston* v *Wellwood* supra who, it will be remembered, interpreted the fiduciary fee doctrine as a qualification on the absolute fee given by the operation of the rule in *Frog's Creditor's*. In this sense the decision in *Mein* v *Taylor* might be described as an example of the application of the doctrine of the fiduciary fee.
[127] (1828) 6 S 1125.
[128] (1870) 7 S.L.R. 548.

disponer's daughter in liferent allenarly and to her children in fee without the interposition of a trust, the point being that "[s]uch a disposition of moveables in liferent is not possible without a trust".[129] Accordingly this want was supplied by implication.[130]

The perpetuity consequences of this line of cases would correspond exactly with those discussed above in section (i).

(iii) The third application of the implied trust principle is somewhat different for it does not involve the notion that the liferenter holds the fee either absolutely or in trust for his children. It had always been the law that where there was a gift to a parent in liferent and to his children nominatim in fee there was no room for the rule in *Frog's Creditors*.[131] There was no danger of a pendency of the fee and therefore no necessity that the parent should hold it in either an absolute or a fiduciary capacity. Difficulties, however, arose in dispositions of an intermediate nature, that is to say in destinations to parents in liferent and to their existing children, who were named, and to any others to be procreated in equal shares. The question here was whether the rule in *Frog's Creditors* operated so as to give the fee of the subjects, in whole or in part, to the parents. The question first came before the courts in *Dykes and Dykes* v *Boyd*[132] where the fee was held to be vested in the named children for the behoof of themselves and those still to be born. The reasons given by the various members of the court differed however and it was not until the case of *McGowan* v *Robb*[133] that the principle was articulated. This case concerned the conveyance of heritage in an antenuptial marriage contract by the wife in favour of her intended husband "and herself and the longest liver of them in conjunct fee and liferent for their liferent use allenarly and to" the children nominatim of the husband by a former marriage and any children to be procreated of this marriage, existing at the death of the longest liver of the spouses, equally among them in fee. It was held that a right of fee was conferred on the children of the first marriage. In the words of Lord Deas:[134]

"An infeftment in the mother's favour on the precept of the marriage contract would have been a good infeftment in the liferent, but in the liferent only. It would not have vested in her the fiduciary fee where there were nomination fiars who could be themselves infeft. But infeftment in favour of the four nominatim fiars in terms of the destination would, undoubtedly have vested the fiduciary fee in them for themselves and the unnamed fiars; and I think infeftment in favour of the survivors of these, if otherwise duly expressed, as the same effect . . . .

Where the destination is in favour of the parents in liferent, for their liferent use

---

[129] per Lord President Inglis at p. 550.
[130] See esp. per Lord Kinloch at pp. 550/551; See also *Rait* v *Arbuthnot* 1892 19 R 687.
[131] 1735 M. 4262.
[132] 3rd June 1813 F.C.
[133] (1862) 1 M. 146; 2 M. 943.
[134] 2 M. at pp. 952/953; See also *Martin* v *Milliken* (1864) 3 M. 326 esp. per Lord Cowan at p. 337:
"When the conveyance is to the parent in liferent and to children natis nominatim and nascituris in fee, the property vests in the party or parties named subject to the claim of the children subsequently born. In such a case neither is the liferent right of the parent enlarged so as to constitute him or her fiar, nor is the vesting of the fee prevented or postponed; there is merely a condition attached to the succession which may become operative and so affect the right of the fiar."

allenarly, and the children unborn or unnamed in fee, the infeftment in favour of the parents, if expede in the appropriate form, so as to include the rights of the children, will be a good infeftment in the fiduciary fee as well as in the liferent. But if the destination be to the parents in liferent for their liferent use allenarly and the existing children nomination and those to be born (and who are consequently unnamed) in fee, infeftment in favour of the children named and the children to be procreated of the said marriage equally, share and share alike in fee, is, I think, a good infeftment in the fee constituting the children nomination infeft fiduciary fiars for themselves and the children who are not named."

Given, then, that in these cases the fee vests immediately, albeit subject to a possible variation of beneficial interests during the lifetime of the parents, the implied trust here created no potential perpetuity problems at all.

Conclusion as to the Common Law Rules

As in English law, the common law rules were not specifically designed to frustrate attempts to create perpetuities. They were more concerned with the regulation of rights as between liferent and fee, or what in England would be described as present and future interests.

Comparison with England, however, is scarcely profitable, since in that country the potential of such rules as anti-perpetuity mcahinery was grasped at a fairly early date. In Scotland there is little evidence of its having been grasped at all until it was too late. By the time the recorded contemplations of their Lordships in *Newlands* and *Allardice* were made on the subject, the rule in *Frog's Creditors* could be avoided virtually at will. From the point of view of the evasion of the rule the provisions of section 8 of the Trusts (Scotland) Act 1921[135] were simply the logical culmination of a process that had been in train for the previous century and a quarter. From a perpetuity point of view, however the provision was irrelevant for by that time statute had provided specific perpetuity rules.

The Statutory Rules

In his commentary on the Rutherford Act[136] George Ross wrote:[137]

"The object of the Act 1848, in regard to Entails, is to assimilate the law of Scotland to that of England, where an estate may be rendered absolutely inalienable during one life, or any given number of lives, in being at the same time . . . .[138] The provisions of the 1848 Act limit the suspension of the vesting of the absolute interest in an estate to the lives of the parties, who were born before the date of the deed creating their interest and until the majority of a party called to the succession who was born after its date."

In point of fact this assimilation in so far as it relates to perpetuity rules is, as we shall see,[139] somewhat superficial. Nevertheless there are very definite points of affinity. For example just as the English perpetuity rules were directed against devices intended to secure the inalienability of entailed property, so the perpetuity provisions of the Act of 1848 were framed with the same anti-avoidance purpose in mind. As Lord President Inglis remarked in *Black* v *Aule*:[140]

---

[135] Statute 11 and 12 Geo. V c. 58.
[136] Statute 11 and 12 Vict. c. 36 [The Entail Amendment (Scotland) Act 1848].
[137] The Law of Entail in Scotland as altered by the Act 1848 (Edinburgh 1848) at p. 70.
[138] *ibid.* at p. 69.
[139] See below Chapter VI.
[140] (1873) 1 R 133 at p. 145.

"Now to carry out these regulations still further, and to secure still more effectually the great object of the statute viz. to prevent entailers from affecting with fetters persons not born, there are some other provisions of the statute which are worthy of attention. I mean particularly 47th, 48th and 49th sections which are directed to prevent an evasion of the leading provisions of the statute, either by the creation of trusts, or by the creation of successive liferents, or by the creation of leasehold rights in succession. All these modes of evading the statute have been anticipated and provided against."

And just as the English perpetuity rules depend on the notion of "lives in being" so the statutory rules of Scots law permit property to be tied up for the duration of the lives of such persons as are living at the date of the coming into effect of the settlement.

However, there the similarities end. Whereas the English rule applies to all (except charitable) settlements of all types of property the Scottish rules cover only such devices and such property as are specifically mentioned by statute.[141] But perhaps the most significant point of difference is the effect of contravening the rules: in England this leads to the invalidity of the infringing limitation, whereas in Scotland the common law example of *Frog's Creditors*[142] is followed with the result that the infringing interest is enlarged so as to become an unencumbered fee.

As might be expected, the provisions of the Rutherford Act applied only to heritage. Further, they related only to deeds dated on or after the passing of the Act, a restriction which was lifted in 1914, after which the provisions were to apply to deeds, whenever executed.[143]

A parallel scheme was applied to moveable and personal property by section 17 of the Entail Amendment (Scotland) Act of 1868[144], a provision which was repealed but re-enacted in substantially the same form as section 9 of the Trusts (Scotland) Act 1921.[145] As with the provisions dealing with heritage it was not intended that the provision should operate retrospectively but, again, it was extended to cover all deeds, although these dated prior to 31st July 1868 are, for the purposes of the provisions, deemed to carry the date 1st October 1924.[146]

Although both sets of provisions are still in force they have now been rendered partially inoperative as regards deeds dated on or after 25th November 1968. These deeds now fall under section 18 of the Law Reform (Miscellaneous Provisions) (Scotland) Act 1968[147] which has the effect of assimilating to a large extent the provisions relating to heritage and moveables into a common code applying to both. Complete assimilation was, perhaps, impossible, given the greater variety of interests that can be created in heritage. The essence of the 1968 legislation is to concentrate on the regulation of the creation of liferents.

It will be remembered that the principal alternative to the strict entail was the trust settlement under which the trust estate would be held for a series of

---

[141] Under post 1968 deeds all types of property are covered.
[142] 1735 M. 4262.
[143] Statute 4 and 5 Geo. V c. 43, section 8 [Entail (Scotland) Act 1914], although such deeds as were affected were deemed to bear the date 10th August 1914.
[144] Statute 31 and 32 Vict. c. 84.
[145] Statute 11 and 12 Geo. V c. 58.
[146] Statute 14 and 15 Geo. V c. 27. section 45 [Conveyancing (Scotland) Act 1924].
[147] Statute 1968 c. 70.

beneficiaries successively in liferent. The interposition of a trust was not, of course, strictly necessary where the subjects were heritable, but it was nevertheless desirable, if only to overcome the problems of the pendency of the fee and the rule in *Frog's Creditors*,[142] and was almost invariably used in practice.[148] Where the subjects were moveable the use of the trust was essential.[149]

Yet in spite of this, the uniformity now achieved by section 18 of the Act of 1968 was conspicuously lacking in the prior enactments. Thus, for example, section 48 of the Rutherfurd Act referred only to the granting of an estate in heritable property "limited to a liferent interest" making no reference to trusts or trust liferents at all, and indeed in *Harvey's Trustees* v *Harvey*[150] it has since been held that the ambit of section 48 "is limited to proper liferents by constitution and .... can have no application to a liferent interest in an estate held by trustees".[151] In practice, however, this would not make a great deal of difference for section 47 would cover the case. The Act of 1868 was more economical. This piece of legislation re-enacted as section 9 of the 1921 Act, made it "[in]competent to constitute or reserve by means of a trust or otherwise a liferent interest in moveable or personal estate in Scotland" otherwise than as provided.

To be caught, then, it is necessary that there be an interest created which can be classified as a liferent. In most cases there is no difficulty at all for the instrument of grant will either define the relevant interest as a liferent in terms or by reference to the rights of enjoyment during the beneficiary's lifetime. Unsurprisingly therefore there are few decisions calling into question the application of the provision by reason of the nature of the interest granted. There was the case of *Drybrough's Trustees* v *Drybrough's Trustees*[152] where the beneficiary was an annuitant. The second Division held this to be outwith section 48 defining liferent so as not to include an annuity, the basis of the distinction being that whereas a liferenter was entitled to the fruits of the subject liferented and to no more, an annuitant had, if necessary, the power to encroach on capital to satisfy his interest.

---

[148] Thus Professor Wood in his "Lectures on Conveyancing" (Edinburgh 1903) writes, at p. 315:
"Deeds containing a direct conveyance of lands or houses to several persons for different interests as of liferent and fee have to a large extent gone out of use. In place of them the modern practice ... is to constitute a title in the persons of the trustees and to confer varying beneficial interests on the parties intended to be benefited, rather than to seek to give them a direct title to the lands. The reasons for this change are numerous but I can only touch upon one or two of them.... [A]s to title, I do not say that there are no cases where it would be right to take a destination; for example in the case of a small house property a destination may be taken to the parents in liferent and, say, a specified child in fee. If the parents die and that child succeeds, there is no doubt some saving of expense in the case of completing the child's title. But if the favoured child dies before the parents, but after infeftment has been taken in terms of the destination, what becomes of the fee? Unless power to make an alteration has been reserved in the deed the fee is beyond the control of the parents. In no circumstances do I think it advisable to take property upon a destination to a parent in liferent and unnamed children in fee. Here you at once raise a question of right as well as title."

[149] See e.g. *Keating* v *Collins* (1870) 7 S.L.R. 548.

[150] 1942 S.C. 582.

[151] *ibid.* at p. 589 per Lord Jamieson.

[152] 1912 S.C. 939. See also *Mackenzie's Trustees* v *Mackenzie* 1922 S.C. 404 and *Baxter* v *Baxter* 1909 S.C. 1027.

A rather more difficult case was that of *Davie* v *Davie's Trustees*[153] which arose out of a trust disposition by which the whole of the settler's estate was conveyed to trustees "to hold the free residue of the trust estate, heritable and moveable until the death of all my children", and in the meantime to pay or to expend the free income therefrom "equally to or for behoof of my said children and the survivors or survivor of them, and the issue of any such of them who might die leaving issue, such issue being entitled equally among them to their deceased parent's share of the free income". The trust then provided that if, at the death of the last surviving child there should be three grandchildren alive, the residue was to be divided among them, but if they were in minority then the trustees were to retain such minors shares until majority, "expending in the meantime such free annual income for behoof of such minors". It was further provided that powers of denuding were to be entirely within the discretion of the trustees.

The pursuer was a grandchild of the settler (and indeed his only descendant). It was held by Lord Low, as a matter of construction, that the pursuer was entitled to the income of the trust fund, there being no other beneficiaries and no direction to accumulate, and that in such a case the pursuer must be in the position of a liferenter so long as the trustees retained the capital.

Up to this point the case is unobjectionable, but Lord Low then went on to grant a declarator to the effect that the pursuer was entitled to the whole estate. Unfortunately, at least as regards the heritage, this decision appeared to be based on section 48 which would seem to be inappropriate in view of the interposition of a trust between the liferent and the estate. And indeed in *Harvey's Trustees* v *Harvey*[154] Lord Justice-Clerk Cooper rejected its authority on this point on the ground that "the report is imperfect, for it appears from an examination of the process, that section 17 of the Act of 1868 and section 47 of the Act of 1848 were also founded upon". This would certainly make more sense of the decision: however, as regards the nature of the pursuer's interest the case would still appear to be authoritative.

Sheill's Trustees v *Sheil's Trustees*[155] was a case under section 17 which concerned a beneficiary whose interest consisted of a contingent fee but with a right to the income arising while the contingency remained unsatisfied. It was held that the beneficiary's right was not a liferent and that accordingly the Act had no application. Again, this in itself can hardly be objected to. The difficulty comes from an oblique reference in Lord Kyllachy's judgement. The point was that the beneficiary's right to income was subject to termination during his lifetime on the satisfaction of the contingency governing the fee. While the case ultimately seems to have been decided on the perfectly proper ground that the beneficiary's interest amounted to a contingent fee and that a contingent fee was not a liferent, Lord Kyllachy approached the matter in a more negative fashion[156] holding that the interest was not a liferent because it had the characteristics of a contingent fee and because it was "less than a

---

[153] (1900) 8 S.L.T. 28 (O.H.).
[154] 1942 S.C. at p. 585.
[155] (1906) 8 F 848.
[156] (1906) 8 F at p. 854.

liferent" in that it might terminate during the lifetime of the grantee. If this is right it means that liferents which are subject to termination or defeasance on the occurrence of some event prior to the liferenter's death would not count as liferents for the purposes of the legislation.

This view seems to run counter to the mainstream authorities which appear to follow the principle that a liferent will not cease to be such merely because it is terminable during the lifetime of the liferenter. There are dicta in two nineteenth century House of Lords cases[157] and the decision of the Court of Session in *Chaplin's Trustee* v *Hoile*[158], which concerned a protective trust where the liferent was subject to forfeiture on any attempt to assign it, to the effect that the interests of the grantees were nevertheless liferents. Admittedly these cases were not concerned with the application of the perpetuity provisions, but it is nonetheless suggested that the principle they embody is to be preferred to that of Lord Kyllachy. The point is that the provisions operate on the existing law. They frame no special definition of liferent, so presumably that obtaining under the ordinary law is appropriate. If this is correct then as terminable or defeasible liferents have been held under the general law to be liferents, there would seem to be no good reason for excluding the provisions in such a case.

It has been said that section 18 of the 1968 Act restricts itself to liferent interests both in moveables and heritage. To this extent it is co-extensive with the scope of the earlier provisions dealing with moveables but is clearly less extensive than the provisions of the Act of 1848. But of these provisions only section 48 is now inoperative: section 18 did not, for example, interfere with the scope of section 49 which provided:

"That where any land or estate in Scotland, shall, by virtue of any tack, assignation of tack or other deed or writing .... be held in lease, either directly or through trustees for his behoof, by a party of full age, born after the date of such tack [etc.] such party shall not in any way be affected by any prohibitions, conditions, restrictions or limitations which may be contained in such tack [etc.], or by which the same, or the interest of such party therein may be qualified, such prohibitions, conditions, restrictions or limitations being of the nature of prohibitions, conditions, restrictions or limitations of entail, or intended to regulate the succession of such party, or to limit, restrict or abridge his possession or enjoyment of such land or estate in favour of any future heir."

The restrictions on the imposition of entail-type conditions is clear enough. What perhaps is less clear is that the section appears to be aiming at a device which might have been used as or alternative to the grant of liferents in succession, namely the grant of successive leases for life, which would not be caught by section 48 as the interest granted would not amount to a liferent.

While section 18 has rendered obsolete section 47 of the 1848 Act to the extent that that section dealt with trust liferents of heritable property, its scope is otherwise unaffected and still has a potentially wide application today. It is drafted along the same lines as section 49 aimed at limitations or restrictions on the possession or enjoyment of heritable subjects held in trust as a result of any conditions, prohibitions, restrictions or limitations contained in the deed which

---

[157] *Campbell* v *Wardlaw* (1883) 10 R (H.L.) 65; esp. per Lord Blackburn at p. 66; *Naismith* v *Boyes* (1899) 1 F (H.L.) 79 esp. per Lord Watson at pp. 80/81.
[158] (1890) 18 R 27.

are intended to have that result. The section clearly has in mind entail-type restrictions. As Lord Mackay commented in *Middleton*:[159]

"The first part of the section takes a declaratory form that a party who fulfils certain conditions as to date of birth and so on, and who is 'in lawful possession, either directly or through any trustees' of land in Scotland 'shall not be in any way affected by any prohibitions, conditions or limitations' obtained in the trust deed 'by which the same or interest of such party therein may bear to be qualified, such prohibitions, conditions, restrictions or limitations being in the nature of prohibitions, conditions, restrictions and limitations of entail'. I pause here to say that this phrase . . . . sets the keynote of the section. It seems to me to be a section striking at prohibitions and restrictions in the nature of entail fetters, but purporting to be set up under the guise of a trust, thereby tending at least to defeat the laws of entail which might perhaps be construed as applying only to direct dispositions in the tailzied form. But the section proceeds . . . . 'or interested to regulate the succession of such party in favour or to limit the restrict or abridge his possession or enjoyment of such land or estate in favour of any future heir'. That completes the sort of trusts that are struck at. For my part I think it very plain that the last words again emphasise the keynote. It is the legal limitation of an heir in possession in favour of future heirs that is the subject struck at."

Middleton was a case of a simple trust designed to admit as beneficiaries heirs of entail, but which, by operation of the trust provisions, sought to restrict the interest of each heir to that of a liferent. Lord Mackay, as Lord Ordinary, held that as the conditions set out in the trust deed were not strictly in accordance with the prohibitions of entail, the case was outwith the scope of section 47. On appeal however this finding was reversed, its being felt that any conditions which fell within the terms of the section would bring the trust within its ambit whether or not such conditions constituted entail fetters.

It will be seen that the section does not define the interests of the beneficiaries that are to come within it. It merely prescribes that there should be "lawful possession" of land in Scotland where the enjoyment is limited by conditions set out in the trust. Clearly a beneficiary who is in possession as a consequence of his beneficial interest[160] under the trust will be caught, assuming the existence of the requisite conditions and restrictions; but what of the case of an object of the trustees' discretion under a discretionary trust who would have no legally recognisable interest at all and where possession would be dependant on the continued exercise of the trustees' discretion in his favour.

The answer would seem to depend on the terms of the discretion and on its exercise. The point is that if the trustees are given an absolute discretion then an exercise of that discretion which simply resulted in factual possession would seem not to bring the section into operation: for even though "lawful possession" might be construed so as to include factual possession, that possession would scarcely be cut down as a result of entail-type fetters. Indeed it can scarcely be said to have been restricted in any sense, since there would in law be nothing that could be cut down, a point which would appear to favour the view that lawful possession for the purposes of this section refers only to possession in pursuance of a beneficial interest.

If this latter view is correct then it follows that any exercise of the trustees'

---

[159] 1929 S.C. 394 at p. 397. See also per Lord Blackburn at p. 400.
[160] See per Ungoed-Thomas J. in *Sainsbury* v *IRC* [1969] 3 All E.R. 919; and the House of Lords in *Gartside* v *IRC* [1968] A.C. 553.

discretion which merely permits possession would be outside the scope of the section, even if the discretion was fenced round with entail-type conditions. Accordingly then it would seem that it is still perfectly possible to create a perpetuity even in land by means of a discretionary trust.[161]

It would seem, in fact, that the only occasion where a discretionary trust would come within the scope of any of the provisions would be if the trustees exercised their discretion in such a way as to create a derivative settlement which itself fell foul of one of the rules. But in such a case it would still leave the original settlement untouched.

Qualifying Beneficiaries

As we shall see below[162] the statutory provisions operate, not by declaring a particular destination void, but by giving to a particular beneficiary, or by providing him with the means of obtaining, an unrestricted fee in the subjects. However, to be so benefited, a beneficiary has to satisfy certain requirements relating to his birth and its relationship with the date of the deed.

If one can glean a common principle as to qualification running through all the provisions, it is that the relevant beneficiary must have been born after the date of the deed creating the liferent, lease or other appropriate interest in his favour. Apparently "born after" in the various provisions is to be given its natural meaning so that a posthumous child, though in utero at the relevant date, will not qualify.[163]

While this is still the position with regard to sections 47 (insofar as the interest is not a liferent) and 49, section 18 of the 1968 Act has modified this with regard to deeds taking effect after 25th November 1968, so that children in utero at the relevant date are now to be treated as being in life then.[164]

Sections 47, 48 and 49 however restrict the benefits to liferenters and others who have attained majority. In *Crichton Stuart's Tutrix*[165] it was attempted to extend the benefit of section 48 to a minor but it was held that it was not within the court's nobile officium to do so. Whereas statutory provisions cover the position with regard to heritage, section 9 is curiously silent as to the position concerning moveables during the minority of a liferenter who prima facie qualified. In *Stewart's Trustees* v *Whitelaw*[166] however Lord Sands felt that the position was the same, holding that section 9 would not apply during the liferenter's minority. Section 18 of the 1968 Act[167] confirms this in respect of the deeds to which it applies.

Perhaps the most difficult part of the law governing qualifications is that relating the beneficiary's birth to the date of the deed. In most ordinary cases there are few problems, a simple comparison being enough, and even in pre-1848 deeds relating to heritage and pre-1868 deeds of moveables again there are few

---

[161] The perpetuity rules governing moveables, of course cannot apply to discretionary trusts, except perhaps in the case of a derivative settlement set up by the exercise of the trustees' discretion.
[162] At p. 271 et seq.
[163] See *Neid's Trustees* v *Dashwood* 1929 S.C. 748 esp. per Lord President Clyde at 751-3.
[164] section 18 (1).
[165] 1921 S.C. 840.
[166] 1926 S.C. 701.
[167] section 18 (1) (b).

problems, the dates being deemed to be 10th August 1914[168] and 1st August 1924[169] respectively. The difficulties arise, especially in the case of heritage, where the deed does not come into operation immediately. Given that virtually all testamentary deeds will be of this type the size of the problem can be seen to be large. Surprisingly, however, only one case has come before the courts. This was that of the *Earl of Moray*[170] which came before Lord Macintosh in the Outer House in 1950. The case was brought under section 47 and concerned a deed whereby the truster had directed his trustees to hold the residue of his estate, heritable and moveable for payment of the annual income therefrom to or for behoof of the successor of individuals who should succeed to his title and dignity, so long as the law might permit. In 1949 part of the trust estate was represented by superiorities and it was sought to utilise section 47 to enable the then Earl to acquire them in fee. This individual had been born in 1894, prior to the original truster's death but after the date of the settlement. As the settlement was testamentary it did not come into operation until the death. It was held by Lord Macintosh that the provisions relating to the date of the deed should be read "literally" so that, on his construction, the petitioner was not in life at the relevant date and therefore had the benefit of the section.

Section 9 operates differently providing that "the date of any testamentary or mortis causa deed being taken to be the date of the death of the granter, and the date of any contract of marriage being taken to be the date of the dissolution of the marriage." Section 18 combines these two approaches as far as liferent settlements are concerned by applying the moveables rules to heritage as well.[171]

Effect

It has been mentioned already that the broad effect of the legislative provisions is to free, or at least provide a means of freeing, a qualifying beneficiary from entail-type fetters. Apart from section 49, however, the provisions do not rest there but go on to enlarge the qualifying interest into a fee. This, apart from the problems attendant upon such enlargement, raises the additional difficulty of third party rights.

(a) Section 49

Section 49 is perhaps the easiest to deal with providing simply a remedy in that ". . . . Such party shall not be in any way affected by any prohibitions . . . . contained in such tack . . . . or by which . . . . the interest of such party therein may be qualified". In other words the lease is not nullified, the interest of the lessee remaining exactly as it was, save that he is freed from the restrictions. Procedurally section 49 differs from the others in that it is defensive; the lessee does not have to go to court or go through any special form to establish this freedom; he merely pleads section 49 as a defence in any action to enforce the restrictions.

---

[168] Entail Act 1914, section 8.
[169] Conveyancing (Scotland) Act 1924, section 45.
[170] 1950 S.L.T. 188.
[171] Section 18 (5).

(b) Section 47

Section 47 provides that a qualifying beneficiary may present a summary petition to the Court of Session "craving the Court to pronounce an act and decree declaring him fee simple proprietor of such land or estate and unaffected by any such conditions...."[172] Again the primary target is the conditions themselves although here any limitations inherent in the interest itself are also overcome by the permitted enlargement. But unlike section 48 and section 9 there is no attempt in the section to render the creation of such interests incompetent, and it is with such attempts that the chief difficulties with regard to the statutory perpetuity rules have been encluntered.

(c) Section 48 and section 9

The difficulties attendant upon the application of these sections lie primarily in their drafting. Each section is in two parts, the first part seemingly prohibiting the creation of liferent interests in favour of persons not in life at the date the deed comes into operation, both then going on to make provision for what is to happen in the event of the prohibition not being complied with.

The two sections are similarly, though not identically worded. As Lord President Clyde said in *Reid's Trustees* v *Dashwood*:[173]

"That section [i.e. section 48] deals with liferents of heritage and is obviously the model on which section 17 of the Act of 1868 (and section 9 of the Act of 1921) was drawn. There are the same or very similar two parts, the same declaration (in the first part) with regard to the competency of making liferent interests in favour only of persons "in life" at the date of the deed and the same apparent restriction (in the second part) of the benefit of the section to persons who (1) attain majority and (2) are 'born' after the date of the deed, but—no doubt because in 1848 heritage could not be the subject of a testament—there is no declaration substituting the date of the death of the granter of the deed for the date of the deed itself."

Given then the similarity in terms and the obvious derivation of section 9 from section 48 how is it that the two have come to be construed differently? To quote Lord President Clyde again:[174]

".... section 48 of the Act of 1848 does not itself convert liferent into fee but only gives the liferenter the power to acquire the fee for himself by means of a petition, similar to that presented by an heir of entail .... for disentail without consents under section 1 of that Act. If the liferenter did not exercise it, the heritage was held in *Crichton-Stuart's* case [175] to pass as directed in the deed; and the declaration in the first part of the section (that it was to be 'competent' in future to make liferents in favour only of persons 'in life' at the date of the deed) was construed neither to make it illegal to confer a liferent on a person born after the date of the deed, nor to render such a liferent if conferred, void, but only to limit the power or 'competence' of the granter to restrict the interest of the disponee to an *inconvertible* liferent within the class of disponees 'born' before the date of the deed.

This construction is, however, impossible of application to the section under consideration in the present case, because the second part of the section by its own terms converts the liferent into a fee. What is given to the liferenter of moveables is not a power to acquire the fee but the fee itself.

What then is the position of a liferenter of moveables born after the date of the

---

[172] per Lord Mackay in *Harvey's Trustees* v *Harvey* 1942 S.C. 582 at p. 588.
[173] 1929 S.C. 748 at p. 752/3.
[174] *ibid.* at p. 753.
[175] 1921 S.C. 840.

testamentary deed but before the date of the testator's death. It may well be that the first part of the section now under consideration falls to be construed differently from the first part of section 48 of the Act of 1848. The terms of the two sections are no doubt so far identical but the subject matter and the context are different. I am inclined to think that the two parts of section 17 of the Act of 1868 (or section 9 of the Act of 1921) must be construed together, in which case I think that the second, as the operative part of the deed must prevail over the first part and must receive effect even though it may not be possible to reconcile it completely with the first or declaratory part."

The essence of the distinction, according to Lord Clyde, is that the words of section 48, though identical in this respect with those of section 9, do not mean what they say; that, in effect, under section 48 it is competent to create liferent interests in favour of those not in life at the date of the deed whereas under section 9 it is not. There are, it will be noticed, two reasons given for this view. The first is that "the subject matter and the context are different". But with the greatest respect this would seem to be inadequate; what are the differences which dictate that heritage should in this respect be treated differently from moveables? Lord Clyde does not mention them and certainly they are difficult to find. And what is different about the overall context?

If the first reason is unsatisfactory the second, that the second part of section 9 "by its own terms converts the liferent into a fee", whereas apparently the second part of section 48 does not, is even more so; for, although admittedly the words of this part of section 48 are different from those of section 9, they would appear to admit of no difference in meaning stating specifically that "the party shall not be in any way affected by any prohibitions, restrictions or limitations which may be contained in such deed . . . . and such party shall be deemed and taken to be the fee simple proprietor of such estate". With all respect to Lord Clyde, it is suggested that these words do exactly the same thing for section 48 as do the relevant words for section 9. Both are followed by what are essentially procedural requirements for going to the court to make up the appropriate title. In both cases these steps are mandatory if an absolute title is to be obtained. What appears to have happened is that in *Crichton-Stuart's* case these procedural requirements have been taken as qualifying the substantive right of the party concerned, a construction which, it is submitted, is wrong.[176]

Yet this, of itself, does not solve the problem of reconciling the two parts of the sections. If "competent" is read literally it would appear to render such liferents as were purported to be created in contravention of the provisions void; but if that construction is the right one, the second part of section 48 would appear to be redundant. Nonetheless it appears to have found some support in the House of Lords in *Muir's Trustees* v *Williams*.[177] Lord Thankerton expressed it in this way:[178]

"[The section] contains two parts, the first of which appears to be declaratory of a prohibition by means of a declaration of what is alone competent. It might have been expressed as a direct prohibition, and, according to the usual canons of construction, it would be tantamount to a direct prohibition. But when you come to the second part which is operative in character, it does not become operative until there is a post-

---

[176] See per Dobie—Liferent and Fee at p. 260 for a supporting view.
[177] 1943 S.C. (H.L.) 47.
[178] *ibid.* at p. 52.

natus of full age.... I will add only that I am unable to agree with [the view] that the Entail Act recognises the competency of creating a liferent in favour of a person not in life at the date of the deed constituting the liferent; it appears to me to have done its best to say exactly the opposite."

If this view is right, it leaves open the position of the appropriate beneficiary until the relevant qualifications have been obtained. If it is not "operative" until then, presumably the liferent granted will in fact be good during this time. If this is correct then it becomes difficult, to reconcile the second part of Lord Thankerton's statement with the first part.

The other view of the word "competent" comes from Lord President Clyde. In *Reid's Trustees* v *Dashwood*[179] he was clearly aware of the difficulties. He said:

"In the first place it is declared to be 'competent' to make a liferent of moveables by deed only in favour of a person who is 'in life' at the date of the deed....

In the second place it is enacted that any moveables which .... may be held in liferent for a person (1) of full age and (2) 'born' after the date of such deed shall belong to such person absolutely and shall be made over to such person accordingly. In this second part of the section there is introduced, by means of parenthetical words .... a direction that, in the case of a testamentary deed, the date of such deed is to be held to be the date of the testator's death.

There is difficulty in apprehending the precise meaning of the word 'competent' and (partly perhaps on that account) in making the two parts of the section fit consistently together. The first part appears to strike—to some effect or other—against a liferent in favour of A who comes into life after the date of the [deed]. It appears that A's liferent stands good, in any case, during his minority notwithstanding the declaration in the first part that it is not 'competent' for the testator to make that liferent; with the result that if A should die without attaining majority the fee of the moveables liferented [to][180] him would pass as directed by the [deed]. Again if A was born after the date of [a] testamentary deed but before the date of the testator's death then— whether or not he has attained his majority—the second part of the section fails of application. But in that case what is the effect to be attributed to the declaration in the first part of the section? In the liferent to be a nullity with the result that the fee passes as directed by the testament, in the same way as it would have done if the statute had not interfered with the liferent at all; or is some less drastic meaning to be given to the word 'competent'?"

In point of fact the Lord President had already answered this question eight years before in relation to section 48 in *Crichton-Stuart's Tutrix*.[181] He said:

"[The section] is in three parts closely related to each other.
(1) It confines the theretofore unrestricted power of a settler effectually to limit the grant of an estate to a liferent to cases in which the selected liferenter is a person living at the date of the grant.
(2) It liberates a person of full age who (*a*) holds an estate .... limited to a liferent and (*b*) was born after the date of the grant, from the limitations, endows him with the rights and powers of a fee simple owner and allows him to establish the fact of his liberation from the limitations by a declarator or petition.
(3) It saves the rights of superiors and security holders, and all other rights derived otherwise than from the deed conferring the liferent.

It will be observed that this enactment in none of its parts makes the grant .... of an estate limited to a liferent interest, unlawful or void. Nor is there in any of them, anything to prevent the grantee .... of an estate so limited from adopting the course of

---

[179] 1929 S.C. 748 at p. 752.
[180] The report actually reades liferented *by*. But presumably this is a mistake for that word would seem to indicate the person creating, as opposed to receiving, the liferent.
[181] 1921 S.C. 810 at p. 843/844.

refraining from availing[182] himself of the rights and powers of a fee simple owner which the statute places within his reach, and apply for a declaration. The object of the enactment indeed is not to make such liferent interests null and void; it is only to disable settlers from making such limitations irremediably effective against the grantee. If the grantee is content with his limited estate and prefers that the settlement should take its course, he is free to act accordingly.[182] The enactment is that 'it shall be *competent* to grant an estate . . . . limited to a liferent interest in favour *only*' of a particular class of persons. This is a different thing from saying that 'it shall be *lawful* to grant a limited estate in favour *only* of that particular class'; and it may be accurately paraphrased thus: 'it shall be in the rightful power (competency) of a settler effectually to restrict the grantee of an estate to a liferent interest in the case only' of grantees belonging to the particular class. Any inconsistency which might at first sight appear to exist between the first and restrictive part of the clause and the reference in the second part to an estate 'held in liferent' . . . . thus disappears."

Section 18 (1) of the 1968 Act manages to avoid these difficulties by concentrating on the operative part, omitting completely any reference to competence, providing:

"Whereby any deed executed after the commencement of this Act there is created a liferent interest in any property and a person who not living or in utero at the date of the coming into operation of the said deed becomes entitled to that interest then—
  (a) if that person is of full age at the date on which he becomes entitled to the liferent interest, as from that date, or
  (b) if that person is not of full age at that date, as from the date on which, being still entitled to the liferent interest, he becomes of full age,
the said property shall . . . . belong absolutely to that person, and, if the property is vested in trustees, those trustees shall, subject as aforesaid, be bound to convey, deliver or make over the property to that person."

Essentially then section 18, with slight modifications as to qualifications, embodies the *Reid's Trustees* v *Dashwood*[183] interpretation of section 9 and applies that across the board.

(d) Third Party Rights

There are two classes of third party rights which might be adversely affected by the enlargement of a liferent into a fee. The first consists of commercial interests, usually encountered in connection with heritage, such as rights in security and any feudal rights appertaining to a superiority over the subjects liferented. Section 9 makes no provision for these commercial interests, for obviously superior's rights would not be relevant in moveable or personal property although rights in security might well be. Presumably any question here would be decided by analogy with section 48 which specifically saves such rights from the operation of the provision. Certainly in post-1968 deeds this position applies irrespective of the nature of the property.[184]

The second class is rather more difficult for it concerns beneficial interests in the property. Two types of interest would appear to be prejudiced: in the first place, obviously, any person to whom the fee was specifically given, but in addition any beneficiaries who had interests limited by or to the duration of the infringing liferent would also be affected adversely. The point provoked

---

[182] This depends on the view rejected above at p. 275.
[183] 1929 S.C. 748.
[184] section 18 (2) (a)—rights in security—and (c)—rights in superiority, although obviously this can only apply to heritage.

discussion in three cases[185] on the 1868 Act, the conclusion being reached that section 17 would not apply if its operation would defeat third party rights. In *Mackenzie's Trustees* v *Mackenzie*[186] this principle was applied by the Lord Ordinary, Lord Blackburn. However on appeal this finding was reversed and the dicta on which it was based disapproved. The basis of this decision was that the section must be construed strictly and that if it was so construed and the interest in question fell within it, the statutory rules must be applied irrespective of the effect on the interests of third parties.

Such a principle, which is not without its difficulties with regard to possible hardship to the third party concerned nevertheless is not without its advantages from the anti-avoidance point of view; a contrary rule would provide a relatively simple way for the provisions to be circumvented.

It is a matter for speculation as to whether this principle applies to heritage as well as moveables, for section 48 is drafted rather differently on this point from section 17 and section 9 of the 1921 Act, containing a specific provision saving interests created independently of the deed by which the liferent in question was created, a provision which is carried forward into section 18 of the 1968 Act and extended to moveables and to trust liferents.[187] However neither section 48, nor section 18 refers to the case of third party interests of a beneficial nature created by the same deed. Given the assimilation effected by the 1968 Act it would seem that it applies to all settlements covered by that Act. It is also suggested that the silence in section 48 on the subject, together with the absence of anything in the provision to indicate that such a rule would not apply (indeed the specific saving of interests created by separate deeds might indicate that it would apply) would seem to favour the general application of the rule in such cases.

Powers of Appointment

The significance of powers of appointment in this context lies in their potential as instruments of avoidance. Thus a settlement might comply with the liferent rules but give a power to a beneficiary to appoint liferent interests to beneficiaries who need not be in esse at the date of the deed.

The first consideration of this question was made by the First Division in *Stewart's Trustees* v *Whitelaw*[188] which concerned a trust settlement by which a testator had directed trustees to hold a sum of money for his four children in liferent for each of them in separate shares and in fee for their respective issue per stirpes. One of the children directed that her provision should be held by her father's trustees for behoof of her children in liferent and for her children's children in fee. The daughter died leaving a child who was born after the death of the testator. The point was that if the liferent so constituted in favour of the child could be construed as issuing from the original settlement, section 9 would

---

[185] *Maccullogh* v *Maccullogh's Trustees* (1903) 6 F (H.L.) 3 per Lord Davey at pp. 6-7; *Shiell's Trustees* v *Shiell's Trustees* (1906) 8 F 848 per Lord Stormonth-Darling at pp. 853/854; *Baxter* v *Baxter* 1909 S.C. 1027 per Lord President Dunedin at p. 1031.
[186] 1922 S.C. 404.
[187] section 18 (2) (b).
[188] 1926 S.C. 701.

have applied so that the child could have claimed the fee. Perhaps unfortunately the point was not specifically decided since the only party interested—the child —did not contest it.

However Lord Sands[189] felt that the matter should be governed by a rule of English law that the operative date should be the date of the settlement where the power, as in this case, was a special power and he cited in support of his contention the case of *Fane* v *Fane*.[190] The rationale of this principle was explained at length by Lord Romer in *Muir's Trustees* v *Williams*.[191] He said:

"If a person be given a general power of appointment over certain property, he is virtually the owner of that property. If and when he exercises the power the interests of his appointees come to them by virtue of, and are created by the deed of appointment. In the case of a special power it is very different. If, for example, property be settled upon trust for A for life and after his death upon trust for such of A's children or remoter issue and in such porportions as B shall by deed appoint, B has no interest in the property whatsoever. He has merely been given the power of saying on behalf of the settler which of the issue of A shall take the property under the settlement and in what proportions. It is as though the settler had left a blank in the settlement which B fills up for him if and when the power of appointment is exercised. The appointees interests come to them under the settlement alone and by virtue of that document. These remarks apply equally well to the case where the donee of a power of appointment has not only the power of saying which of the class shall take under the trust, but also the power of saying what interests they shall take. This would be the case if, in the instance that I have given, the limitation after A's life interest were for such of the children or remoter issue of A in such proportions and for such estates and interests as B shall by deed appoint. If and when B executes the power the settlement will, in accordance with the principle be read thereafter as if the property had been thereby limited to the appointees for the several estates and interests specified in the deed of appointment."

To this might be added the words of Lord Macmillan:[192]

"I think [it to be] a sound principle of construction . . . . that 'where a testator gives a power of appointment under which the donee of the power may appoint among a limited class to a liferent of part of the testator's estate, the validity of the appointment must be judged as if the exercise of the power were read into the will of the granter of the power . . . .' Finally, if it is not competent to constitute directly a liferent in favour of a post natus, it is not competent to do so indirectly by delegation. Such a liferent cannot competently be constituted 'by means of a trust or otherwise'. What is not competent per direction is not competent per obliquium."

This principle was apparently followed in the unreported sequel to *Stewart's Trustees* v *Whitelaw* in 1932 by Lord Pitman in the Outer House.[193]

The next case in which the matter arose was *Burns' Trustees* v *McKenna*[194] where again the discussion was obiter but Lord Justice-Clerk Aitchison and Lord Wark both held that this principle was the correct one to be applied in such cases.

In *Muir's Trustees* v *Williams*[195] this issue was vital. The Second Division reviewed the existing cases, found they were not bound by any of them, and refused to apply the principle, holding that the better date was the date of the

---

[189] *ibid.* at pp. 719-720.
[190] [1913] 1 Ch. 404 esp. per Buckley L.J. at pp. 413, 414.
[191] 1943 S.C. (H.L.) 47 at p. 58/59.
[192] *ibid.* at p. 55.
[193] *Whitelaw* v *Stewart's Trustees* 1932 (unreported).
[194] 1940 S.C. 489.
[195] 1942 S.C. 5 (Ct. of Sess.); 1943 S.C. (H.L.) 47.

exercise of the power. Lord Justice-Clerk Cooper[196] delivered a strong attack on the principle, rejecting its introduction as unnecessary Anglicisation[197], which was in any event unacceptable because, in his view, it was derived from the technicalities of the English rule against perpetuities, a rule which had no place in, and whose influence ought to be excluded from Scots law.

Lord Wark[198] was obviously much impressed by this, for he recanted, stating that his opinion in Burns' case had been wrong on this point and that he now supported the Lord Justice-Clerk. As did Lord Jamieson. Accordingly the Second Division held that the operative date was the date of the exercise of the power and not the date of the settlement.

The case then went to the House of Lords who unanimously reversed the decision of the Court of Session and re-asserted the rule, holding that its origin was not to be found in the specialties of the English rule against perpetuities and that it was of general application. Lord Thankerton indeed[199] went into the precedents and attempted to show that this rule of construction had a place in Scots law irrespective of any suggested English importation. This view he founded on a passage in McLaren[200] and on a dictum of Lord Moncrieff in *Marshall's Trustees* v *Findlay*[201] that, "in a case in which a person vested with a power of appointment exercises that power such an exercise confers rights of succession which flow from the maker of the power and not from the party which exercises it".

That the principle had been re-asserted as good law in Scotland was confirmed by the majority of the Court of Session[202] and a unanimous House of Lords[203] in *Malcolm's Trustees* v *Malcolm* where it was held that the rule applied where the power of appointment was reserved to the truster and not given to a third party.

There was, in fact, an alternative ratio for the rule adumbrated by Lord Thankerton and approved by the other members of the House in *Muir's* case This was to the effect that what the truster had done was to have conveyed to his trustees the whole estate for his grandson in fee, and his successor could not, therefore be said to have constituted or reserved the relevant liferent by the subsequent appointment; that the subsequent deed was not the constitution of a liferent but the limitation or restriction of a fee which the truster had assigned and had no power to withdraw. In the words of Lord Macmillan:[204]

"What the testator did by his trust-disposition and settlement was, in effect, to confer on his grandchildren an interest in a share of his estate, leaving it to his son to say, if he chose that this interest should be restricted to a liferent."

In *Malcolm's Trustees* v *Malcolm*, before the Court of Session it was pleaded that this was the only true ratio decidendi of *Muir's* case and that as the truster had reserved to himself the power in the case before them *Muir's* case had no

---

[196] 1942 S.C. at pp. 11-15.
[197] See above at Chapter II.
[198] 1942 S.C. at pp. 15-17.
[199] 1943 S.C. (H.L.) at p. 53.
[200] Wills and Succession vol. ii section 2048.
[201] 1928 S.L.T. 560 at p. 561.
[202] 2nd Division—Lord Mackay dissenting; 1948 S.L.T. 549.
[203] 1950 S.C. (H.L.) 17.
[204] 1943 S.C. (H.L.) at p. 55.

application. The majority however refused to accept this, holding, as did the House of Lord's that both rationes were valid and that under both the truster's power should be viewed as having been given by the original settlement.

Accordingly then it is settled law as far as section 9 (and presumably section 47 as well) is concerned that the effects of the Scottish perpetuity statutes cannot be evaded by means of a special power of appointment.[205] This rule has been carried forward into post 1968 settlements by section 18 (5) (c) of the 1968 Act so that where a special power of appointment is validly exercised in favour of a person not in esse at the date of the instrument creating the power, so as to confer on that person an interest in liferent, that interest will be enlarged into a fee immediately, if the appointee is of full age, or if he is not of full age, on his attaining it.

---

[205] Clearly the provisions could be evaded by means of a general power of appointment. But as such a power would, by definition, invest the donee with the right to appoint the property in favour of himself, from a perpetuity point of view, any attempt to avoid the legislation by this means would be self-defeating.

CHAPTER V

ACCUMULATIONS

HOWEVER independent might have been the development of most of the law of perpetuities in Scotland, it is an undoubted fact that the law governing accumulations of income has come from England,[1] both in the specific rules applicable to accumulations under Scottish trust settlements and in the raison d'etre for those rules. Ironically, it was not the achievement of the Modern Rule against Perpetuities that led to the framing of special rules to deal with accumulations of income, but rather its failure; specifically its failure, in the eyes of contemporary opinion in England, to deal adequately with the will of Peter Thellusson.[2]

Traditionally, the treatment of accumulations by Scottish commentators has tended to begin and end with the Thellusson Act,[3] the amendments to it and the judicial interpretation of it. It is accepted as an English imposition, and the implication that accompanies such acceptance is that accumulation settlements also came to Scotland from the South. Accordingly, then, it would appear to be proper to look first at the English developments and to examine whether, and if so, how they correspond with events in Scotland.

The Origins of Accumulation Settlements in England

The underlying principle of the accumulation trust is essentially that of compound interest; that not only is capital invested so as to produce income profits, but that these income profits, instead of being distributed, are themselves invested and added to capital. Given that England was a commercial country where this principle was practised every day in banking and other transactions it is perhaps surprising that accumulation settlements appeared comparatively late. Indeed the first true accumulation cases did not come before the courts until the second quarter of the eighteenth century.

The contemporary authority on accumulation settlements was Hargrave who was senior (and unsuccessful) counsel for the children in the *Thallusson case*[4] and who wrote at length on the problems surrounding the origins of such settlements and who drew on this learning to found his arguments before the Court of Chancery and the House of Lords. Although his arguments failed to establish his client's case his statement as to the origin and early development of accumulation settlements was apparently accepted. Certainly it has been accepted by legal historians[5] although its application in the *Thellusson case* has been criticised.[6]

---

[1] See above Chapter II.
[2] See Morris & Leach "The Rule against Perpetuities" (2nd Ed. 1962) at pp. 303-306; G. W. Keeton "Social Change in the Law of Trusts" (1958) Ch. 4; "The Thellusson Case and Trusts for Accumulation" (1970) 21 N.I.L.Q. 131; "Modern Developments in the Law of Trusts" (1971) Ch. 17.
[3] 39 & 40 Geo. III. c. 98 subsequently named the Accumulation Act 1800.
[4] *Thellusson* v *Woodford* (1799) 4 Ves. 227; (1805) 11 Ves. 112 (H.L.).
[5] Esp. Holdsworth—History of English Law vol. vii at pp. 228-231.
[6] See Keeton 21 N.I.L.Q. 131.

The substance of Hargrave's view is that trusts designed to secure the accumulation of income arose out of constructions put upon legacies and gifts of residuary personalty where the vesting of the capital of the fund had been postponed and where the intermediate income had been left undisposed of by the testator. The courts affected to construe gifts of the corpus of the fund as carrying, by implication, the intermediate income, but that until such time as the stated contingency should be satisfied the income should be accumulated in the hands of the trustees, whereupon it should be transferred with the capital when an interest in that vested. Upon such directions of the court settlors founded elaborate settlements directing expressly that accumulation should take place (and therefore enjoyment postponed) during such periods before the relevant interest vested. In *Thellusson* v *Woodford*[7] Hargrave put it this way:

"However, the practice of posthumous accumulation has, I confess, by some means insinuated itself. During infancy, such a trust is scarce more than a restraint upon expenditure almost necessarily incident to that situation. On that account, perhaps, a trust for the same purpose escaped observation. This might lead to attempts at the same thing for a short time afterwards, and in a way independant both of minority and mental incapacity. Thus, insensibly, trust[s] of accumulation obtained some sort of footing. At length, I believe, even respectable lawyers have been led to suppose it allowable to annex trust[s] of accumulation to executory devise[s] . . . . [with regard to] the intermediate profits between the death of the testator and the vesting of the executory devise."

It must be remembered, when considering Hargrave's argument in this case, that he was seeking to upset the trust and was therefore seeking to show how the court could act to the benefit of his clients. His approach was to attempt to show that the practice of settling funds for accumulation, and the cases in which that practice had been upheld were discreditable by suggesting that the practice had crept in through the back door and, where it had been sanctioned by the court, without proper consideration having been given to it. As we know, this tactic failed: the point was that by the time of *Thellusson* v *Woodford* the issue, at least as far as the Chancery was concerned, was beyond recall. Thus counsel for the trustees in the original suit submitted:[8]

"It is surprising that it should be doubted whether the attention of this Court has been given muct to accumulation. There are many cases in which accumulation has been directed by the Court, because the testator has expressly directed it; others in which it has been directed not for that reason but because the will contains indications of such an intention; and others in which the attention of the Court has been so much drawn to the legality of the accumulation directed as to fix the period beyond which it shall not go.[9] There are many cases in which the attention of the Court has not been called to the subject; which is to be accounted for upon this; that, large as the property may have been, there was no provision to argue a point so well settled."

The earliest reported decision was *Studholme* v *Hodgson*[10] which concerned a bequest of residuary personalty to an infant, with the vesting postponed until

---

[7] (1799) 4 Ves. at p. 264.
[8] *ibid.* at p. 285.
[9] Counsel then cited two late examples, *the Case of Lady Denison's Will*, at the Rolls, 11th July 1787 before Lord Kenyon M.R. which was unreported but given the title *Harrison* v *Harrison* in the Register Book, which concerned a real estate fund, and the very recently decided *Webb* v *Earl of Shaftesbury*, otherwise *Earl of Shaftesbury* v *Arrowsmith*—Trinity Term 1789 unreported.
[10] (1734) 3 P.Wms. 300.

the attainment of majority. There were no directions as to the destination of the income during this period but Lord Talbot L.C. decided that the income should be accumulated and added to the capital. This decision was followed by Lord Hardwicke L.C. in *Green* v *Ekins*[11] in 1742 and was applied subsequently in *Butler* v *Butler*[12], *Travanion* v *Vivian*,[13] *Bullock* v *Stones*[14] and *Gibson* v *Rogers*.[15]

Essentially in these cases the court was filling in a gap left by the testator. In *Mole* v *Mole*[16] that gap had been filled in by the draftsman, the will containing express directions to accumulate. The court upheld the validity of the direction, as it did in *Hawkins* v *Combe*.[17]

In *Green* v *Ekins,* Lord Hardwicke had drawn a distinction between personalty and realty, but even in respect of real estate a similar process was going on. To quote Hargrave again:[18]

"[Trusts for accumulation have] insensibly sprung up under the shelter of executory devise and trusts of the like nature.[19] Cases have occurred both for real and personal estate; not cases of accumulations; but controverted cases of executory devise and testamentary trusts without any express words to explain to whom the intermediate profits of the devised property should belong; and cases in which the great point was whether the boundary line of executory devise was exceeded, and in cases in which the point as to intermediate profits was merely incidental and secondary. These cases also arising on devises of residuary estate, the courts of equity were in some instances, and the courts of law, on reference to them from the former courts for opinion in others, were tempted by the comprehensive force of the words 'residue' and 'residuary' to construe them, as carrying the intermediate profits to the executory devise or legatee. In this way Chancery decided for itself in *Chapman* v *Blissett*[20] before Lord Talbot in 1735. In the same way Lord Hardwicke and the other judge of the King's Bench certified to Chancery in *Stephens* v *Stephens*[21] in the following year. Thus while the judges of both courts seemed to be settling the boundaries of executory devise, and to be only incidentally deciding that an unborn person was intended to be legatee of the intermediate profits instead of a living person, they in reality sanctioned a trust of accumulation; because if the intermediate profits were to go to the future devisee or legatee, they were necessarily to be saved and accumulated for him."

The decisions in *Chapman* v *Blissett* and *Stephens* v *Stephens* were applied in 1749 in *Hopkins* v *Hopkins*[22] and again in the following year in *Gibson* v *Lord Mountford*[23] where the court not only prescribed the destination of the intermediate rents and profits but expressly directed that they should be accumulated until vesting day.[24]

As in the personalty cases the examples of express directions came towards

---

[11] (1742) 2 Atk. 473.
[12] (1744) 3 Atk. 58.
[13] (1752) 2 Ves. Sen. 430.
[14] (1754) 2 Ves. Sen. 521.
[15] (1750) 1 Ves. Sen. 485.
[16] (1758) 1 Dick. 310.
[17] (1783) 1 Bro. C.C. 335.
[18] Jurisconsult Exercitations: i, 311-312.
[19] See above—Chapter II.
[20] (1735) Cases. temp. Talbot 145.
[21] (1736) *ibid*. 228.
[22] (1749) 1 Ves. Sen. 268.
[23] (1750) 1 Ves. Sen. 485.
[24] See also *Perry* v *Phelips* (1798) 4 Ves. 108.

the end of the century, specifically in 1786 in the case of *Lady Denison's will*.[25] Here the testatrix had two nieces, both very young, one of them being not more than four or five at the date of the will. The will contained directions to the effect that the residue of her personal estate should be invested in the purchase of land, and that the rents and profits of the land to be purchased, and of certain other real estate held by her at the date of her death, should accumulate until there should be a second son of the body of the eldest niece, such son's interest to vest on his majority. (There were default provisions following upon this). It was contended that the limitation was too remote and further that the accumulation provisions were bad as being unlawful. Lord Kenyon, however, felt that the law was such that the accumulation could not be prevented. As was pointed out in the *Thellusson case*, this accumulation was still going on at the date of the Thellusson litigation. Accordingly then, by the time the Thellusson will was contested there was authority, binding upon the Chancery Court to the effect that accumulations were good provided the period of accumulation did not exceed that permitted by law for the settlement of property.[26] As Hargrave afterwards concluded:[27]

"We gather, firstly, that the origin of trusts for accumulation is of comparatively modern date, there being no traces of such trusts, either express or implied, to be met with much before the middle of the eighteenth century. Secondly, that the first recorded cases of what has been aptly styled 'posthumous avarice' arose as soon as the extension of commerce and progress of trade had brought personal property into importance. Thirdly, that from the middle of the eighteenth century these dispositions had gradually taken a wider range extending from gifts of residuary personalty to real estate and after having primarily engrossed only the surplus income during minorities, had thence extended to the entire income and for longer periods, under cover of an executory devise of the 'rest and residue', but that shortly before the end of the eighteenth century avowed and express trusts for accumulation commensurate with executory devise had made their appearance; although until Mr. Thellusson's experiment, this mania accumulandi, or Sinking Fund Enthusiasm, does not seem to have led men to grasp at more than one life, or at most two lives, and a minority, such life or lives being the life or lives of the parent or parents of the person to be beneficially entitled."

This last remark of Hargrave's raises a further and perhaps broader point concerning the origin of accumulation settlements. Whatever the conveyancing loopholes that made possible the validity of trusts for accumulation we have seen that the bulk of activity in setting up such settlements with express directions to accumulate occurred in the 1780s. This coincided with a significant development in public finance in Britain in the setting up by Pitt in 1786 of a Sinking Fund. The theory, suggested above by Hargrave and followed subsequently by Keeton, was that the creators of accumulation settlements were merely applying to private fortunes a principle that had been dignified by its adoption by government: specifically that Thellusson and others were founding their settlements on the principle of the Sinking Fund. Keeton describes it as follows:[28]

"Annual appropriations were to be invested and accumulated at compound interest until the sum realised was sufficient to pay off the National Debt. Unfortunately,

---

[25] *Harrison* v *Harrison* cited above at note 9.
[26] i.e. The Perpetuity Period.
[27] "Treatise on the Thellusson Act" at pp. 56-67.
[28] (1970) 21 N.I.L.Q. at p. 153.

England was on the eve of a prolonged struggle with France, during which the rate of interest on Government borrowing rose to an amount exceeding the earnings of the Sinking Fund. It was not until 1812 that it was noticed that the interest on the money borrowed to appropriate to the Sinking Fund exceeded its yield, but in the early years of its existence the possibilities of the Fund undoubtedly influenced a number of testators of whom Thellusson[29] was the chief. If the idea of accumulation could be used to pay off the National Debt, it could be used with similar advantages for private benefit."

This view is not entirely without difficulty if only because some of the settlements, and indeed the cases upon them[30] clearly antedated the establishment of the Sinking Fund. What probably happened was that the idea of accumulation was generally gaining favour as the middle classes increased their influence throughout the eighteenth century and that the settlements of this mercantile class simply gave positive expression to it, having the same ultimate aim attributable to most creators of perpetuities.[31] Its employment by the government in 1786 merely added respectability to a device already employed in the private sector, but such use by the government may well have increased its popularity.

Accumulation Settlements in Scotland

Unfortunately the origins and derivation of accumulation settlements in Scotland are not so well documented as they are in the South: there was apparently no one like Hargrave who had a sufficiently large chip on his shoulder about the subject.[32] However, from the cases, a few inferences can be drawn.

---

[29] Keeton goes on to suggest two further reasons applicable in the case of Peter Thellusson. He writes: (*ibid*. at pp. 154-155) "This [i.e. the Sinking Fund] may not have been the only episode of public finance which influenced Thellusson in making his will, a draft of which was said to have existed some time before 1790. In that year Pitt, needing additional finance, informed the Governors of the Bank of England (of which Peter Isaac Thellusson [Peter Thellusson's son] was a director) that the balances of unclaimed dividends on government stock in the hands of the Bank had been constantly increasing and at that date amounted to £547,000. He therefore suggested that the Governor might use them, The Governors and directors strenuously opposed this, and petitioned the Commons. urging that the agents of many foreigners, including the Thellussons, were extensively interested in the unclaimed funds, that only £190,000 had been undistributed for more than three years, and that the unclaimed sums were neither forgotten nor their owners unknown. Substantial sums, it may be surmised, were held by the Thellussons and others on behalf of French investors. In spite of the Bank's protests however, Pitt secured £500,000 of these balances in perpetual loan, in return for a guarantee in case of claims. That the British Government eventually profited substantially from this compulsory surrender through the destruction of French depositors under the guillotine during the Terror is not open to doubt. In 1790, however, no one foresaw this, and it has been suggested that Peter Thellusson wished to build up a fund that would protect his family against claims when the French Revolution had spent itself, and when peace returned to Europe.

This may have been a contributory factor . . . . but it is not the main reason for this remarkable will . . . . [T]here was a much more important object, and it was this which provoked such a burst of hostility from the English upper classes. This was the age when East and West India merchants were steadily translating their wealth into land, and were founding noble families. This was exactly what Thellusson intended. The family name must be perpetuated, but there must be at least one coronet in the family, with extensive landed estates to support it . . . . Peter himself never entered the portals of the House of Lords, although Peter Isaac became Baron Rendlesham in 1805. At this point the elder Peter's intentions seemed well on the way to fulfilment."

[30] See especially *Mole* v *Mole* (1758) 1 Dick. 310 and *Hawkins* v *Combe* (1783) 1 Bro. C.C. 335. And in the *case of Lady Denison's Will*, the will antedated the setting up of the Sinking Fund.

[31] See above Chapter I; and Chapter V note 29.

[32] See Keeton's remarks esp. 21 N.I.L.Q. 131 et seq.

In the first place the number of accumulation settlements prior to the passing of the Thellusson Act appears to have been small; and the numbers do not appear to increase substantially until towards the middle of the nineteenth century. Indeed by the time of McLaren's Law of Trusts and Trust Settlements[33] the number was still small, the author being able to cite only five Scottish cases on the subject, a large portion of his treatment being drawn from English sources.[34] This approach would clearly tend to support the view that the law governing accumulations in Scotland has its origins in the South.

However, in spite of this, there are a very small number of Scottish accumulation settlements which ante-date the Accumulations Act. These have little in common with the cases coming before the English courts; indeed there do not appear to be any examples of the Scottish courts being asked to pronounce on the destination of intermediate income arising prior to the vesting of a contingent interest before 1800; still less is there any decree of the court ordering such income to be accumulated until vesting.

And yet there is nevertheless an affinity between the legal sources which permitted the development of accumulation settlements in England and those which provided the legal background in Scotland. In England, it will be remembered, accumulation settlements grew out of types of executory devise and bequest. In all these cases a supplementary (in the early cases, a primary) consideration was whether the limitation was bad for perpetuity. In other words the accumulation settlement grew out of the development of the general law of perpetuities. In Scotland a not dissimilar process seems to have taken place. We have seen that in *McNair*[35] the principle of perpetuity was accepted by analogy with entails[36] and mortifications.[37] So, too, the first accumulation settlements were to be found in entails and mortifications.

The earliest example is the case of Barholm settlements[38] which came before The Court of Session in 1752. The background here was the practice of some entailers of directing that any surplus income produced by the entailed estate should not accrue to the heir of entail in possession but should be employed by him in the purchase of additional lands which were to be entailed on the same terms and conditions as, and thereby added to, the original entail. In a sense this was a form of accumulation settlement, but was relatively ineffective in view of the facts that the forms of words used were often permissive[39] and not mandatory, but that, even if mandatory, the directions were easily avoided by the heir of entail's arranging his affairs in such a way as to make the occurrence of a surplus most unlikely.

---

[33] Edinburgh 1863.
[34] These are the cases directly related to points arising from the Act or from the common law. In addition McLaren mentioned three others from the general Scots law of Succession on peripheral matters. He also cites *McNair* (see note 35) which was not an accumulation of the orthodox type, the income there being accumulated for seven year periods, at the end of which it was to be distributed.
[35] 1791 Bell's Cas. 547.
[36] See above Chapter III.
[37] *ibid*.
[38] *McCullogh* v *McCullogh* 1752 5 W & S 547 Note: The settlement is set out above in Chapter III.
[39] Often expressed in terms such as "It is my hope that" or "my desire that".

The Barholm settlements extended this practice by not only making the direction to purchase additional lands mandatory, but also by providing that, with the exception of small amounts to be paid to specified beneficiaries, the entire income produced was to be used to purchase more land which was to be put under strict entail. Admittedly the ultimate time for distribution would vary from beneficiary to beneficiary and the estate so accumulated was to be fragmented among the entailer's remote descendants, but nonetheless this settlement amounted to a deliberate attempt at accumulation.

It should be noted that the idea of using current income to increase the corpus of the entailed estate was not a notion peculiar to Scotland; it was an accepted practice to provide for the setting aside of a portion of the income of a tenant for life under English strict settlements. Where the Barholm settlements were unique however, was the virtually all-embracing nature of the accumulation. The income involved was not the surplus, was not even a portion, but was primarily the whole of the rents and profits produced by the estate and additions thereto, with such sums as were actually paid out being a deduction therefrom. In a sense, therefore, it constituted not merely an extension of existing practice, but a departure to the extent that the "surplus" principle had been reversed.

We have seen that the pursuer pleaded that the law should not allow such[40] "preposterous provisions, locking up estates for ages, securing from them the least possible advantage to his family and leaving his immediate descendants in poverty and ignorance".

The Court accepted this argument, but unfortunately the basis of its decision is unclear. The only report of the judgement is that of Lord Elchies who wrote:[41]

"This was a question of reducing two most ridiculous entails and trust rights whereby excepting small aliments to the heir, the rents were to be applied for many years in purchasing other estates and [settling] them in the same manner. We all agreed to reduce the whole deeds."

When, however, the case was sought to be relied on to reduce the accumulation provisions of the Strathmore entail[42] it was rejected by Lord Brougham on the basis that the settlements of Barholm were unintelligible being[43] "mixed up with such a mass of clauses, impossible to be construed, that very nonsense of itself constitutes a material specialty, and prevents the case from applying as an authority to another case where no such specialty exists".

Imperfect as the reports of this case are, it is the only one to have come before the courts prior to the Act of 1800 where the subject matter was undeniably a settlement specifically designed for the increase of the capital by the principle of accumulation. The reports mention two other, rather shadowy, instances where the settlement may have been by way of an accumulation trust. The first was that of Lady Betty Cunningham's settlement which was referred

---

[40] 5 W & S at p. 184 (Note).
[41] Elch. "Tailzie" No. 48.
[42] *Strathmore's Trustees* v *Strathmore* 1831 5 W & S 170.
[43] *ibid.* at p. 196.
[44] 1791 Bell's Cas. 547.

to in *McNair* v *McNair*[44] by counsel as "differing from the present in that the annual produce was withdrawn from the use of the heirs unless under particular circumstances".[45] There is nothing, however, in *McNair's case* to indicate that the income so withdrawn was accumulated. The case in any event was never actually decided, the action being compromised and the trust funds divided under the declaration of an arbiter.[46]

The other was the settlement of Lord Hyndford which was referred to in *McNair's case* and was discussed in a little more detail by Lord Brougham in *Strathmore's Trustees* v *Strathmore*.[42] The difficulty about this is the treatment afforded to it by Lord Brougham for, at first mention, the Lord Chancellor appears to cite it in connection with general observations about perpetuities as an instance of a settlement which was apparently upheld in part but which had a tendency to perpetuity. But he then proceeds to use it as a foundation for his observations on accumulation trusts.[47]

There is one other known example of an eighteenth century trust for accumulation. This has nothing to do with the purchase of lands for settlement under entail but constitutes one of the examples cited in *McNair* as a valid perpetual trust. It was in fact the settlement of John Watson in 1781 for the endowment of a hospital in Edinburgh. Apparently a sum of £4,700 was directed to be accumulated by the trustees, such accumulation realising £90,000 in 1822.[48]

In spite of these eighteenth century examples it would seem that the legality of an accumulation trust as such was not really brought into question until the *Strathmore case*. There was of course the decision in the *Barholm case* but that, irrespective of whether Lord Brougham's assessment of the settlement is correct, involves points of difficulty. The first is that there is no evidence that the Court of Session addressed its attention to the question of the legality of an accumulation at all. It may well be, of course, that this is what Lord Elchies was referring to when he described the settlements as "ridiculous". But it seems just as likely that, in view of the pleas of the pursuer, the court had in mind the economic effects of the provisions on the immediate and not so immediate family of the settler. And then there is the problem that the deeds were reduced as being "inextricable", which tends to support Lord Brougham's opinion of the case.

The first case, then, reported at any length, which considers the legality of accumulation trusts under the law of Scotland was that of *Strathmore's Trustees* v *Strathmore*[42] which concerned a direction to accumulate the rents of an estate for the term of thirty years, or until the death of the longest liver of two persons named in the settlement, for the purpose of investing the sums so accumulated in the purchase of lands to be entailed. As we have been, Lord

---

[45] *ibid*. at p. 551.
[46] Per Lord President Campbell; *ibid*. at p. 552 "The only similar case is Lady Betty Cunningham's and there the trust was to continue in force only for so many generations. I do not know that a decision was given in that case. But it came into Court; and either by the advice of friends or in consequence of what passed here, it was submitted, and the funds divided under the declaration of an arbiter".
[47] (1831) 5 W & S at p. 197.
[48] See per Note of Lord Cuninghame in *Ogilvie's Trustees* v *Kirk Session of Dundee* (1846) 8 D at p. 1234.

Brougham refused to apply the *Barholm case* on the basis that the irrationality apparent there was absent from the Strathmore settlement which displayed the "plain, consistent and distinct intention[49] of the framer of the deeds". The Hyndford settlement, however was less easy to dispose of. After citing the passages from *McNair* where the settlement was commented upon, Lord Brougham continued:[50]

"I have looked into the papers of the Hyndford case and they raise the impression that the trust was to endure for a longer period of time than by possibility this could. This was not a deed for 25 years, except in one of two alternatives happening; but nevertheless the deed was supported, if I am to take the statement of Lord President Campbell. He says it may be supported in so far as it was temporary, for special purposes; and what possibly may reconcile the books on the subject is, that it was supported as regards the temporary part, and set aside only as regards the perpetuity. Here it is not contended that the perpetuity should be supported, nor is that contention necessary to support the judgement of the Court below."

From this Lord Brougham drew the conclusion that there was nothing inherently illegal about accumulation trusts in Scotland if within the limits described above, that the accumulation should be for a "special purpose" and should not endure in perpetuity. He elaborated this last point:[50]

"I do not mean to say that there may not be an extremely good ground for setting aside an accumulation which is to go on for ever, and I do not consider that we are bound to say how long or short a period money or land may accumulate in Scotland .... I must say .... [however] that it would be very desirable to have the rule fixed by positive statute in Scotland as Lord Loughborough's Act did in England."[51]

The said Act was extended to heritable property in Scotland by section 41 of the Entail Amendment (Scotland) Act 1848[52] and in *Keith's Trustees* v *Keith*[53] the question arose as to whether that provision operated retrospectively. The case concerned a direction to the trustees of a settlement to retain the management of certain heritable estates until the death of the party named, if she should die childless, or if she should have children, until the majority of her elder surviving child, during which period the rents and profits of the estate were to be collected and laid out in the purchase of lands in Scotland which were then to be entailed. The argument concerned the operation, as stated, of section 41 of the Rutherfurd Act, its being assumed, in consequence of Lord Brougham's judgement in the *Strathmore case* that the accumulation directions in the settlement were valid at common law.

Both the limits as to purpose and time were considered by the First Division in *Mason* v *Skinner*[54] which concerned a settlement which provided for the accumulation of rents from heritable properties for an indefinite period and for purposes which were not expressed with any clarity, but intended for the benefit of the Scottish Episcopal Church. The court referred the matter to an accountant as to the practicability of implementing the directions and on receiving his adverse report reduced the settlement, Lord Fullerton summing

---

[49] 5 W & S at p. 195; See above Chapter III at note 294.
[50] *ibid*. at p. 198/199.
[51] Lord Loughborough's Act (The Thellusson Act) only extended to moveables in Scotland at this time.
[52] The Rutherford Act; 11 & 12 Vict. s. 36.
[53] (1857) 19 D 1040.
[54] (1844) 16 Jur. 422.

up the position in this way:[55]

".... [A]ccumulations must have a definite object. The beneficial interests must merge immediately as in the case of a charitable endowment. Here not only is the fund to continue for ever, but the accumulations also are to continue for ever, and without any definite object, making it impossible for any court to carry the testator's intentions into effect. It is in fact a mere emulous accumulation."

Again however there was no attempt to fix any precise time limit, the members of court acquiescing in the view of the Lord Ordinary, Lord Cuninghame, that an accumulation intended for "too distant a contingency" would be ineffectual at common law.[57] Two points strike one in reading through the reports of these cases. The first is the tendency to discuss accumulations in terms of general perpetuities.

This is particularly noticeable in the *Strathmore case*, and indeed in *Mason v Skinner*, especially in Lord Cuninghame's Note, the tendency is present also. Doubtless this was why it could still be seriously contended in *Suttie v Suttie's Trustees*[58] that private trusts generally might be bad for perpetuity. The second point, which is derived from this is that, as far as the effects of perpetuity were concerned,[57] trusts which directed the accumulation of income were special: They were affected by a remoteness principle in a way that no other trust in Scots law was. We have seen that the courts never attempted to fix a hard and fast rule as to what might and what might not be too remote save that an accumulation which went on for ever was bad. No one ever attempted to define what "too distant a contingency" meant. And of course there was scarcely any need to do so, for four years after *Mason v Skinner* statutory control was extended which made such deliberations of the common law virtually redundant.

Objections to Accumulation Settlements

In their chapter on accumulations Morris and Leach write:[59]

"The Thellusson Act was rushed through Parliament in a panic, one year after the Thellusson dispositions had been upheld by the Court of Chancery, at a time when people had an almost superstitious fear of the power of compound interest. They were shocked at what they regarded as the heartlessness of the will, and fearful lest the great Thellusson whirlpool might drain into its vortex all the wealth of the country.

We know that these fears were exaggerated. The accumulation did not produce one tenth of the amount of the most conservative estimate. Modern opinion tends to regard the testator's scheme as patehtic rather than heartless and to dismiss the whole episode as a commentary on the vanity of human wishes. After all, Peter Thellusson did not leave his wife and children destitute—he divided well over £100,000 between them before disposing of his residue.

But the Thellusson Act remains to this day as a memorial to the shock which one man's testamentary dispositions administered to contemporary opinion."[60]

---

[55] *ibid.* at p. 425.
[56] *ibid.* at p. 423.
[57] For further discussion of the implications of this case see above at Chapter I; and Chapter III.
[58] 1846 18 Jur. 442.
[59] "The Rule against Perpetuities" (2nd Ed. 1962) at pp. 303-304.
[60] Certainly the Thellusson will has been the birth of much emotional criticism both judicially and otherwise. For a commentary on this see Keeton (1970) 21 N.I.L.Q. 130 et seq.

Of the reasons for that shock the Act itself says very little mearly contenting itself with a recital that

". . . . it is expedient that all dispositions of real or personal estates whereby the profits and produce thereof are directed to be accumulated, and the beneficial enjoyment thereof if postponed, should be subject to the restrictions hereinafter contained . . . ."[61]

Fortunately, there are the writings and pleadings of Hargrave. His "Treatise on the Thellusson Act" contains a long and at times emotional diatribe on the evils of accumulation settlements. Most of these reproduce the standard arguments against perpetuities[62] with the added dimension that an accumulation went even further, resulting in "the causeless disinhersion of unoffending families . . . . produced by the dazzling prospect of remote but apparently boundless aggrandisement, presented by accumulation at compound interest for nearly a century".[63]

In point of fact the theme of his argument in his "Treatise" is simply a development of his submissions to Lord Loughborough in the Court of Chancery which Vesey's Report rendered thus:[64]

"The consequence of not overruling the legality of these trusts must be that executory devise may be applied to prevent all alienation of property for 120 or even 140 years; and by combining it with accumulation it may be possible to prohibit all beneficial enjoyment during the same period. Such a combination of trust of accumulation with executory device could not be endured without the most glaring and dangerous mischief to the community by locking up an immense property and the income of it for many years to the great injury of the commerce, the revenue and the wealth of the country; by monopolizing and reducing into a state of mortmain the landed estates of the Kingdom to a great extent, and by giving at the end of that period, possibly to one individual, a property producing a revenue equal to the Civil List upon a moderate calculation. This may be imitated in other instances and carried to a much greater extent upon the principles which must be established by a judgement in favour of these trusts. But by a combination of accumulation with executory devise, even confining the latter to its proper limits, the incidental public mischief would be very great by affording very probable means of protracting accumulations for half a century."[65]

One of the things which comes through from this, as from all Hargrave's considerations of the matter, is an apparent discrepancy between the basis of his argument and the real issue. The basis of his argument is primarily legal principle, and, if that is insufficient, the principle of public policy. But the real

---

[61] 39 & 40 Geo III c. 98 preamble.
[62] See above Chapters I, II and III.
[63] "Treatise on the Thellusson Act" at pp. 62/3.
[64] 4 Ves at p. 280.
[65] See per Keeton "Modern Developments in the Law of Trusts" at p. 221. "[Hargrave] repeats the error which appears throughout his consideration of the *Thellusson case,* whether in court or in publication. [He] fails to distinguish between the denial of beneficial enjoyment to the successor, until the estate vests, and the investment and management of the property by the trustees. But it is not difficult to detect in this and in other passages of his work, the dislike of the landowners for the increasingly numerous and wealthy commercial and industrial families, of whom the Thellusson family was an outstanding example. Finally it should be noticed that much of Hargrave's denunciation of trusts for accumulation, on the ground of injury to commerce, could have been applied equally to strict settlements of land, as their history in the nineteenth century, and the piecemeal legislation in respect of them, was to show." (See above, Chapter III).

issue was not either of these: the real issue was size,[66] and the law had not yet arrived at the stage where it was prepared to frown upon an arrangement simply because it created an agglomoration of assets in excess of what it considered to be appropriate.

So instead the case was fought on the basis of legal principle and on the basis of public policy: and was lost. Indeed the policy argument was most emphatically rejected in a rather surprising statement from Lord Eldon.[67] He said:

"In truth there is no objection to accumulation upon the policy of the law applying to perpetuities; for the rents and profits are not to be locked up, and made no use of, for the individuals or the public. The effect is only to invest them from time to time in land; so that the fund is, not only in a constant cause of accumulation, but in a constant course of circulation."

What is surprising is the difference in attitude adopted in this case when compared with the ordinary perpetuity situations. It would appear to the present writer that the "fund" in both cases is in exactly the same position; either it has been invested and is thereby producing income or is of itself producing income. But in neither case is *it* circulating. In both cases *it* is static, albeit producing further wealth. The only difference is that in an accumulation trust, there is provision for a compulsory application of income in a specified way, as opposed to the unrestricted, and possibly dissipatory, options open to an income beneficiary under an ordinary settlement. It is submitted that, if the policy of the law with regard to perpetuities had foundation, then the same considerations apply to accumulations; indeed, perhaps even more so in view of the prescribed conversion of income into capital and thereby increasing the amount of the fund subject to fetters.

Rules against Accumulations

The Accumulation Rules, as they apply in Scotland are at present contained almost entirely in two legislative provisions, section 5 of the Trusts (Scotland) Act 1961[68] and section 6 of the Law Reform (Miscellaneous Provisions) (Scotland) Act 1966.[69] The former of these two provisions is a repeal and re-enactment, with amendments, of almost all of the then existing legislation on the subject, going back to the Thellusson Act itself; the latter

---

[66] See per Lord Brougham L.C. in *Strathmore's Trustees* v *Strathmore* (1831) 5 W & S at p. 192.

"By the will of Mr. Thellusson, he had intended, from motives of family pride, to accumulate property to an immense amount. It was calculated that the fund might probably reach 100 millions before it could be enjoyed; and it was said that in thirty years, which was the lowest period you could then look forward to, it would amount to eighteen or nineteen millions. Alas! the calculation of those who thus commented on that will were as vain as the wishes of the testator himself for it is a fact worth mentioning, to show the value of such perspective views of accumulation, that the Court of Chancery having got possession of the property, this great accumulation is now under £500,000."

McLaren in his "Law of Trusts" repeats the fallacy that Thellusson was a millionaire (at p. 116); in fact his estate at his death was worth approximately £800,000, and the residue that was to be accumulated about £600,000.

[67] (1805) 11 Ves. at p. 147.
[68] Statute 9 & 10 Eliz II c. 57.
[69] *ibid*. 1966 c. 19.

contains the counterpart for Scotland of the accumulations provisions of The Perpetuities and Accumulations Act 1964 which concerned England only.

A consideration of the Accumulation Rules seems to fall into five parts: first, the legislation; second, its scope; third, the periods of accumulation permitted under the Rules; fourth, invalid directions and their consequences; and fifth, the termination of accumulations.

The Legislation

(a) *The Thellusson Act*

The first legislation was, of course, the Thellusson Act,[70] and it might be helpful to set out its provisions:

"1. .... Be it enacted .... That no person or persons shall, after the passing of this Act, by any deed or deeds, surrender or surrenders, will, codicil, or otherwise howsoever, settle or dispose of any real or personal property, so and in such manner that the rents, issues profits or produce thereof shall be wholly or partially accumulated; for any longer term than the life or lives of any such grantor or grantors, settlor or settlors; or the term of twenty one years from the death of any such grantor, settlor, devisor or testator, or during the minority or respective minorities of any person or persons who shall be living, or in ventre sa mère at the time of the death of such grantor, devisor or testator; or during the minority or respective minorities only of any persons who, under the uses or trusts of the deed, surrender, will or other assurances, directing such accumulations, would, for the time being, if of full age, be entitled unto the rents, issues and profits, or the interest dividends or annual produce so directed to be accumulated; and in every case where any accumulation shall be directed otherwise than aforesaid, such direction shall be null and void, and the rents, issues, profits and produce of such property so directed to be accumulated, shall so long as the same shall be directed contrary to the provisions of this Act, go to and be received by such person or persons as would have been entitled thereto if such accumulation had not been directed.

2. Provided always .... That nothing in this Act contained shall extend to any provision for payment of debts of any grantor, settlor or devisor, or other person or persons, or to any provision for raising portions for any child or children of any person taking any interest under any such conveyance, settlement or devise, or to any direction touching the produce of timber or wood upon any lands or tenements; but that all such provisions and directions shall and may be made as if this Act had not been passed.

3. Provided also .... That nothing in this Act contained shall extend to any dispositions respecting heritable property within that part of Great Britain called Scotland.

4. Provided also .... That the restrictions in this Act contained shall take effect and be in force with respect to wills and testaments made and executed before the passing of this Act, in such cases only where the devisor or testator shall be living, and of sound and disposing mind, after the expiration of twelve calendar months from the passing of this Act."

Perhaps surprisingly, in view of the express exclusion of heritage in Scotland and the consequent implication that Scottish moveables were covered, it has been suggested by Bell[71] that the Act's application at all to Scotland was doubtful. No ground or attempted justification is given for this view, expressed as it is in a footnote;[72] but presumably it is based on an idea that the Act is not expressly stated as applying to Scotland and therefore, in spite of section 3, does not so apply.

---

[70] *ibid.* 39 & 40 Geo. III c. 98.
[71] Bell's Commentaries (7th Ed. McLaren) at p. 37, footnote 39.

This view, it should be stated, was not shared by Baron David Hume[73] or by the later editors of Erskine;[74] and it was not shared by the Courts, its being accepted by Lord Brougham in *Strathmore's Trustees* v *Strathmore*[75] in 1831 and stated by the Court of Session in *Keith's Trustees* v *Keith*[76] that Scottish moveables were covered.

No indication is given as to why Parliament saw fit to exempt heritage in Scotland from the operation of the Act. In *Strathmore's Trustees*[75] two suggestions were made. The first was that the statute proceeded upon a principle of English law, namely the recognition of the period of twenty-one years after lives in being, beyond which restraint of property is not allowed for fear of perpetuity. This, quite clearly, is true as far as the general background to the Act is concerned, and indeed was accepted as such by Lord Brougham. The second suggestion however was more specific. It was put forward by counsel for the appellant in the following terms:[77]

"No doubt the statute contains the exception, that 'nothing in this act contained shall extend to any disposition respecting heritable property within that part of Great Britain called Scotland', but this exception was introduced because it was unnecessary to extend the protection of the statute to Scotland, seeing that the common law of that country was in itself sufficient to prevent undue accumulation. Surely the exception could not have been made for insuring in Scotland, in a worse shape, the existence of the evil thus corrected in England."

The foundation for this argument was the decision in the *Barholm case*[78] reducing the deeds which made provision for accumulations there. As we have seen, however, Lord Brougham refused to apply this case, or to treat it as authoritative: certainly he refused to regard it as settling any principle governing the validity of accumulations.

However the same point was restated in *Mason* v *Skinner*[79] by Lord Cuninghame, again founding himself on the *Barholm case,* and here the Inner House did not dissent from the view of the Lord Ordinary.[80] The reason for the difference of treatment became academic some four years later with the extension of the Act to heritable property.

In the forty-eight years during which the distinction had relevance there was only one case before the courts which appeared to turn on it. This was *Ogilvie's Trustees* v *Kirk-Session of Dundee*[81] which concerned a bequest of £2,000 payable out of the general residue of the deceased's estate. The testator

---

[72] However this would appear to conflict with the statement in footnote 2 on p. 36.
[73] Lectures vol. V p. 193 (Stair Soc. vol. 18).
[74] See III. ix. 14, Notes.
[75] (1831) 5 W & S 170.
[76] (1857) 19 D 1040.
[77] 5 W & S at pp. 182-185.
[78] (1752) 5 W & S (Note) at pp. 180-185.
[79] (1844) 16 Jur. 422.
[80] In the *Strathmore case* (at p. 193) Lord Brougham appeared to favour the explanation that the omission in the Act came from a combination of two factors: first, the general background of accumulations in the English law of perpetuities, a background which was not shared with the law of Scotland, and secondly, that Parliament had specifically declared its intentions with regard to Scotland in the Act. But, with respect, this last seems to be begging, rather than answering the question as to the reasons for the different treatment of heritage and moveables.
[81] (1846) 8 D 1229.

directed that this sum be invested in Government Stock and the interest it earned to be reinvested in the Funds, such accumulations to continue for a hundred years. It was held that, although the general residue contained heritage, the source of the intended accumulations was the £2,000 itself; this was moveable property and so was outwith the scope of the exception.

This decision was relied upon and followed in *Keith's Trustees* v *Keith*[82] which concerned a conveyance by the settler of the general residue of his estate to trustees on trust to invest his estate in the purchase of lands, the rents of which were to be accumulated until the death of his daughter; and again invested in lands with power to make intermediate purchases. It was attempted to bring this case within the exception on the basis that the accumulations after each purchase were the produce of lands. The Court however rejected this, finding that this submission referred to the manner of accumulation, which was immaterial; what was important was the source of the fund, which was moveable estate. As such the Act was held to apply. As Lord Ardmillan stated:[83]

"The test of the application of the rule, or the exception, in the Thellusson Act, is to be found in the character of the property of which the rents and profits are directed to be accumulated. In this case it was a 'residue' of general estate, heritable and moveable, in England and in Scotland. Lands in Scotland are to be purchased with the accumulated fund, and the rents of the purchased lands, or in other words the annual proceeds of the produce of the accumulations, are to be again accumulated until the period arrives for winding up the trust and executing an entail of the Scottish landed estate. But the nucleus or centre of the accumulations, around which the rents and proceeds are to be wound as they annually arise, was the residue of the whole estate conveyed to the trustees; and, except in so far as regards the heritable property in Scotland so conveyed, this process of accumulation appears to the Lord Ordinary to be opposed to the enactments of the Thellusson Act, and therefore to be only legal for twenty-one years after Lord Keith's death. The decision in the case of *Ogilvie's Trustees* [v] *Kirk-Session of Dundee* .... in which the Thellusson Act was applied by the Court, though heritable subjects in Scotland were conveyed as part of a general estate, of which 'the balance' was directed to be accumulated for a hundred years, is not opposed to the view now expressed. In that case the trustees had a power of sale which it was necessary to exercise in order to create the balance, which formed what the Lord President called[84] the 'nest egg of the accumulations', or 'the foundation of the fund'. The attempt to bring the case within the exception in the Thellusson Act failed, and the rule of that Act was enforced. In the present case the foundation of the fund to be accumulated, and that which gave a character to the subsequent accumulations, was (in so far as it did not consist of heritable property in Scotland) within the rule of the Thellusson Act; and if, in order to bring it within the exception, it were only necessary to provide that the accumulated funds should be invested in land in Scotland, of which the rents should continue to be accumulated, this would substantially be to set nought the provisions of the statute. It is not from considering the object [for which] the accumulations are to be applied, but from considering the character of the property

---

[82] (1857) 19 D 1040.
[83] *ibid*. at pp. 1053/1054.
[84] per Lord President Boyle at p. 1240: "The general estate of the truster is to be brought into such a shape as to leave a balance, and then the £2,000, or the remainder of the balance, as the case may be, is to be applied as therein directed. £2,000 is what the truster contemplates as the balance. That was to be the nest egg of this accumulation. The truster did not contemplate leaving a heritable estate as the foundation of the fund with which the projected institution was to be established. He contemplated a moveable fund. I therefore cannot find that the bequest for the proposed accumulation .... was within the exception in the The[l]lusson Act."

from which the accumulations are to be gathered, that any just criterion can be obtained for applying the rule or the exception in the Thellusson Act[85] prior to the recent statute of her present Majesty."[86]

(b) The Rutherfurd Act[86]

Given that the stated object of the Act was to assimilate the law of entail in Scotland with that of England[84] it is unsurprising that the law relating to accumulations of income deriving from heritage in Scotland should also be anglicised. Thus section 41 provided.

"And whereas an Act was passed in the 39th and 40th years of His Majesty King George the Third, instituted an Act to restrain all Trusts and Directions in Deeds or Wills whereby the Profits or Produce of Real or Personal Estate shall be accumulated, and the beneficial enjoyment thereof postponed beyond the time therein limited[87] . . . . be it enacted that[88] . . . . the said Act shall in future apply to heritable property in Scotland."

In *Keith's Trustees* v *Keith*[89] the question arose as to whether that part of the estate which consisted of heritable property in Scotland was subject to the restrictions on accumulation introduced in 1848, the settlement having been made before then. It was held that the words "in future" could not be construed as applying to existing accumulations and that accordingly the accumulation in this case was not caught.

(c) The Accumulations Act 1892[90]

It will have been noted that the classical accumulation fund to be used in the purchase of real or heritable property for the purpose of entailing it[91] was a not infrequent part of nineteenth century conveyancing practice in Scotland. The Act provides:

"No person shall after the passing of this Act, settle or dispose of any property in such manner that the rents, issues, profits or income thereof shall be wholly or partially accumulated for the purchase of land only for any longer period than during the minority or respective minorities of any person or persons who under the uses or trusts of the instrument directing such accumulation would, for the time being, if of full age, be entitled to receive the rents, issues, profits or income as directed to be accumulated."

The Act then restricted such accumulations even more than those to which only the Thellusson Act applied permitting only one period of accumulation instead of the four allowed under the original Act and can be regarded as one of the reforming enactments of that period concerning settled estates. There appears to have been only one decision of the Scottish courts on this Act. This was the case of *Robertson's Trustees* v *Robertson's Trustees*[91a] which concerned a direction whereby trustees were, on the expiry of a trust liferent, to hold the

---

[85] Citing Hargrave—"Treatise on the Thellusson Act" at p. 19.
[86] The Entail Amendment (Scotland) Act 1848, statute 11 & 12 Vict. c. 36.
[87] See above Chapter III.
[88] Denotes words repeated by Statute Law Revision Act 1891.
[89] (1857) 19 D. 1040.
[90] 55 & 56 Vict. c. 55.
[91] For some reason, which is unexplained in their book, Morris and Leach describe this practice as "a particularly loathsome manifestation of post-humous vanity". (at p. 272).
[91a] 1933 S.C. 639.

residue of an estate for a further period of fifteen years, accumulating the income from the fund, adding it to capital and using the whole in purchasing heritage to be entailed on a series of heirs. It was held that the period of accumulation stipulated was not that allowed in the Act and that therefore the direction to accumulate was void. However it was stressed that it was only the direction that was affected and not the settlement as a whole, which otherwise remained intact.

The only English decision relevant to Scotland would appear to be that of Maugham J. in *Re Knapp*[92] to the effect that any duality in the direction to accumulate will exclude the Act. The case concerned a testator who had left his entire estate in trust for Scarborough Municipal Charities, with a direction that the income from investments should be accumulated for twenty-one years, or so long as the law would allow, and from that time "the interest only of my investments will be applied for the purchase of land and the building thereon of almshouses for the aged poor of Scarborough". It was held that the English successor of the 1892 Act, section 166 (1) of the Law of Property Act 1925,[93] did not apply.

(d) The Entail (Scotland) Act 1914[94]

It will be remembered that section 2 of the Thellusson Act excepted from the restrictions on accumulation trusts whereby the fund was to be accumulated for the payment of debts, for the raising of portions for the children of the testator or of beneficiaries, or arising out of timber growing. Section 9 of the Entail (Scotland) Act 1914 repeals this section providing:

"The second section of the Accumulation Act 1800 shall not apply to Scotland; and the restrictions in the said Act contained shall take effect and be in force with respect to any provision or direction in operation at the passing of this Act, to which, but for the enactment of this section, the said second section would continue to apply, as if the date of the execution of the deed, will codicil, or other writing where in such provision or direction is contained had been the passing of this Act."

Contemporary opinion appears to have been mixed as to the desirability of this particular reform. As to the abolition of the exemption regarding debts there was little doubt that this was a much welcomed measure. As one commentator put it:[95]

"They result in trusts going on for ever and becoming inextricable. Further the intention is frustrated, for just as fast as the trustees (if they can do so at all) extinguish a debt which is bearing a comparatively low rate of interest, the expectant heir piles up another debt on his expectancy and at a much higher rate, and probably with the additional expense of life survivance."

However the same commentator felt that the abolition of the exemptions for the latter two categories (portions and timber) was a retrograde step as both, in his view, served a useful purpose. But with respect, from English experience, it is suggested that this abolition has been something of a blessing, for the intricacies of defining the term "portion" and of applying the section generally have in England produced a body of law which is as unsatisfactory and

---

[92] [1929] 1 Ch. 341.
[93] Statute 15 Geo. V. c. 20.
[94] *ibid.* 4 & B Geo. V c. 43.
[95] 1913 S.L.R. (News) 233 at p. 241. The article is unattributed.

inconsistent as it is voluminous,[96] and to have avoided this cannot but have been beneficial.

(e) The Trusts (Scotland) Act 1961[97]

In England the Thellusson Act and its amending statute were repealed and their substance brought up to date and re-enacted in modern form in the Law of Property Act 1925,[93] sections 164-166. In the Outer House decision in 1930 it was suggested that this repeal had extended to Scotland also. The case was *Henderson's Trustees* v *Anderson*[98] which concerned the effect of the 1925 Act on the Scottish application of the Powers of Appointment Act 1874.[99] In a remark, which was clearly obiter, Lord Moncrieff said:[100]

"It may be noted, if, only as an additional point of interest, that the 7th Schedule of the Act of 1925 contains also a general repeal of the Thellusson Act, without a relative re-enactment of its provision in the body of the statute of which Scotland can take advantage. It would appear to follow that the Courts in Scotland are henceforth to be powerless to control existing and future trusts for accumulation."

This was quickly seized upon and in the following year there were three actions before the Inner House,[101] in which both Divisions affirmed that the Thellusson Act was still operational as far as Scotland were concerned, disapproving Lord Moncrieff's dictum.

The updating of the Thellusson Act in Scotland was effected by section 5 of the Trusts (Scotland) Act 1961 which provided:

"(1) The following provisions of this section shall have effect in substitution for the provisions of the Accumulations Act, 1800, and that Act is hereby repealed.

(2) No person may by any will, settlement or other disposition dispose of any property in such manner that the income thereof shall be wholly or partially accumulated for any longer period than one of the following, that is to say—

(a) the life of the grantor; or
(b) a term of twenty-one years from the death of the grantor; or
(c) the duration of the minority or respective minorities of any person or persons living or in utero at the death of the grantor; or
(d) the duration of the minority or respective minorities of any person or persons who, under the terms of the will, settlement or other disposition directing the accumulation, would for the time being, if of full age, be entitled to the income directed to be accumulated.

(3) In every case where any accumulation is directed otherwise than as aforesaid, the direction shall, save as hereinafter provided, be void, and the income directed to be accumulated contrary to this section, go to and be received by the person or persons who would have been entitled thereto if such accumulation had not been directed.

(4) For avoidance of doubt it is hereby declared that, in the case of a settlement or other disposition inter vivos, a direction to accumulate income during a period specified in paragraph (d) of subsection 2 of this section shall not be void nor shall the accumulation of income be contrary to this section, solely by reason of the fact that the period begins during the life of the grantor and ends after his death.

---

[96] See Morris & Leach at pp. 281-289; Keeton "Modern Developments in the Law of Trusts" at pp. 250-263.
[97] Statute 9 & 10 Eliz. II c. 57.
[98] 1930 S.L.T. 346.
[99] Statute 37 & 38 Vict. c. 37.
[100] 1930 S.L.T. at p. 348.
[101] *Smith's Trustees* v *Gaydon* 1931 S.C. 533; *Chisholm's Trustees* v *Menzies* 1931 S.N. 41; *Lindsay's Trustees* v *Lindsay* 1931 S.C. 586, per Lord Justice Clerk Alness at p. 588.

(5) The restrictions imposed by this section apply to wills, settlements and other dispositions made on or after the twenty-eighth day of July, eighteen hundred, but, in the case of wills, only where the testator was living and of testamentary capacity after the end of one year from that date.

(6) In this section 'minority' in relation to any person means the period beginning with the birth of the person and ending with his attainment of the age of twenty-one years, and 'grantor' includes 'settlor', and, in relation to a will, the testator."

It will be seen that this Act does not go as far as sections 164 to 166 of the Law of Property Act 1925 in that it repeals only the Thellusson Act, leaving apparently intact, albeit seemingly redundant in view of the general application of this section, section 41 of the Rutherfurd Act;[102] nor does it attempt to modify the provisions of the Accumulations Act 1892 nor the Entail (Scotland) Act 1914. However for all purposes, apart from accumulations directed with the object of investing the accumulated funds in the purchase of lands, section 5 is now the primary code.

(f) The Law Reform (Miscellaneous Provisions) (Scotland) Act 1966[103]

In England the code provided by the Law of Property Act was supplemented in 1964 by section 13 of the Perpetuities and Accumulations Act[104] which gave effect to certain recommendations in the Law Reform Committee's Fourth Report.[105] The primary recommendation was the provision of two additional periods of accumulation. Section 6 of the Law Reform (Miscellaneous Provisions) (Scotland) Act 1966 makes similar provision for trusts governed by the law of Scotland. It provides:

"(1) The periods for which accumulations of income are permitted by section 5 of the Trusts (Scotland) Act 1961 shall include—

(a) a term of twenty-one years from the date of the making of the settlement or other dispositions, and

(b) the duration of the minority or respective minorities of any person or persons living or in utero at that date,

and a direction to accumulate income during a period specified in paragraph (a) or paragraph (b) of this subsection shall not be void, nor shall the accumulation of income be contrary to the said section 5, solely by reason of the fact that the period begins during the life of the grantor and ends after his death.

(2) The restrictions imposed by the said section 5 shall apply in relation to a power to accumulate income whether or not there is a duty to exercise that power, and they shall apply whether or not the power to accumulate extends to income produced by the investment of income previously accumulated.

(3) This section shall apply only in relation to instruments taking effect after the passing of this Act, and in the case of an instrument made in the exercise of a special power of appointment shall only apply where the instrument creating the power takes effect after the passing of this Act."

Since it was passed, the operation of this section has been before the courts only once, in connection with subsection (3). The court was asked to accede to a petition by a Mr. J. S. Aikman[106] for the variation of the provisions of a trust

---

[102] Although section 41 is still apparently in force its operation would appear to be incompetent as it refers specifically to the Act of 1800 which is repealed by section 5.
[103] Statute 1966 c. 19.
[104] Statute 1964 c. 55.
[105] 1956 Cmnd. 18.
[106] *James Sutherland Aikman—Petitioner* 1968 S.L.T. 137.

under section 1 of the Trusts (Scotland) Act 1961 so as to provide, inter alia, for the accumulation of income from the trust fund for a period of twenty-one years, as permitted by section 6 (1) (a) of the 1966 Act. The question was as to the operative date: if the accumulation was treated as running from the date of the original trust deed the accumulation directed would be incompetent as the deed took effect prior to the passing of the 1966 Act; on the other hand if the accumulation could be treated as running from the date of the court's interlocutor then the provisions of section 6 (1) (a) would be available, and the accumulation would be competent. It was held that in the case before them that the relevant date was that of the interlocutor. But Lord President Clyde qualified this in a statement of principle, saying:[107]

"The subsection adds a further period to that provided in the 1961 Act in which accumulations can be legal. But it confines the added period to twenty-one years from the making of the settlement. The additional power, therefore, could only be involved in the present case if the date of the making of the settlement is the date upon which our interlocutor approving the arrangement is pronounced. In the present case we are of the opinion that this is clearly so since the arrangement fundamentally and almost completely supersedes the original trust provisions and in effect makes a new settlement. In the case of other arrangements under the 1961 Act, it may well be that the arrangement would not constitute the making of a new settlement but the mere modification of an existing one. If so the new provision in the 1966 Act may not have the same effect, and the terminus a quo of the twenty-one years may remain the date when the original trust was set up."

Scope of the Legislation

In his "Treatise on the Thellusson Act",[108] Hargrave states that dispositions within the scope of the Act should have two characteristics; first, there should be a direction to accumulate the trust income and secondly, that the beneficial enjoyment of that income should be postponed.

The Act of 1800, in fact, uses the term "direction" only in a descriptive sense, referring to earlier words setting out the types of disposition to which it applied. The Act of 1961 continues this, section 5 (2) detailing the dispositions which are to be subject to restrictions and section 5 (3) then referring to these as "directions to accumulate". It would seem to follow that, wherever such a direction to accumulate is present, given the nature of an accumulation, the necessary consequence is that the beneficial enjoyment of the income subject to that direction is postponed.[108a] As a result, therefore, it is suggested that the scope of the legislation really covers two things: first, whether or not there is an arrangement which amounts to an accumulation and secondly whether the provision of the deed or other appropriate instrument constitutes a direction to accumulate.

(a) Accumulations

The cases in which the courts have decided that an arrangement amounts to an accumulation fall into two classes. The first is the obvious one where the

---

[107] *ibid.* at p. 141.
[108] at p. 72.
[108a] See Keeton—Modern Developments in the Law of Trusts at pp. 228/230. This rule will apply except in rare situations such as that in *Re A.E.G. Unit Trust (Managers) Ltd.'s Deed* [1957] Ch. 415. See below.

income of the trust fund is received by the trustees and is invested in assets which are then added to the capital of the fund. Both the income produced by the original corpus together with that produced by the accumulations are subsequently invested in further assets which are in turn added to the capital of the trust fund. This type of scheme amounts to an accumulation at compound interest and is the usual type of case that comes before the courts. Both income and capital here are completely withdrawn from the beneficial enjoyment of the beneficiary and the arrangement is clearly within the scope of the legislation. If the powers of the trustees are limited in such a way that the accumulations may only be invested in the purchase of land, then not only will the arrangement be subject to control, but it will be subject to that control prescribed by the Act of 1892 which allows accumulations only for one specified period.[109]

It occasionally happens, however, that the settlor directs that the income produced by the trust fund shall be invested in assets which are then added to capital but that the income produced by these additions may be enjoyed beneficially. In other words the capital is continually being supplemented by the income produced by the original corpus of the trust fund, but the beneficiary is also getting a continually increased income benefit as the additions to the accumulated fund increase. This type of scheme is a simple accumulation, which occurs very rarely in practice and, indeed, which has yet to produce a case for decision by the Scottish courts. In England however, there have been a number of instances where eventually, after some hesitation, it was decided that the Act applied. In *Re Hawkins*[110] Sargant J. explained. He said:

"Is this addition of surplus income to the capital of the residuary estate an accumulation within the Thellusson Act? On this point there has been a great difference of judicial opinion, *Crawley* v *Crawley*[111] would seem to be based on the view that such an addition of income to capital was not an accumulation. And Farwell J. in *Re Pope*[112] has, in terms, decided that a simple addition of income to capital is not an accumulation, either in ordinary parlance or within the Thellusson Act. On the other hand Malins V-C in *Re Phillips*[113] took a diametrically opposite view. And in the comparatively recent case of *Re Cababe*,[114] Neville J. has expressed his strong preference for the view of Malins V-C. In this state of the authorities I am free to follow my own judgement, which is in favour of the view of Malins V-C and Neville J. Such a recurrent addition as this seems to me plainly to amount to an accumulation, though it is a simple accumulation only, and not a compound accumulation. And, to my mind, the definition of accumulation from the Oxford Dictionary which Farwell J. has quoted in *Re Pope* is in favour of this view of the meaning of the word rather than in favour of the view of Farwell J. Further, it should be noticed that the Thellusson Act speaks of either total or partial accumulation, and is, in terms, aimed at preventing too great a postponement of beneficial enjoyment. It seems to me that a piling up of the income of property—even though the income of the additions to the growing pile is left at liberty—is at least a partial accumulation, and that such a process results in the

---

[109] See *Robertson's Trustees* v *Robertson's Trustees* 1933 S.C. 639 where an accumulation which would have been valid under the Thellusson Act was declared void on the Act of 1892.
[110] [1916] 2 Ch. 570 at p.577.
[111] (1835) 7 Sim. 427.
[112] [1901] 1 Ch. 64.
[113] (1880) 49 L.J. Ch. 198.
[114] (1914) 59 Sol. Jo. 129.

postponement of the beneficial enjoyment of the property within the meaning of that Act, since I cannot think that property is enjoyed beneficially in any real sense if income is hoarded and all that is left for enjoyment is the income of the hoard."[115]

It should be noted that even if one takes a different view from that of Sargant J. as to whether or not the beneficial enjoyment of the property is withheld, for trusts in Scotland, now governed by the 1961 Act, such simple accumulations would seem to be caught, section 5 (2) specifically referring to "partial accumulations" but making no mention whatever of postponement of beneficial enjoyment.

A third type of scheme which has been considered by the courts is where the income from the trust fund, pursuant to a power given to the trustees, is withdrawn from the enjoyment of the beneficiaries under the trust and is collected by the trustees, but is not added to capital. Such a situation came for decision by the Court of Session in *Lindsay's Trustees-Petitioners*[116] where the trustees were authorised to "set aside and accumulate" the balance of income from the residue of the trust fund for a specific purpose, but were not empowered to apply the capital for that purpose. It was held that the sums set aside by the trustees amounted to "savings of income" and, as such, were not accumulations within the meaning of the Thellusson Act.[117]

It seems clear from this case that the mere designation by the settler of a scheme as an "accumulation" will not of itself render that scheme subject to the legislation. Similarly the omission of that word will not negative the legislation's application. The basic question remains whether the directed scheme, however it be labelled,[118] amounts to an accumulation within the terms of the legislation.

The first thing that appears from the legislation is that, to come within it, the subject of the scheme must be of an income nature, the Act of 1800 referring to "rents, issue, profits or produce", and the Act of 1961 simply mentioning "income". Accordingly then, if what is set aside is treated by the law as being of a capital nature the restrictions should not apply. Thus in *Ranken's Trustees* v *Ranken*[119] it was held that the accumulation of certain mineral rents paid by the lessees of a coalfield while the coal remained unworked was outwith the scope of the Thellusson Act, such rents being of a capital nature, in accordance with the principle laid down by the House of Lords in *Campbell* v *Campbell's Trustees*.[120]

But even if the subject of the scheme is properly treated as income the above analysis indicates that a distinction might be drawn between those schemes whereby the income garnered by the trustees is added to the corpus of the fund, and those where it is not. Can it be said, then, that where the scheme is such

---

[115] Followed by Astbury J in *Re Garside* [1919] 1 Ch. 132.
[116] 1911 S.C. 584.
[117] Applied by Lord Guthrie (although not by Lord Salvesen and Lord Justice-Clerk Macdonald) in *Mitchell's Trustees* v *Fraser* 1915 S.C. 350 at p. 357.
[118] "The statute does not require that the accumulation must . . . . be directed to be made in any particular words or form", per Lord Ormidale in *Maxwell's Trustees* v *Maxwell* (1877) 5 R 249 at p. 251. See also *Royal Bank of Scotland* v *Inland Revenue* 1977 S.L.T. 45.
[119] 1908 S.C. 3.
[120] (1882) 10 R (H.L.) 65.

that the sums accumulated are appropriated to some special purpose, leaving intact (and not being added to) the corpus, the Act will not apply? Certainly there is English authority for such a proposition. In *Vine* v *Raleigh*[121] the Court of Appeal held that a direction to accumulate income which was to be applied in repairing and improving buildings on land was outwith the Act of 1800, at least in so far as improvements which could properly be defrayed out of income.[122] And in *Re Hurlbatt*[123] Warrington J. held that a direction to accumulate the income from one quarter of a residuary trust fund to provide a "reserve" out of which the trustees could be indemnified in certain events was equally held to be free of the statutory restrictions, as was a similar provision whereby a portion of the rents of certain leaseholds were to be accumulated to replace the capital that would be lost on the falling in of the leases.[124]

However, a question arises as to the position if the purpose of an accumulation of income is such that although the accumulations themselves are not added to capital, they are directed to be used in a way which will result in the capital being increased. Certainly this type of arrangement differs from both simple and compound accumulations in that there is no direct addition. And yet, the same economic result could be achieved by this indirect method as by an orthodox accumulation. There is one dictum of Lindley L.J. in *Vine* v *Raleigh*[125] to the effect that where an accumulation trust has for its purpose the improvement of property, and such improvement would have the consequence of increasing the value of the property then that would be within the scope of the legislation.

Yet, apart from that, although the cases achieve a kind of consistency, that consistency seems to lack a conceptual basis. Thus, for example, suppose income is not accumulated in the ordinary sense of being added to capital, but instead, is utilised in the purchase of an asset which is or will or may at a later date fall into the trust fund; does this arrangement come within the Act? On the one hand there is the case of *Smyth's Trustees* v *Kinloch*[126] which concerned a trust provision whereby trustees were empowered to purchase lands for the trust, incurring debts in the process, and applying surplus income from the trust fund to pay off those debts. It was held by the Court of Session that, even if the trustees were acting lawfully in executing this arrangement such surplus payments could only continue for twenty-one years from the testator's death, as they constituted accumulations within the meaning of the Thellusson Act. Lord Ormidale explained the decision in this way. He said:[127]

"And, again, even if, according to any reasonable construction of his trust deed the granter in the present instance could be held to have empowered his trustees to purchase lands by borrowed money to be paid off by accumulation of the rents or revenues of the trust estate, after a lapse of twenty-one years, I should entertain very little doubt that such accumulation would be struck at by the statute. Were it otherwise, the enact-

---

[121] [1891] 2 Ch. 13.
[122] See also *Re Mason* [1891] 3 Ch. 467.
[123] [1910] 2 Ch. 553.
[124] *Re Gardiner* [1901] 1 Ch. 697.
[125] [1891] 2 Ch. 13 at p. 26.
[126] (1880) 7 R 1176.
[127] *ibid*. at p. 1185.

ments of the statute might be very easily evaded and accumulation might go on for an indefinite length of time. Just suppose that in the present instance the trustees had shortly before the expiry of the twenty-one years, in virtue of powers given to them to that effect, purchased lands in the extent of £200,000, or some other very large sum, with borrowed money, to be repaid out of the accumulation of subsequent rents and revenues of the trust estate, for, it might be, a very long period of time before the lapse of twenty-one years from its commencement, I cannot doubt that such an accumulation would be an evasion of the statute and consequently illegal."

This question of evasion and the concomitant bona fides were very much in the minds of the English judges in deciding that appropriations of income accumulations for specific purposes were outwith the scope of the legislation. Thus in *Re Mason*[128] Stirling J. took the view that a trust for accumulation was valid so far as it was a bona fide provision for the performance of the specified trusts, and that accordingly it was not within the Thellusson Act, but that when the purposes were fulfilled, the general accumulation trust did fall within it.[129]

But on the other hand there are the life assurance cases, which, at first sight, would seem to fall clearly within the Act in that they do provide for the accumulation of income which is applied for the acquisition of an asset and that asset will, in time, fall into the general trust fund, thus increasing its value. And yet in two English cases, and one decision of the Second Division of the Inner House in Scotland, the payment of the premiums necessary to keep up the life policies have been held to be outwith the Thellusson Act.

The first of the English cases was *Bassil* v *Lister*[130] which concerned a direction in a will to pay out of the income of the estate the premiums on a life policy effected by the testator on the life of a third party. The Vice-Chancellor, Sir George Turner, held that these premium payments made out of the income of the estate did not fall within the Act. In view of the reliance that has been placed on his judgement, it would seem to be proper to set it out at length. He said:[131]

"The dry question I propose to determine is whether a direction given by a will, to pay out of the income of the testator's property the premiums upon a policy of insurance, effected by the testator upon the life of another person, is valid for the whole of the life insured, or only for the term of twenty-one years after the death of the testator. The question depends wholly upon the statute, for there is no doubt that at common law the direction would have been perfectly good, a circumstance not to be disregarded in construing the statute, although not, I think, too much to be relied on, as the Court, I apprehend, in putting a construction upon the statute, must have regard not merely to the pre-existing state of the law, but to the evil which had arisen from it, and which the statute was intended to remedy. Bearing in mind these views, it is necessary, I think, in order to arrive at a sound conclusion upon the present question, to consider the statute with reference to its origin, its enactments and its spirit and intent.

.... It had its origin in dispositions for the accumulation of rents and profits qua rents and profits and not in dispositions having any reference whatever to any bargains or contracts entered into for other purposes than the mere purpose of accumulation.

.... It was said in argument that the payment of the income to the insurance company in the present case was itself an accumulation; that the company are recipients of the income for the purpose of accumulation; that what was done was the same

---

[128] [1891] 3 Ch. 467.
[129] See also *Re Gardiner* [1901] 1 Ch. 697.
[130] (1851) 9 Hare 177.
[131] *ibid.* at p. 180-184.

thing as if the rents were paid to an individual to accumulate in his hands, and to be paid over at the death of the life insured. . . . . [B]ut I do not see how the payment of the premiums to the insurance company out of the income is an accumulation of the income. The premiums when paid to the insurance company become part of their general funds, subject to all their expenses; and, although, it is generally true that the funds in the hands of the companies do generally produce accumulations, it is impossible to say what accumulations arise from any particular premium.

It was said that it was an accumulation as to the estate, because the estate receives back a certain sum upon the death of the party whose life was insured; but what the estate receives back is not the accumulations of the income, but a sum payable by the office, by contract with the testator; and is this an accumulation within the meaning of the statute? The history of the statute goes far to show that it is not; and I think the language of the enactment confirms that view.

The enactment is that no person shall settle or disopse of real or personal estate so and in such manner as that the grants, profits, income or produce shall be accumulated beyond the prescribed periods: and these are words which admit of a clear, plain, common-sense interpretation, as referring to the accumulation of rents, profits and income qua rents, profits and income. Why is the Court to put a strained construction upon them, and cut down the undoubted right which existed before the statute, beyond what the language of the statute, in its ordinary interpretation, imparts? It is said that the Court ought to do so, because the spirit and intent of the statute was to prevent accumulations and the suspension of the beneficial enjoyment; but this argument appears to me to beg the question; for it assumes that what the Petitioner here calls an accumulation, suspending the beneficial enjoyment, was an accumulation intended to be prevented by the statute."

This decision was severely criticised by Jarman,[132] largely on the basis that the decision of the testator constituted a "direction to accumulate". However, as was pointed out by Lord Justice-Clerk Moncrieff in *Cathcart's Trustees* v *Heneage's Trustees*[133] Jarman's criticism tended to assume that the scheme constituted an accumulation to which the Act applied, without actually showing that it was.

Both the decision of Sir George Turner and the criticism of Jarman were placed before Chitty J. in *Re Vaughan*[134] who felt that he was bound by *Bassil* v *Lister*. Then later in the same year a case arose in Scotland on similar facts, save that in this case, it was the trustees, and not the testator, who effected the insurance. The Second Division, by a majority held that the Act did not apply. The Lord Justice-Clerk was content to follow the two decisions of the English courts, adding simply that, in his view the premiums were not accumulated, but rather that they were expended, which was the converse, adding that "All accumulation must carry with it a progressive increase in the aggregate of the accumulated product. In this case the lapse of time simply carried with it an increasing burden . . . ."[135]

Lord Rutherford Clark, while stating that, in his personal opinion, the Act should apply, was content to acquiesce in the line adopted by the Lord Justice-Clerk.[136] Lord Young was more certain, not referring at all to the English decisions. He said:[137]

---

[132] Wills, see Eighth Ed. pp. 408-411.
[133] (1883) 10 R 1205.
[134] (1883) W.N. 89.
[135] (1883) 10 R at p. 1215/6.
[136] *ibid.* at p. 1220.
[137] *ibid.* at p. 1217.

"The annual payments made under [the contracts of insurance] are not accumulations of income, they are simply periodical payments of contract debts well entered into, and I think we would be allowing ourselves to be misled, if we were to hold that this constitutes a saving up of income."

But if one accepts this, should not the same be true of the debts incurred by the trustees in *Smyth's Trustees* v *Kinloch*.[138] It was this point which was seized upon by Lord Craighill[139] in his dissenting judgement, holding that the case was not governed by the English decisions but by the prior decision of the Court of Session.

As far as Scotland is concerned, then the majority view was that the English rule would apply, so that premiums paid to keep up a life policy do not constitute accumulations within the legislation.[139a]

Yet this principle is not without its difficulties. The essence of the view is really that for the Act to apply it is the very garnerings themselves that are to be added to capital, and that "indirect" accretions to the corpus are not sufficient. But this, as will be seen, is not consistent with the view of Lindley L.J. in *Vine* v *Raleigh*[140] where the increase was rather of the value of the original corpus and not in the form of an addition to that corpus. And in *Smyth's Trustees* v *Kinloch* it was not the income that was added to capital; nor even was the produce of that income. It was, as in the life insurance cases, a separate asset. Further, Sir George Turner's point about the premium payments being mixed in with the general funds of the insurance company would appear to apply equally well to the payments under the debts in *Smyth's Trustees*.

It is submitted that the life assurance cases cannot truly be reconciled with either Lindley L.J.'s dictum or the Court of Session's decision in *Smyth's Trustees* v *Kinloch*. Of the two views it is possible to justify the exclusion of the Act in these cases on the ground that what is received is in fact a capital sum to which the Act clearly has no application. But to accept this view is to invite attempts at evasion. Whatever criticisms may be levelled at *Smyth's case*, it does have the merit of being wide enough to cover any such attempts. Of course, the bona fides rule suggested in some of the English cases could be brought into play here, but this would involve inquiries into motive and intention which are notoriously difficult and indecisive.

It is suggested that on the pure construction of the Act, the principle adopted in *Bassil* v *Lister* is probably right, and that *Smyth's Trustees* v *Kinloch* proceeds on a fear of the Act being evaded. But if this view, that accumulations to which the Act applies should be direct accumulations is correct, it is difficult to see how Lindley L.J.'s dictum can stand.

The decision in *Bassil* v *Lister* was applied in, perhaps, an even more surprising case, that of *Re A.E.G. Unit Trust (Managers) Ltd's Deed*[141] which concerned a unit trust scheme under which undistributed balances of income were to be added to capital. It was held that this was not a scheme to which the legislation was meant to apply, and further that the legislation was ineffectual

---

[138] (1880) 7 R 1176.
[139] (1883) 10 R at p. 1219.
[139a] But see *Royal Bank of Scotland* v *Inland Revenue* 1977 S.L.T. 45.
[140] 2 Ch. 13 at p. 26.
[141] [1957] Ch. 415.

in this situation in that, even if it did apply, because of the right of the unit holders to put an end to the scheme and withdrew their capital, on such withdrawal they would be free to embark upon the same scheme as was rendered void after the appropriate period. Perhaps the relevant factor here was that in no sense could it be said that the beneficial enjoyment of the fund was postponed[142] since both the distributed income was available annually and the accumulations simply accrued in such a way as to increase the value of the unit holder's investment which could be encashed at any time.

It is suggested then that the rules governing the application of the legislation can be summarised in the following propositions.
- (a) Where the scheme is such that accumulations of income are to be added directly to the corpus of the fund, the legislation will apply, unless the right or interest of the party entitled to the corpus is such that beneficial enjoyment is not postponed as a result of the scheme.
- (b) That where the accumulations are not to be added to the corpus of the fund the scheme is outwith the scope of the Act, provided that it is directed in good faith and is not aimed at avoidance of the restrictions.
- (c) That accretions to the fund which are received as capital are outwith the scope of the legislation, whether or not financed by payments out of current income and that accordingly such payments may continue beyond the statutory periods, provided that such schemes are directed in good faith.

(b) Directions to Accumulate

It has been mentioned that the phrase "direction to accumulate" occurs in the legislation as a description of the substantive provision which sets out those trusts to which the legislation applies. On this basis one would imagine that where an express provision in a deed covered the accumulation of income, the legislation would apply whether that provision was mandatory, that is, imposed a duty on the trustees to accumulate, or merely permissive in that it gave the trustees only a power so to do. In England it has been held that a mere power to accumulate is within the legislation, although in the relevant case, *Re Robb*[143] the non-exercise of the power would have given rise to a trust to accumulate. In Scotland however the case law is not so clear, if only because there has been no decision in which this question was addressed directly by the courts.

There are really three types of clause where the relationship between trusts and powers to accumulate occur. The first creates comparatively little difficulty. This occurs where the terms of the deed are such that the trustees are under an obligation to accumulate subject to a power to advance or distribute some income in favour of specified beneficiaries. In this case clearly there is a direction to accumulate, and this was so held in *Watson's Trustees* v *Brown*[144] where the terms of a trust deed directed that a share of residue was to go to a specified beneficiary contingently upon his attaining the age of twenty-five. There was

---

[142] Although this specific requirement is not present in s. 5 of the 1961 Act nor in s. 164 of the Law of Property Act 1925.
[143] [1953] Ch. 459.
[144] 1923 S.C. 228.

no express direction as to income during the meantime save that the trustees were given power to advance for the maintenance of the beneficiary. It was held, unsurprisingly that there existed an implied direction to accumulation which was not affected by the presence of the power.

The second type of clause carries the relationship one stage further. It is exemplified by a provision similar to the first type save that the whole of the income is subject to the power to advance, the effect being simply that the trustees, in a negative way are given a discretion as to whether or not to accumulate. In effect, the trustees are in the same position vis a vis their treatment of the income arising as when they are given a specific discretion either to distribute or to accumulate. In *Watson's Trustees* the power to advance potentially covered the whole of the income and, as has been pointed out, it was held by the court that a direction to accumulate existed.

The third type is simply a progression from the last two, namely a direction to distribute subject to such accumulations as are made under a discretionary power. In *Stewart's Trustees* v *Whitelaw*[145] it appeared to be assumed that the Act would apply although no discussion was directed specifically to the point.

In point of fact it would seem proper that powers should be so covered, not so much because of their inherent nature, but because they would appear to fall within the general rule as to directions, that if accumulation occurs as a necessary consequence of the provisions of the settlement, the terms of settlement embodying that necessity constitute a direction.[146] And, at least with regard to instruments taking effect after the passing of the 1966 Act there appears to be no doubt, section 6 (2) enacting for Scotland the provisions of section 13 (2) of the (English) Perpetuities and Accumulations Act 1964 stating explicity that a power "whether or not there is a duty to exercise that power" is subject to the legislation.

From an early period in Scotland it was accepted that the legislation covered implied, as well as express, directions to accumulate. In some of the early English cases[147] a distinction had been drawn between express directions, which were within the scope of the Act, and accumulations which arose by implication, which were not. However this distinction was held inapplicable in the 1850's[148] and when the first Scottish case on the subject, *Lord* v *Colvin*[149] came for decision in 1860 it was this latter line that was followed. As Lord Ivory said:[150]

"If there had been express words in the deed, it could not have been disputed; but it is said that it requires positive direction, or at least the distinction between that and what was said is so very thin that I can hardly follow it. It is not necessary that there be express words of direction, as I read the statute and as I understand the statute to have been read in the sister country where many questions of this sort have arisen. For,

---

[145] 1926 S.C. 701. See also *Blair* v *Curran* (1939) 62 C.L.R. 464 where a similar assumption was made.
[146] See below with regard to implied directions to accumulate.
[147] *Elborne* v *Goode* (1844) 14 Sim, 165; *Corporation of Bridgenorth* v *Collins* (1847) 15 Sim 538.
[148] *Tench* v *Cleese* (1855) 6 D.H. & G. 453; reversing (1854) 19 Beav. 3.
[149] (1860) 23. D. 111.
[150] *ibid.* at p. 126.

if by the inevitable operation of the directions which the deed gives to the trustees as to their dealing with and management of the estate, accumulation must take place in the extrication of the testator's mind, the necessary implication to be gathered from this is as clear as the most express direction. The statute uses the word "direction", but not throughout. . . . . It is clear from this [in reading the statute] that the evil to be prevented was the partial accumulation and the postponement of the beneficial interest in any party. The question therefore is whether the natural and necessary operation of this deed is not to produce the accumulation prohibited."

Lord Deas's judgement was more elaborate and in the course of it a discussion of the nature of "directions" was entered into. His Lordship said:[151]

"If the Act were to be held inapplicable wherever there was no express direction to accumulate, it would be easy in all cases to evade its operation. If it were held to be inapplicable wherever it did not appear that the testator had it in view to evade it, that would also favour evasion by involving an inquiry into what was paving in the testator's mind, which could not be satisfactorily answered. . . . . I think it is enough that the deed is so conceived that, to carry out its purposes in the event which has happened, there must, necessarily, be accumulation for a period beyond the twenty-one years.

The Act, in its primary and substantive enactment, does not use the terms 'direction' or 'directed' at all. It bears 'that no person or persons shall, after the passing of this Act, by any deed or deeds, surrender or surrenders, will, codicil or otherwise howsoever, settle or dispose of any real or personal property, so and in such manner that the rents, issues, profits or produce thereof shall be wholly or partially accumulated for any longer term than the issues of any such granter or granters, settler or settlers, or the term of twenty-one years from the death of any such granter, etc.' Now, pausing there, the testator has done the very thing prohibited. He has settled or disposed of his property 'so and in such manner' that the rents, issues and profits thereof must be accumulated—if the will is to have effect in its terms—for more than twenty-one years after his death. No doubt the Act goes on to speak of the party who would take but for the deed 'direction such accumulations' and to enact that 'in any case where any such accumulation shall be directed otherwise than as aforesaid, such direction shall be null and void' and the annual proceeds 'directed to be accumulated contrary to the provisions of this Act' shall go to those who would have been entitled thereto 'if such accumulation had not been directed'. But all this shows, to my mind, what it is the statute regards as a direction to accumulate—viz. a settlement or disposal of property 'so and in such manner that the rents, issues, profits or produce thereof shall be wholly or partially accumulated for any longer term' than the life of the granter, or twenty-one years after his death, etc. which, as I have already said, is the very thing the testator has done."

In a sense, then, "direction" would appear to be something of a misnomer for the situation coming within the legislation, implying as that word does, some form of instruction which, in its execution brings about the result of accumulation. No doubt that was what was envisaged by Lord Loughborough in framing the Thellusson Act; but in addition the term has come to take in also the historical antecedents[152] of the express direction, the necessary consequence and the direction by the Court.[153] Accordingly, in Scots and in English law, if it could be shown that the necessary consequence of implementing the terms of the trust was that an accumulation would follow, then these terms could be

---

[151] *ibid.* at pp. 136/137.
[152] In England. See above.
[153] See *Shaw* v *Rhodes* (1835) 1 Ny & Cr. 135: but see per contra *Moss's Trustees* v *Bramwell* where court order adopting an actuary's scheme for equitable compensation which involved accumulation was held by the House of Lords to be outwith the Act. See below at p. 342 et seq.

said to constitute a direction to accumulate which would bring into operation the provisions of the Act.

Thus in *Lord* v *Colvin*[154] the testator made a gift of property which carried the intermediate income, but in respect of which the vesting was postponed. It was held that this constituted an implied direction to accumulate and was therefore within the terms of the Thellusson Act. In *Pursell* v *Elder*[155] the House of Lords in a Scottish appeal had to consider the situation where the intermediate income of property had not been disposed of. The English rule was adopted, Lord Westbury saying:

"But this consequence arises, that the surplus income remaining in the hands of the trustees until the ultimate disposition takes effect must be invested and the proceeds and dividends of the investment must follow the principal and therefore, of necessity from the character of the gift, there will result in law, though it be not declared in the deed a trust for accumulation."

Indeed the lack of any provision for the disposition of intermediate income has become the classic situation of an implied direction to accumulate in Scotland.[156] In *Hutchison* v *Grant's Trustees*[157] there was a slight variation in a trust-settlement which contained a direction to trustees to hold the testator's estate for his daughter in liferent, and on her death to convey the fee to her issue. The daughter claimed and received legitim, whereupon the trustees retained and accumulated the income from the remaining estate so as to compensate the estate for the withdrawals from it that were necessary in order to satisfy the daughter's legal rights. It was held that, irrespective of the fact that, at the end of twenty-one years, the accumulations had failed to replace the withdrawn capital, the accumulation was a necessary consequence of the provisions of the trust deeds and as such was within the scope of the Thellusson Act which accordingly rendered void any accumulations outwith the twenty-one year period. This decision was followed seven years later in *Innes's Trustees* v *Bowen*[158] on almost exactly similar facts. In 1936, however, the House of Lords distinguished these two cases holding that in the case before it the accumulation in impletation of a scheme for equitable compensation was not a necessary consequence of the terms of the trust deeds. The case was *Moss's Trustees* v *Bramwell*[159] which also concerned a claim for the satisfaction of legal rights. Here a testator had directed that his residuary estate should be divided into three parts, the first part going to his wife in liferent, and upon her death or remarriage to her daughter in liferent and to the daughter's children in fee. The two other parts were to go to the testator's two daughters (by his first marriage) in liferent

---

[154] (1860) 23 D. 111.
[155] (1865) 4 Macq. 992 at p. 994.
[156] See *MacKenzie's Trustees* v *MacKenzie* (1877) 4 R 962; *Maxwell's Trustees* v *Maxwell* (1877) SR 249; *Smyth's Trustees* v *Kinloch* (1880) 7 R 1176; *Campbell's Trustees* v *Campbell* (1891) 18 R 2; *Elders Trustees* v *Treasurer of Free Church of Scotland* (1892) 20 R 2; *Logan's Trustees* v *Logan* (1896) 23 R 849; *Lee's Trustees* v *Fringies* (1897) 34 S.L.R. 613; *Moon's Trustees* v *Moon* (1899) 2 F 201; *Hutchison* v *Grant's Trustees* 1913 SC 1211; *Mitchell's Trustees* v *Fraser* 1915 SC 350 at p. 356; *Innes's Trustees* v *Bowen* 1920 SC 133; *Watson's Trustees* v *Brown* 1923 SC 228; *Stewart's Trustees* v *Whitelaw* 1926 SC 701; *Carey's Trustees* v *Rose* 1957 SC 252.
[157] 1913 SC 1211 (O.H.).
[158] 1920 SC 133.
[159] 1936 SC (H.L.) 1.

and to their issue in fee. There were further provisions directing that those beneficiaries who elected to claim their legal rights to the estate should forfeit the interests and benefits given to them under the will, such interests and benefits to accresce to the other beneficiaries. The widow elected to claim her legal rights and in so doing considerably diminished the residuary estate. A scheme of equitable compensation was approved by the court which involved accumulation of part of the annual income of the forfeited portion for behoof of the fiars until the death or remarriage of the widow. It was held by the House of Lords, reversing the Second Division, that the Thellusson Act had no application in that the accumulations were not directed by the will of the testator either expressly or by necessary implication, distinguishing *Hutchison* v *Grant's Trustees* and *Innes's Trustees* v *Bowen* on the ground that in those two cases it was found by the court that the form of compensation was contemplated by the testator within the language employed in the respective trust deeds, but that in the instant case, while it might be assumed that some form of compensation would be employed, there was nothing in the will to indicate what that form would be. As such it could not be said to contemplate an accumulation, which was therefore not a necessary consequence of the provisions of the will but rather an independent result of the terms of the scheme an approved by the court.

At first sight it seems difficult to find any reality in the distinction drawn by the House of Lords; both cases were, after all, concerned with the provision of equitable compensation in the events (which happened) of nominated beneficiaries claiming their legal rights to the estate instead of accepting the benefits allocated under the will; and in neither case was there any suggestion in the will of an accumulation taking place. If there is a distinction to be made, it is apparently that in *Moss's Trustees* v *Bramwell* the testator made specific provision as to what was to happen to the forfeited share of a specified beneficiary whereas in *Hutchison* v *Grant's Trustees* (and in *Innes's Trustees* v *Bowen*) no such provision existed, either for forfeiture or for allocation of any forfeited share. In the latter case the effect of electing to take the legal rights was that "temporarily, at all events . . . . her liferent interest was set free. As there was not a forfeiture clause she was entitled, on the estate being recouped in the amount that she had taken out in respect of her legal claims, to be restored to her interests under the will is to enjoy the remainder of her life interest".[160] As such the life interest went back to the estate and, there being no provision for dealing with it under the terms of the will it was added to capital under the ordinary law. As Lord Dundas stated in *Innes's Trustees* v *Bowen*:[161]

"Now, I think we are bound to assume on the part of this truster (as of every other Scots truster) a knowledge of the general law of Scotland, and particularly of the right of a daughter to claim legitim, and the legal results of such a claim in regard to the administration of the estate. The position is not substantially different from what it would have been if the truster had added to her bequest of the liferent such words as these: 'And if my daughter shall elect to claim her legal rights, then the income of the residue shall be accumulated, and applied towards the equitable compensation of those prejudged by her said claim until the capital sum paid to her in the name of legitim shall be made good to my estate'."

[160] 1913 SC at p. 1214 per Lord Moncrieff.
[161] 1920 SC at p. 140. Approved by the House of Lords in *Moss's Trustees* v *Bramwell*.

In *Moss's Trustees* v *Bramwell* this result was obviated by the forfeiture clause and the complementary provisions which went with it. These made provision for such forfeited rights to accresce the other beneficiaries accepting the will for the same interests of liferent, fee or otherwise as had been set out in the primary provisions of the will. There was therefore no gap in the sense that there was in the two earlier cases, no liferent piling up income which was to be used for the benefit of the trust and which under the general law necessarily produced an accumulation.

Nonetheless an accumulation did result in the latter case, albeit as a result of a scheme produced to get around the practical difficulties of implementing the forfeiture and forfeiture-related provisions. Could not the testator be taken to have comprehended these? The House thought not. As Lord Thankerton put it:[162]

"In the present case there could be no knowledge of the part of the testator of the particular form which the equitable compensation was to take or that it involved accumulation. The Court itself did not know until the reports of the actuary had been received. . . . . How then can the testator be held to have known that the present scheme would inevitably follow, or how could a direction for the present scheme be written into the settlement on the lines adopted by Lord Dundas."

In this case, given that the scheme suggested by the actuary was not the only one that might have been adopted[163] but merely the most expedient, the distinction would appear to have substance. But what if it transpired that there was only one practicable scheme by which the testator's intention could be implemented? Could it be said that the testator should be "constructively" aware of it, as he is deemed to be of the legal effects of the terms of the deeds he executed? In *Moss's Trustees* v *Bramwell* only Lord Macmillan appeared to envisage this possibility. Commenting on the scheme before him, he said:[164]

"I cannot see how it can be said in law that Mr. Lidstone's [i.e. the actuary] scheme was the necessary result of the directions given by the testator for the disposal of Lady Moss's forfeited provisions. The author of the scheme was Mr. Lidstone, not the testator, and it was the Lord Ordinary, not the testator, who put it into operation. It was no doubt a workable and probably the best and most practicable, method of carrying out the testator's directions as the Lord Ordinary construed them. But I do not think that this method was by necessary implication directed by the testator; indeed I should hesitate long to attribute to Sir Edward Moss any conception that such a scheme would be evolved to effectuate his directions. *That might not matter if the method chosen was, in the circumstances, the inevitable result of the directions he had given.* But I have already shown that, while the method was an expedient one, and doubtless the most workable one, it cannot be said as a matter of law to be the necessary result of the testator's directions as construed."

The implication then is that where the scheme was not the result of choosing one of several possible schemes, but involved the application of one such, and one such only, scheme then legal necessity might be implied so as to construct such provisions as constituting directions to accumulate.[165]

---

[162] 1936 SC (H.L.) at p. 9.
[163] See per Lord Macmillan *ibid.* at pp. 10/11.
[164] *ibid.* at p. 11.
[165] Sed quaere, whether this would be a necessity of law, as opposed to a necessity of fact, and, indeed, whether this would make any difference. It is suggested that probably it would not, since the rule requires simply that accumulations be a necessary consequence, apparently either of law or of fact.

These cases serve to illustrate the principal difficulty with the doctrine of "implied direction"; namely where the line is to be drawn? The legal principle that to constitute an implied direction the accumulation must be a necessary consequence is in Scotland at least, as old as the doctrine itself. The judgements in *Lord* v *Colvin* stress the element of necessary consequence, with the result that if this were to be absent the legislation would not apply. The problem therefore where accumulation has taken place is to consider which circumstances will be considered as extraneous and so not as the necessary consequence of the provisions of the trust deed?

Although this distinction has been much canvassed it has only twice[166] been applied by the Scottish courts. The first occasion was in a case before the Second Division, namely *Mitchell's Trustees* v *Fraser*.[167] The case concerned a provision in a trust-disposition and settlement whereby the testator's residuary estate was given to trustees who were directed "from time to time, as they think proper, to make such special payments out of the free residue and remainder of my estate to such of my children or children's children as they may think most deserving, with special instructions to relieve any of them who may appear to be in want, provided always that they have not brought themselves into such circumstances by their own misconduct. My great desire is to assist merit and thrift and not to acknowledge indolence or folly". There being no further directions as to the disposal of residue, the income therefrom was accumulated for a period of twenty-one year's from the testator's death, the trustees not making any distribution owing to the fact that they were not satisfied that any cases existed which warranted payment out of the trust funds. It was held by the court that the accumulation of income was due, not to the directions of the testator, but to the extraneous circumstance that no occasion for payments out of income had yet arisen. The grounds for so holding were set out at length by Lord Salvesen:[168]

"The testator neither directed accumulation, nor, so far as I can see, did he contemplate it. On the contrary he appointed his trustees to make payments not merely out of the income, but out of the capital of the estate. It is true that they have not done so: the reason which they allege being 'that they were not satisfied that any cases existed which warranted payment out of the trust funds on the ground of want or special merit'. Personally, I think that if they had applied their minds to their duties in the proper spirit they would not have found so much difficulty in executing their trust duties. But whether this be so or not, the fact that there have been accumulations beyond twenty-one years has not resulted from a direction, express or implied; nor do I think that the accumulation was a necessary consequence of the directions given. It has resulted entirely from something extraneous to the deed, namely, the inability of the trustees to find proper objects of the testator's bounty. One can conceive of a case of a testator directing the income of his estate to be paid to a certain beneficiary, whom, though alive, the trustees are unable to find, with the result that for more than twenty-one years the income accumulates in their hands. Could it be said that such an accumulation was struck at by the statute? I apprehend not. The statute itself uses the words: 'In every case where any accumulation shall be directed, otherwise than

---

[166] Excluding *Lindsay's Trustees* 1911 SC 584 which really concerned whether the arrangement amounted to an accumulation, not whether the instructions amounted to a direction.
[167] 1915 SC 350.
[168] *ibid.* at pp. 357/358: Approved by Lord Dundas in *Innes's Trustees* v *Bowen* 1920 SC at p. 141.

as aforesaid, such direction shall be null and void, and the rents, issues, profits and produce of such property so directed to be accumulated, contrary to the provisions of this Act, go to and be received by such person or persons as would have been entitled thereto if such accumulation had not been directed'. Now there is no direction here to accumulate after the lapse of twenty-one years, any more than during the currency of twenty-one years; and I see no ground why the trustees should not have paid the whole income of the twenty-second year to any of the testator's children or grandchildren who appear to be in want, and who had not disentitled themselves to assistance by their own misconduct. There is every likelihood that during the continuance of this trust such beneficiaries will emerge; and the fact of accumulation beyond twenty-one years is not due to any direction of the testator, but to the accident that there have been no objects on which his bounty could be bestowed. The same thing might occur if a testator gave instructions to trustees to pay the annual income of the fund to persons, within a given parish who happened to be attacked by cancer, or some less common malady, and no such person existed, during a period exceeding twenty-one years. In the case of *Lord* v *Colvin* Lord President McNeill[169] expressly contemplated accumulation beyond twenty-one years resulting from the operation of law 'as may happen in regard to minority', and plainly implied that such an accumulation would not be struck at by the statute, although exceeding twenty-one years."

It is perhaps significant that the other decision which bases itself on the doctrine of necessary consequence, *Moss's Trustees* v *Bramwell*[170] makes no reference to this case, and further that in the subsequent decisions[171] in which *Mitchell's Trustees* v *Fraser* has been sought to be applied the courts have come to explain it on other ground. Thus, for example in *Innes's Trustees* v *Bowen*, Lord Dundas explained the decision thus:[172]

"The recent decision of this Division in *Mitchell's Trustees* is not, I think in any way discrepant. I gather that the Court considered that the fee of the residue had vested in the testator's issue, as a class, subject to the trustees direction in administering the benefit to those of the class whom they might think 'most deserving'. In *Lord* v *Colvin*[173] the Act was held to apply because the necessity for accumulating income arose, in the opinion of the learned judges, from the provisions of the settlement in the circumstances which had occurred, as I think it clearly did in the case before me. It was pointed out (e.g. per Lord Ivory, at p. 127) that a different situation would arise, as in the case, e.g. of a lunatic, it might be necessary as a matter of prudent administration, to accumulate, beyond the period of twenty-one years, the bulk of the income of an estate which actually belonged to him. So, again, in *Mitchell's Trustees* Lord Salvesen figured[174] the case of an absentee, not known to be dead, to whom, if alive, the estate belonged. But no such situation is, as I have explained, here present; for the fee of the estate was not, when the twenty-one years expired, and is not yet, vested in anyone."

According to Lord Dundas, then, the basis of the decision in *Mitchell's Trustees* v *Fraser* was not so much that the accumulation came about as the result of an extraneous factor, per se, but rather that it related to the interests of beneficiaries which were vested and not contingent. An examination of the judgements in *Lord* v *Colvin* from which the necessary consequence doctrine derives also shows that the circumstances contemplated in which an accumulation by trustees would not be a necessary consequence related to cases where

---

[169] (1860) 23 D at p. 124.
[170] 1936. SC (H.L.) 1.
[171] See per *Watson's Trustees* v *Brown* 1923 SC 228; *Innes's Trustees* v *Bowen* 1920 SC 133
[172] 1920 SC at p. 141.
[173] (1860) 23 D 111.
[174] 1915 SC at p. 357.

the beneficiaries had vested interests. Thus, in Lord Ivory's judgement, which was the most detailed on this point, the following passage occurs:[175]

"It was said that, not being an express direction, and not being an implied direction in the sense to which I have just been speaking that the accumulation is truly an act of the law, by which the trustees must accumulate. It is not an act of law in the sense of the law being the source of the duty. The duty originates in the deed, and is to be fulfilled in the terms of the deed. There is no general law regarding the subject. It is the will of the testator. But there is a misapprehension in the use which has been made of that observation, for the illustration which was given was that to which your Lordship has already alluded,—the case of trustees or curators acting for pupils, or for persons otherwise incapacitated from managing their own estates, lunatics and such like, when the trustees are compelled to manage the estate which they have been intrusted with, that all the produce may be gathered together and dealt with as a portion of the estate eventually to be extricated. Well, that is very fine. There is no direction there, and it is in such a case that the law interposes; but the distinction lies here, that in the case of an estate that has fallen to a minor as a fee simple estate, burdened with no contingency, no directions, no accumulations, so far as the deed goes, then the estate is pure and simple. It is an estate which belongs to him after the death of the testator from the first; and the Thellusson Act does not deal with accumulations in the interests of a party to whom the estate itself belongs and who is in in the beneficial enjoyment as well as in the vested right to the whole estate. The case there is the case of funds of the successor being placed in such a situation that it is necessary to throw the protection of the law over them. The trustees, or the receivers of Court, or whoever else is placed in charge, must deal with the estate, so that all the beneficial results from that estate shall fall to the party whose the estate is. But that is not at all the kind of case which the Thellusson Act points at."

This background to and interpretation of the principle applied by the Second Division in *Mitchell's Trustees* v *Fraser*[176] raises two questions. The first is whether the cause of extraneous circumstances which takes the accumulation outwith the legislation is limited to cases where the beneficiaries have vested interests. While there was no mention of such a limitation in *Moss's Trustees* v *Bramwell*[177] it is nonetheless a fact that the relevant interests there were vested; and further, the first of the examples given by Lord Salvesen in his statement of the principle,[178] namely that of the last beneficiary is also a case of an interest which has vested. And, of course, if the interpretation of *Mitchell's Trustees* v *Fraser* is correct, then this too would exemplify such a correlation. It must also be stated that in England the principle is stated in terms of the consequences of accumulations where the beneficiary has a vested interest rather than in terms of extraneous circumstances.[179]

If this view is right, then the second question comes sharply into focus, namely whether on this basis the case of *Mitchell's Trustees* v *Fraser* has been rightly decided and correctly interpreted. The point is whether, in truth, the beneficiaries in that case had vested interests. The judgements of the members

---

[175] (1860) 23 D at p. 127.
[176] 1915 SC 350.
[177] 1936 SC (H.L.) 1.
[178] 1915 SC at pp. 357/358.
[179] See Morris and Leach at pp. 276-278; Keeton—Modern Developments in the Law of Trusts at pp. 236-239. Subject to one exception, *Lombe* v *Stoughton* (1841) 12 Sim. 304 which concerned a bequest for a specific purpose, namely the erection of a mansion house on land where owing to the refusal of the tenant for life to approve the plan the purpose could not be carried out until more than twenty-one years after the death of the testator.

of the court make no analysis of these interests at all and the Lord Ordinary, Lord Skerrington, in his opinion[180] referred to them as "contingent". With the greatest respect it is suggested that, given the terms of the direction to the trustees empowering them "from time to time, as they think proper, to make such special payments out of the free residue . . . . to such of [the class of beneficiaries] as they shall think most deserving, with special instructions to relieve any of them who appear to be in want", it is difficult to ascribe any vested right to the beneficiaries—indeed it is difficult to ascribe any contingent right either for even if they so satisfy the conditions of membership no beneficiary is to have any interest at all until the trustees exercise their discretion in his favour. If this be a correct assessment of the beneficiaries' rights then, given that cases where the intermediate income is not dealt with until vesting have been held[181] to constitute implied directions to accumulate, the instant case would appear to fall within this class, with the result that it should be subject to the restrictions of the legislation.[182]

It is perhaps to be regretted that the term "direction to accumulate" was ever included in the Act of 1800 and still more that it has been retained in the Act of 1961, for if nothing else it is something of a misnomer which has only added complexity to an already complex subject. Misnomer it is because direction is usually taken to imply an action, an instruction which if implemented has a consequence; whereas in fact it is not the action or instruction which is important as far as the operation of the legislation is concerned, but rather the consequence. While it is true that this consequence must necessarily result from the provisions of the deed it remains that the primary factor is the consequence and it is from that that the process of and questions arising out of applying the legislation arise.

The Legislative Restrictions

It will be remembered that the Act of 1800 sought only to regulate, rather than to prohibit, the practice of accumulation and accordingly sought in no way to affect the validity or nature of the beneficial interests given under the settlement as do the perpetuity rules applicable in England and Scotland respectively. All the Act did was to limit accumulation by defining the periods during which it was permissible. It is these provisions and their consequences that now fall to be considered.

(a) The Periods of Accumulation

Four periods were prescribed by section 1 of the Thellusson Act[183] and these were carried forward to form the basis of section 5 of the Trusts (Scotland) Act 1961.[184] To these section 6 of the Law Reform (Miscellaneous Provisions) (Scotland) Act 1966[185] added two more.

---

[180] 1915 SC at pp. 351/352.
[181] See cases cited above at note 156.
[182] The second example of Lord Salvesen's, the bequest to such members of a village as became afflicted with cancer, etc. would not seem to be at one with the situation here since in that example the interests of the beneficiaries depended on their cancerous state rather than on the exercise of the trustees' discretion in their favour.
[183] Statute 39 & 40 Geo. III c. 98.
[184] *ibid.* 9 & 10 Eliz. II c. 57.
[185] *ibid.* 1966 c. 19.

The six periods are:
(i) The life of the grantor or settlor;
(ii) A term of twenty-one years from the death of the grantor, settlor or testator;
(iii) The duration of the minority or respective minorities of any person or persons living or in utero at the death of the grantor, settlor or testator;
(iv) The duration of the minority or respective minorities only of any person or persons who, under the limitations of the instrument directing the accumulation would, for the time being, if of full age, be entitled to the income directed to be accumulated;
(v) A term of twenty-one years from the date of the making of the disposition;
(vi) The duration of the minority or respective minorities of any person or persons in being at that date.

Periods (v) and (vi), having been introduced by the 1966 Act apply only to deeds taking effect after the passing of that Act. (i) "The first period", said Lord Parker of Waddington,[186] "contemplates the case of a man who settles his property otherwise than by will, in which case he may direct that the rents and profits be accumulated during his life—The settlor cannot direct an accumulation during his life and some further period".

This principle came to be considered in Scotland in *Stewart's Trustees* v *Stewart*,[187] which concerned an inter vivos trust with an accumulation provision which came into effect during the truster's lifetime. It was held that the only valid period during which the income could be accumulated was from the date of the coming into force of the accumulation to the death of the truster, the court expressly following two earlier English decisions in *Re Lady Rosslyn's Trust*[188] and *Jagger* v *Jagger*.[189] *Stewart's Trustees* v *Stewart*[187] was followed two years later in *Union Bank of Scotland* v *Campbell*[190] where the principle was expressed in somewhat wider terms to the effect that if a direction to accumulate was contained in an inter vivos trust and had an immediate operation, period (*a*) was the only appropriate one to apply. These two cases were in turn followed in *Russell's Trustees* v *Russell*[190a] and *Lady Gibson's Trustees, Petitioners*.[190b]

As a result of the wide language used in these cases it came to be assumed that wherever there was a direction to accumulate in an inter vivos settlement it would be terminated on the death of the truster unless it had been tied to a minority which has expired in the meantime. Consequently where an accumulation was tied to a minority, but one which did not cease until after the truster's death it came to be felt that the accumulation would nonetheless be curtailed

---

[186] In *Re Cattell* [1914] 1 Ch. 177 at p. 186.
[187] 1927 SC 350.
[188] (1848) 16 Sim. 391.
[189] (1883) 25 Ch. D. 729.
[190] 1929 SC 143.
[190a] 1959 SC 148.
[190b] 1963 SC 350.

at the date of death. Indeed in *McIver's Trustees* v *IRC*[190c] Lord Fraser was emphatic that "there was clear authority to the effect that where, under a direction to accumulate income contained in an inter vivos deed, accumulations began during the grantor's life and that accumulations after his death were illegal".

In this case a fund was transferred to trustees with a direction that they were to retain it and accumulate the income from it until his son attained the age of twenty-two years. The grantor died when the son was sixteen and the trustees were assessed for estate duty on the basis that the accumulation provisions became illegal on the grantor's death as the appropriate accumulation period was the life of the grantor. The trustees on the other hand held that the appropriate period was period (iv) as the accumulation period was defined by reference to the son's age and the period was consistent with the grantor's intention was that one which permitted accumulation during the son's minority. As a matter of construction the trustees failed. As Lord Kissen explained:[190d]

"The words 'during a period specified in paragraph [iv]' cannot be applied to the provisions in the deed as that accumulation could take place beyond the truster's life. Apart from that, the terms of and the language employed in the deed point clearly in my opinion to the view that the truster must have intended that the accumulation of revenue was to continue until his death. His overriding intention . . . . was that accumulation was to continue until his son reached the age of twenty-two years. That intention could not have been carried out by the application of . . . . period . . . . [iv] because the accumulation would necessarily have ended when the son had reached the age of twenty-one years, even if the truster was then alive. The only possibility of accumulation continuing until the son reached the age of twenty-two years was the truster's survivance to that time."

The trustees had founded their argument on section 5 (4) of the Act of 1966 which provided:

"For the avoidance of doubt it is hereby declared that, in the case of a settlement or other disposition inter vivos, a direction to accumulate income during . . . . period . . . . [iv] shall not be void, nor shall the accumulation of the income be contrary to this section, solely by reason of the fact that the period begins during the life of the grantor and ends after his death."

Both Lord Kissen and Lord Fraser treated this section as altering the pre-1961 law, as opposed to merely clarifying it. Certainly there had been no cases decided in Scotland in which an accumulation which has begun during the grantor's lifetime had been permitted to continue after his death, and there were of course the dicta in *Stewart's Trustees* v *Stewart* and the *Union Bank Case*. But, with respect, wide though these dicta are, they were made in the context of and indeed applying the principle that the accumulation periods cannot be aggregated together. There is nothing, in either of them, it is submitted, which would justify an extension of this to the effect that in an inter vivos deed, if another period was appropriate, it should be cut short by the death of the grantor. However, having said that, it must be admitted that in *Russell's Ttustees* v *Russell*[190a] this contextual point was not taken, the judgement of the Lord Presi-

---

[190c] [1973] S.T.C. 398 at p. 403; See also per Lord Kissen at p. 401 ". . . . in inter vivos deeds accumulation of income was illegal after the death of the grantor of such a deed". Now reported 1974 S.L.T. 201.
[190d] [1973] S.T.C. at p. 401.

dent in particular applying the dicta without qualification.[190e]

Yet whatever the effect of section 5 (4) on the previous law, the decision in *McIver's Case* would seem to restrict its application to these cases where the terms of the deed specifically direct an accumulation for the relevant minority. Certainly any direction contemplating an excess would appear, on Lord Kissen's reasoning, automatically to make period (*a*) the appropriate one. (ii) Unlike period (i) this accumulation period applies to both inter vivos and mortis causa deeds, provided, of course, that the direction to accumulate is to take effect from the grantor's death. The actual date of death is excluded from the term so that income falling due on the twenty-first anniversary of the death can be accumulated.[191]

In *Ogilvie's Trustees* v *Kirk Session of Dundee*[192] it seems to have been assumed that in the case of all testamentary deeds no accumulation which did not involve a minority could continue beyond the twenty-first anniversary of the death. However in *Maxwell's Trustees* v *Maxwell*[193] it was held that this period renders illegal directions to accumulate after the twenty-first anniversary of the date on which the direction became operative. In this case the accumulation was directed to begin only after the lapse of certain annuities. The testator had died in 1841, but the annuities had continued to be paid until Whitsuntide 1856. Thereafter the trustees accumulated the requisite portion of the residuary income until 1877. It was held by the court that any accumulation after this date would be null and void.

This case was cited as authority for the proposition that where the direction to accumulate became operative after the date of the death of the grantor then although the period of accumulation was limited to twenty-one years in toto, it need not cease on the twenty-first anniversary of the death. In *Campbell's Trustees* v *Campbell*[194] however the Lord Ordinary, Lord Kincairney, refused to follow *Maxwell's case* on this point, writing:[195]

".... it is to be observed that [in *Maxwell's case*] prior accumulations were not challenged and the question put to the Court was only whether the direction was void as from Whitsunday 1877. The Court could, and did, decide nothing else. Probably attention was not drawn to the legality of the prior accumulations, and I do not find that any of the judges indicated an opinion on the point."

The Second Division accepted the Lord Ordinary's assessment (by a majority) and held that, in the case of period (ii), whenever the direction came into operation, the accumulation could not continue beyond the twenty-first anniversary of the grantor's death.[195a]

In *Stewart's Trustees* v *Whitelaw*[196] an accumulation was directed by a power of appointment which took effect several years after the coming into operation of the parent deed on the death of a testator. The question for the

---

[190e] It should be mentioned that because of other factors present in the case the end result would have been the same.
[191] *Gorst* v *Lowndes* (1841) 11 Sim. 434.
[192] (1846) 8 D 1229.
[193] (1877) 5 R 248.
[194] (1891) 18 R 992; See also *Barbour* v *Rudge* 1947 SN 100.
[195] *ibid.* at p. 997/998.
[195a] See also *Carey's Trustees* v *Rose* 1957 SC 252.
[196] 1926 SC 701; confirmed in respect of post 1966 deeds by section 6 (3).

court, inter alia, was as to the operative date from which the period was to run. If it was the date of the power, as this was geared to the duration of the minority of the beneficiary the accumulation would accordingly continue for twenty-one years from the date of the coming into operation of the power; if on the other hand the relevant date was the date of the parent deed, period (ii) would apply so that the accumulation would have to terminate on the twenty-first anniversary of the death. It was held, following English authority[197] that the relevant date was the date of the deed under which the power had been created so that the accumulation period ran from the death of the testator.

(iii) At its extreme limit this period can only exceed that prescribed in period (ii) by a few months. Often it will not do that. Again the principle that the cut-off date is the end of the minority applies, irrespective of when the direction to accumulate became operative. In *Union Bank of Scotland* v *Campbell*[198] the question arose as to whether, in the case of an inter vivos trust containing a non-specific direction to accumulate, the appropriate period was period (i) or period (ii). It was held that in such a case, in the absence of a precise nomination as to the period to be employed, there were no valid grounds on which period (iii) could be used, and that accordingly, the appropriate period was (i).[199]

(iv) The period here referred to is that of the minority or respective minorities of beneficiaries. The period would seem to be applicable to a beneficiary whether he was in life or not at the date the deed came into operation. If it were otherwise then period (iv) would be superfluous, adding nothing to period (iii). Indeed it could be argued that this period was more restrictive, confining the relevant minorities to those of persons who but for the accumulation would, if of full age, be entitled to receive the income accumulated.

This qualification would seem to contemplate such beneficiaries who are entitled to "a present gift of the fund itself"[199a] which in *Russell's Trustees* v *Russell*[199b] was defined as someone whose interest had vested absolutely, if not from the date of the gift, at least before the termination of the accumulation. In this case there was a defeasance clause, which was held to prevent absolute vesting until the date specified for payment. In *McIver's case* this principle was applied as an alternative ground for the inapplicability of period (iv).[199c]

A typical case where the application of period (iv) is appropriate would seem to be where the accumulation is directed to follow some intervening interest. As Lord President Clyde explained in *Carey's Trustees* v *Rose*:[200]

---

[197] *Fane* v *Fane* [1913] 1 Ch. 404.
[198] 1929 SC 143.
[199] per Kay J in *Jagger* v *Jagger* (1883) 25 Ch. D at p. 773—"It is clear that this part of the Act refers only to a direction to accumulate when such accumulation is to begin from the date of the grantor's death; and to say that the accumulation may begin at the date of the settlement whilst the grantor is living and continue during his lifetime and afterwards during the minorities of the children is, in effect to contend that the Act is cumulative, that is to say, that you may take one of the periods and apply it after a previous one had been exhausted." Approved per Lord Justice-Clerk Alness in the *Union Bank case*, 1929 SC at p. 150.
[199a] See below.
[199b] 1959 SC 148.
[199c] See [1973] S.T.C. at pp. 401/2 (per Lord Kissen) and at pp. 404/5 (per Lord Fraser).
[200] 1957 SC 252 at pp. 257/258.

"The prohibition in relation to the fourth period however deals with a quite different situation. A testator may provide for the income of part, or the whole of his estate being enjoyed by a liferenter or some intervening interest, and he may direct that on the death of the liferenter or the termination of that intervening interest that income is to be accumulated for a beneficiary who on attaining majority is to be entitled to the accumulated funds. It would be quite inequitable to seek to apply the prohibition in relation to the second period in such a case, so as to prohibit all accumulations after twenty-one years from the testator's death, for the direction in this case might not begin to operate until after these twenty-one years had passed. . . . . Where the direction to accumulate only begins to operate, owing to the existence of an intervening interest, some years after the date of the testator's death, the prohibition relating to the fourth period comes into operation and, while sanctioning accumulations during the beneficiary's minority, prohibits any further accumulation after that beneficiary becomes twenty-one years of age."

As it would appear unnecessary for the relevant beneficiary to be in esse at the date of the deed it would seem that by framing a deed in such a way that accumulations were to take place during the minorities of successive beneficiaries a series of accumulations would be possible, which in toto would continue for long in excess of twenty-one years.[201] However it would appear that if period (iv) is to be applicable and the beneficiary is unborn at the date of the deed, there has to be, if not an intervening interest, at least some intervening trust purpose. In the only English case where this has been permitted, *Re Cattell*[202] there was an intervening trust purpose. But in *Re Taylor*[203] where there was an implied direction to accumulate income for such of the children of a married woman as should attain the age of twenty-one, the woman being childless at the date of the deed, the court directed accumulation for twenty-one years from the testator's death, and negatived an argument that the accumulation could only begin on the birth of a child and continue during its minority. And in *Re Watt's Will Trusts*,[204] where an accumulation was directed during the minority of the children of A, the capital and accumulations of the fund going to them at twenty-one, it was held that period (iv) was inappropriate here because the income of the whole fund was directed still to be subject to accumulation after some of those entitled to share in it had attained majority. The appropriate period here was held to be the third period and accordingly therefore the accumulation had to be restricted to the minority of the children living at the testator's death.

We have seen that section 5 (4) of the Trusts (Scotland) Act 1961[205] relates specifically to period (iv) declaring, "for the avoidance of doubt" that a direction to accumulate for this period is not to be considered in breach of the legislation solely by reason of the fact that the period begins during the life of the grantor and ends after his death.

The provision now makes it clear that, if the direction be sufficiently explicit to make it clear that period (iv) is appropriate, the mere fact that it is to begin

---

[201] *Re Cattell* [1914] 1 Ch. 547 (C.A.) not following dicta in *Haley* v *Bannister* (1819) 4 Mood 275; *Ellis* v *Maxwell* (1841) 3 Beav. 587; *Bryan* v *Collins* (1852) 16 Beav. 14; *Jagger* v *Jagger* supra.
[202] [1907] 1 Ch. 567 per Neville J.
[203] [1901] 2 Ch. 134 approved by Lord President Clyde at 1957 SC at p. 258.
[204] [1936] 1 All ER 1555.
[205] See above.

during the grantor's lifetime will not operate to invalidate it.[206]

It will be recalled that accumulation governed by the Accumulations Act 1892[207] are restricted to this period alone.

(v) This period, introduced by the Act of 1966 provides the counterpart for deeds inter vivos to that available for testamentary disposition under period (ii). To date there has been only one case before the courts in which this period has figured, that of *J. S. Aikman, Petitioner*[208] which is discussed above.

(vi) The second additional period introduced by the 1966 Act is a counterpart to period (iii) although this of course applies only to inter vivos settlements.

(b) Choice of Period

In settlements where there are present express directions to accumulate it is usual to specify which of the six periods is intended to apply to the settlement. In many cases, however, either because the period specified is inappropriate or illegal as being in contravention of the legislation, and where the direction to accumulate is implied, it has to be ascertained which period is appropriate to the particular direction.

There is, perhaps, only one basic principle and that is that only one period can be selected. As Lord Ormidale put it in *Union Bank of Scotland* v *Campbell*.[209]

"It must, I think, be held to have been finally ascertained as a matter of construction, that any one, but not more than one, of these periods can be selected by the settlor. In re *Lady Rosslyn's Trust*[210] the argument appears to have been submitted to the Vice-Chancellor (Sir L. Shatwell) but rejected by him, that the settlor was entitled to take more than one, or the whole four periods as making one aggregate period. And his construction of the section appears to have been consistently followed[211] and the periods held to be, not cumulative to any extent, but exclusive.'

That being the case questions then arise as to which of the periods is applicable in any given case and what factors are taken into account in making the choice?

In most cases it will be apparent from the provisions of the trust deed that at least one, and probably two (or now four) of the periods will be inappropriate as being irrelevant to those provisions. The ultimate decision will usually be between two periods and is almost always arrived at by a process of elimination. In *Re Bourne's Settlement Trusts* the case arose out of an inter vivos settlement where the choice of period lay between (i) and (iv), and Lord Greene's judgement exemplifies the process that has been consistently applied both in England and in Scotland. He said:[212]

"The problem which the legislature has laid down for the Court under this section is in any particular case to discover the period which is appropriate for the particular

---

[206] See also per Lord Kissen (at p. 401) and Lord Fraser (at pp. 403/3) in *McIver* v *I.R.C.* [1973] S.T.C. 398.
[207] See above.
[208] 1968 S.L.T. 137.
[209] 1929 SC 143 at p. 156.
[210] (1848) 16 Sim. 381.
[211] See *Jagger* v *Jagger* (1883) 25 Ch. D 729 at 731 per Kay J. In *Re Errington* (1897) 76 L.T. 616; In *Re Cattell* [1907] 1 Ch. 567 per Neville J; and [1914] 1 Ch. 177 per Lord Parker of Waddington.
[212] (1946) 115 L.J. Ch. 152 at p. 154.

case. The first thing to do is to look at the date from which, according to the settlement, the accumulations are to begin. In the present case they are to begin at once. Accordingly, paragraph [ii] can be put out of the way altogether because it says this: 'A term of twenty-one years from the death of the grantor, settlor or testator'. This cannot possibly be appropriate to a settlement which directs the accumulation to begin, not on the death of the settlor but immediately the settlement is executed. Similarly, paragraph [iii] which I need not read, also disappears out of the picture. The controversy is between paragraphs [i] and [iv]. Evershed J. [at first instance] held that the appropriate provision is [i], namely 'the life of the grantor or settlor'. Counsel for the first seven defendants argues that the appropriate provision is [iv], the duration of the minority or respective minorities only of any person or persons who, under the limitations of the instrument direction the accumulations, would, for the time being, if of full age, be entitled to the income directed to be accumulated. He says that that is the 'appropriate' period because it is possible to fit in the whole of the provisions of this deed so as to be consistent with the language of that paragraph. Evershed J. rejected that view and held that the life of the grantor or settlor, being the only one then left, must be taken as the proper period."[213]

This passage also gives some indication as to the factors to be taken into account in choosing the period, or more specifically in working through that process of elimination. The basis, as Lord Greene remarks, must be the instrument itself, and the construction to be put on it in the events which have happened; it is from the instrument alone that guidance must be sought. But suppose, applying such a test, a result is arrived at which, although it seems reasonable enough as a matter of pure construction, appears to be at odds with the settlor's intention to accumulate, as that is expressed through the whole tenor of the deed? The answer seems to be that intention gives way to construction. As Lord Ormidale said in the *Union Bank case*:[214]

"The competition is between [i] and [iii] and in my opinion it must be decided in favour of [i]. It may well be that to come to this conclusion is to frustrate the intention of the grantor to a greater extent than by holding that period [iii] is applicable to the direction to accumulate. But the intention of the grantor is of little account. As Kekewich J. says in *Errington*—perhaps a little too broadly: 'The Thellusson Act was passed to destroy intention'. In the present case what I go on mainly is that the declaration of trust is an inter vivos deed, and that it commenced to operate during [the settlor's] life and not from the date of his death."[215]

However in spite of the rather general and indefinite nature of the principles just adumbrated it would seem possible to formulate a few practical rules of guidance:[215a]

---

[213] See also e.g. per Lord Justice-Clerk Alness and Lord Ormidale in *Union Bank of Scotland v Campbell* 1929 SC at pp. 154 and 156 respectively and per Lord President Clyde in *Carey's Trustees v Rose* 1957 SC at p. 257.

[214] 1929 SC at p. 156; See also *McIver's Trustees v I.R.C.* [1973] S.T.C. 398.

[215] But see per Upjohn J. in *Re Ransome* [1957] Ch. 348 at pp. 361-2 dealing with the English restatement of the accumulation periods in section 164 (1) of the Law of Property Act 1925.

"The test is stated to be that you have first to determine which of the four periods set out in section 164 the testatrix has seemingly selected, determining that question according to the language employed and the facts of the case. That seems to me an artificial and difficult test. The trouble in this case and in most cases dealing with the rule against accumulations is that the testatrix here has given directions clearly not having the rule in mind at all. The competing periods in this case are [periods (ii) and (iii)] . . . . Neither [period] fits in, in the least degree with the directions of the testatrix . . . ."

Upjohn J. proceeded to choose period (ii) on the basis that, of the two, the result that would flow from it would be less incompatible with the testatrix's intention.

[215a] Derived from the cases discussed above.

1. Where the settlement is to take effect on the grantor's death, then
   (*A*) periods (i), (v) and (vi) can have no application, and
   (*B*) the normal period will be period (ii) unless there can be established a direct link between the accumulation and a minority.
   (*C*) If the accumulation can be directly linked to a minority the competition will be between (iii) and (iv). If the accumulation is directed for:
      (1) the minority of an individual beneficiary or beneficiaries, who need not be in esse at the date of death the appropriate period will be (iv),
      (2) the minorities of persons forming a group, the accumulation to terminate on the majority of the youngest member the appropriate period will be (iii),
      (3) any other case of a minority the appropriate period will be (iii).
2. Where the settlement is to take effect inter vivos, then
   (*A*) periods (ii) and (iii) can have no application;
   (*B*) if a direct link between the accumulation and minority can be established the competition will be between (iv) and (v). If the accumulation is directed for:
      (1) The minority of an individual beneficiary or beneficiaries, who need not be in esse at the date of the deed, the appropriate period will be (iv),
      (2) the minorities of persons forming a group, the accumulation to terminate on the majority of the youngest member, the appropriate period will be (vi),
      (3) any other case of a minority, the appropriate period will be (vi).
   (*C*) where such a direct link is established periods (iv) or (vi) will not be inappropriate merely because the accumulation begins during the lifetime of the grantor but ends after his death.
   (*D*) Where no such link can be established the competition will be between periods (i) and (v). There is no indication which the courts will tend to prefer. As a matter of practice, if the direct period of twenty-one years is appropriate, it is likely to be spelled out in the deed, if only because of the estate duty implications of period (i). Accordingly, it is suggested, though without much confidence, that unless there is such specific reference, or such a context as to make a specific reference superfluous, the appropriate period will be (i).
3. In ascertaining the above the basic working document will be the trust provisions governing the accumulation, read in the light of the events which have happened.

Contravention of the Restrictions

In most cases of contravention of the statutory restrictions the excesses have occurred either through accident or ignorance, being expressed in the drafting

---

[216] See for example the words of Upjohn J. in *Re Ransome* supra at note 215.

of the deed.[216] In some cases however deliberate attempts have been made to get around the restrictions.

In the first part of the nineteenth century, this was fairly easy to do, heritage being excluded from the operation of the Thellusson Act by section 3. But, as we have seen, the Rutherfurd Act[217] abolished that exemption.

In England the chief attempts at evasion have come by trying to make use of the exception from section 2 in that draftsmen would try to clothe a direction for accumulation in the trappings of a fund for the payment of debts or the raising of portions. A substantial part of the mass of English case law dealing with the rule against accumulations is derived from these attempts, with the courts trying to ascertain the dividing line and apply it to the various settlements confronting them.[218] Some attempts were made in Scotland and there are a few nineteenth century cases where the scope of section 2 figures prominently.[219] However with the repeal of section 2, as far as Scotland is concerned, by the Entail (Scotland) Act 1914[220] this has long since ceased to be a problem.

Of more seriousness perhaps were the nineteenth and early twentieth century attempts to use the period permitted by the Act as cumulative rather than as exclusive. These attempts were aided by the writings of Hargrave[221] who expressed the view that there was nothing in the legislation to prevent a grantor selecting more than one period if he so wished, and to employ these periods successively so as to produce an aggregate period in excess of any of the periods specified in the Act. Jarman[222] on the other hand was firm in the view that the periods were exclusive and that accordingly only one could be properly chosen. As we have seen[223] the courts adopted this latter view.

In *Maxwell's Trustees* v *Maxwell*[224] the possibility of avoiding the restrictions by obtaining requisite consents was explored. The case concerned a trust-disposition and settlement which contained provisions directing an accumulation in favour of certain charities. The direction was such that the duration of the accumulations would have exceeded the periods permitted under the Thellusson Act with the result that they became illegal. However the trustees entered into an arrangement with the heir at law (who would have been entitled to any surplus revenues) under which the latter ratified and confirmed the provisions of the settlement. The question was whether this ratification operated as a personal bar so as to stop the heir from maintaining that the accumulations were illegal. Were the court to accept this, clearly an indirect way of evading the restrictions would have been found. The court however refused to do so. As Lord Ormidale put it:[225]

"No private arrangement or consent to defeat the provisions of the Thellusson Act, which, as is well-known, was dictated by public policy, and had for its object

---

[217] The Entail Amendment (Scotland) Act 1848; statute 11 & 12 Vict. c. 36, section 41.
[218] See Morris and Leach at pp. 281-289; Keeton, "Modern Developments in the Law of Trusts" at pp. 250-263.
[219] See *Moon's Trustees* v *Moon* 1899 2 F 201; *Hutchison* v *Grant's Trustees* 1913 SC 1211.
[220] Statute 4 & 5 Geo. V c. 43, section 9.
[221] Treatise on the Thellusson Act at pp. 138-142.
[222] Wills (2nd Ed. 1855) vol. i at p. 248.
[223] See above.
[224] (1877) 5 R 248.
[225] *ibid.* at p. 254.

the repression of public evils, can be entertained and given effect to by the Court. Were it otherwise, I can readily understand that the Act might, without much difficulty, be so entirely defeated as to render it of no more effect than if it had been repealed."

A rather more intricate method was employed in the comparatively recent case of *Lady Gibson's Trustees, Petitioners*.[226] This concerned an inter vivos trust under which accumulations had been directed which became illegal on the death of the truster. Under the rules as to surplus income[227] the excess accumulations would have fallen to be dealt with under the residue clause of the truster's will. However the terms of the clause were such that they amounted to a direction to return the income to the inter vivos trustees to be added to the capital of that fund. The broad effect would have been that, by her will, the truster was authorising the inter vivos trustees to continue to accumulate the income of the property settled in their hands for a period in excess of the life of the grantor, thus attempting to produce a cumulative effect by two, instead of one, instruments. The court however would have none of it. Lord Sorn expressed the position succinctly. He said:[228]

"[The clause in the will provided] the very same direction, in fact, as that which is contained in the inter vivos trust itself and which has become illegal for those trustees to carry out.

In my view a grantor cannot get over the disabling effect of the Accumulation Acts by executing a second deed directing illegal accumulations to be returned to the trustees acting under the first deed so that they may be accumulated in the very way which has become illegal."[229]

However, whether the contravention of the legislative restrictions be caused by ignorance, bad drafting or deliberate attempts at evasion a finding of contravention will involve certain consequences, specifically as to the effects on the provisions of the trust and the interests thereunder, as to the destination of excessive accumulations, and as to their nature in the hands of the recipients. It is to these consequences that we now turn.

(a) Effects of Contravention on the Trust Provisions

Section 1 of the Thellusson Act provided that "in every case where any accumulation shall be directed otherwise then as aforesaid, such direction shall be null and void".[230] The primary question, then, where the court was faced with an infringing direction was as to the extent of the nullity: was it null and void ab initio, so that no income could be validly accumulated or was it to be treated as valid for the appropriate statutory period, but void only as to any excess?

The first case after the passing of the Act to come before the courts concerning a direction in contravention of the statutory provisions was *Griffiths* v *Vere*[231] where Lord Eldon chose the latter course, holding that if the accumulation directed in fact exceeded the permitted period, it was to be void only for the excess, so that income might be validly accumulated for the appropriate

---

[226] 1963 SC 350.
[227] See below.
[228] 1963 SC at p. 355.
[229] See also *Stewart's Trustees* v *Whitelaw* 1926 SC 701 for the position governing the use of special powers of appointment in possible attempts to extend the period of accumulation.
[230] Carried forward as s. 5 (2) of the 1961 Act.
[231] (1803) 9 Ves. 127.

period. This decision was followed three years later by Sir William Grant in *Langdon* v *Simon*[232] and was accepted thereafter'[233]

The first Scottish case where the point came to be considered was *Ogilvie's Trustees* v *Kirk Session of Dundee*[234] where the English decisions were applied. As Lord Fullerton said:

". . . . the statute does not annul the bequest, it only annuls the direction to accumulate for more than a certain period. That point is ruled by the English decisions referred to: so that in this case the only result of holding the statute to apply will be to carry the bequest to the Kirk Session free from any obligation to accumulate after the number of years fixed by the statute shall expire. For I see no intelligible distinction between the present and the English cases. It may always be said that when a testator directs an accumulation for a certain number of years, that number of years forms an essential element in his calculations, and, that if that is cut short there is no certainty that he would have directed any accumulation at all. But that view has been disregarded in England. I think we must do the same here."

And, as in England, this principle has never been questioned since.[235]

It will be recalled that the provisions of the Accumulation Act 1892[236] differ somewhat from those of the Thellusson Act, not only as regards the permitted periods, but also as regards contravention. Thus while the Act of 1800 spoke of "directions" being null and void the Act of 1892 simply recited the stark prohibition that "No person shall . . . . settle or dispose of any property" in such a way as to contravene the provisions of that Act: there were no indications as to the consequences of contravention. Accordingly when a case came before the courts, this difference was seized upon as an argument for suggesting that the Act of 1892 produced a different result. The court however rejected this argument, largely on the basis that the result it would produce, namely the invalidity of the settlement itself, was unacceptable. As Lord President Clyde put it:[237]

"The first question in this case arises upon the meaning and effect of the Act of 1892. The frame of the enactment in that statute differs from the Thellusson Act. The Thellusson Act made it illegal to accumulate for more than a statutory period, and declared that any illegal accumulations should be disposed of as if the testator had never directed them to be made. The Act of 1892 proceeds on the principle of declaring illegal any settlement of property which is framed in such a manner as to direct accumulation for the purpose of purchasing land; and it does not say anything about what is to happen to the accumulations which are directed in a settlement of that kind. The argument is that whereas under the Thellusson Act the settlement remains in effect except as regards the direction to accumulate; under the Act of 1892 the whole settlement (or at least that part of it which deals with the property in question) is rendered illegal if it contains a direction to accumulate with a view to the purchase of land. I confess I do not understand why the Act of 1892 took the form it did, especially when the draftsman must have had before him the well-known form of the Thellusson Act. But I am unable to attribute to the Legislature—merely

---

[232] (1806) 12 Ves. 295.
[233] *Haley* v *Bannister* (1819) 4 Madd. 275; *Crawley* v *Crawley* (1835) 7 Sim 427; *Miles* v *Dyer* (1837) 8 Sim 330; *O'Neill* v *Lucas* (1838) 2 Keen 313; *Eyre* v *Marsden* (1838) 2 Keen 564; *Pride* v *Fooks* (1839) 2 Beav. 430; *Williams* v *Nixon* (1840) 2 Beav. 472; *Blease* v *Burgh* (1840) 2 Beav. 221; *Webb* v *Webb* (1840) 2 Beav. 493.
[234] (1846) 8 D 1229 at pp. 1242-3.
[235] See *Elder's Trustees* v *Free Church of Scotland* (1892) 20 R 2.
[236] See above.
[237] In *Robertson's Trustees* v *Robertson's Trustees* 1933 SC 639 at p. 645.

because of the adoption of that particular form—any idea so drastic as that, because the settlement (or that part of it which deals with the property in question) contains a direction to accumulate with a view to the purchase of land, the settlement (or that particular part of it) is to be wholly null and void. I think that the statute goes no further than to annul the directions to accumulate."

This statement of principle however simply raises the question that was initially present in the early cases on the Thellusson Act, namely, to what extent is the direction a nullity—in its entirety, or merely as regards the excess? The case itself was decided on the basis of the latter view, thus equating, as did Lord Clyde, the effects of the Acts of 1800 and 1892.[238]

This interpretation of the legislation, vitiating the direction to accumulate only in so far as it contravenes the periods laid down, should necessarily have the effect that nothing else under the trust is affected.[239] Certainly there seems to be a general principle that the curtailment of an accumulation under the statute will not affect beneficial interests under the trust. The principle was propounded by Lord Westbury L.C. in *Green* v *Gascoigne* as follows:[240]

"I take it that the words of the statute .... must be construed to mean 'if such excessive accumulations had not been directed'; and, so holding, the meaning of the words is brought to this,—as if the accumulations had been directed for twenty-one years only. Now, I apprehend that I am not at liberty to apply or use the statute so as in any manner to accelerate the enjoyment of any gift or disposition contained in the will. Neither can I use the statute for the purpose of giving to any term or description contained in the will a meaning which it would not have had if the trust for accumulation were good, instead of bad. Although the trust for accumulation is cut down and reduced to a limited period, the whole of the rest of the will remains, in point of disposition, in point of the meaning, effect and true interpretation of its language, precisely as if there had been no such operation performed by the statute."

This principle was acknowledged as having been received into Scots law by Lord Justice-Clerk Moncrieff in *Maxwell's Trustees* v *Maxwell*[241] and has been applied by the First Division in *MacKay's Trustees* v *MacKay*[242] and in *Wilson's Trustees* v *Glasgow Royal Infirmary*.[243] However its application is not entirely without difficulty for there exists a line of cases where the curtailment of the accumulation has undoubtedly produced an immediate enjoyment of a gift which would otherwise have been delayed until the end of the accumulation period. This line begins with *Ogilvie's Trustees* v *Kirk Session of Dundee*[244] where a sum of £2,000 was bequeathed to trustees to accumulate the income therefrom for a hundred years whereupon the resultant sum was to be given to the Kirk-Session in order that they might build a hospital. After the accumu-

---

[238] See per Lord Blackburn at pp. 646/7; "..... the effect .... is to prohibit any further accumulations after that person has reached majority".
[239] In England, such directions also have to satisfy the Rule against Perpetuities which, as we have seen, has a more drastic effect, if contravened. Accordingly even though an accumulation might be struck down by the Act only to the extent that it was exceissve, if it also contravened the perpetuity rule it would be wholly void (See per Morris and Leach at pp. 301-303). This added requirement does not, of course, apply to Scotland where *its* rule against perpetuities has no effect on accumulation trusts.
[240] (1865) 34 L.J. Ch. 268 at p. 271.
[241] (1877) 5 R 248 at p. 250.
[242] 1909 SC 139.
[243] 1917 SC 527.
[244] (1846) 8 D 1229.

O

lation had been curtailed the Kirk-Session claimed the whole fund and the court upheld that claim on the basis that there was no one else who could have been entitled. This decision was applied in *Mackenzie* v *Mackenzie's Trustees*[245] where the entire income of a fund was directed to be applied in the purchase of an entailed estate, and, until the purchase, to be divided in the proportions of three quarters to the first institute of entail and the remaining quarter to accumulate. Again, on the curtailment by the Act, the enjoyment of the accumulated fund was immediate.

In *Maxwell's Trustees*[241] the Lord Justice-Clerk rationalised these two lines of cases as follows:
"If the fund directed to be accumulated is not subject to any present gift then the right of the eventual beneficiary will not be accelerated or arise at the term of twenty-one years. . . . . But if there be a present gift of the fund itself, and the directions to accumulate be only a burden on the gift, then the burden will terminate at the expiration of twenty-one years, and the gift will become absolute in the person of the donee."[246]

In this case a testator had directed her trustees, after the lapse of certain annuities to create a fund for the payment of charitable bequests, by means of an accumulating investment. It was held that this gave the charities a present interest in the fund and that, as the accumulation was a mere burden on this, its discharge after twenty-one years, meant that the bequest could now be enjoyed by the charities.

In *Mackay's Trustees* v *Mackay*[242] although the interests were vested, payment was postponed until the beneficiaries attained majority. It was held that, as such, there was no present gift of the fund and so there would be no acceleration. Similarly in *Wilson's Trustees* v *Glasgow Royal Infirmary*[243] enjoyment was postponed until the death of the testator's widow and accordingly the curtailment of accumulation was held not to accelerate this, there being on present gift.

In all cases, then, the question would seem, as indicated by Lord Westbury,[247] to be a matter of the construction of the trust provisions to ascertain whether or not, but for the accumulation there was in existence a present gift. A difficulty arises, however, where the enjoyment is clearly postponed, but where the reason for that postponement is to allow the income from the fund to be accumulated. An example would be where trustees were directed to accumulate until a specified sum had been achieved, and thereupon to distribute. So in *Colquhoun* v *Colquhoun's Trustees*[248] the sum required to be achieved was £25,000. It was

---

[245] (1877) 4 R 962.
[246] Citing Turner L.J. in *Combe* v *Hughes* (1865) 34 L.J. Ch. at p. 344—"I think the general rule may well be taken to be this: If there is an absolute gift, and then a series of limitations modifying that gift, so far as the limitations do not extend, the absolute gift remains. If on the other hand there be no absolute gift, but merely a series of limitations, then of course the limitations only can take effect, and what is not reached by the limitations is not disposed of".
[247] See also per Lord Langdale in *Eyre* v *Marsden* (1838) 2 Keen 569 at 574—"The statute, it appears to me, was not intended to operate, and does not operate, to alter any dispositions made by the testator, except his direction to accumulate. Striking that out, everything else is left as before, and all the other directions of the will, as to the time of payement, substitution or any contingencies are to take effect according to the true construction of the will unaltered by the effect of the statute".
[248] (1892) 19 R 946.

held however that the beneficiary was entitled to take such accumulations as had accrued at the end of the permitted period. Lord McLaren explained his decision thus:[249]

"[The designated] sum can never be realised, because further accumulations are rendered impossible by the operation of the Thellusson Act, and it seems to me, that the accumulated fund should, in these circumstances, be treated as having already attained its maximum amount, and should be given to the person designated in the instrument as the person to whom payment was to be made at the end of the period of accumulation."

The problem with a case such as this is that it comes from a situation which sits astride the dividing line drawn by Lord Moncrieff. On the one hand there was clearly no present gift here. The requirement of raising £25,000 operated as a postponement in just the same way that a requirement that payment be delayed until majority or death would. The only difference is that in the former case the curtailment of the accumulation by the statute would ensure that payment was delayed for ever, whereas in the latter case the date for payment had, sooner or later, to arrive. It is perhaps this which distinguishes *Colquhoun* v *Colquhoun's Trustees* from the other cases where there is no present gift; but at the same time it hardly places it within the category of *Ogilvie's Trustees*[250] and *Maxwell's Trustees*,[251] for in these cases there cannot be said to have been any acceleration, or any change in the interests of the beneficiaries under the trust. In *Colquhoun's case* there was both, a plain acceleration and a change in the gift: a bequest of £25,000 is not a gift of something less. And yet, had the court's decision gone the other way the change would have been even greater: a vested interest would have been defeated by the operation of the Act.

On balance then it seems that the decision in *Colquhoun's case* was the right one, but for entirely negative reasons; because a rule was not applied rather than because it was. If for no other reason, this should characterise the decision as an individual case which cannot, and clearly does not, exemplify the rule's operation.

There is one further complication in this area of the law, arising not from the interests granted, but rather from the beneficiary or beneficiaries to whom it is granted. While it is not unreasonable that if the beneficiary, under the terms of the trust, is not to be ascertained until the date fixed for the accumulation to finish, the curtailment of that accumulation by the statute will not accelerate the date for ascertainment[252] (and therefore enjoyment), difficulties arise in the case of a class gift. Thus, for example, suppose that the terms of a trust direct an accumulation period at the termination of which the class is to be ascertained. Clearly, if the accumulation is curtailed, on the principle of *Campbell's Trustees* v *Campbell*[252] this should not alter the ascertainment date, especially if the class consists of children or other descendants, if only because of the possibility of

---

[249] *ibid.* at p. 953.
[250] (1846) 8 D 1229.
[251] (1877) 5 R 248.
[252] *Campbell* v *Campbell's Trustees* (1891) 18 R 992 where an accumulation was directed, after which termination a deed of entail was directed to be executed in favour of an institute and series of heirs ascertainable only at the date fixed by the truster for the termination of the accumulation.

additions to the class in the meantime. However if that possibility is removed, because, say, of the physical impossibility of future births in the given case, would not it be reasonable to allow the beneficiaries to take on the curtailment of the accumulation? In the English case of *Re Deloitte*[253] it was held that as there was no legal presumption against child-bearing the class could not be said, in law, to have closed, whatever the defacto position, with the result that payment would have to be delayed until the date stipulated in the trust.

On the other hand it is doubtful whether the principle in *Re Deloitte* ever obtained in Scotland.[254] And certainly it has been held in another context that the principle on which *Re Deloitte* proceeded, that there was no legal presumption against child-bearing, would not be applicable where the only interests to be prejudiced were those of children[255] who were unborn and could not be born because of the age of the woman in question. Accordingly, in such cases, it would seem that the courts in Scotland would permit acceleration even though the gift would not be a present gift, in Lord Moncrieff's sense, and would not even be a gift which had vested absolutely, being subject to potential (if not actual) defeasance in part.

By way of confirmation, it is to be noted that the rule in *Re Deloitte* was abolished in England by section 14 of the Perpetuities and Accumulations Act 1964[256] but that this particular measure was excluded from the Scottish accumulation reforms which came with the Act of 1966, although the other reforms of the law of accumulations effected by the English Act were implemented: presumably its inclusion was felt to be unnecessary.

(b) Destination of Surplus Income

After nullifying directions not conforming to the restrictions set out in the first part, the latter part of section 1 of the Thellusson Act[257] enacted that "the rents, issues, profits and produce of such property so directed to be accumulated, shall, so long as the same shall be directed contrary to the provisions of this Act, go to and be received by such person or persons as would have been entitled thereto if such accumulation had not been directed".

While the section clearly applies to income freed by the Act, in *Mason's Trustees* v *Mason*[258] the question arose as to whether it applies to accumulations made by the trustees after the permitted period had expired, the point being that at the time the action was brought they were no longer in the form of rents and profits. It was held that the illegal accumulations were so covered, the fact that they had been made illegally not having changed their character as income.

As we have seen, the broad effect of this section has been simply to curtail accumulations at the end of the appropriate period, but otherwise to leave

---

[253] [1926] 1 Ch. 56.
[254] Mackenzie-Stuart "Law of Trusts" (Edinburgh 1932) at p. 95 suggests that it did.
[255] See *G.* v *G.'s Trustees* 1936 SC 837 (before a Court of seven judges) and *A.* v *B.'s Trustees* 1941 S.L.T. 193. For the historical background to this principle see Henderson on Vesting (2nd Ed.) at p. 309 and cases cited there.
[256] Statute 1964 c. 55.
[257] Re-enacted as section 5 (3) of the Trusts (Scotland) Act 1961.
[258] (1899) 2 F 201.

everything as it was before so that the destination of any surplus income, whether accumulated or not, will depend, not on the statute, but on the provisions of the trust. As Lord Ormidale said in *Smyth's Trustees* v *Kinloch*:[259]
"The result of the decisions is to hold the deed as containing and to read it as if it had contained, an express clause providing that all accumulations of rents and profits shall cease on the expiry of twenty-one years, without saying more and without containing any provisions as to the person or persons to whom the rents accruing after twenty-one years shall go."

Depending as they do on the provisions of their individual trust deeds, the cases really involve two problems: first, whether the surplus income goes to the beneficiary taking the accumulated fund, and second, if it does not, as to its ultimate destination.

With regard to the first of these, the issues involved are almost exactly similar to those encountered in ascertaining whether the statutory intervention operated so as to accelerate the enjoyment of the gift. While the consideration above was concerned with enjoyment of capital, if the income of that capital could be enjoyed by the postponed capital beneficiary there would be an effective, if partial, acceleration which might carry with it[260] the capital as well. As we saw, the basic distinction was whether the gift amounted to a "present gift" of the fund: if it did the accumulation was treated simply as a charge on the gift, which fell away when the accumulations were curtailed by statute, so that the fund could be taken immediately by the beneficiaries entitled to it. Such a gift carries with it the surplus income. The question therefore is what is necessary to constitute a present gift of the capital of the fund. In *Wilson's Trustees* v *Glasgow Royal Infirmary*[261] Lord Skerrington put forward the following analysis. He said:

"It has been said that the question whether income set free by the operation of the Thellusson Act belongs to the legatee of the corpus which produces the income or falls into intestacy depends on whether such legatee has or has not an absolute vested right to his legacy. That however is an incomplete statement of the law. Absolute vesting is indeed a condition of success on the part of the legatee, but something more is required. A legatee, whether specific or general or residuary, whose legacy falls to be paid or delivered at a postponed date is not necessarily and in all circumstances entitled to receive the intermediate income even though his right to the corpus is absolutely vested in him. It is always a question of intention, depending on the express or implied directions of the testator, whether such a legatee is entitled to claim the fruits accruing prior to the date fixed for payments or delivery of the legacy. It follows that where a direction to accumulate income has become null and void by the operation of the Thellusson Act, the legatees of the corpus cannot successfully claim the income set free by the statute unless he can show that he has a gift of that income which remains valid notwithstanding that the direction to accumulate has become void and ineffectual."

The primary requirement, then, is for "absolute vesting", for without this no beneficiary has the right to compel the trustees to pay off the capital of the fund to him, and similarly no power to put the trustees under an obligation with regard to the payment of income. Thus beneficiaries whose interests are contingent will have no such right, not will those whose interests have vested but

[259] (1880) 7 R 1176 at p. 1180.
[260] See below.
[261] 1917 SC 527 at p. 532.

are subject to defeasance in whole or in part.[262] Accordingly gifts in favour of a class of persons, where the class has not closed at the appropriate date will carry neither the right to enforce payment of capital, nor an entitlement to surplus income since the interests of all members of the class at that date are liable to be defeated in part by the addition of new members.[263]

It would seem that the appropriate date for ascertaining whether the interest has vested absolutely is the date of the curtailment of the accumulation.[264] Accordingly it would appear that an interest need not have vested at the coming into operation of the deed so long as it vested before the statutory period had expired. Thus a class gift would be enforceable and would carry the surplus income if the class had closed in fact by the date of the curtailment,[265] even though it had clearly not closed at the date of the deed.

However, as Lord Skerrington has indicated, absolute vesting alone may not be sufficient if the intention of the truster, as expressed in the deed, is against present enjoyment. The difficulty is that the very fact of a provision for accumulation involves postponement: how then does one sort out a postponement which is simply a burden on a present gift from one which is something more? If the cases throw up any principle of demarcation at all, it seems to be that if the identity of the beneficiary or the particular interest to be taken is described in the deed by reference to a specific date then, the gift will not be a present gift and will not, in the absence of a specific direction to the contrary, carry any entitlement to surplus income.

It will be remembered that in *Campbell's Trustees* v *Campbell*[266] the court found that there was no present gift of an accumulated fund where the identity of the beneficiary was to be established at a date fixed by the truster. In *Elder's Trustees* v *Treasurer of the Free Church of Scotland*[267] a similar decision was arrived at specifically with regard to surplus income. The case concerned a provision in a will for an annuity to be paid to the testator's wife with the surplus income produced by the trust fund to be accumulated during her lifetime, and at her death the trustees were to utilise various sums to finance certain projects for the Free Church. The widow survived the testator by more than twenty-one years and the question arose as to the destination of the surplus income then arising. It was held that as the projects were subject to selection by the trustees, who were not to exercise their power of selection until the widow's death, the surplus income did not go along with the corpus. Lord Justice-Clerk Mac-Donald explained the decision in the following terms. He said:[268]

"The question is one of construction and we must look at the whole deed. Now, giving it the best construction I can, I think that there is no present right on the part of [the Free Church] to payment of the income, which can no longer be accumulated in consequence of the Thellusson Act. There are some cases in which the residuary

---

[262] See *Weatherhall* v *Thornburgh* (1878) 8 Ch. D 261 per James L.J. at p. 269. Approved in *Smith* v *Glasgow Royal Infirmary* 1909 SC 1231; See now *Russell's Trustees* v *Russell* 1959 SC 148 and *McIver's Trustees* v *I.R.C.* [1973] S.T.C. 398; 1974 S.L.T. 201.
[263] As in *Re Deloitte* [1926] 1 Ch. 56.
[264] per Lord President Dunedin in *Smith* v *Glasgow Royal Infirmary* supra at p. 1236.
[265] c.f. *Re Deloitte* supra. In view of *G's Tees* supra at note 255 in Scotland the position to be taken account of would be the de facto and not necessarily the de jure one.
[266] (1891) 18 R 992.
[267] (1892) 20 R 2.
[268] *ibid.* at p. 7.

legatee is so distinctly described in the will that he is entitled to the sums which fall under the residuary clause, and cannot be any longer accumulated. . . . . But this is certainly not the case. I think that in this case the residuary legatee is not at present ascertainable. No legatee is so pointed out that we can say that we are certain who the legatee is who must take."

In *Smith* v *Glasgow Royal Infirmary*[269] it was not the identity of the beneficiary, but rather precisely what that beneficiary should take that was to be fixed at a date specified by the truster. Here there were gifts of income to certain annuitants, after the death of the last of which the residue was to go to the Glasgow Royal Infirmary. Surplus income was directed to be accumulated for specified purposes, but these were rendered illegal after twenty-one years by the Thellusson Act. Here the bequest to the Infirmary undoubtedly vested absolutely and there was no question of establishment of identity. But nonetheless the gift was not to carry with it the surplus income. As Lord Kinnear said:[270]

"I entirely agree that if there had been a gift of residue in the larger sense, by which a testator gives to a residuary legatee his whole estate subject to certain purposes, some of which may have failed, the accumulations which are rendered illegal by the Act would simply have been directed to be devoted to purposes which have failed, and having failed, would fall within the residuary gift which, although it was the word 'residuary', defines the estate which the so-called residuary legatee is to take by reference to the position of the funds in the trustees' hands at a specific date."

This decision was applied in *Wilson's Trustees* v *Glasgow Royal Infirmary*[271] on similar facts.

However it is suggested that the principle, as stated by Lord Kinnear may be too wide. The point is surely not so much the specific date (although that in itself would seem to distinguish these lines of cases from most of those where the court has found a present gift) but that the specific date is related to an extraneous event, an event which does not depend upon the accumulation, but rather upon which the accumulation is made to depend. By way of contrast in *Ogilvie's Trustees* v *Kirk Session of Dundee*[272] the accumulation was directed for a hundred years; a date unconnected with anything except the accumulation and which, when declared void under the Act, was instrumental in the finding of a present gift. In *Maxwell's Trustees* v *Maxwell*[273] there was not even a date provided, the accumulation seemingly to continue in perpetuity. Again the gift was held to be a present gift of capital carrying the income with it.

Rather more doubtful is the case of *Colquhoun* v *Colquhoun's Trustees*[274] where the accumulation was governed not by date but by amount, the direction being that the accumulation was to continue until a specified sum had been accumulated. Here there was clearly no present gift in any real sense, the court in effect accelerating payment of the fund and thereby of the income produced by it. This rather individual decision was emulated in an Outer House decision in 1938. In *Donaldson's Trustees* v *H.M. Advocate*[275] the direction was to accu-

---

[269] 1909 SC 1231; following *Weatherall* v *Thornburgh* (1878) 8 Ch. D 261.
[270] *ibid*. at pp. 1237/8.
[271] 1917 SC 527.
[272] (1846) 8 D 1229.
[273] (1877) 5 R 248.
[274] (1892) 19 R 946.
[275] 1938 S.L.T. 106 (O.H.).

mulate income until £1,000 had been amassed. However here Lord Russell preferred to rely on *Ogilvie's Trustees and Maxwell's Trustees* holding, as a matter of construction that the terms of the will conferred a present gift.

In *Mackenzie* v *Mackenzie's Trustees*[276] the testator had left an entailed estate in trust, with directions to his trustees to purchase with his residuary estate land adjoining the entailed property. Until such purchase was effected the trustees were directed to pay three-quarters of the income to the heir of entail and to accumulate the balance which was to be added to the residue. On the twenty-first anniversary of the death the purchase had still not been made, whereupon the accumulations were curtailed by the statute. It was held that the heir of entail was entitled to the surplus income under the principle in *Lord Stair* v *Stair's Trustees*[277] to the effect that income arising from a fund subject to a direction that it was to be employed in the purchase of land to be entailed belonged to the heir of entail.

The most recent case is that of *Dowden's Trustees* v *Governors of Merchiston Castle School*[278] where the possibility of postponement of enjoyment arose from a codicil to the testator's will setting up a series of annuities which were charged on residue and which was framed in such a way as to contemplate the accumulation of surplus income until the death of the last annuitant. The statutory period expired three years before this death and the trustees transferred to a suspense account the surplus income arising during this time. The question arose as to who was entitled to these surpluses. On the basis of *Smith* v *Glasgow Royal Infirmary*[269] and *Wilson's Trustees*[271] it was argued that the codicil operated so as to provide a postponement with the result that the surplus income would not go with the corpus of the residuary fund. The court however rejected this, Lord Justice-Clerk Grant explaining:[279]

"[This argument] proceeded on the basis that *Smith* v *Glasgow Royal Infirmary* and *Wilson's Trustees* v *Glasgow Royal Infirmary* are directly in point in the circumstances here. In both those cases the residue appears to have already vested in the residuary legatees at the date when the accumulation of surplus income became illegal, but it was not suggested that they were entitled to payment of the capital at that date. In each case the gift of residue took the form of a direction to pay on the death of an annuitant or annuitants. There was no present gift of the residue and the residuary legatees rights could not be accelerated by the operation of the Thellusson Act. And, although the residue clauses disposed of income which could be legally accumulated, they did not dispose of the accumulation which became illegal. The latter income accordingly fell into intestacy.

As I read the testamentary writings in the present case, however, the situation is markedly different. Under [the original will] there is an absolute and unqualified gift of the residue as at [a date prior to the expiry of the accumulation period]. The codicil does not affect that except in so far as it directs a postponement of payment until the death of the last surviving annuitant. So far as this direction involves the retention by the trustees of sufficient capital to secure the payment of the annuity or annuities, it is valid and effective. The retention of the balance of the capital is, however, a very different matter. Under the codicil the income from that balance is merely to be accumulated and ultimately to be paid over to the residuary legatees who have an already unqualified and absolute right to the fee, and there are no trust purposes which

---

[276] (1877) 4 R 962.
[277] (1826) 4 S 488.
[278] 1965 SC 56.
[279] *ibid.* at pp. 65/66.

cannot be secured without the retention of the fee in the hands of the trustees. In these circumstances . . . . [the residuary legatees] are entitled to demand payment of the free balance of the residue."[280]

For the surplus income to go with the capital, then, there needs to be a present unqualified gift of that capital. If there is not such a gift what happens to the surplus income?

The answer would seem to depend on whether the settlement was to take effect inter vivos or mortis causa. If the settlement took effect inter vivos then the permissible periods for accumulation would end either at the death of the settlor or twenty-one years from the date of the settlement, whichever was held to be appropriate to the particular settlement. In the case of the latter period, if it elapsed prior to death there would appear to be little problem as, subject to an express provision in the deed, surplus income would be undisposed of and would result to the settlor during his lifetime. If he still possessed any, or was due any, at the date of his death this would form part of his estate and would pass accordingly.

If the first period applied so that the accumulations ceased on death the same principle has been held to apply.[281] In this particular case however a problem might arise if the inter vivos settlement which directed the accumulation also covered the settlor's estate on death. The question is whether the surplus income passes as on intestacy or forms part of the estate covered by the settlement. As in all matters concerned with the destination of surplus income the matter depends on the provisions of the particular deed.[282] If the deed is so widely drawn as to include the settler's entire estate of which he stood possessed at the date of death then there seems little doubt that the surplus income would be dealt with under the settlement; if the deed were not so widely drawn, it would pass as on intestacy.

If the second accumulation period applied but in such circumstances that the settlor died before the twenty-one years had elapsed, then if the circumstances were such that surplus income were to arise it would presumably fall into his estate and be dealt with either under the residuary clause of his will or on intestacy as the case may be.

On the other hand if the settlement is testamentary different principles will apply, and the result will vary according to whether what is given is a specific fund or a gift of residue.

If the subject of the accumulations is income arising from a specific fund then, subject, as always, to any direction in the will, income freed from a direction to accumulate will fall into residue. In *Watson's Trustees* v *Brown*[283] this result ensued when accumulations on an invested legacy were curtailed by the statute. However in this case only one-half of the residue had vested with the consequence that the income released by the statute was held to be payable as to one-half to the beneficiary whose right had vested, and as to the other half,

---

[280] See also cases discussed above.
[281] *Union Bank* v *Campbell* 1929 SC 143; *Russell's Trustees* v *Russell* 1959 SC 148.
[282] *Union Bank* v *Campbell* supra at pp. 152/3 per Lord Justice-Clerk Alness.
[283] 1923 SC 228; See also *Storie's Trustees* v *Gray* (1872) 1 R 953.

to such persons as would be entitled on intestacy.[284]

If however the gift is a residuary one then prima facie any surplus income will pass as on intestacy. The reasoning behind this is simply that the effect of curtailment releases income which, in the absence of express direction, will be undisposed of. If it is undisposed of as far as the residuary estate is concerned it cannot be dealt with under the will. As such it must fall outside the scope of the will and so be dealt with as on intestacy.[285] As Lord Ivory stated in *Lord* v *Colvin*:[286]

"[T]he parties entitled to prohibited accumulations are those who would have taken ab intestato at the time of the testator's death. The question raised necessarily involves the principle of intestacy. There are no directions in the deed for the disposal of these accumulations, other than that they shall remain in the hands of the trustees, to be dealt with along with corpus, when the time for dealing with both arises. There is no beneficial enjoyment, no right or interest in anybody whatever. In the face of this, the statute enacts that the accumulations, in so far as prohibited by the statute, are to be received by such person or persons as would have been entitled to them if the accumulations had not been directed. That is, in other words, just saying that they are to be dealt with on the footing of intestacy. They are the fruits of an estate which belonged to an intestate. They are a parcel of that estate, necessarily connected with it, and not appropriated by the testator; which is just saying that they would have fallen within his succession if not otherwise dealt with."

Prior to the passing of the Succession (Scotland) Act 1964,[287] where surplus income fell to be dealt with as on intestacy, a further problem arose as to whether the party to take was to be the heir at law or the heirs in mobilibus. The general rule was that if the accumulations comprised rent or other produce of heritage only, then they passed to the heir at law. However the particular person who filled that description was ascertained, not at the date of death, but at the date each payment became due.[288] If however the accumulations derived from moveable estate[289] then the appropriate beneficiaries were the heirs in mobilibus[290]

---

[284] The reason for this finding was that the latter half could not be added to the share of residue which had not yet vested because this would de facto amount to an accumulation which would not apparently be covered by any of the periods stipulated under the Act. See also *Lady Gibson's Trustees Petitioners* 1963 SC 350.

[285] See *Lord* v *Colvin* (1860) 23 D 111; *Pursell* v *Elder* (1865) 4 Macq. 992 (H.L.); *Cathcart's Trustees* v *Heneage's Trustees* (1883) 10 R 1205; *Campbell's Trustees* v *Campbell* (1891) 18 R 992; *Elder's Trustees* v *Free Church of Scotland* (1892) 20 R 2; *Logan's Trustees* v *Logan* (1896) 23 R 848; *Moon's Trustees* v *Moon* (1899) 2 F 201; *Mackay's Trustees* v *Mackay* 1909 SC 139; *Smith* v *Glasgow Royal Infirmary* 1909 SC 1231; *Hutchison* v *Grant's Trustees* 1913 SC 1211; *Wilson's Trustees* v *Glasgow Royal Infirmary* 1917 SC 527; *Watson's Trustees* v *Brown* supra; *Robertson's Trustees* v *Robertson's Trustees* 1933 SC 639; *Pyper's Trustees* v *Leighton* 1946 S.L.T. 255 (O.H.); *Carey's Trustees* v *Rose* 1957 SC 252; *Lady Gibson's Trustees Petitioners* 1963 SC 350.

[286] (1860) 23 D 111 at p. 127.

[287] Statute 1964 c. 41.

[288] *Campbell's Trustees* v *Campbell* (1891) 18 R 992; *Logan's Trustees* v *Logan* (1896) 23 R 848; *Moon's Trustees* v *Moon* (1899) 2 F 201; *Hunter's Trustees* v *Edinburgh Chamber of Commerce* 1911 2 S.L.T. 287 (O.H.); *Watson's Trustees* v *Brown* 1923 SC 228; *Mairs' Curator Bonis* v *Inland Revenue* 1932 SC 151; *Robertson's Trustees* v *Robertson's Trustees* 1933 SC 639; *Pyper's Trustees* v *Leighton* 1946 S.L.T. 255 (O.H.).

[289] *Lord* v *Colvin* (1860) 23 D 111. Rents of heritage accumulated in the hands of the trustees during such period as the statute allows and reduced into their possession for the purposes of the trust are moveable, and surplus income derived therefrom is disposed of as moveable estate and does not go to the heir at law even though it is indirectly the proceeds of heritage. See *Wilson's Trustees* v *Glasgow Royal Infirmary* 1917 SC 527 (and cases cited there) for a critique of the rule.

[290] i.e. next of kin.

ascertained as at the date of death. As the 1964 Act[291] largely abolished the special position of the heir at law with regard to heritage this problem can no longer arise, the surplus income now going to the heirs in mobilibus.

There is one exception to this general rule that surplus accumulations from a residuary estate fall to be dealt with as on intestacy and this occurs in the rare case where the testator specifically provides for the event, and in effect creates a second residue, albeit containing exactly the same interests as the main residuary disposition. Lord President Dunedin described them in *Smith* v *Glasgow Royal Infirmary* as follows:[292]

"A residuary clause may be conceived in such terms as will, by means of present gift, embrace everything, and there are cases of their description where there is a residuary clause which gives to the residuary legatee, by way of present gift everything that has not otherwise been disposed of. Then, of course, any accumulation as to which there is no direction will fall within the residuary clause."[293]

(c) Receipt of Surpluses

A final question arising from the situation brought about by a contravention of the statutory restrictions concerns whether the income freed by the statute from the accumulation falls to be treated in the hands of the ultimate recipient as income or as capital. The point has significance in two situations: first, if they are to be treated as income, the payments will form part of the recipient's total income and so be potentially liable to income tax; and second, where the released income passes to a settlement under which there are interests in liferent and in fee. This last case will occur, for example, where the excessive accumulation is from a specific fund and the surpluses fall into residue which has been thus settled; or where the excessive accumulations arise under an inter vivos settlement and fall to be treated as part of the residuary estate of the settlor which has been thus settled.[294]

In *Mair's Curator Bonis* v *Inland Revenue*[295] surplus income from an accumulated fund of heritage passed to the heir at law who sought to reclaim the income tax that had been paid on it by the trustees. The Revenue on the other hand claimed that, whatever its position in the hands of the trustees, as far as the beneficiary was concerned he received it as capital. It was held by the First Division that the sums paid over to the heir at law, having originated as the annual value of heritage, were of an income nature and remained so. The court distinguished a dictum of Lord Curriehill in *Lord* v *Colvin*[296] where the view was expressed that in relation to moveables the sums were received as capital on the basis that undisposed of moveable property vests in the heir in mobilibus at the testator's death as a universitas. "The pail may, at the date of the testator's death, seem to be quite empty (just as may a residue pail) but the

---

[291] section 1.
[292] 1909 SC 1231 at p. 1236.
[293] See also per Lord Maugham in *Berry* v *Geen* [1938] AC 575 at p. 582.
[294] In a Canadian case, *Re Wood* (1961) 28 D.L.R. (2d) 583 a further circumstance emerged, namely where an excessive accumulation of residue had been directed, but when the next of kin died after the testator's death, but before the curtailment of the accumulation having settled his residuary estate by will on A for life, with remainder to B in fee.
[295] 1932 SC 151.
[296] (1860) 23 D 111 at p. 133.

pail, such as it is, passed to the heir in mobilibus, and anything that may subsequently drop into it, however unexpectedly belongs to him."[297] In *Mair's case* the distinguishing factor was the temporary nature of the heir at law's interest, ceasing as it did on his death and not forming part of his estate.

If this distinction had any validity, it is of course now redundant with the assimilation of heritage and moveables as regards devolution on intestacy,[298] as a result of which the principles governing moveables would now apply. Two points however might be made at this juncture: first, that the decision in *Mair's case* runs counter to the general line of authority in Scotland holding as it does (albeit with regard to moveable estate) that such sums are received as capital; and second, that one commentator at least,[299] feels that in subsequent similar cases, even with regard to moveables, the decision in this case would be followed, although it must be stated that he gives no reasons for this view.

The Scottish authority referred to consists of the dictum of Lord Curriehill above mentioned and the decision of the Second Division in *Union Bank of Scotland* v *Campbell*[300] which concerned an inter vivos settlement under which the settler's residuary estate was conveyed at his death on trust for A in liferent and B in fee. The Act curtailed the accumulations at the death of the settlor whereupon the excessive accumulations fell into residue and the question arose as to whether the liferentrix was entitled to them as they fell in (i.e. as income) or only to the revenue from them (i.e. as capital). The court held that she was entitled only to the revenue from them. As Lord Ormidale put it:[301]

"It must be borne in mind that no part of the capital of the 'trust-estate' constituted by the declaration of trust is vested in the settlement trustee. What he does come to hold was, no doubt, income in the hands of the other trustee, and that is the reason why the latter had to eject it from his 'trust-estate'; but the settlement trustee ingathers it as capital just as he does the other items of the testator's estate, and it becomes subject, just like the rest of the testator's estate to its provisions, and only to the provisions of the testator's will."

The essential point about this decision was that there existed in effect two trusts—the inter vivos settlement and the will trust and—that while the trustees of the first no doubt received the surpluses as income, when these were passed as part of the estate to the trustees of the second, they become capital in the second trustees' hands.

It was argued that this was effectively adding capital, and therefore instituting a further accumulation and a battery of English cases[302] were cited to the effect that such additions constituted a simple accumulation[303] which was caught by the Act. The court however managed to distinguish these on the basis that they dealt with single testamentary trusts and not the combination which confronted the court here. As Lord Ormidale said:[304]

---

[297] Per Lord Sands, 1932 SC at p. 156.
[298] Succession (Scotland) Act 1964 s. 1.
[299] Dobie—"Liferent and Fee" at p. 268.
[300] 1929 SC 143.
[301] *ibid.* at p. 158.
[302] *Crawley* v *Crawley* (1835) 7 Sim. 427; *Re Pope* [1901] 1 Ch. 64; *Re Phillips* (1880) 49 L.J. Ch. 198; *Re Cababe* (1914) 59 S.J. 129; In *Re Hawkins* [1916] 2 Ch. 570; *Re Garside* [1919] 1 Ch. 132.
[303] See above.
[304] 1929 SC at p. 159.

"[I]n each and all of them the question under consideration was in connexion with one deed only—a will, itself containing a clause of direction to accumulate; and, as a matter of fact, in each of them the maximum period of twenty-one years had elapsed during which income had been accumulated. Further, the surplus income in these cases was true income from first to last—the estate which produced it being in the hands of the same trustees—and was received by them as income of the estate. In my opinion these cases are of no assistance. They do not appear to deal directly with the matter in hand. In none of them had the surplus income in fact become residue of the testator's estate as here."

In *Lady Gibson's Trustees, Petitioners*,[305] as in the *Union Bank* case there was an inter vivos trust directing an accumulation coupled with a will. Here however the residuary clause of the will directed that the residuary estate be transferred to and held by the trustees of the inter vivos settlement on the trusts of that settlement. To give effect to that provision would undoubtedly have sanctioned a double accumulation. The court therefore held that the surplus income was to pass as on intestacy. There was no discussion, however, as to how this was to be received; presumably as capital as it became part of the testator's estate, albeit ineffectually disposed of, and as part of that estate passed.

The distinction would appear to centre around this point; whether or not the surpluses are received as part of someone's estate, for it would seem to be this fact of death, and its consequent effect of capitalising the deceased's assets of whatever nature, that is decisive. In *Lord* v *Colvin*[306] it was on this point that Lord Curriehill's remarks were based. He said:

"Since, in this class of cases the income of a trust estate, when not disposed of by the testator during the period while the beneficial right to the capital of the trust estate has not vested in any one, is held to consist of the testator's intestate estate, and is succeeded to by his representatives ab intestato, it follows that, according to the regulating principle of intestate succession, the right to the whole of such revenue vests a morte testoris in these legal representatives. In such cases the right vests in the legal representatives . . . . in consequence of the estate itself being vested in trustees for their behoof. And what so vests in them is the whole of the intestacy, including the undisposed of revenues, during all the period while the beneficial right to the capital may remain in suspense. The parties who are in the position of being the legal representatives at the time of the testator's death, and when the right to the intestate succession vests have right to all the revenue which may become due during the whole of the period while the capital may be held in suspense, although they may die during its currency; because all of it, from first to last is equally included in the intestate succession of the defunct. The right itself, although the subject of it may so become payable by instalments at different periods of time, is a unum quid; and it vests at once and entirely in the representatives of the defunct immediately on his death. The circumstance that the subject of a right consists of annual payments is quite consistent with the right itself being such a unum quid, and indivisible as to succession. This is exemplified by the case of annuities; for if a person having right to an annuity, payable during the continuance of another person's life, dies intestate, what his legal representative succeeds to is the right of annuity itself during the whole of its currency and not merely such instalments thereof as may become payable during his own lifetime.[307] And an annuity although in other respects it differs from a right to the income of the trust estate in the class of cases we are considering, serves to show that a right may be a unum quid, although the subject of it may consist of instalments

---

[305] 1963 SC 350.
[306] (1860) 23 D 111 at pp. 132/3.
[307] This was the point of difference stressed by the court in *Mair's Curator Bonis* v *Inland Revenue* 1932 SC 151.

payable during an indefinite period of time. Were it otherwise, such an intestate succession of even personal estate would consist of a series of successive liferent rights; and instead of each liferenter, after the first deriving his right from his immediate predecessor, according to the rule of intestate succession, all of them would derive it successively from the same predecessor . . . .

To the extent to which he may have so disposed of the income, his intestate estate would of course be diminished. But it would only be diminished in extent. Its nature or legal character, so far as left unaffected by the settlement, would not be changed and would still be intestacy; and as his intestate succession, the right thereto would vest immediately on his death in the parties who would then be his legal representatives, and would be subject to their disposal. If, in such a case, the period of suspense of the right to the capital should continue for a period of thirty years, and the testator had disposed of the instalments of the posthumous income for the first twenty-one years of that period, but not for the remainder of that period, the instalments of the remaining nine years would still retain their character of intestacy, and belong to those who would be in the position of being his legal representatives at the time of his death."

Accordingly then the position would seem to be that unless there is this transfer from an inter vivos trust into the estate of the settlor the surplus income will retain its income character in the hands of its recipient, whether that recipient be an individual or another inter vivos trust (unless of course the provisions of this latter trust expressly capitalise it). Similarly if there is a transfer from testamentary trust to a beneficiary or to another trust (but not another estate) the surplus income will retain its character as income, the fact and consequences of death not intervening.

Termination of Accumulations

We have seen that from the line of cases beginning with *Ogilvie's Trustees* v *Kirk-Session of Dundee*[308] where there is a present gift of the fee which has vested in the beneficiary prior to the curtailment of the accumulation by the Act, that curtailment operates so as to discharge the duty to accumulate enabling the beneficiaries entitled to take both the gifted property and the income it produces. What this line of cases does not do, however, is to enable the beneficiary to put an end to the accumulation itself within the statutory period. Power to do this would seem to arise only in cases governed by the rule in *Miller's Trustees* v *Miller,*[309] a principle which was described in that case by Lord McLaren in the following terms:[310]

"Ever since I knew anything of the law of trusts, I have considered it to be a settled, and indeed an elementary proposition that where trustees hold property for a person in fee, that is a simple trust which the court will execute by divesting the trustees at the suit of the person interested. It seems to me that a beneficiary who has an estate in fee has by the very terms of the gift the same right of divesting the trustees, and so putting an end to the trust, which the truster himself possessed, because under a gift in fee the grantee acquires all the right in the property which the truster had to give. It seems to me to be not only an unsound proposition in law, but a logical impossibility that a person should have an estate in fee and that some other person should at the same time have the power of withholding it. This I understand to be a well-settled principle. It is laid down by writers of authority on the law of England and I have never had any doubts about its being the law of Scotland." . . . .

---

[308] (1846) 8 D 1229.
[309] (1890) 18 R 301.
[310] *ibid.* at pp. 310/311.

The principle was further explained by Lord President Balfour, Lord Adam, Lord McLaren and Lord Kinnear in a joint opinion in *Yuill's Trustees* v *Thomson*[311] in the following terms:

"The principle .... is that when a vested, unqualified and indefeasible right of fee is given to a beneficiary of full age, he is entitled to payment of the provision notwithstanding any direction to the trustees to retain the capital of the provision, and to pay over the income periodically, or to apply the capital or income in some way for his benefit. The proposition was qualified in the opinion of Lord President Inglis by the addition that, where there are trust purposes to be served which cannot be secured without the retention of the vested estate or interest of the beneficiary in the hands of the trustees, the rule cannot be applied, and the right of the beneficiary must be subordinated to the will of the testator. This is a necessary qualification because there may be contingent liabilities, the amount of which cannot be precisely ascertained, and for which it may be necessary to retain such a sum as the trustees judge to be sufficient.

The rule only applies to a gift of an absolute or unqualified right of fee, because of the fee is burdened with annuities or other charges a sufficient sum must be retained to provide for these charges out of the income of the portion retained. Further the rule presupposes an indefeasible right of fee because it may be that where, as in the case of *Chambers' Trustees* v *Smith*,[312] the trustees are empowered in certain circumstances, as in their discretion, to reduce the right of fee to a liferent, it may be their duty to retain the fund until they shall be satisfied that the necessity will not arise for exercising the power."

The case of *Miller's Trustees* v *Miller* was not of itself concerned with accumulations, and though accumulations figured in *Yuill's Trustees*, that decision is not of much assistance on the point at issue because the accumulations there had been curtailed by the operation of the Thellusson Act. Such Scottish authority as there is is indecisive and, by and large, at variance with the established rule in English law[313] that where the requirements for the application of the principle are satisfied as regards the beneficiary's interest "a direction to accumulate the income is only a mode of preventing the person from enjoying the property, which can have no effect".[314]

The point of variance seems to be the view that a direction to accumulate is itself a trust purpose[315] and therefore that any application of the principle of *Miller's Trustees* would be incompetent as the direction to accumulate would bring it within Lord President Inglis' qualification. The principal proponent of this view was Lord Watson in his opinion in *Muirhead* v *Muirhead*[316] an opinion with which the other members of the House of Lords concurred. The case concerned an annuity payable out of the income of the residuary fund, with a direction to accumulate the balance of such income not utilised in servicing the annuity. In point of fact the principle in *Miller's case* was held to be inapplicable because the interests of the residuary beneficiaries had not yet vested; but Lord Watson addressed himself with regard to the direction to accumulate as follows. He said:[317]

---

[311] (1902) 4 F 915 at p. 819.
[312] (1878) 5 R (H.L.) 151.
[313] *Saunders* v *Vautier* (1841) 4 Beav. 115.
[314] per James L.J. in *Weatherall* v *Thornburgh* (1878) 8 Ch. D 261 at p. 269.
[315] per Lord Moncrieff in *Yuill's Trustees*, 1902 4 F at p. 828.
[316] (1890) 17 R (H.L.) 45.
[317] *ibid.* at p. 48.

"It seems to me that, apart from other considerations, an insuperable bar to the respondents' demand for present distribution is to be found in the fact that the testator has given a positive direction that accumulations of revenue shall be continued until the death of his widow. They endeavour to meet that obvious difficulty by arguing that the accumulation was intended to secure his widow's annuity and was not meant to serve any other purpose, but the direction is express and unqualified, and neither the context of the deed nor the circumstances of the trust lend probability to the argument."

The implication then is that if the direction were "express and unqualified" and not connected with the annuity, that would be sufficient to negative the application of the principle in *Miller's case*.

Lord Watson's remarks were addressed in connection with the earlier decision of the Second Division in *Lucas' Trustees* v *The Lucas Trust*.[318] In this case trustees were directed to accumulate income during the lifetime of the truster's widow, who was an annuitant on the estate, and the accumulations together with the capital of the trust were to form a fund which was to be vested in certain trustees for the establishment of a charitable foundation to be called "The Lucas Trust". There were also certain contingent interests ascertainable only at the widow's death. The widow repudiated the annuity and as a result it was held that the trustees of The Lucas Trust were entitled to immediate payment "subject to existing and contingent interest". The problem with this decision is that there were apparently no judgements given, the report containing only the interlocutor. But Lord Watson commented on this case:[319]

"The differs from the present in this important respect, that the trustees of the charity, and they alone, were entitled to the estate and its accumulations, so that the the transfer to them could not prejudice any beneficiary. But it was the plainly expressed intention of the testator that the residue increased by accumulations until his widow's decease, and no lesser amount should be employed in launching his charitable scheme, and I entertain a doubt whether the Court was justified in giving the estate to the administrators of the Lucas Trust without imposing upon them the duty of accumulation as directed by the truster."

Several points arise out of those statements. In the first place, it must be remembered that they were obiter and in no sense necessary for the decision, and as such are not binding in respect of future decisions. In the second place, it should be recalled that the context in which the remarks were delivered was one of showing that the interests of the residuary legatees had not vested and that the arguments and analyses in the judgement were directed to that end. If read in that light much of the difficulty arising from the generalised language used disappears.[320] And lastly, and this perhaps is the most crucial, Lord Watson's view seems to be based on the paramountcy of the principle of giving effect to the expressed intention of the truster. Now *Muirhead* v *Muirhead* was decided a few months before *Miller* v *Miller's Trustees*[321] and in this latter case the basis of the arguments employed by the minority judges was this self-same principle of the weight to be given to the truster's intention. Having failed in

---

[318] (1881) 8 R 502.
[319] (1890) 17 R (H.L.) at p. 49.
[320] Compare the statements of Lord Hunter in *Mowbray's Trustees* v *Mowbray's Executors* 1931 SC 595 at p. 599.
[321] 1890 18 R 301.

Miller's case, which has been upheld many times subsequently,[322] it is suggested that Lord Watson's arguments can be discounted.

However if so discounted we are left with a principle which has never properly been applied by the courts to terminate an accumulation in Scotland, except in one case, in which judgements were apparently not delivered. In this situation, given that there exists a parallel principle in English law,[323] it is suggested that the English rule, that accumulations can be terminated where the beneficiary has a present unqualified and indefeasible right in fee, be applicable in Scotland also. This, however, raises in all cases the primary question as to the nature of the interest which must be decided, as in *Muirhead* v *Muirhead*,[324] before there can be any possibility of applying the principle of *Miller's Trustees*. As in so many areas of the law governing accumulations the question is ultimately one of construction.[325]

---

[322] See *Yuill's Trustees* v *Thomson* (1902) 4 F 815; *Coats' Trustees* v *Coats* (1903) 5 F 401; *Macculloch* v *Macculloch's Trustees* (1903) 6 F (H.L.) 3; *Watson's Trustees* v *Watson* 1913 SC 1133; *Compton's Judicial Factor* v *Barnardo's Homes* 1917 SC 713; *Graham* v *Graham's Trustees* 1927 SC 388; *Merchiston Castle School* 1965 SC 56; See also Dobie on Liferent and Fee at p. 12 and cases cited there.
[323] The rule in *Saunders* v *Vautier* (1841) 4 Beav. 115.
[324] (1890) 17 R (H.L.) 45.
[325] Compare the differing treatments by the House of Lords on two cases on similar facts illustrating this point.—*Wharton* v *Masterman* [1895] AC 186 and *Berry* v *Geen* [1838] AC 575

Chapter VI

RULES AND PERPETUITIES

In the preceding chapters we have traced the rise and fall of the perpetuity from its historical roots up till the present day. It will have been seen that the idea of perpetuity flourished, especially in Scotland, during the eighteenth and nineteenth centuries. And yet during the latter part of this period, on both a national and family level the continuance of perpetuities came to be regarded first as irrelevant and then as positively harmful.[1]

The demise of the perpetuity began with the destructibility of the entail. Once this had been achieved the trust form had been employed with increasing frequency in attempts to attain the same ends. And yet in this employment were the seeds of destruction of the whole perpetuity concept, for trustees either acquired or were given powers of sale the exercise of which necessitated alienation. This was emphasised in the reforms of the later nineteenth century remodelling the laws of England and Scotland as regards settled estates. The settled estate was no longer to be considered as something, the sanctity of which must not be violated; it had become just one form of capital which, like any other, could be exchanged, disposed of or otherwise dealt with for the benefit of those entitled under the settlement.

With this the settlement itself no longer acted so as to hinder commerce in land or in any other asset. It is perhaps symbolic that in 1925[2] the first perpetuity, the English entail, was considered to be so purged of its perpetuity implications that it was made available for the settlement of personal as well as real property.

The reasons for this change have in part been discussed already.[3] The pressures imposed by the legislation, the positive economic damage inflicted on those intended to benefit all played their part. Perhaps they were instrumental in ending the belief in the utility of primogeniture. Certainly the notion gained acceptance that younger children were no less worthy of their parents' bounty than the eldest son and with the dramatic increases in the taxation both of income and capital that have taken place during the present century the practice of fragmentation of family assets has been seen to have advantages in the preservation of family wealth such that make adherance to the strict rules of primogeniture and the consolidation of assets implicit therein sheer folly. Indeed whereas the idea of the perpetuity embodied the notion that ownership, albeit of a limited kind, was to be protected and even enforced, the present feeling is that the divesting of ownership, while retaining some measure of control, is the most that can be done to protect the family. For the danger is now seen as coming no longer from the family itself but from the Government.

Given then this reversal of attitudes questions arise as to the part played by the perpetuity rules in this and of their relevance at the present day.

---

[1] See above at Chapter I and Chapter III.
[2] Law of property Act 1925, section 130.
[3] See especially Chapter I and Chapter III.

The Role of the Rules against Perpetuities

It is sad, given the trust placed in them that the Rules against Perpetuities appear to have played little part in this reversal of attitudes. Indeed given the process of settlement and resettlement that was widely adopted during the latter part of the nineteenth and early twentieth centuries it might be asked whether they had any significant effect at all in the curbing of the effects that flowed from perpetuities.

To this latter question the answer must be in the affirmative: the mere existence of the device of resettlement would seem to indicate that. While it is true that they came to be allowed for in arrangements made, they nevertheless had the effect of making the fulfilment of the settler's aim dependent, not only on his draftsman, but on the acceptance by future generations of his aims, for without their co-operation, the retention of family wealth on the lines laid down by him was impossible.

The very process of settlement and resettlement can in a sense be seen as a half-way house to the position that applies at the present day. While on the one hand the original settler's directions might serve as guidelines, the process permitted deviations to take into account changes of circumstances. At the present day flexibility is all, or almost all. Settlements are drafted giving powers of variation and termination to trustees to employ as they think best for the beneficiaries in the circumstances.

And these circumstances are very largely dictated by fiscal considerations. Gone are the balmy days of 1878/79 when, with income tax at a standard rate of 2d in the £, it was hoped to be able to abolish it altogether. By 1916 this had risen to five shillings in the pound; by 1940 to eight shilling and sixpence. In addition there was supertax of three shillings and sixpence in 1916 and the surtax rate for 1940 was up to nine shillings and sixpence. At the present day taxation of income rises to eighty-three per cent on the top slice[4] plus an investment income surcharge of fifteen per cent where appropriate. Capital taxes again did not begin to bite until the current century began to unfold. Under the Finance Act of 1894[5] the rate of estate duty on an estate of over a million pounds was only eight per cent. By 1914 this had increased to twenty per cent[6] and by 1940[7] to fifty-two per cent, with a rate of sixty-five per cent for estate of over two millions. Just prior to its replacement by capital transfer tax the effective top rate of estate duty was approximately eighty per cent.[8]

Given these figures it will be seen that the deaths of two or more entailed proprietors or liferenters in possession within a short time would diminish the available fund to such a degree that the only true beneficiary would be the Exchequer.

Apart from purely fiscal considerations the reforms of 1925[9] in England confirmed the practice of dividing parents' estates equally among their children,

---

[4] Finance Act 1974, section 761.
[5] Section 17.
[6] Finance Act 1914, section 12 and First Schedule.
[7] Finance Act 1940, section 16 and Sixth Schedule.
[8] Finance Act 1971 section 61(1).
[9] Administration of Estates Act 1925 section 46.

only entailed estates going to the heir at law, a position that was emulated in Scotland in 1964[10], albeit in a slightly different way.

The Relevance of Perpetuity Rules at the Present Day

As external factors would appear to be responsible for the unwillingness to create perpetuities at the present day the question of the continued relevance of perpetuity rules comes into focus. Given that the property settled is in no way inalienable any effect the rules have must be in connection with the beneficial interests created under the settlement and any justification for their retention must lie here.

In a recent work on English Property Law one writer felt that he had found it. He wrote:[11]

"In so far as it prevents the creation of remote future interests the rule still has a useful, though limited, function. It is true that death duties are now a powerful disincentive to the creation of such interests, but there needs also to be some absolute barrier to the occasional attempts of eccentric autocrats to rule other people's lives from their graves . . . . My own guess is that the Rule is, generally, beneficial . . . . in that it probably helps the legal advisers of testators and others to persuade their clients not to indulge in the creation of fanciful trusts."

Morris and Leach make substantially the same point. They write:[12]

"Another reason for the Rule . . . . seems to the present authors to be far more realistic. It is that 'the Rule against Perpetuities strike a fair balance between the desires of members of the present generation, and similar desires of succeeding generations, to do what they wish with the property they enjoy!'[13] It is a natural human desire to provide for one's family in the foreseeable future. The difficulty is that if one generation is allowed to create unlimited future interests in property, succeeding generations will receive the property in a restricted state and thus be unable to indulge the same desire. The dilemma is thus precisely what it has been throughout the history of English law, namely how to prevent the power of alienation being used to its own destruction. In this idea of compromise between two competing policies—freedom of disposition by one generation and freedom of disposition by succeeding generations —the Rule against Perpetuities seems to the present authors to find its best justification."

It is difficult to refute statements such as this, and indeed applying them to Scotland it would appear that the Scottish rules of liferent enlargement effect this compromise with a clarity which the Modern Rule in England lacks. However if both rules, English and Scottish, were abolished it is suggested that it is unlikely that attempts would be made to create interests reaching into the mists of the uncharted future and still less that such interests, even if created, would be given effect to.

As to the first, the obvious disincentives to such creation are fiscal. Even if the instrument chosen was a discretionary trust the probability of the imposition of a wealth tax[14] and the certainty of a deemed disposal every few years[15] giving rise to a charge under a capital transfer tax would act as deterrents to all but the most stupid. And even in the case of the most stupid who might

---

[10] Succession (Scotland) Act 1964 section 2.
[11] Eric Poole "English Property Law" (1973) at pp. 317/318.
[12] The Rule against Perpetuities (2nd Ed. 1962) at p. 17.
[13] Quoting Lewis M. Simes "Public Policy and the Dead Hand" (1955) at p. 58.
[14] Green Paper "Wealth Tax" (1974) Cmnd. 5705.
[15] Finance Act 1975 Schedule 5 para. 12.

override all advice there exist now in Scotland[16] and in England[17] powers to vary the provisions of trust settlements so that in practice the creation of limited interests reaching out into the future need not, and in all probability would not, operate to break this compromise. It is therefore suggested that the existence of rights to vary the beneficial interests granted under trusts dispenses with the need for any "absolute barrier" which might be provided by the perpetuity rules.

Similar objections can be raised against other justifications for the existence of a Rule. Thus, for example, the American Law Institute[18] propounds the view that perpetuity rules prevent the undue concentration of wealth in the hands of a few. Given that opinions will differ as to what amounts can be said to constitute an "undue concentration" and as to how many comprise "a few",[19] while this may have been true in the past, and may even have been a reason[20] for the promotion of a policy of free alienation, the same end can now be effected by taxation, and in particular by the taxation of capital. If the concentrations of wealth that exist today are held by some to be unduly large this state of affairs would seem to have arisen in spite of the existence of perpetuity rules. In other words for those who believe that wealth is unduly concentrated in the hands of a few the perpetuity rules have manifestly failed: for those who do not they are likely to attribute the reason to such external factors as the scope and levels of twentieth century taxation rather than to the existence and operation of perpetuity rules.

Professor Simes, who has been perhaps the leading modern apologist for the existence of a perpetuity rule, states in general terms that it is socially desirable that the wealth of the world should be controlled by its living members and not by the dead.[21] In such general terms this proposition is difficult to fault. But then he proceeds to elaborate his argument. An example of the Perpetuity Rule's furthering this objective, he says, is that the Rules effectively restrict the limitations that can be created behind private trusts: that as trustees investment powers are narrower than those of absolute owners, if something like a perpetuity rule did not operate to limit the duration of such trusts, too much private capital would be tied up and would not be available for the financing of new economic enterprises.

Several things can be said about this. In the first place the investment activities of trustees are becoming increasingly similar to those of private individuals. Modern investment clauses, particularly where large amounts of capital are involved, tend to be drawn in such a way that trustees are empowered to invest the trust fund "as if they were absolute owners thereof". In the second place funds for the type of investment envisaged by Professor Simes—the examples he gives are of investment in jet propulsion and atomic energy—tend to come in large part from the government and from corporate funds. Given this,

---

[16] Trusts (Scotland) Act 1961, section 1.
[17] Variation of Trusts Act 1958.
[18] Restatement of Property, vol. iv (1944) p. 2129.
[19] See e.g. Atkinson "Unequal Shares" (1972); Polanyi and Wood "How Much Inequality" (1974).
[20] See above Chapter II.
[21] "Public Policy and the Dead Hand" at pp. 59-60.

the part played by private trusts is minimal and so the effect of the existence of a perpetuity rule, if it had any effect at all, would also be minimal.

Professor Simes gives another example. He says:[22]

"To meet the changing and unforeseeable economic conditions of each generation, there should be some free flow of property between capital investment and consumer's goods.... if depression strikes, so that beneficiaries of trusts need to invade the corpus, or if inflation becomes rampant, so that the amount of trust income becomes inadequate, the beneficiary cannot use the capital of the trust."

In other words, according to Professor Simes, a perpetuity rule tends to prevent a continued freezing of capital. There is, indeed, a great deal of truth in this, and in Chapters I and III there are examples of the effects of this freezing of capital. However the question still remains as to whether in the fiscal climate of the present day the scope of existing taxes and the imminence of their being supplemented by others does not perform the same function more efficiently; that whereas the perpetuity rules inhibited concentration over long periods, present day fiscal legislation positively promotes fragmentation.

Indeed from what we have said it might be felt that such legislation has taken over the function of the perpetuity rules with regard to perpetual settlements. However this point must not, perhaps, be pressed too far, for this effect is produced by specific types of taxation, direct taxation attacking at progressively high rates concentrations of income, transfers of capital, and soon, no doubt concentrations of capital per se. If ever there were a shift of emphaiss to consumer taxation such that the weight of the Revenue's attack is lifted from the possession of wealth and placed on its expenditure and employment then the situation would clearly be different. Quite how likely such a fundamental change is is unknown, and probably unknowable. Certainly during the late nineteen sixties and for the first few years of the current decade various politicians from all the main parties stated their support for such a change. But the recent revertion to an obsessive egalitarianism would tend to discount the implementation of such a change in the immediate future.

If rules against perpetuities have any relevance at the present day it would seem to be as reserve weapons to guard against the effects of such a change. Certainly, of all the jurisdictions in which perpetuity rules exist, and in which reforms have been made over the last fifty or so years, few, if any, have been in favour of complete abolition. Most have been concerned merely to eradicate anomalies; others have recast the form and nature of their rules; but all of these have accepted without demur[23] the need for the existence of a perpetuity rule, even in a climate of high direct taxation. It may be that it is considered that taxation is such a fluid instrument that it cannot be trusted permanently to police perpetuities. If this is the case then certainly the possession of a perpetuity rule, albeit as a second line of defence, would seem to be desirable.

As for the rules against accumulations, these constituted the first real stage to prevent the undue agglomeration of wealth. Whereas the perpetuity rules operated on wealth already acquired, the accumulation rules operated in a modest way to prevent the acquisition of too much and for too long. In a sense,

---

[22] "Is the Rule against Perpetuities Doomed?—The Wait and See Doctrine" (1953) 52 Mich L. Rev. 179 at p. 192.

[23] See for example Fourth Report of the English Law Reform Committee 1956 para 4.

directed as they were, against size, they were forerunners of the monopolies legislation of today, which enshrines the principle that the sheer size of a concentration of wealth may be harmful and needs to be regulated. So long as this principle is observed its application to private fortunes may not be out of place.

Whether the present cost of the rules is appropriate however is another question. Certainly they are extremely complex and provide a number of traps for the draftsman, not only in that they can operate so as to frustrate the obvious intention of the settler, but also until recently that they could harm the intended beneficiaries, giving rise as they did to estate duty liability.

But long term accumulations, like perpetuities, are anachronistic. From this study it will have been seen that the idea of perpetuity flourished, especially in Scotland, during an age in which attempts to establish perpetual settlements reflected the prosperity, the stability, the hope and above all the confidence of that period. Indeed the assumption that a settler could and should be able to carve out the future for limitless generations embodies that confidence to the point of arrogance. At the present day in an age that displays little of that stability and even less of that hope and confidence such assumptions seem rather pathetic.

THE STAIR SOCIETY

Instituted in 1934 *to encourage the study and advance the knowledge of the History of Scots Law*

OFFICE-BEARERS 1979

President: THE RT. HON. LORD AVONSIDE

Vice-President: PROFESSOR GORDON DONALDSON, M.A., PH.D., D.LITT., HON. D.LITT., F.B.A.

Chairman of Council: JOHN IMRIE, LL.D.

Vice-Chairman: SHERIFF J. IRVINE SMITH, LL.B.

Council: ROBERT SUTHERLAND, W.S.; PROFESSOR I. D. WILLOCK; D. A. O. EDWARD, Q.C.; D. C. NEILLANDS, ADVOCATE; W. D. H. SELLAR; PROFESSOR W. A. J. WATSON; ALAN HARDING; J. M. PINKERTON, ADVOCATE; PROFESSOR D. M. WALKER, Q.C.; PROFESSOR M. C. MESTON; MISS L. BROWN.

Literary Director: PROFESSOR W. A. J. WATSON, M.A., LL.B., D.PHIL.

Secretary: G. R. THOMSON, T.D., B.L., PH.D., S.S.C., 2 St. Giles' Street, Edinburgh EH1 1PU

Treasurer: I. R. GUILD, W.S., 16 Charlotte Square, Edinburgh EH2 4YS

Auditor: G. R. LINDSAY BROWN, C.A.

Secretary for the U.S.A.: JOHN H. TUCKER, Jnr., B.A., LL.B., LL.D.

CONSTITUTION

1. The Society shall be called 'The Stair Society'.

2. The object of the Society shall be to encourage the study and advance the knowledge of the history of Scots Law especially by the publication of original documents, and by the reprinting and editing of works of sufficient rarity or importance.

3. Membership of the Society shall be constituted by payment of the annual subscription, and shall cease if this be in arrear for one year.

4. The amount of the annual subscriptions shall be fixed by the Council from time to time, and shall be payable in advance on 1st January in each year.

5. The management of the affairs and funds of the Society shall be vested in a Council consisting of the President, Vice-President, a Chairman, a Vice-Chairman and not more than ten ordinary elected members.

6. The President, Vice-President, Chairman and Vice-Chairman shall be elected annually at the Annual General Meeting, to hold office for the following calendar year, and shall be eligible for re-election. Those elected at the Inaugural Meeting shall hold office until 31st December, 1935.

7. The ordinary members of Council elected at the Inaugural Meeting shall hold office from that date. At every Annual General Meeting thereafter the Society shall elect members to fill any vacancies on the Council that may have occurred, or that may be due to occur at the end of the year, members so elected to hold office from the ensuing 1st of January. The original members of Council shall hold office until 31st December, 1939, and, at the Annual General Meeting to be held in Novemner 1939, all of these members, except two (selected by agreement or by lot), shall be eligible for re-election. The two so selected shall retire as at 31st December following, and shall not be eligible for re-election for one year. Thereafter at each Annual General Meeting two of the ordinary members of Council shall retire as at 31st December following, and shall not be eligible for re-election for one year. The two members to retire annually shall be those who have the longest continuous period of service, and, as among those of equal service, shall be selected by agreement or by lot.

8. In addition to the elected members, the Council shall have power to co-opt as additional members of Council any member of the Society who, in their opinion, may be fitted to render special service in promoting the work of the Society. Such co-opted members shall hold office for such period, not exceeding five years, as the Council may in each case determine. At no time shall the co-opted members of Council exceed three in number.

9. The Society at the Inaugural Meeting, and thereafter at the Annual General Meeting, shall appoint a Literary Director or Directors, a Secretary and a Treasurer, and such other officers as may from time to time be deemed necessary, who shall be subject to the direction of the Council in the performance of their duties, and who shall receive such remuneration as the Council may determine. Those so appointed shall not be members of Council, but may be invited to attend any meeting of Council.

10. Any casual vacancies in the offices of President, Vice-President, Chairman, Vice-Chairman or elected members of the Council, or among the officers of the Society, may be filled up by the Council, appointments so made to be for the period till the 31st of December following the next Annual General Meeting.

11. In any year in which a volume is published each member who has paid his subscription for that year shall be entitled to receive one copy.

12. The Annual General Meeting shall be held between 1st November and 31st March at such time and place as may be fixed by the Council. If the Meeting is not held until after 31st December in any year, office-bearers and members of Council then due to retire shall remain in office until the Meeting is held. The Council may also at any time call a Special General Meeting of the Society, and shall do so on a requisition from not less than ten members, which shall specify the object for which the Meeting is to be called. Seven days' notice shall be given of all General Meetings.

13. The Constitution of the Society as contained in these Rules may be amended at any General Meeting on twenty-one days' notice of the proposed amendments being given to the Secretary and included in the Agenda circulated for the Meeting.

PUBLICATIONS OF
THE STAIR SOCIETY

1. AN INTRODUCTORY SURVEY OF THE SOURCES AND LITERATURE OF SCOTS LAW. By various authors. With an introduction by The Rt. Hon. Lord Macmillan, P.C., LL.D., Lord of Appeal in Ordinary. 1936.

1a. AN INDEX TO VOLUME NO. 1, compiled by James Cowie Brown, M.A., LL.B., Ph.D., was issued in 1939.

2. ACTA CURIAE ADMIRALLATUS SCOTIAE, 6th September 1557—11th March 1561-2. Edited by Thomas Callander Wade, M.A., LL.B., Solicitor, Falkirk. 1937.

3. HOPE'S MAJOR PRACTICKS, 1608-1633. Edited by The Rt. Hon. James Avon Clyde, LL.D., formerly Lord Justice-General of Scotland and Lord President of the Court of Session. Vol. 1. With portrait. 1937.

4. HOPE'S MAJOR PRACTICKS, 1608-1633. Edited by The Rt. Hon. James Avon Clyde, LL.D., formerly Lord Justice-General of Scotland and Lord President of the Court of Session. Vol. II. 1938.

5. BARON DAVID HUME'S LECTURES, 1786-1822. Edited and annotated by G. Campbell H. Paton, M.A., LL.B., Solicitor, and Assistant to Professor of Law in the University of Glasgow. Vol. I. With portrait. 1939.

6. LORD HERMAND'S CONSISTORIAL DECISIONS, 1684-1777. Edited by F. P. Walton, K.C.(Quebec), LL.D., Hon. Fellow, Lincoln College, Oxford, formerly Director, Royal School of Law, Cairo. With Biographical Sketch of Lord Hermand by James Fergusson. With portrait. 1940.

7. ST. ANDREWS FORMULARE, 1514-1546. Text transcribed and edited by Gordon Donaldson, M.A., Ph.D., and C. Macrae, M.A., D.Phil. Vol. I. 1942.

8. ACTA DOMINORUM CONCILII, 26th March 1501—27th January 1502-3. Transcribed by J. A. Crawford, M.A., LL.B., Advocate. Edited with an Introduction by The Rt. Hon. James Avon Clyde, LL.D., formerly Lord Justice-General of Scotland and Lord President of the Court of Session. 1943.

9. ST. ANDREWS FORMULARE, 1514-1546. Edited by Gordon Donaldson, M.A., Ph.D., with Prefatory Note by David Baird Smith, C.B.E., LL.D. Vol. II. 1944.

10. THE REGISTER OF BRIEVES, 1286-1386, as contained in the Ayr MS., the Bute MS., and Quoniam Attachiamenta. Edited by The Rt. Hon. Lord Cooper, LL.D., Lord Justice-Clerk. THOMAS THOMSON'S MEMORIAL ON OLD EXTENT. Edited by J. D. Mackie, C.B.E., M.C., M.A., Professor of Scottish History and Literature in the University of Glasgow. 1946.

11. REGIAM MAJESTATEM AND QUONIAM ATTACHIAMENTA, based on the text of Sir John Skene. Edited and translated with Introduction and Notes by The Rt. Hon. Lord Cooper, LL.D. 1947.

12. THE JUSTICIARY RECORDS OF ARGYLL AND THE ISLES, 1664-1705. Transcribed and edited, with an Introduction, by John Cameron, M.A., LL.B., Ph.D. 1949.

13. BARON DAVID HUME'S LECTURES, 1786-1882. Edited and annotated by G. Campbell H. Paton, M.A., LL.B., Solicitor. Vol. II. 1949.

14. ACTA DOMINORIUM CONCILII ET SESSIONIS, 1532-1533. Edited by Ian H. Shearer, M.A., LL.B., Advocate. 1951.

15. BARON DAVID HUME'S LECTURES, 1786-1822. Edited and annotated by G. Campbell H. Paton, M.A., LL.B., Advocate and Lecturer in the History of Scots Law in the University of Glasgow. Vol. III. 1952.

16. SELECTED JUSTICIARY CASES, 1624-1650. Edited and annotated by Stair A. Gillon, B.A., LL.B., Advocate. 1953.

17. BARON DAVID HUME'S LECTURES, 1786-1882. Edited and annotated by G. Campbell H. Paton, M.A., LL.B., Advocate and Lecturer in the History of Scots Law in the University of Glasgow. Vol. IV. 1955.

18. BARON DAVID HUME'S LECTURES, 1786-1822. Edited and annotated by G. Campbell H. Paton, M.A., LL.B., Advocate and Lecturer in the History of Scots Law in the University of Glasgow. Vol. V. 1957.

19. BARON DAVID HUME'S LECTURES, 1786-1822. Edited and annotated by G. Campbell H. Paton, M.A., LL.B., Advocate and Lecturer in the History of Scots Law in the University of Glasgow. Vol. VI. 1958.

20. AN INTRODUCTION TO SCOTTISH LEGAL HISTORY. By various authors. With an Introduction by The Rt. Hon. Lord Normand, P.C., LL.D., Lord of Appeal in Ordinary, 1947-53. 1958.

21. THE PRACTICKS OF SIR JAMES BALFOUR OF PITTENDREICH. Edited by Peter G. B. McNeill, M.A., LL.B., Ph.D., Advocate. Vol. I. 1962.

22. THE PRACTICKS OF SIR JAMES BALFOUR OF PITTENDREICH. Edited by Peter G. B. McNeill, M.A., LL.B., Ph.D., Advocate. Vol. II. 1963.

23. THE ORIGINS AND DEVELOPMENT OF THE JURY IN SCOTLAND. By Ian D. Willock, M.A., LL.B., Advocate and Professor of Jurisprudence in the University of St. Andrews. 1966.

24. WILLIAM HAY'S LECTURES ON MARRIAGE. Transcribed, translated and edited by The Right Rev. Monsignor John C. Barry, M.A.(Cantab.), D.C.L. (Rome), Rector of St. Andrew's College, Drygrange, Melrose; Consultor to the Pontifical Commission for the Revision of the Code of Canon Law. 1967.

25. THE JUSTICIARY RECORDS OF ARGYLL AND THE ISLES. 1664-1742. Edited by John Imrie. Vol. II. 1969.

26. MISCELLANY I. By various authors. With a Preface by The Rt. Hon. Lord Clyde, LL.D., Lord Justice-General and Lord President of the Court of Session. 1971.

27. SELECTED JUSTICIARY CASES, 1624-1650. Edited with an Introduction by J. Irvine Smith, M.A., LL.B., Advocate, Sheriff of Lanarkshire at Glasgow. Vol. II. 1972.

28. SELECTED JUSTICIARY CASES, 1624-1650. Edited with an Introduction by J. Irvine Smith, M.A., LL.B., Advocate, Sheriff of Lanarkshire at Glasgow. Vol. III. 1974.

29. THE MINUTE BOOK OF THE FACULTY OF ADVOCATES. 1661-1712. Edited by John M. Pinkerton, Clerk of Faculty. Volume I. 1976.

30. THE SYNOD RECORDS OF LOTHIAN AND TWEEDDALE, 1589-1596. Edited with an Introduction by Dr. James Kirk of the Department of Scottish History, Glasgow University. 1977.